DAY HIKING
North
Cascades

D0198961

Previous page: Foggy Lake from Del Campo Peak

Opposite: North Twentymile Peak

Larches in October

Rugged shoulder of Church Mountain

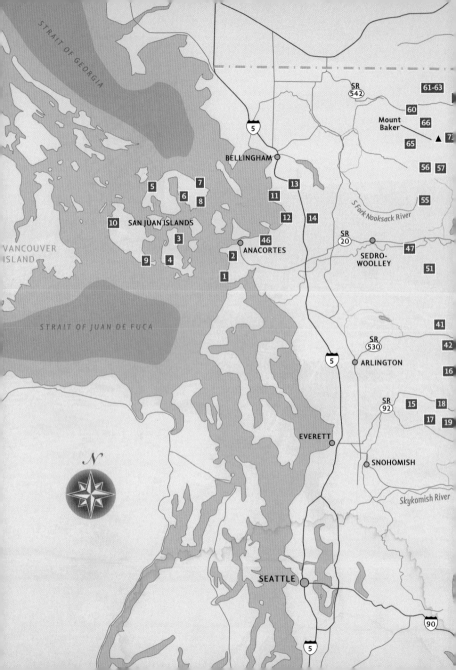

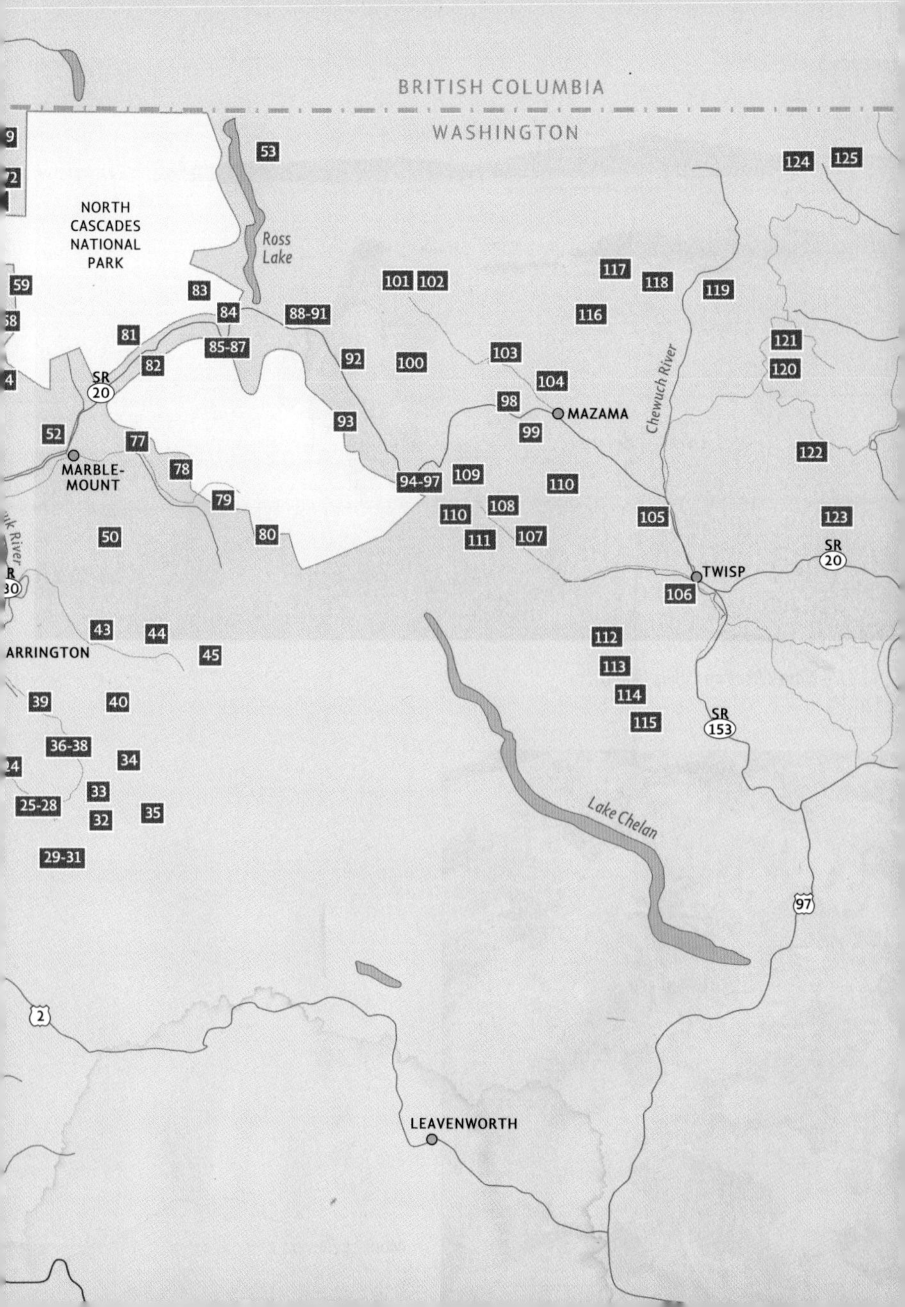

BRITISH COLUMBIA

WASHINGTON

9

2

53

NORTH
CASCADES
NATIONAL
PARK

Ross
Lake

124 | 125

59

58

83

101 | 102

117

118

119

81

84

88-91

116

4

82

85-87

92

100

103

121

120

SR
20

93

98

104

MAZAMA

Chewuch River

52

77

99

122

MARBLE-
MOUNT

78

94-97

109

110

105

123

50

79

110

108

SR
20

80

111

107

106

TWISP

43

44

112

ARRINGTON

45

113

39

40

114

115

SR
153

36-38

34

24

33

Lake Chelan

25-28

32

35

29-31

97

k River

R
30

2

97

LEAVENWORTH

Shark Reef on Lopez Island

Monkey flowers

Skyline Divide

South Fork Cascade River

DAY HIKING

North
Cascades

mount baker/mountain loop highway/san juan islands

Craig Romano

THE MOUNTAINEERS BOOKS

THE MOUNTAINEERS BOOKS
*is the nonprofit publishing arm of The Mountaineers Club, an
organization founded in 1906 and dedicated to the exploration,
preservation, and enjoyment of outdoor and wilderness areas.*

1001 SW Klickitat Way, Suite 201, Seattle, WA 98134

© 2008 by Craig Romano

All rights reserved

First edition: first printing 2008, second printing 2010

No part of this book may be reproduced in any form, or by any electronic, mechanical, or other
means, without permission in writing from the publisher.

Manufactured in Canada

Copy Editor: Julie Van Pelt
Cover and Book Design: The Mountaineers Books
Layout: Mayumi Thompson
Cartographer: Moore Creative Design
All photos by the author unless otherwise noted.

Cover photograph: *Autumn larches* (Photo by Alan Bauer)
Frontispiece: *Mount Baker from Dock Butte*

Maps shown in this book were produced using National Geographic's *TOPO!*
software. For more information, go to *www.nationalgeographic.com/topo.*

Library of Congress Cataloging-in-Publication Data
Romano, Craig.
  Day hiking North Cascades / by Craig Romano. — 1st ed.
    p. cm.
  ISBN-13: 978-1-59485-048-6
  ISBN-10: 1-59485-048-8
 1. Hiking—Washington (State)—Guidebooks. 2. Hiking—Cascade Range—Guidebooks.
3. Hiking—Washington (State)—San Juan Islands—Guidebooks. 4. Washington (State)—
Guidebooks. 5. Cascade Range—Guidebooks. 6. San Juan Islands (Wash.)—Guidebooks. I. Title.
GV199.42.W2R66 2007
796.5109797—dc22

                                     2007041014

♻ Printed on recycled paper
ISBN (paperback): 978-1-59485-048-6
ISBN (ebook): 978-1-59485-256-5

Table of Contents

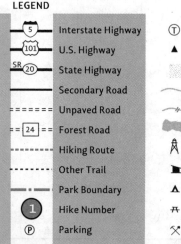

LEGEND

5	Interstate Highway	Ⓣ	Trailhead
101	U.S. Highway	▲	Summit
SR 20	State Highway		Sand/Mud
	Secondary Road		River/Stream
=======	Unpaved Road		Falls
== 24 ==	Forest Road		Lake
---------	Hiking Route		Lookout Tower
---------	Other Trail		Ranger Station
—·—·—	Park Boundary	∆	Campground
1	Hike Number	🎋	Picnic Area
Ⓟ	Parking	⚒	Mine site

Hikes at a Glance

HIKE	DISTANCE (ROUND–TRIP)	DIFFICULTY	HIKEABLE ALL YEAR	KID-FRIENDLY
ISLANDS AND PUGET SOUND				
1. Deception Pass	5 miles	1	x	x
2. Sugarloaf	2.5 miles	2	x	x
3. Spencer Spit	1.75 miles	1	x	x
4. Shark Reef Sanctuary	1 mile	1	x	x
5. Turtleback Mountain	3 miles	3	x	x
6. Cascade Lake	2.7 miles	2	x	x
7. Mount Constitution/Mountain Lake	6.7/3.9 miles	3/2	x	x
8. Obstruction Pass	1.2 miles	1	x	x
9. Mount Finlayson	3.5 miles	2	x	x
10. Young Hill/Bell Point	2/1.5 miles	2/1	x	x
11. Fragrance Lake	5.5 miles	2	x	x
12. Oyster Dome	6.5 miles	3	x	
13. Pine and Cedar Lakes	5 miles	3	x	
14. Squires Lake	2 miles	2	x	x
MOUNTAIN LOOP HIGHWAY				
15. Lime Kiln Trail	7 miles	2	x	x
16. Tin Can Gap	12 miles	4		
17. Mount Pilchuck	5.4 miles	3		
18. Heather Lake	4.6 miles	2		x
19. Lake Twentytwo	5.4 miles	3		x
20. Pinnacle Lake	3.8 miles	3		x
21. Ashland Lakes	5.5 miles	2		x
22. Boardman Lake	2 miles	1		x
23. Bald Mountain	10 miles	3		
24. Independence and North Lakes	7 miles	4		x
25. Big Four Ice Caves	2.2 mles	1		x
26. Perry Creek	8 miles	4		
27. Mount Dickerman	8.6 miles	4		
28. Headlee Pass and Vesper Lake	7 miles	5		
29. Gothic Basin	9 miles	4		
30. Silver Lake	12 miles	4		x
31. Glacier Basin	12.5 miles	5		
32. Goat Lake	10.4 miles	3		
33. Bedal Basin	5.2 miles	4		

DOG-FRIENDLY	HISTORICAL	BEACH HIKING	WILDERNESS	OLD-GROWTH	SOLITUDE	WILD-FLOWERS	ALPINE VIEWS	CAR CAMP NEARBY
	X	X						X
X								X
	X	X						X
		X						
X						X	X	
X	X							X
X	X			X			X	X
X		X						X
X	X	X				X		
X	X	X				X		
X								X
							X	X
X								
X								
X	X							
			X	X		X	X	
	X			X			X	
X								
X				X				X
				X				X
X				X	X			X
X				X				X
X				X	X		X	
X				X	X			
	X					X		
X				X		X	X	
						X	X	
	X			X		X	X	
	X			X		X	X	
X	X		X	X			X	
	X		X		X	X	X	
X	X		X	X				
	X		X	X	X	X	X	X

HIKE	DISTANCE (ROUND–TRIP)	DIFFICULTY	HIKEABLE ALL YEAR	KID-FRIENDLY
34. Round Lake	11 miles	5		
35. North Fork Sauk River/Red Mountain	10/2 miles	2/3		
36. Mount Pugh	11 miles	5		
37. Peek-a-boo Lake	5 miles	3		
38. Beaver Lake	4 miles	1	x	x
39. Old Sauk River Trail	6 miles	1	x	x
40. Crystal Lake	9 miles	4		
WEST SLOPE				
41. Mount Higgins	9 miles	4		
42. Boulder River	8.6 miles	2	x	x
43. Huckleberry Mountain	12 miles	5		
44. Green Mountain	8 miles	4		
45. Sulphur Moutain	10 miles	5		
46. Padilla Bay	4.8 miles	1	x	x
47. Rasar State Park	3 miles	1	x	x
48. Rockport State Park	3 miles	1	x	x
49. Sauk Mountain	4.2 miles	3		
50. Slide Lake	2.5 miles	1		x
51. Gee Point	3 miles	4		
52. Cow Heaven	10 miles	4		
53. Hozomeen Lake	7.4 miles	2		x
54. Anderson/Watson Lakes	4/6 miles	3/3		x
55. Blue Lake/Dock Butte	1.5/3.5 miles	1/3		x
56. Park Butte	7.5 miles	3		x
57. Scott Paul Trail	8 miles	3		
58. Baker Lake	9 miles	2	x	x
59. Baker River	5 miles	2	x	x
MOUNT BAKER HIGHWAY				
60. Horseshoe Bend	2.4 miles	1	x	x
61. Canyon Ridge	6 miles	3		x
62. Excelsior Peak	6.5 miles	3		x
63. Church Mountain	8.5 miles	5		
64. Welcome Pass and the High Divide	8 miles	5		
65. Heliotrope Ridge	5.5 miles	3		
66. Skyline Divide	9 miles	3		x
67. Yellow Aster Butte	7.5 miles	4		
68. Winchester Mountain	3.5 miles	3		
69. High Pass	4 miles	3		
70. Nooksack Cirque	7 miles	3		

DOG-FRIENDLY	HISTORICAL	BEACH HIKING	WILDERNESS	OLD-GROWTH	SOLITUDE	WILD-FLOWERS	ALPINE VIEWS	CAR CAMP NEARBY
			X	X	X	X	X	X
X			X	X				
	X		X	X		X	X	
X				X				
X	X			X				
X				X				X
X			X		X			
X				X	X		X	
X			X	X				
X			X	X	X		X	
	X		X			X	X	X
			X	X	X	X	X	X
X								X
X	X							X
X				X				X
	X					X	X	X
X			X	X				
	X			X	X		X	
X				X	X		X	
X			X	X	X			X
			X	X			X	
X				X		X	X	
	X			X		X	X	X
X				X		X	X	X
X								X
			X		X			X
				X				X
X				X	X	X	X	
				X		X	X	
				X		X	X	X
			X	X	X	X	X	X
			X	X		X	X	
X			X			X	X	
			X			X	X	
	X		X			X	X	X
	X		X		X	X	X	X
			X	X	X			X

HIKE	DISTANCE (ROUND–TRIP)	DIFFICULTY	HIKEABLE ALL YEAR	KID-FRIENDLY
71. Goat Mountain	11 miles	5		
72. Hannegan Peak	10.4 miles	4		
73. Chain Lakes	8 miles	3		x
74. Table Mountain	3 miles	2		
75. Ptarmigan Ridge	10 miles	4		
76. Lake Ann	8.2 miles	4		x
NORTH CASCADES				
77. Lookout Mountain/Monogram Lake	9.4/9.8 miles	5/5		
78. Hidden Lake Lookout	9 miles	4		
79. Middle/South Fork Cascade River	9/10 miles	3/3		
80. Cascade Pass and Sahale Arm	12 miles	4		x
81. Thornton Lakes/Trappers Peak	10.2/10.6	5/5		
82. Skagit River	1.8 miles	1	x	x
83. Sourdough Mountain	11 miles	5		
84. Diablo Lake	7.5 miles	2		x
85. Pyramid Lake	4.5 miles	2		
86. Thunder Knob	3.8 miles	2	x	x
87. Thunder Creek	12 miles	3		x
88. Happy-Panther Trail	12.4 miles	2		
89. Ruby Creek	6.5 miles	2		x
90. Crater Mountain	14 miles	5		
91. Canyon Creek	7 miles	3		
92. East Creek	8 miles	3		
93. Easy Pass	7 miles	5		
94. Maple Pass	7.2 miles	3		x
95. Cutthroat Pass	10 miles	3		x
96. Stiletto Peak	14 miles	5		
97. Blue Lake	4.4 miles	3		x
98. Driveway Butte	8 miles	4		
99. Cedar Falls	3.5 miles	2		x
100. Tatie Peak/Grasshopper Pass	5/11 miles	3/3		x
101. Windy Pass	7 miles	2		x
102. Silver Lake	11 miles	4		
EAST SLOPE				
103. Lost River	8 miles	2		
104. Goat Peak	5 miles	3		x
105. Patterson Mountain	3.7 miles	3		x
106. Lookout Mountain	3 miles	3		x
107. Scatter Lake	8.5 miles	5		

DOG-FRIENDLY	HISTORICAL	BEACH HIKING	WILDERNESS	OLD-GROWTH	SOLITUDE	WILD-FLOWERS	ALPINE VIEWS	CAR CAMP NEARBY
X			X			X	X	X
X			X			X	X	X
	X		X			X	X	
							X	
			X				X	
X			X	X				
					X	X	X	X
	X					X	X	X
X			X	X	X			X
			X			X	X	
			X	X			X	X
X								X
X			X		X	X	X	X
								X
				X				X
X								X
X				X				X
X	X				X			X
X	X			X	X			
	X		X		X	X	X	
X	X			X	X			
X	X				X			
						X	X	
				X		X	X	
X						X	X	
			X	X	X	X	X	
							X	X
					X	X	X	X
					X			X
X						X	X	X
X						X	X	X
X			X		X	X	X	X
X			X		X			X
X						X	X	
						X	X	
					X	X	X	
			X		X	X	X	X

HIKE	DISTANCE (ROUND-TRIP)	DIFFICULTY	HIKEABLE ALL YEAR	KID-FRIENDLY
108. North Lake	9.8 miles	3		
109. Copper Pass	10 miles	4		
110. Twisp Pass	9 miles	3		
111. Louis Lake	10.5 miles	3		
112. Libby Lake	11 miles	4		
113. Crater Lakes	8.6 miles	3		
114. Eagle Lakes	12 miles	4		
115. Sunrise Lake	13 miles	4		
116. Copper Glance Lake	6 miles	4		
117. Burch Mountain	10 miles	4		
118. Black Lake	8 miles	2		x
119. North Twentymile Peak	13 miles	5		
120. Tiffany Mountain	6 miles	3		x
121. Tiffany Lake	3 miles	1		x
122. Golden Stairway	6 miles	3		
123. Beaver Lake	2 miles	1		x
124. Horseshoe Basin	12 miles	3		
125. Disappointment Peak	5 miles	3		

DOG-FRIENDLY	HISTORICAL	BEACH HIKING	WILDERNESS	OLD-GROWTH	SOLITUDE	WILD-FLOWERS	ALPINE VIEWS	CAR CAMP NEARBY
X			X		X			X
X			X		X	X	X	X
			X			X	X	X
X			X		X			X
	X		X		X		X	X
X				X	X			
					X		X	
					X	X	X	
	X			X	X	X	X	X
X			X		X	X	X	
X			X					X
	X				X	X	X	X
X						X	X	
X								X
X					X	X	X	
X								
X			X			X	X	X
X					X	X	X	X

Acknowledgments

In addition to my trusty pickup truck and several (now well-worn) pairs of hiking shoes, the following people's help and support were essential for writing this book.

First, a big *grazie* to all the great people at The Mountaineers Books, especially publisher Helen Cherullo and Hally Swift for giving me the opportunity to be a part of this exciting day-hiking series. *Grazie* to Kate Rogers, too, for her support. *Mille grazie* to Mary Metz for her encouragement and for listening to my rants about creating maps and profiles—and for being so understanding and flexible concerning my deadlines. I promise never to move house again while working on a manuscript! I especially want to thank my editor, Julie Van Pelt, whose professionalism and attention to detail

has contributed to making this book a finer volume. I look forward to working with you on my next book—I hope you can handle more of my bad puns and my tendency to alliterate a lot.

I also want to acknowledge guidebook pioneers Ira Spring and Harvey Manning for their inspiration and invaluable knowledge. It is an honor to walk in their bootprints. And to my series partners, Alan Bauer and Dan Nelson, I am both honored and pleased to be in your company.

Lastly, but most importantly, I want to thank my wife Heather for believing in me and supporting me while I worked hard on yet another manuscript. Thanks for hiking with me, too, to so many of the special places in this book. And *mille, mille grazie* for all of the shoulder massages after my long nights at the keyboard.

Preface

I first stepped foot (actually wheel) in Washington State in April 1980. I had bicycled across the country from my home state, New Hampshire, and entered the Evergreen State in Pacific County. I immediately fell in love with the raw beauty and expansive wild tidal flats of Willapa Bay. The Washington that I first experienced was the Washington I had always imagined—a land of big timber, big rivers, and a big coastline.

In July 1985 I returned to the state and got off the roads and onto the trails—destination North Cascades! My first hike, to Cutthroat Pass, yielded stunning alpine views and an up-close and personal encounter with four mountain goats. The next day I headed for Sourdough Mountain. The grueling trail delivered me to resplendent meadows, glistening snowfields, and a drop-dead view of cobalt Diablo Lake. A friendly fire lookout—a Jack Kerouac protégé—greeted me with an ice-cold beer. It didn't take long for me to become enamored with these wild and awesome mountains.

I came back for more hiking in the summer of 1989, and I never left. There was just too much wild country to explore and I became determined to see it all. And as a guidebook writer I'm trying my darnedest to do just that. I'm fortunate to be able to return to the North Cascades pretty much whenever I want to, and Cutthroat Pass remains as special to me today as it was a quarter of a century ago.

Unfortunately, most of my fellow humans will probably never experience the soothing and inspiring beauty of Cutthroat Pass and the countless other special places in this gorgeous corner of the world. Many have chosen a path leading them away from nature. Sad indeed, for as our world continues to urbanize, its denizens grow more sedentary, materialistic, and disconnected from the natural world. Life for many on this course has lost its real meaning. Nature may need us to protect it from becoming another urban center, but we need nature to protect us from the encroaching world of meaningless consumption.

Henry David Thoreau proclaimed, "In wildness is the preservation of the world." And I would like to add, "In wildness also is the salvation of our souls, the meaning of life, and the preservation of our humanness." So shun the mall, turn off the TV, skip the casino, and hit the trail. I've lined up 125 magnificent hikes to help you celebrate nature, life, the incredible landscapes of the North Cascades region, and you. Yes, you! Go take a hike. Celebrate life and return from the natural world a better and more content person.

If I'm preaching to the choir, help me then to introduce new disciples to the sacred world of nature. For while we sometimes relish our solitude on the trail, we need more like-minded souls to help us keep what little wildlands remain. Help nature by introducing family members, coworkers, your neighbors, children, and politicians to our wonderful trails. I'm convinced that hiking is not only good for our wild and natural places (people will be willing to protect them), but is also good for us (it helps us live healthy and connected lives).

Enjoy this book. I've enjoyed writing it. I'm convinced that we can change our world for the better, one hike at a time. I hope to see you on the trail.

Introduction

Modern life is full of irony. Technology was supposed to set us free, but instead of doing more of our work for us, it has only enabled us to do more work. Americans are working now more than ever, and for many this is a necessity as the costs of health care, energy, education, housing, and food continue to rise. For others, working harder is a choice as they quest after the Joneses. But do we really need a 2500-square-foot home (for two people), a big vehicle (that was made for combat but is used for grocery shopping), and all the latest gizmos, contraptions, and clutter (what happened to phones for phone calls?) that we don't have time for anyway, because we're too busy working to pay them off? Americans are working more hours each year, with less vacation time taken, than they have at any time since World War II.

This helps explain why more and more hikers these days are foregoing multiday backpacking trips in favor of daylong outings. With fewer free hours to devote to the outdoors, many hikers seem to favor trail excursions that can be done as day hikes. But even if you aren't pressed for time, perhaps you prefer day hikes to backpacking for other reasons. For one thing, you can travel farther and with more ease than if you were schlepping a 50-pound pack. Day hikes also generally require less planning and fewer hassles when it comes to all of the permits (if any) that might be required these days to recreate on our public lands.

So to help all you hurried and busy or travel-light hikers get your wilderness fixes, turn to this new Day Hiking series. The series sets out to find the best routes in each region that can be enjoyed as day trips. Of course, depending on where you live, some destinations may

be too far for you to travel to, hike, and travel back from in a day. In that case, look at these trips as daily excursions you can make from that weeklong cabin rental or from a three-day weekend at a car campground. Again, no backpacking is necessary.

The book you are now holding focuses on hiking routes found throughout the North Cascades and the San Juan Islands—basically, all the good day hikes from the Canadian border south to the Mountain Loop Highway and east from the San Juans to the Okanogan River. You'll find short walks close to population centers and all-day treks deep into wilderness areas. Beaches, islands, riversides, lakefronts, old-growth forests, alpine meadows, mountaintops, and fire lookouts—they're all in here. Hikes in national parks, national forests, wilderness areas, state and county parks. Hikes perfect for children, friendly to dogs, accessible year-round, popular and remote. New trails, historical trails, and revitalized trails. Where to find wildlife, where to escape crowds, and where to get the best bang for your boot. It's all included in this packed with adventure volume.

The North Cascades region is home to incredible biological diversity. With some of the largest contiguous tracts of wilderness in the Lower 48, wildlife flourishes here. Wolves, grizzly, lynx, wolverines, mountain goats, spotted owls, marbled murrelets, and a myriad of other rare and endangered species still inhabit this wild corner of planet earth. The only pod of orcas (killer whales) in the continental United States plies the waters surrounding the San Juan Islands.

The North Cascades themselves are a dramatic mountain range: jagged and craggy,

Opposite: Admiring the view on Mount Pilchuck

bred from fire (volcanic in origin and still active), and draped in ice (containing half the glaciers in the Lower 48). The range contains huge lakes, long free-flowing rivers, sprawling alpine meadows, and some of the largest tracts of virgin forest remaining in the contiguous United States.

The North Cascades is a land of great climatic contrasts too, from pockets of rain forest on western slopes to pockets of desert steppe on eastern slopes. Nearly 700,000 acres of this special landscape is protected in national parkland. More than 1.5 million acres is protected as federal wilderness, guaranteeing that it will remain in a wild and natural state in perpetuity.

The area is rich in human history too. First peoples, European explorers, French-Canadian voyageurs, African, Asian, and European American pioneers and homesteaders all traveled through these mountains and along the region's waterways. Humans of all walks have hunted, mined, fished, and harvested the region's great natural resources. In many cases their marks scarred the land. In many other cases the land recovered. Traces of past dreams and schemes can be found throughout this vast area.

And what better way for you to explore this special corner of the American landscape than by taking a hike through it? There are hundreds of miles of trails that traverse the greater North Cascades region, assuring no shortage of day-hiking options. I've lined up 125 of the very best for you.

USING THIS BOOK

These Day Hiking guidebooks strike a fine balance. They were developed to be as easy to use as possible while still providing enough detail to help you explore a region. As a result, *Day Hiking: North Cascades* includes all the information you need to find and enjoy the hikes, but leaves enough room for you to make your own discoveries as you venture into areas new to you.

What the Ratings Mean

Every trail described in this book features a detailed "trails facts" section. Not all of the details are facts, however.

Each hike starts with two subjective ratings: each has a **rating** of 1 to 5 stars for its overall appeal, and each route's **difficulty** is rated on a scale of 1 to 5. This is subjective, based on the author's impressions of each route, but the ratings do follow a formula of sorts. The overall rating is based on scenic beauty, natural wonder, and other unique qualities, such as solitude potential and wildlife-viewing opportunities. Here are the guidelines I followed for the North Cascades region:

***** Unmatched hiking adventure, great scenic beauty, and wonderful trail experience

**** Excellent experience, sure to please all

*** A great hike, with one or more fabulous features to enjoy

** May lack the "killer view" features, but offers lots of little moments to enjoy

* Worth doing as a refreshing wild-country walk, especially if you're in the neighborhood

The **difficulty** rating is based on trail length, the steepness of the trail, and how difficult it is to hike. Generally, trails that are rated more difficult (4 or 5) are longer and steeper than average. But it's not a simple equation. A short, steep trail over talus slopes may be rated 5, while a long, smooth trail with little elevation gain may be rated 2. In the North Cascades, here's what the difficulty ratings mean:

5 Extremely difficult: Excessive elevation gain and/or more than 6 miles one-way, and/or bushwhacking required

4 Difficult: Some steep sections, possibly rough trail or poorly maintained trail

3 Moderate: A good workout, but no real problems

2 Moderately easy: Relatively flat or short route with good trail

1 Easy: A relaxing stroll in the woods

To help explain the difficulty ratings, you'll find the **round-trip mileage**, total **elevation gain**, and **high point** for each hike. The distances are not always exact mileages—trails weren't measured with calibrated instruments—but the mileages are those used by cartographers and land managers (who have measured many of the trails). The elevation gains report the cumulative difference between the high and low points on the route—in other words, the total amount you will go up on a hike. It's worth noting that not all high points are at the end of the trail—a route may run over a high ridge before dropping to a lake basin, for instance.

The recommended **season** is another tool to help you choose a hike. Many trails can be enjoyed from when they lose their winter snowpack right up until they are buried in fresh snow now the following fall. But snowpacks vary from year to year, so a trail that is open in May one year may be snow-covered until mid-July the next. The hiking season for each trail is an estimate, and before you venture out it's worth contacting the land manager to get current conditions.

To help with trip planning, each hike lists which **maps** you'll want to have on your hike, as well as who to **contact** to get current trail conditions. Hikes in this guidebook reference USGS topographical maps or Green Trails maps, which are based on the standard 7.5-minute USGS maps. Both USGS and Green Trails maps are available at most outdoor retailers in the state, as well as at many National Park Service and U.S. Forest Service visitors centers.

Important **notes**, if any, follow. These consist of information pertinent to your planning, such as trail restrictions or whether a trailhead parking pass is required.

GPS coordinates for each trailhead are

Mount Shuksan

also provided—use this both to get to the trail and to help you get back to your car if you get caught out in a storm or wander off-trail.

Finally, **icons** at the start of each hike description provide you with a quick shorthand for the trip's highlights. Kid-friendly hikes are generally easier, pose few if any obstacles, and often consist of natural features that should intrigue and engage youngsters. A dog-friendly hike is one on which dogs are not only allowed, but is a trip that usually will be easy on the paws and that has adequate shade and water. A beachcombing hike is one that is either on or to a beach. Do leave all living organisms for the health of our coastal ecosystems and for others to enjoy, though. Hikes with especially abundant seasonal wildflowers are also spotlighted. Historical hikes highlight the region's human story in mining relics, fire lookouts, and early settlements. Endangered Trails are threatened due to lack of maintenance, motorized encroachment, or other actions detrimental to their existence. Saved Trails, on the other hand, are reasons to rejoice—these hikes have been revived and restored, often by passionate hikers just like you.

 Kid-friendly

 Dog-friendly

 Beachcombing

 Wildflowers

 Historical

 Endangered Trail

 Saved Trail

The route descriptions themselves provide detailed descriptions of the hike and some of the things you might find along the way, including geographic features, scenic views, flora and fauna potential, and more. Thorough driving directions get you to the trailhead, and options for extending your trip round out most hikes so that those looking for more can add miles or even days to their outing.

Of course, you'll need some information long before you ever leave home. So, as you plan your trips, consider the following several issues.

PERMITS, REGULATIONS, AND FEES

As our public lands have become increasingly popular, and as both federal and state funding has declined, regulations and permits have become necessary components in managing our natural heritage. It's important that you know, understand, and abide by them. To help keep our wilderness areas wild and our trails safe and well maintained, land managers—especially the National Park Service and U.S. Forest Service—have implemented a sometimes complex set of rules and regulations governing the use of these lands.

Generally, any developed trailhead in Washington's national forests (Oregon too) fall under the Region 6 forest pass program. Simply stated, in order to park legally at these designated national forest trailheads, you must display a Northwest Forest Pass decal in your windshield. These sell for $5 per day or $30 for an annual pass good throughout Washington and Oregon (which constitute Region 6).

Concerning Washington's national parks, popular access points in Olympic and Mount Rainier require a national park entrance fee, currently $15 for a one-week pass, $30 for an annual pass, or $50 for an annual pass that covers national parks nationwide. There are no entrance fees in the North Cascades National Park Complex.

Your best bet if you hike a lot in both national parks and forests is to buy an America the Beautiful Pass for $80 (sold through the Park Service and by the U.S. Geological

Survey at *http://store.usgs.gov/pass*). This annual pass grants you and three other adults in your vehicle (children under sixteen are admitted free) access to all federal recreation sites that charge a day-use fee. These include national parks, national forests, national wildlife refuges, and Bureau of Land Management areas, not only here in Washington but throughout the country. Currently there is no day-use charge at Washington's state parks.

I know that who charges what can get confusing, which is why the America the Beautiful Pass makes sense (see "Whose Land Is This?" below). Even if you don't hike much, all park and forest pass monies go directly to the agencies managing our lands. It is money well spent. You can purchase passes at national park and forest visitors centers and Northwest Forest Passes can be purchased from many area outdoor retailers as well. Passes are good for one year from the day of purchase.

WHOSE LAND IS THIS?

Almost all of the hikes in this book are on public land. That is, they belong to you and me and the rest of the citizenry. What's confusing however, is just who exactly is in charge of this public trust. Over a half dozen different governing agencies manage lands described in this guide.

The largest of the agencies, and the one managing most of the hikes in this book, is the U.S. Forest Service. A division of the Department of Agriculture, the Forest Service strives to "sustain the health, diversity, and productivity of the Nation's forests and grasslands to meet the needs of present and future generations." The agency purports to do this under the doctrine of "multiple-use"—the greatest good for the greatest number. However, supplying timber products, managing wildlife habitat, and developing motorized and nonmotorized recreation options have a tendency to conflict with each other. Several areas within the national forests, however, have been afforded stringent protection as federal wilderness areas, which bar development, roads, and motorized recreation (see "The Untrammeled North Cascades" in the East Slope section).

The National Park Service, a division of the Department of the Interior, manages nearly 700,000 acres of land in the North Cascades as North Cascades National Park, Ross Lake National Recreation Area, and Lake Chelan National Recreation Area (the San Juan Island National Historical Park is also administered by the Park Service). The Park Service's primary objective is quite different from the Forest Service. To wit: "to conserve the scenery and natural and historical objects and the wildlife therein and to provide for the enjoyment of the same in such a manner and by such means as will leave them unimpaired for the enjoyment of future generations." In other words, the primary focus of the Park Service is preservation.

Other public lands you'll encounter in this book are Washington's state parks, managed primarily for recreation and preservation; Washington Department of Natural Resources lands, managed primarily for timber harvesting, with pockets of natural area preserves; national estuarine reserves established to protect coastal habitat; and county parks, which are often like state parks but on a regional level.

It's important that you know who manages the land that you'll be hiking on, for each agency has its own fees and its own rules (like for dogs: generally no in national parks, yes in national forests, and yes but leashed in state parks). Confusing, yes? But it's our land and we should understand how it's managed for us. And remember that we have a say in how our lands are managed, too, and can let the agencies know whether we like what they're doing or not.

Self-arrest practice!

WEATHER

Mountain weather in general is famously unpredictable, and in the North Cascades, with its multitude of microclimates, you'll be completely baffled (or intrigued) trying to figure it out. Weather patterns west and east of the Cascade crest are two different stories. The western slopes are characterized by a marine climate, influenced by prevailing winds off of the Pacific Ocean. Rainfall is heavy from November to April, with higher altitudes receiving much of that precipitation in snow. Summers are generally temperate, with extended periods of no or low rainfall. Mid-July through early October is generally a delightful time to hike the region.

East of the Cascade crest, weather patterns are representative of a continental climate, with cold winters (snowfall heavy at high elevations) and hot, dry summers. As storm clouds move eastward and are pushed up over the mountains, they cool and release their moisture. Peaks closer to Puget Sound wring the most moisture, Mount Baker being one of the best wringers of them all. The big volcano, second only to Rainier as most glaciated Cascade peak, holds the distinction of being one of the snowiest places on earth. During the winter of 1998–99, 1140 inches (95 feet) of snow fell on Baker, setting a new world record for annual snowfall. Trails on and near the mountain that summer never melted out.

The San Juan Islands enjoy temperate weather and low rainfall year-round (snowfall is rare) thanks to being in the rain shadow of the

Olympic Mountains. On any given day it can be sunny on Mount Constitution on Orcas Island, pouring rain on Mount Pilchuck, snowing on Mount Baker, sunny on Tiffany Mountain, and downright hot on Patterson Mountain. Plan your hike according to your weather preference.

But no matter where you hike in the region, always pack raingear. Being caught in a sudden rain and wind storm without adequate clothing can lead to hypothermia (loss of body temperature), which is deadly if not immediately treated. Most hikers who die of exposure (hypothermia) do so not in winter, but during the milder months when a sudden change of temperature accompanied by winds and rain sneak up on them. Always carry extra clothing layers, including rain and wind protection.

While snow blankets the high country primarily from November to May, it can occur anytime of year. Be prepared. Lightning is rare along the west slopes, but quite common during the summer months east of the Cascade crest. If you hear thunder, waste no time getting off of summits and away from water. Take shelter, but not under big trees or rock ledges. If caught in an electrical storm, crouch down, making minimal contact with the ground, and wait for the boomer to pass. Remove your metal-framed pack and ditch the trekking poles.

Other weather-induced hazards you should be aware of are the results of episodes of rain and snow. River and creek crossings can be extremely dangerous to traverse after periods of heavy rain or snowmelt. Always use caution and sound judgment when fording.

Be aware of snowfields left over from the previous winter's snowpack. Depending on the severity of the past winter, and the weather conditions of the spring and early summer, some trails may not melt out until well into summer or not at all. In addition to treacherous footing and difficulties in routefinding, lingering snowfields can be prone to avalanches or slides. Use caution crossing them.

Mount Pugh summit

WHEN A RIVER RUNS WILD

One thing can be said about the North Cascades: like all ecosystems, the region is in a state of constant flux. Life. Death. Decay. Rebirth. It's all part of the circle of life. Sometimes flux comes slowly, and change is subtle. Other times its pace is swift, leaving in its wake a totally altered state. Thus was the case of the wind- and rainstorms of November 2006.

Mother Nature apparently was in the mood for a little rearranging. She unleashed a fury of storms, causing rivers to jump their banks, stands of ancient trees to uproot, and tons of rock and soil to come crashing down from the mountains. Not only did these storms significantly change the landscape in some areas, they inflicted record damage on the trails and roads that traverse it.

The storms of November 2006 were unprecedented. In some areas of Mount Rainier National Park over 18 inches of rain fell in a 36-hour period. June Lake in the Mount Saint Helens National Monument set the state's 24-hour rainfall record, receiving 15.2 inches. And throughout much of the North Cascades a similar story unfolded: the road and trail damage was both grand in scope and in the amount of money needed for repair. In all, over $70 million worth of damage was assessed by national parks and forest officials in western Washington.

While Mount Rainier sustained the brunt of the wreckage, the Darrington Ranger District in the Mount Baker–Snoqualmie National Forest— home of the Mountain Loop Highway—was also severely affected. The storms left nearly 70 percent of the district's trails inaccessible, including popular destinations like the Big Four Ice Caves, Pinnacle Lake, Monte Cristo, and the North Fork Sauk River. The Suiattle River Road, which provides access to Green Mountain, Sulphur Mountain, Crystal Lake, and Huckleberry Mountain, also sustained considerable damage. Ravaged by floods in 2003, the road was slated to reopen in 2007 until the storms in 2006 levied a heavy additional toll. When and if the road will reopen is now uncertain. The problem is money—or lack of it.

Since the end of major timber harvesting in western Washington's national forests in the early 1990s, Congress has starved the U.S. Forest Service of monies for trail and road maintenance. To many in the hiking community, the storms of 2006 rang out as the death knell for many of our trails and roads. We must tell our elected officials to adequately fund *our* Forest Service and to release money to repair this unprecedented damage. We can and must also do more than write letters—pitching in with trail advocacy groups like the Washington Trails Association to assist with trail repairs, picking up where the government leaves off.

As far as hiking to your favorite destinations, it is imperative that you contact the appropriate park or forest ranger districts to inquire about trail and road status before setting out. Enjoy the trails you can hike, and speak out for funding restoration of those you can't. Funding shortfalls and inclement weather will always be challenges to our trails, but hikers that advocate for their stomping grounds should never be in short supply—get involved!

Opposite: Hiking with kids

ROAD AND TRAIL CONDITIONS

In general, trails change little year to year. But change can and does occur, and sometimes very quickly. A heavy storm can cause a river to jump its channel, washing out sections of the trail or access road in moments. Windstorms can blow down trees across trails by the hundreds, making the paths unhikeable. And snow can bury trails well into the summer. Avalanches, landslides, and forest fires can also bring serious damage and obliteration to our trails. The record rainfall in November 2006 caused significant flooding that inflicted substantial damage on North Cascades trails and access roads. Many of these trails and roads remain closed as financially strapped land managers grapple with insufficient resources to restore them.

With this in mind, each hike included in this book lists the land manager's contact information so you can phone the agency prior to your trip and ensure that your chosen road and trail are open and safe to travel.

On the topic of trail conditions, it is vital that we thank the countless volunteers who donate tens of thousands of hours to trail maintenance each year. The Washington Trails Association (WTA) alone coordinates upwards of sixty thousand hours of volunteer trail maintenance each year.

As enormous as the volunteer efforts have become, there is always a need for more. Our wilderness trail system faces ever-increasing threats, including (but by no means limited to) ever-shrinking trail funding, inappropriate trail uses, and conflicting land-management policies and practices.

With this in mind, this guide includes trails that are threatened and in danger of becoming unhikeable. These Endangered Trails are marked with a special icon in this book. On the other side of the coin, we've also been blessed with some great trail successes in recent years, thanks in large part to that massive volunteer movement spearheaded by WTA. These Saved Trails are marked, too, to help show you that individual efforts do make a difference. As you enjoy these Saved Trails, stop to consider the contributions made by your fellow hikers that helped protect our trail resources.

WILDERNESS ETHICS

As wonderful as volunteer trail maintenance programs are, they aren't the only way to help save our trails. Indeed, these on-the-ground efforts provide quality trails today, but to ensure the long-term survival of our trails—and the wildlands they cross—we all must embrace and practice sound wilderness ethics.

Strong, positive wilderness ethics include making sure you leave the wilderness as pure or purer than it was when you found it. As the adage says, "take only pictures, leave only footprints." But sound wilderness ethics go deeper than that, beyond simply picking up after ourselves when we go for a hike. Wilderness ethics must carry over into our daily lives. We need to ensure that our elected officials and public-land managers recognize and respond to our wilderness needs and desires. If we hike the trails on the weekend, but let the wilderness go neglected—or worse, allow it to be abused—on the weekdays, we'll soon find our weekend haunts diminished or destroyed. Protecting trails and wild areas is a full-time job—and one with many rewards, as any hiker can tell you.

TRAIL GIANTS

I grew up in rural New Hampshire and was introduced to hiking and respect for our wildlands at a young age. I grew to admire the men and women responsible for saving and protecting many of our trails and wilderness areas as I became more aware of the often tumultuous history behind the preservation efforts.

When I moved to Washington in 1989 I immediately gained a respect for Harvey

Manning and Ira Spring. Through their pioneering 100 Hikes guidebooks, I was introduced to and fell in love with the Washington backcountry. I bought the whole series and voraciously devoured them on the trail and on the sofa. I joined the Mountaineers Club, the WTA, and other local trail and conservation organizations so that I could help a little to protect these places and carry on this legacy for future generations.

While I never met Ira Spring, I was honored to work on his last book after he passed away (*Best Wildflower Hikes in Washington*). I believe 100 percent in what he termed "green bonding." We must, in Ira's words, "get people onto trails. They need to bond with the wilderness." This is essential in building public support for trails and trail funding. When hikers get complacent, trails suffer.

And while I often chuckled at Harvey Manning's tirades and diatribes as he lambasted public officials' short-sighted and misguided land practices, I almost always tacitly agreed with him. Sometimes I thought Harvey was a bit combative, a tad too polarizing, perhaps even risked turning off potential allies. On the other hand, sometimes you have to raise a little hell to get results.

As you get out and hike the trails you find described here, consider that many of these trails would have long ago ceased to exist without the phenomenal efforts of people like Ira Spring, Harvey Manning, Louise Marshall, Robert Wood, and Greg Ball, not to mention the scores of unnamed hikers who joined them in their push for wildland protection, trail funding, and strong environmental stewardship programs.

When you get home, take a page from their playbook and write a letter to your congressperson or state representative, asking for better trail funding. Call your local Forest Service office to say you've enjoyed the trails in their jurisdiction and that you want these routes to remain wild and accessible for use by you and your children.

If you're not already a member, consider joining an organization devoted to wilderness, backcountry trails, or other wild-country issues. Organizations like the Mountaineers Club, Washington Trails Association, Volunteers for Outdoor Washington, Washington's National Park Fund, Conservation Northwest, and countless others leverage individual contributions and efforts to help ensure the future of our trails and the wonderful wilderness legacy we've inherited. Buy a specialty license plate for Washington's national parks or state parks and let everybody on the way to the trailhead see what you value and are willing to work for.

TRAIL ETIQUETTE

We need to not only be sensitive to the environment surrounding our trails, but to other trail users as well. Many of the trails in this book are open to an array of uses. Some are hiker-only, but others allow equestrians and mountain bikers too (only a couple of hikes in this book are open to motorbikes).

When you encounter other trail users—whether they are hikers, climbers, runners, bicyclists, or horse riders—the only hard-and-fast rule is to follow common sense and exercise simple courtesy. It's hard to overstate just how vital these two things—common sense and courtesy—are to maintaining an enjoyable, safe, and friendly situation when different types of trail users meet.

With this Golden Rule of Trail Etiquette firmly in mind, here are other things you can do during trail encounters to make everyone's trip more enjoyable:

- **Right-of-way.** When meeting other hikers, the uphill group has the right-of-way. There are two general reasons for this. First, on steep ascents, hikers may be watching the trail and not notice the approach of descending hikers until they are face-to-face. More importantly, it's easier for descending hikers to break their stride and step off the trail than it is for those who have gotten into a good climbing rhythm. But by all means if you are the uphill trekker and you wish to grant passage to oncoming hikers, go right ahead with this act of trail kindness.

- **Moving off-trail.** When meeting other user groups (like bicyclists and horseback riders), the hiker should move off the trail. This is because hikers are more mobile and flexible than other users, making it easier for them to step off the trail.

- **Encountering horses.** When meeting horseback riders, the hiker should step off the downhill side of the trail unless the terrain makes this difficult or dangerous. In that case, move to the uphill side of the trail, but crouch down a bit so you don't tower over the horses' heads. Also, make yourself visible so as not to spook the big beastie, and talk in a normal voice to the riders. This calms the horses. If hiking with a dog, keep your buddy under control.

- **Stay on trails,** and practice minimum impact. Don't cut switchbacks, take shortcuts or make new trails. If your destination is off-trail, stick to snow and rock when possible so as not to damage fragile alpine meadows. Spread out when traveling off-trail; don't hike in line if in a group, as this greatly increases the chance of compacting thin soils and crushing delicate plant environments.

- **Obey the rules** specific to the trail you are visiting. Many trails are closed to certain types of use, including hiking with dogs (North Cascades National Park) or riding horses.

- **Hiking with dogs.** Hikers who take dogs on the trails should have their dog on a leash or under very strict voice command at all times. And if leashes are required (such as in all state parks) then this *does* apply to you. Too many dog owners flagrantly disregard this regulation, setting themselves up for tickets,

hostile words from fellow hikers, and the possibility of losing the right to bring Fido out on that trail in the future. Remember that many hikers are not fond of dogs on the trail. Respect their right not to be approached by your loveable lab. A well-behaved leashed dog, however, can certainly help warm up these hikers to your buddy.

- **Avoid disturbing wildlife,** especially in winter and in calving areas. Observe from a distance, resisting the urge to move closer to wildlife (use your telephoto lens). This not only keeps you safer, but it prevents the animal from having to exert itself unnecessarily fleeing from you.

- **Take only photographs.** Leave all natural things, features, and historical artifacts as you found them for others to enjoy.

- **Never roll rocks off trails or cliffs.** You risk endangering lives below you.

These are just a few of the things you can do to maintain a safe and harmonious trail environment. And while not every situation is addressed by these rules, you can avoid problems by always remembering that *common sense and courtesy are in order*.

Remember, too, that anything you pack in must be packed out, even biodegradable items like apple cores and pistachio shells. "Leave only footprints, take only pictures," is a worthy slogan to live by when visiting the wilderness.

Another important Leave No Trace principle focuses on the business of taking care of business. The first rule of backcountry bathroom etiquette says that if an outhouse exists, use it. While you may be tempted not to (they really aren't that bad—we're not talking city public restrooms here), remember that they help keep backcountry water supplies free from contamination and the surrounding countryside from turning into a minefield of human waste decorated with toilet-paper flowers. Composting privies can actually improve the environment. I once spent a summer as a backcountry ranger in which one of my duties was composting the duty. Once the "stew" was sterile, we spread it on damaged alpine meadows, helping to restore the turf.

When privies aren't provided, the key factor to consider is location. Choose a site at least 200 feet from water, campsites, and the trail. Dig a cat hole. Once you're done, bury your waste with organic duff, sticks, rocks, and a Microbes at Work sign (just kidding about the last one).

Water

As a general rule you should treat all backcountry water sources. There is quite a bit of debate on how widespread nasties like *Giardia* (a waterborne parasite) are in water sources. New evidence suggests that the threat is greatly overblown. However, it's still better to assume that all water is contaminated. You don't want to risk it. I have contracted giardiasis on several occasions (in places as diverse as Paraguay and Vermont) and it's no treat—especially for the people around you.

Treating water can be as simple as boiling it, chemically purifying it (adding tiny iodine tablets), or pumping it through a water filter and/or purifier. (Note: Pump units labeled as filters generally remove everything but viruses, which are too small to be filtered out. Pumps labeled as purifiers use a chemical element, usually iodine, to render viruses inactive after filtering all the other bugs out.)

Cleanup

When washing your hands, rinse off as much dust and dirt as you can in just plain water first. If you still feel the need for a soapy wash, collect a pot of water from a lake or stream and move at least 100 feet away. Apply a tiny bit of biodegradable soap to your hands, dribble on a little water, and lather up. Use a bandana or towel to wipe away most of the soap, and then rinse with the water in the pot.

WILDLIFE
The Bear Essentials

The North Cascades is one of the best places in Washington for observing bears. While an extremely small population of grizzlies struggle to survive in the greater North Cascades ecosystem (see "Bearly Making It" in the Tiffany Highlands section), the bear you're most likely to see is the ubiquitous black bear. Your encounter will probably involve just catching a glimpse of his bear behind. Bears tend to prefer solitude to human company, generally fleeing long before you have a chance to get too close.

There are times, however, when a bear doesn't hear (or smell) your approach, or when it is more interested in defending its food source or its young than in avoiding a confrontation. These instances are rare, and you can minimize the odds of an encounter with an aggressive bear by heeding the following:

- **Hike in a group** and hike only during daylight hours.
- **Talk or sing as you hike** (Frank Sinatra or Johnny Cash tunes work well). If a bear hears you coming, it will usually avoid you. When surprised, however, a bear may feel threatened. So make noises that will identify you as a human—talk, sing, rattle pebbles in a tin can—especially when hiking near a river or stream (which can mask more subtle sounds that might normally alert a bear to your presence).
- **Be aware** of the environment around you, and know how to identify bear sign. Overturned rocks and torn-up deadwood logs often are the result of a bear searching for grubs. Berry bushes stripped of berries—with leaves, branches, and berries littering the ground under the bushes—show where a bear has fed. Bears will often leave claw marks on trees and, since they use trees as scratching posts, fur in the rough bark of a tree is a sign that says "a bear was here!"

Tracks and scat are the most common signs of bear's recent presence.

- **Stay away from abundant food sources and dead animals.** Black bears are opportunistic and will scavenge food. A bear that finds a dead deer will hang around until the meat is gone, and it will defend that food against any perceived threat.
- **Keep dogs leashed and under control.** Many bear encounters have resulted from unleashed dogs chasing a bear: The bear gets angry and turns on the dog. The dog gets scared and runs for help (back to its owner). And the bear follows right back into the dog owner's lap.

Docile Orcas Island deer

- **Leave scented items at home**—the perfume, hair spray, cologne and scented soaps. Using scented sprays and body lotions makes you smell like a big, tasty treat.

Occasionally the bruin may actually want to get a look at *you*. In very rare cases (and I repeat, rare), a bear may act aggressively. To avoid an un-bear-able encounter, heed the following advice, compliments of fellow guidebook writer and man of many bear encounters, Dan Nelson:

- **Respect a bear's need for personal space.** If you see a bear in the distance, make a wide detour around it, or if that's not possible (i.e., if the trail leads close to the bear), leave the area.
- **Remain calm** if you encounter a bear at close range. Do not run, as this may trigger a predator-prey reaction from the bear.
- **Talk in a low, calm manner** to the bear to help identify yourself as a human.
- **Hold your arms out from your body,** and if wearing a jacket hold open the front so you appear to be as big as possible.
- **Don't stare directly at the bear**—the bear may interpret this as a direct threat or challenge. Watch the animal without making direct eye-to-eye contact.
- **Slowly move upwind** of the bear if you can do so without crowding the bear. The bear's strongest sense is its sense of smell, and if it can sniff you and identify you as human, it may retreat.
- **Know how to interpret bear actions.** A nervous bear will often rumble in its chest, clack its teeth, and "pop" its jaw. It may paw the ground and swing its head violently side to side. If the bear does this, watch it closely (without staring directly at it). Continue to speak low and calmly.
- **A bear may bluff-charge**—run at you but stop well before reaching you—to try to intimidate you. Resist the eager desire to run from this charge, as that would turn

the bluff into a real charge and you will *not* be able to outrun the bear (black bears can run at speeds up to 35 miles per hour through log-strewn forests).

- If you surprise a bear and it does charge from close range, **lie down and play dead.** A surprised bear will leave you once the perceived threat is neutralized. However, if the bear wasn't attacking because it was surprised—if it charges from a long distance, or **if it has had a chance to identify you and still attacks—you should fight back**. A bear in this situation is behaving in a predatory manner (as opposed to the defensive attack of a surprised bear) and is looking at you as food. Kick, stab, punch at the bear. If it knows you will fight back, it may leave you and search for easier prey.
- **Carry a 12-ounce (or larger) can of pepper spray bear deterrent**. The spray—a high concentration of oils from hot peppers—should fire out at least 20 or 30 feet in a broad mist. Don't use the spray unless a bear is actually charging and is in range of the spray.

This Is Cougar Country

Very few hikers ever see cougars in the wild. I've been tracked by them, but in all of my hiking throughout North and South America I have yet to see one of these elusive kitties. Shy and solitary, there are about 2500 to 3000 of them roaming the state of Washington. The North Cascades support a healthy population of *Felix concolor*.

While cougar encounters are rare in the North Cascades, they do occur. To make sure the encounter is a positive one (at least for you), you need to understand these wild cats. Cougars are curious (after all, they're cats). They will follow hikers simply to see what kind of beasts we are, but they rarely (almost never) attack adult humans.

If you do encounter a cougar, remember that cougars rely on prey that can't, or won't, fight back. Fellow guidebook writer, Dan Nelson, is a Washington State University Cougar who also grew up in cougar country (the Blue Mountains of southeast Washington). He offers the following advice should you run into one of these cats:

- **Do not run!** Running may trigger a cougar's attack instinct.
- **Stand up and face it.** Virtually every recorded cougar attack of humans has been a predator-prey attack. If you appear as another aggressive predator rather than as prey, the cougar will back down.
- **Try to appear large.** Wave your arms or a jacket over your head.
- **Pick up children and small dogs.**
- **Maintain eye contact** with the animal. The cougar will interpret this as a show of dominance on your part.
- **Back away slowly** if you can safely do so.
- **Do not turn your back** or take your eyes off the cougar. Remain standing.
- **Throw things,** provided you don't have to bend over to pick them up. If you have a water bottle on your belt, chuck it at the cat. Wave your trekking pole, and if the cat gets close enough, whack it *hard* with your pole.
- **Shout loudly.**
- **Fight back** aggressively.

And you can minimize the already slim chances of having a negative cougar encounter by heeding the following:

- **Do not hike or run alone** (runners look like fleeing prey to a predator).
- **Keep children within sight** and close at all times.
- **Avoid dead animals.**
- **Keep dogs leashed and under control.** A cougar may attack a loose, solitary dog, but a leashed dog next to you makes two foes for the cougar to deal with—and cougars are too smart to take on two aggressive animals at once.
- **Be alert** to your surroundings.
- **Carry a walking stick** or trekking poles.

GEAR

No hiker should venture far up a trail without being properly equipped. Starting with the feet, a good pair of boots can make all the difference between a wonderful hike and a blistering affair. Keep your feet happy and you'll be happy.

But you can't talk boots without talking socks. Only one rule here: wear whatever is most comfortable, unless it's cotton. I prefer a synthetic liner under a wool sock. Cotton is a wonderful fabric, but not the best to hike in. When it gets wet, it stays wet and lacks any insulation value. In fact wet cotton sucks away body heat, leaving you susceptible to hypothermia. Still, I encounter hundreds of hikers who prefer jeans and cotton T-shirts—my preference for campground wear, but not for the trails.

While the list of what you pack will vary from what another hiker on the same trail is carrying, there are a few items everyone should have in their packs. Every hiker who ventures into the woods should be prepared to spend the night out with emergency food and shelter. Mountain storms can whip up in a hurry, catching fair-weather hikers by surprise. What was an easy to follow trail during a calm, clear day can disappear into a confusing world of fog and rain—or snow. Therefore, every member of the party should pack the Ten Essentials, as well as a few other items that aren't necessarily essential, but that would be good to have on hand in an emergency.

The Ten Essentials

1. **Navigation (map and compass):** Carry a topographic map of the area you plan to be in and knowledge of how to read it. Likewise, a compass—again, make sure you know how to use it.
2. **Sun protection (sunglasses and sunscreen):** Even on wet days I always carry sunscreen and sunglasses; you never know when the clouds will lift. At higher elevations your exposure to ultraviolet rays is much more intense than at sea level. You can easily burn on snow and near water. Protect yourself.
3. **Insulation (extra clothing):** It may be 70 degrees Fahrenheit at the trailhead, but at the summit it's 45 and windy. Also, storms can and do blow in rapidly. In the high country it can snow anytime of the year. Be sure to carry raingear, wind gear, and extra layers. If you get injured or lost, you won't be moving around generating heat, so you'll need to be able to bundle up.
4. **Illumination (flashlight/headlamp):** If caught after dark, you'll need a headlamp or flashlight to be able to follow the trail. If forced to spend the night, you'll need it to set up emergency camp, gather wood, and so on. Carry extra batteries and bulbs too.
5. **First-aid supplies:** At the very least, your kit should include bandages, gauze, scissors, tape, tweezers, pain relievers, antiseptics, and perhaps a small manual. It is also recommended that you get first-aid training through a program such as MOFA (Mountaineering Oriented First Aid).
6. **Fire (firestarter and matches):** If forced to spend the night, you can build an emergency campfire to provide warmth. Be sure you keep your matches dry. I use sealable plastic bags. A candle can come in handy too.
7. **Repair kit and tools (including a knife):** A knife is helpful, a multitool is better. You never know when you might need a small pair of pliers or scissors, both of which are commonly found on compact multitools. A basic repair kit should include such things as nylon cord, a small roll of duct tape, some 1-inch webbing and extra webbing buckles (to

fix broken pack straps), and a small tube of superglue. A handful of safety pins can work wonders too.

8. **Nutrition (extra food):** Always pack in more food than what you need for your hike. If you are forced to spend the night, you'll be prepared. Better to have and not need than the other way around. I also pack a couple of energy bars for emergency pick-me-ups.

9. **Hydration (extra water):** I carry two full 32-ounce water bottles all the time, unless I'm hiking entirely along a water source. You'll need to carry iodine tablets or a filter, too, so as not to catch any waterborne nasties like *Giardia*.

10. **Emergency shelter:** This can be as simple as garbage bags, or something more efficient like a reflective space blanket. My poncho doubles as an emergency tarp.

TRAILHEAD CONCERNS

Sadly, the topic of trailhead and trail crime must be addressed. As urban areas continuously encroach upon our green spaces, societal ills follow along. While violent crime is extremely rare (practically absent on most of our public lands, thankfully), it is a grim reminder that we are never truly free from the worst elements of society.

But by and large our hiking trails are safe places—far safer than most city streets. Common sense and vigilance, however, are still in order. This is true for all hikers, but particularly so for solo hikers. (Solo hiking sparks much debate over whether it is prudent or not. I hike solo 90 percent of the time, reaping rewards of deep reflection, self-determination, and a complete wilderness experience. You must decide for yourself.) Be aware of your surroundings at all times. Leave your itinerary with someone back home. If something doesn't feel right, it probably isn't. Take action

by leaving the place or situation immediately. But remember, most hikers are friendly, decent people. Some may be a little introverted, but that's no cause for worry.

By far your biggest concern should be with trailhead theft. Car break-ins, sadly, are a far too common occurrence at some of our trailheads. Do not—absolutely under no circumstances—leave anything of value in your vehicle while out hiking. Take your wallet, cell phone, and listening devices with you, or better yet, don't bring them along in the first place. Don't leave anything in your car that may appear valuable. A duffle bag on the back seat may contain dirty T-shirts, but a thief may think there's a laptop in it. Save yourself the hassle of returning to a busted window by not giving criminals a reason to clout your car.

If you arrive at a trailhead and someone looks suspicious, don't discount your intuition. Take notes on the person and his or her vehicle. Record the license plate and report the behavior to the authorities. Do not confront the person. Leave and go to another trail.

While most car break-ins are crimes of opportunity by drug addicts looking for loot to support their fix, organized bands intent on stealing IDs have also been known to target parked cars at trailheads. While some trailheads are regularly targeted, and others rarely if at all, there's no sure way of preventing this from happening to you other than being dropped off at the trailhead or taking the bus (rarely an option, either way). But you can make your car less of a target by not leaving anything of value in it.

ENJOY THE TRAILS

Most importantly, though, be safe and enjoy the trails in this book. They exist for our enjoyment and for the enjoyment of future generations of hikers. We can use them and protect them at the same time if we are careful with our actions, as well as forthright with our demands on Congress and state legislators to continue and further the protection of our state's wildlands.

Throughout the twentieth century, wilderness lovers helped secure protection for many of the lands we enjoy today. As we enter the twenty-first century, we must see to it that those protections continue and that the last bits of wildlands are also preserved for the enjoyment of future generations.

If you enjoy these trails, get involved! Trails may wind through trees, but they don't grow on them. Your involvement can be as simple as picking up trash, educating fellow citizens, or writing Congress or your state representatives a letter. All of these seemingly small acts can make a big difference. Introduce children to our trails. We need to continue a legacy of good trail stewards. At the end of this book you'll find a list of organizations working on behalf of our trails and wildlands in Washington. Consider getting involved with a few of them.

Happy hiking!

A NOTE ABOUT SAFETY

Safety is an important concern in all outdoor activities. No guidebook can alert you to every hazard or anticipate the limitations of every reader. Therefore, the descriptions of roads, trails, routes, and natural features in this book are not representations that a particular place or excursion will be safe for your party. When you follow any of the routes described in this book, you assume responsibility for your own safety. Under normal conditions, such excursions require the usual attention to traffic, road and trail conditions, weather, terrain, the capabilities of your party, and other factors. Keeping informed on current conditions and exercising common sense are the keys to a safe, enjoyable outing.

—The Mountaineers Books

Opposite: View from Oyster Dome

islands and puget sound

Fidalgo Island

Gateway to the San Juan Islands, Fidalgo is also blessed with breathtaking coastal scenery, rolling hills, forests and wetlands teeming with wildlife, and an excellent trail system. Nearly half of the island is protected in parks and preserves traversed by miles of trail. Lying within the Olympic Mountains rain shadow, Fidalgo makes for an excellent hiking destination during the dreary winter months. And unlike the San Juans long haul, Fidalgo is a quick getaway, no ferry crossing required.

1 Deception Pass Headlands

RATING/ DIFFICULTY	ROUND-TRIP	ELEV GAIN/ HIGH POINT	SEASON
★★★★/1	5 miles	350 feet/ 110 feet	Year-round

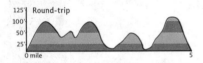

Map: Green Trails Deception Pass/Anacortes Community Forest Lands No. 41S; **Contact:** Deception Pass State Park, (360) 675-2417, *www.parks.wa.gov*; **Notes:** Dogs must be leashed. Trails are kid-friendly but require caution and supervision around coastal cliffs; **GPS:** N 48 25.013, W 122 39.070

Rugged coastal headlands, placid coves, tidal pools teeming with crusty critters, towering ancient evergreens, and breathtaking views of the Olympic Mountains—Deception Pass State Park packs it in. And with waterfront campsites and easy access from Pugetopolis, it's easy to see why Deception Pass is Washington's most popular state park (over three million annual visitors). This hike samples the park's rugged northern headlands, delivering spectacular views of straits and bays and of Deception Pass itself, with its treacherous waters and majestic bridge.

GETTING THERE

From Burlington (exit 230 on I-5), head west on State Route 20 for about 12 miles to the junction with the SR 20 spur (which continues to Anacortes). Turn left on SR 20 (signed for Oak Harbor) and continue for 5 miles, turning right onto Rosario Road just after passing Pass Lake. Proceed 100 yards, then turn left (signed for Bowman Bay), following this park road 0.4 mile to day-use parking at the Civilian Conservation Corps Interpretive Center (if this lot is full, park at the nearby boat launch lot). Water and restrooms available.

ON THE TRAIL

With over 4000 acres and nearly 40 miles of trails, Deception Pass State Park offers far more than the small section this hike passes through. But what a section! From the CCC Interpretive Center you'll travel out and back to Rosario Head and then likewise for Lighthouse Point and Lottie Point. First, visit the CCC center to gain an appreciation of what FDR's Depression-era program did for our country. Hardworking corps were stationed right here at Deception Pass, transforming this corner of Washington into a prime state park. Trails, campgrounds, and sturdy structures throughout the park are all part of their legacy.

The trail for Rosario Head takes off west from the interpretive center. Under a canopy of stately firs and madronas, the well-built trail climbs 100 feet up a steep hillside flanking Bowman Bay. Pass a series of fine outlooks before slowly descending, reaching Sharpe Cove in 0.75 mile. Now, make the 0.3-mile loop around Rosario Head using caution: 50-foot cliffs on the west side drop straight to Rosario Strait. Savor views across salty waters to the San Juan Islands and the Olympic Mountains.

Sunsets are spectacular. Retrace your steps to the interpretive center.

Continue hiking south, now, along the sandy beaches of Bowman Bay. Pass the boat launch and pier. A short steep climb of about 50 feet slows your momentum—a necessary detour around a rocky impasse. As the trail drops back to sea level, an unsigned trail takes off left for Pass Lake. Continue right, soon coming to another junction. The trail left heads 0.5 mile along Lottie Bay before climbing and looping around Lottie Point, providing outstanding views of the narrow channel separating Fildalgo from Whidbey Island: Deception Pass.

Return to the junction and head left via a tombolo (a spit connecting an island or offshore rock with the mainland, created by wave-carried sedimentation) to Lighthouse Point. Enter an old-growth Douglas-fir forest, and in

about 0.25 mile come to an unsigned junction, the beginning and end of a 1-mile loop.

Head left to grassy bluffs that offer stunning views of Deception Pass. Carry on, climbing above a rocky cleft. Along the loop, several side trails lead to jaw-dropping viewpoints out to lonely Deception Island and a vast waterway. Back into thick timber, the trail descends, closing the loop. Return to your vehicle or continue exploring the park. Be sure to thank the CCC.

EXTENDING YOUR TRIP

With nearly 40 miles of trails, you'll not tire of hiking options in this gorgeous state park. Pass Lake Trail is a good choice, while across Deception Pass on Whidbey Island, North Beach, Goose Rock, and Hoypus Point all make fine destinations. Just up Rosario Road is Sharpe Park, where a 0.5-mile trail leads

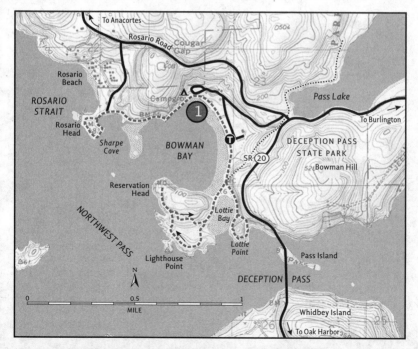

to a magnificent headland towering 400 feet above Rosario Strait. With all these trails, you may want to camp a night, but don't forget to make a reservation.

2 Sugarloaf

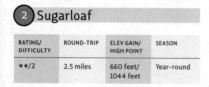

RATING/ DIFFICULTY	ROUND-TRIP	ELEV GAIN/ HIGH POINT	SEASON
★★/2	2.5 miles	660 feet/ 1044 feet	Year-round

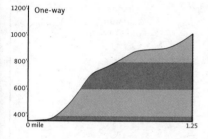

Map: Green Trails Deception Pass/Anacortes Community Forest Lands No. 41S; **Contact:** City of Anacortes Parks and Recreation, (360) 293-1918, *www.cityofanacortes.org/parks.asp*; **Notes:** Dogs must be leashed. Some trails are multiuse. Smoking prohibited; **GPS:** N 48 28.037, W 122 37.804

From this little summit in the heart of Fidalgo Island, enjoy an eagle's-eye view of the San Juan Islands, the Olympic Mountains, Whidbey Island, and Vancouver Island. Enjoy too, big trees, mossy ledges, and sunny slopes. Sweet little Sugarloaf sits in the center of the 2800-acre Anacortes Community Forest Lands—a miniwilderness just minutes from the city's downtown. And though hiking to this delectable destination is indeed short and sweet, there are miles of adjoining trails if you're craving more adventure.

Opposite: Deception Pass headlands

GETTING THERE

From Burlington (exit 230 on I-5), head west on State Route 20 for about 12 miles to the junction with the SR 20 spur. Turn left on SR 20 (signed for Oak Harbor) and continue for 1.8 miles, turning right onto Campbell Lake Road. Follow this road for 1.5 miles to the vintage Lake Erie Grocery. Bear right onto Heart Lake Road, continuing for 1.4 miles. Turn right where a sign indicates "MT Erie Viewpoint" and drive a couple of hundred feet to a parking area and trailhead kiosk (elev. 380 ft) (don't turn to the right up Mount Erie Road).

ON THE TRAIL

There are over 20 miles of trails crisscrossing and zigzagging across the Anacortes Community Forest Lands. They are all well marked, but without a map you'll have a heck of a time figuring them out. Study the map on the back of the kiosk. Better yet, get yourself one—either the map published by Green Trails or the Anacortes park department (sold by area merchants) will work. Note that many of the forests are multiuse, meaning you'll be sharing space with horses, mountain bikes, and yes, even a few motorbikes (I can't understand why these last are allowed). By and far the largest group of users are hikers like you, so you'll feel right at home.

Begin on Trail No. 215 through a wet draw graced with a few big impressive cedars. In 0.25 mile, near a handsome tree, come to a junction with Trail No.320. This hiker-only trail heads to Heart Lake, one of the nicest natural features in the community forest lands. You, however, are heading to Sugarloaf, so bear right and continue on Trail No. 215.

The warm-up is over. The path now changes gears, shifting into a steep climb. Doug-firs replace cedars. Ferns and moss line the way. At 0.5 mile, encounter another junction, where you

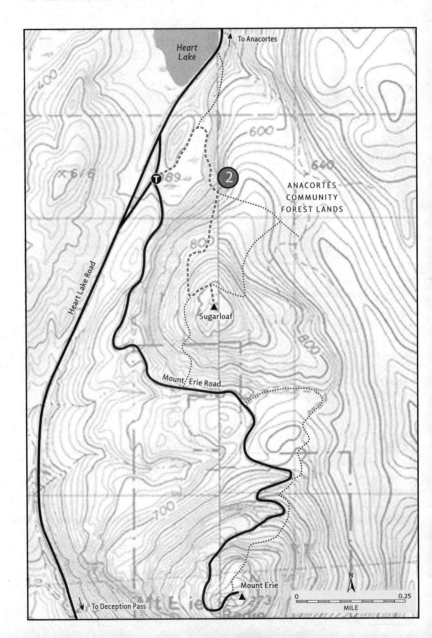

stay to the right on Trail No. 215. Under a canopy of mature Douglas-firs, the trail wastes little time reaching the summit block, working its way up and around a series of mossy ledges.

At 1 mile is another trail junction. Turn left, leaving Trail No. 215 for Trail No. 226. One final short push and you're on top of the 1044-foot loaf. But, where are those sweet views that were promised? Head to the right down Trail No. 238 (it loops from Trail No. 226), and in five minutes you'll be staring out over Whidbey, Vancouver, and the San Juan islands. Enjoy views, too, out to the Cascades from this shelf of sun-kissed grassy ledges. The big blob in front of you is Mount Erie, highest point on Fidalgo Island. The views from that 1273-foot peak are indeed fine, but its summit road may leave a bad taste in your mouth. Savor instead the sweet scenic serenity of Sugarloaf.

EXTENDING YOUR TRIP
There are many options for extending your hike in the Anacortes Community Forest Lands. Take Trail No. 215 down to the Mount Erie Road, then locate the trail to Erie's summit just a couple of minutes up the road. Despite summit towers and parking lots, the views are quite spectacular, especially over Deception Pass. Nearby Whistle Lake makes a kid-friendly destination. This quiet body of water is reached via a 0.75-mile hike from a trailhead off of O Avenue, which is north of the Sugarloaf hike.

San Juan Islands
A cluster of islands sprinkled between the straits of Georgia and Juan de Fuca, the San Juan Islands are surrounded by some of the most stunning coastal scenery in all of North America. With rugged rocky coastlines, sandy spits, forested mountains punctuated with pastures and ponds and a handful of villages you'd swear were plucked right out of New England, the San Juans are Washington's most charming place. Day hikers will find plenty of agreeable terrain here and some of the best-groomed trails in the Northwest. They'll also find some of the best weather, thanks to the Olympic

Maritime view from Suglarloaf

Mountains capturing rain-filled clouds and wringing them out before they pass over the islands. Wildlife teems on these rural islands too, and chances are good you may see the only orca whale population in the continental United States. Bustling in summer, the islands are quiet in winter and just as delightful.

3 Spencer Spit

RATING/ DIFFICULTY	ROUND-TRIP	ELEV GAIN/ HIGH POINT	SEASON
★★★/1	1.75 miles	60 feet/ 60 feet	Year-round

Map: USGS Blakely Island; **Contact:** Spencer Spit State Park, (360) 468-2251, *www.parks* *.wa.gov*; **Notes:** Dogs must be leashed. Park facilities closed late autumn until early spring. If road gated, park on shoulder and walk park road 0.4 mile to trailhead or take trail that goes right from gate 0.4 mile to spit; **GPS:** N 48 32.175, W 122 51.558

Cast your cares to the salty breezes while venturing onto this wide beach of sand and polished stones. A delightful hike any time of year, Spencer Spit is a dynamic environment always in flux. Amble along this protruding point in Lopez Sound watching for playful seals, probing shorebirds, surf-riding waterfowl, and majestic eagles hovering above. The

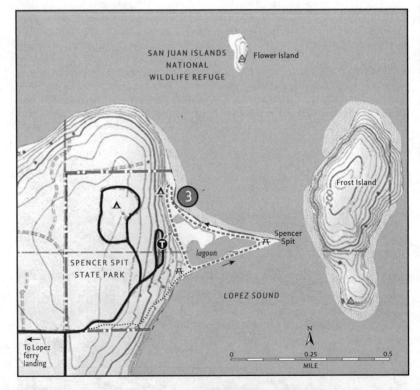

Winter hike at Spencer Spit

hike is short, but you'll want to linger long, for Spencer Spit is one of the finest beaches in the San Juans.

GETTING THERE

Take the Washington State Ferry from Anacortes to Lopez Island. From the Lopez ferry landing, follow Ferry Road south for 1.2 miles. Turn left onto Port Stanley Road and drive 2.4 miles. Turn left onto Baker View Road (signed for "Spencer Spit"), reaching the state park boundary in 0.6 mile. Continue for another 0.4 mile to the day-use area and trailhead (elev. 60 ft). Water and restrooms available.

ON THE TRAIL

It's a short jaunt to the beach, and all downhill. Immediately upon leaving the trailhead, come to a junction. Turn right and make a beeline straight for the picnic area at the base of the spit. Homesteaded in the 1880s by the Spencer and Troxell families, the area is still graced with fruit trees and other remnants of their tenure. Passive bunnies also abound. Be careful not to twist an ankle in one of their burrows. It can be a hare-oing experience! In 1967 the spit and adjacent uplands, 138 acres in all, were transferred to Washington State Parks.

Time to explore the spit. If the tide is high, stick to the wide trail; otherwise, scamper over a hedgerow of beached logs to the beach. It's a 0.4-mile glorious walk to the tip of the spit, where Frost Island teasingly tempts to be touched. If the spit ever expands enough to embrace the island, a land formation known as a tombolo will be created. The channel separating these two landforms, however, is deep and swift moving, so the likelihood of this happening is not great.

Check out the log cabin at the tip of the spit. A 1978 replica of a 1913 structure, it was constructed of driftwood logs. Now return via the north shore of the spit. Watch for playful harbor seals and water-plying ferries. Scan Flower Island for avian activity. Admire a beautiful backdrop dominated by Orcas Island's Mount Constitution.

At 0.25 mile from the cabin, come to a creek draining the spit's interior lagoon. Expect wet feet crossing the creek. Don't enter the lagoon; it's a sanctuary for breeding, nesting, and feeding birds. Continue along the beach another 0.25 mile, coming to a walk-in campground. Turn south, following a lagoon-hugging trail back to the picnic area and then back to your vehicle. En route, let muck-darting herons and shrub-scratching towhees entertain you.

EXTENDING YOUR TRIP

A couple of miles of trail traverse the park's woodlands and make for a nice extension to your hike. Consider spending the evening at Spencer Spit's appealing campground (reservations necessary in summer). Nearby Odlin County Park and Upright Channel State Park also offer good woodland romps and excellent beach hiking. In low tides, hike the 1.25-mile shoreline between the two parks for spectacular San Juan Islands scenery and fine ferry, eagle, and seal watching.

4 Shark Reef Sanctuary

RATING/ DIFFICULTY	ROUND-TRIP	ELEV GAIN/ HIGH POINT	SEASON
★★★/1	1 mile	70 feet/ 100 feet	Year-round

Map: USGS Richardson; **Contact:** San Juan County Parks, (360) 378-8420, www.co.san-juan.wa.us/parks; **Notes:** Dogs must be leashed; **GPS:** N 48 27.760, W 122 56.240

Take a short and sweet stroll through shoulder-high salal and stately timber to a shoreline teeming with marine life. One of the best spots on Lopez Island for seal watching, the Shark Reef Sanctuary also ranks supreme for observing birds. Easy to hike, breathtakingly scenic, and biologically diverse, Shark Reef makes for an excellent destination for nascent hikers and young'uns yearning for discovery.

GETTING THERE

Take the Washington State Ferry from Anacortes to Lopez Island. From Lopez ferry landing, follow Ferry Road south for 2.2 miles to a junction with Center Road. Bear right onto Fisherman Bay Road and drive 5 miles, passing Lopez Village. Turn right onto Airport Road. In 0.4 mile, turn left onto Shark Reef Road and drive another 1.8 miles to Shark Reef Sanctuary (0.1 mile beyond the Burt Road junction). Privy available.

ON THE TRAIL

Originally a military post, then a Washington State Department of Natural Resources tract, the Shark Reef Sanctuary was nearly stripped of its mature timber in 1980. But island residents petitioned the state, arguing that the 39-acre parcel is more valuable as an outdoor laboratory than as a woodlot. And they're right. The land was transferred to San Juan County Parks and has become one of Lopez's most popular hiking destinations.

On good trail, set out through thick forest carpeted in salal. A handful of old firs, a rarity on Lopez, grace the way. Raucous gulls and amplifying surf announce you're getting close to shore. In 0.25 mile, and after a short descent, emerge on an opening above the beautiful and bustling-with-life San Juan Channel. The views are good, but they get better. Continue hiking south for another 0.25 mile to an area of ledges and grassy bluffs framed by windblown pines.

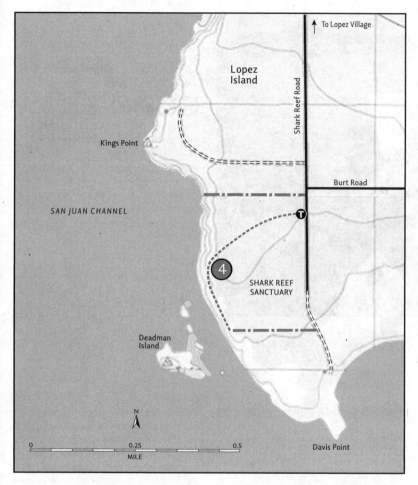

Find yourself a sunny sitting spot and start taking it all in. Across the channel, Mount Finlayson (Hike 9) rises above the golden lawns of Cattle Point on San Juan Island. Dallas Mountain, the highest point on that island, peeks just to the northwest. Look south to an Olympic skyline, capped in white and hovering above the Strait of Juan de Fuca. Directly in front of you in the channel below are Dead-man Island and a series of reefs and offshore rocks. Shark Reef is actually to the north and not visible from this point. No matter—the landmarks in sight are teeming with life.

Tenacious oystercatchers sift through freshly exposed tidal pools. Lumbering sea lions and lethargic harbor seals bask and look on. Kingfishers scout and eagles soar while cormorants cut through choppy currents. It's not a bad show

Hiker soaking up sun and scenery at Shark Reef Sanctuary

and performances are repeated throughout the day, year-round.

⑤ Turtleback Mountain

RATING/ DIFFICULTY	ROUND-TRIP	ELEV GAIN/ HIGH POINT	SEASON
★★★★/3	3 miles	830 feet/ 930 feet	Year-round

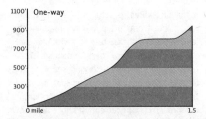

Map: USGS Eastsound; **Contact:** San Juan County Land Bank, (360) 378-4402, www .co.san-juan.wa.us; **Notes:** Dogs must be leashed. Please respect adjacent private property by not leaving trail; **GPS:** N 48 38.489, W 122 58.625

⭐👪🪝⚙️ *It's a shell of a nice view from Orcas Island's Turtleback Mountain. From an open knoll on the turtle's "head" known as Ship Peak, set your sights asail to a magnificent maritime mélange of islands, harbors, headlands, and water-plying vessels. Recently spared from subdivision, the 1578-acre Turtleback Mountain Preserve promises to be one of the San Juan Islands' prime hiking destinations.*

GETTING THERE

Take the Washington State Ferry from Anacortes to Orcas Island. From the Orcas ferry landing follow Orcas Road (Horseshoe Highway) 2.5 miles north. Turn left onto Deer Harbor Road, continuing for 2.2 miles. Turn right onto dirt Wild Rose Lane and proceed 0.1 mile to a small parking lot with information kiosk (elev. 100 ft).

ON THE TRAIL

Officially opened to the public in January 2007, land managers for the Turtleback Mountain Preserve are working on a management plan for the 1578-acre property. Once it's completed, expect it to include a few miles of new hiking trail. In the meantime, though, hiking in the preserve is limited primarily to existing woods roads. The hike to the Ship Peak overlook, perhaps the best viewing venue on the preserve, is open and is accepting interested hikers.

Start by walking up dirt Wild Rose Lane for 500 feet to a gated road on your right signed "Turtleback South Trail." Under a canopy of Doug-fir, madrona, and Garry oak, follow the trail—a winding woods road—upward. In 0.6

mile reach a telephone line and a direct view down to West Sound.

Continue climbing, traversing an open shrubby slope reminiscent of a southern Appa-lachian bald. As the trail increases in steepness, your determined stride will slow to a turtle's crawl. But what's the hurry? Look around—the expanding views are breathtaking. In 1 mile

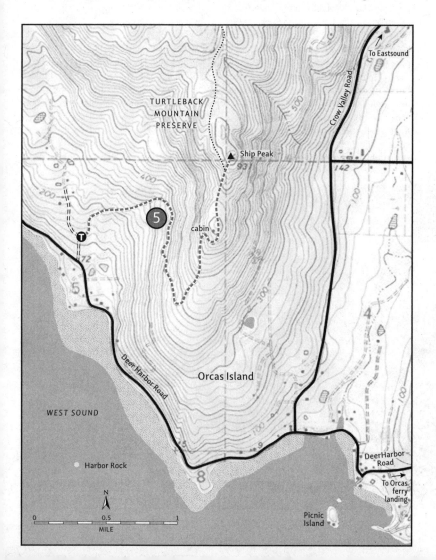

reach an old cabin (elev. 800 ft) perched on a point and providing pure panoramic pleasure. Look south to glistening waters punctuated by the San Juans, their ramped and plucked topography courtesy of retreating glaciers from a few millennia ago. Look west to Canada's Gulf Islands and a backdrop of craggy Vancouver Island summits and ridges. Sunsets from this point are spectacular.

For Ship Peak, locate a trail taking off in forest behind the cabin. Follow it for 0.2 mile, descending to a signed junction. The trail left leads 0.75 mile across the wooded spine of the Turtleback (a wood turtle?) connecting with the Center Loop Trail (an old road). Head right instead for 0.3 mile, climbing open mossy ledges adorned with oak to the 930-foot Ship Peak overlook. East Sound, West Sound—and Mount Constitution rising over the rolling pastures of Crow Valley—what a view! And what a preserve this is too—respect it and protect it.

EXTENDING YOUR TRIP

The preserve's North and Center Loop trails are old woods roads primarily traveling through forest. However, the Waldron overlook, a sheer ledge (watch children and dogs here), offers an impressive view of Waldron Island and makes a worthwhile hike. Follow the North Trail (accessible from the Crow Valley Road) 1.25 miles, climbing 700 feet to reach the overlook.

West Sound from Ship Peak overlook

SAVING THE TURTLE

In the 1920s, prominent ship builder and former Seattle mayor Robert Moran donated more than 3500 acres of spectacular Orcas Island property to the state to be established as a park. Today Moran State Park protects over 5000 acres of old-growth forest, pristine lakeshore, and scenic mountaintops in one of Washington's priciest and most-threatened-with-development scenic corners. But fortunately, Moran's legacy would not be the last grand land protection initiative to help retain Orcas Island's rural charm and natural heritage.

In 2006, 1578 acres of Turtleback Mountain were permanently removed from real-estate listings and added to the public trust, protecting one of the last large undeveloped tracts left in all of the San Juan Islands. And what a tract! But perhaps more impressive than Turtleback's spectacular island vistas is how rapidly concerned citizens mobilized to protect it.

The property was put up for sale in the summer of 2005 by a private foundation. It was immediately eyed by residential and resort developers. To many island residents and visitors alike, the thought of this familiar landmark being marred by second homes and condominiums was unbearable. A partnership of conservation organizations sprang up to raise the funds necessary to purchase the property. Spearheaded by the San Juan Preservation Trust, the Trust for Public Land, and the San Juan County Land Bank, the partnership raised $18.5 million in just six months. It was the largest fundraising campaign ever undertaken in San Juan County.

In January 2007 the Turtleback Mountain Preserve was officially opened to the public. The San Juan County Land Bank now owns it, while the San Juan Preservation Trust retains a conservation easement on the land, ensuring that the area will remain in a natural state and open to the public in perpetuity.

6 Cascade Lake

RATING/ DIFFICULTY	LOOP	ELEV GAIN/ HIGH POINT	SEASON
★★/2	2.7 miles	100 feet/ 400 feet	Year-round

Maps: USGS Mount Constitution, park map from entrance kiosk; **Contact:** Moran State Park, (360) 376-2326, www.parks.wa.gov; **Notes:** Dogs must be leashed; **GPS:** N 48 39.373, W 122 51.330

With its three campgrounds, shaded picnic area, paddle-boat concession, and inviting beaches, Cascade Lake is the hub of outdoor activity in Orcas Island's sprawling Moran State Park. And an attractive trail circling the lake makes this beautiful body of water a hiker's favorite as well. While definitely one of the more popular hiking destinations within the 5200-acre park, opportunities for tranquility do exist at Cascade. Early mornings and evenings are quiet, with good prospects for observing wildlife, while winter casts an especially peaceful pall on the lake. Kids will love this hike no matter the time of year.

GETTING THERE

Take the Washington State Ferry from Anacortes to Orcas Island. From the Orcas ferry landing follow Orcas Road (Horseshoe Highway) 9 miles north to the village of Eastsound. Continue east on Crescent Beach Drive for 1 mile to an intersection. Turn right (south) onto Olga Road and proceed 3.25 miles to Moran State Park. Pass through the entrance arch, and in 0.25 mile come to the Cascade Lake Day-Use Area (elev. 350 ft.). Park on either side of the road. Water and restrooms available.

ON THE TRAIL

Starting in the day-use area, take a moment to admire the rustic picnic shelter, one of many structures in the park, including the trails and their elegant signposts, that were built by the Civilian Conservation Corps during the Great Depression. Begin your loop hike by heading counterclockwise, crossing Cold Creek in a stand of big ol' cedars.

Hugging the lakeshore the delightful trail passes through marshy areas and over ledges teetering on waters' edge. Ignore a trail lead-

ing right, unless you're intent on visiting the Rosario Resort, former home of Robert Moran (who donated much of Moran State Park to the people of Washington) and now on the National Register of Historical Places.

At 1 mile reach another junction. The trail right circles Rosario Lagoon on a 0.75-mile brushy and muddy route. Head straight instead, crossing the lagoon on an attractive bridge. Now in tall timber, continue along the lake, taking in views of the broad south face of Mount Constitution rising above. Scan the water for playful otters.

At 1.5 miles reach the South End Campground. Avoiding the temptation to drop in on someone's barbeque, pick up the trail again near campsite number 1. Hugging the lake once more the trail heads north, crossing the park office road, then veering away from the water.

Soon afterward the trail crosses Olga Road (use caution crossing), coming to a junction. The trail right leads 0.75 mile to Cascade

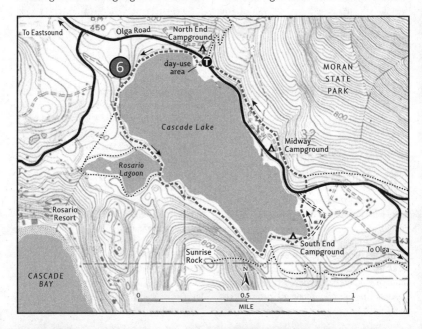

Evening serenity on Cascade Lake

Falls, a worthwhile side trip. Head left instead to close the loop, skirting the Midway Campground and arriving back at the day-use area, 0.75 mile from the junction.

EXTENDING YOUR TRIP
There are over 30 miles of hiking trails in Moran State Park, providing plenty of options for extending this loop or creating new ones. Add Cascade Falls to this hike for a 4-mile loop. Consider making the short but steep (0.75 mile one-way, 500-foot elevation gain), rugged side trip to Sunrise Rock for an eagle's-eye view of the lake. Spend a night or two camping at the park, but be sure to make reservations if visiting in the summer.

7 Mount Constitution and Mountain Lake

Mount Constitution

RATING/ DIFFICULTY	LOOP	ELEV GAIN/ HIGH POINT	SEASON
★★★★★/3	6.7 miles	1500 feet/ 2410 feet	Year-round

Mountain Lake

RATING/ DIFFICULTY	LOOP	ELEV GAIN/ HIGH POINT	SEASON
★★/2	3.9 miles	50 feet/ 950 feet	Year-round

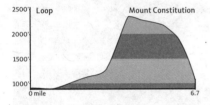

Maps: USGS Mount Constitution, park map from entrance kiosk; **Contact:** Moran State Park, (360) 376-2326, www.parks.wa.gov; **Notes:** Dogs must be leashed; **GPS:** N 48 39.416, W 122 49.080

Enjoy an easy, kid-friendly near-level woodland stroll around one of the largest lakes in the San Juans or a heart-pounding ascent up the islands' highest point. From Mount Constitution's unique stone tower savor stunning views of snow-capped peaks and emerald islands spanning from British Columbia's Garibaldi all the way to Rainier. After fawning and awing, walk along the edge of precipitous cliffs gazing at the twinkling waters of Mountain Lake 1000-feet below. This is the heart of Moran State Park, and when it comes to pure scenery, wildlife observations, and top-notch trails, you'll be hard-pressed to find an area surpassing this.

GETTING THERE

Take the Washington State Ferry from Anacortes to Orcas Island. From the Orcas ferry landing follow Orcas Road (Horseshoe Highway) 9 miles north to the village of Eastsound. Continue east on Crescent Beach Drive for 1 mile to an intersection. Turn right (south) onto Olga Road and proceed 3.25 miles to Moran State Park, passing through the entrance arch. Continue for 1.25 miles, then bear left onto Mount Constitution Road. Follow this paved narrow road for just over a mile to the Mountain Lake turnoff. Turn right, coming to a parking area and ranger station in 0.25 mile (elev. 925 ft). Water and restrooms available.

ON THE TRAIL

For both loops, begin by walking 0.25 mile down a dirt road to the boat launch. Here, the trail takes off north, hugging the western shore of Mountain Lake. This section of trail is named for Bonnie Sliger, a popular Youth Conservation Corps supervisor who tragically died in a fall in 1977.

Skirting the placid shoreline graced with mature timber, keep your eyes and ears tuned for woodpeckers, eagles, ducks, and osprey. Watch too for kingfishers and heron. While you're scoping for birds, a few of Moran's ubiquitous black-tailed deer will probably be watching you.

In 1.25 miles reach a junction. To continue circling 200-acre Mountain Lake, proceed right. Meandering along pristine shoreline, the trail carries on with its easy journey. A small ledge requiring a climb of 50 feet or so is the only break from near-level hiking on the entire loop. At 3.25 miles reach a small dam at the lake's southern tip. From this point enjoy good views of Mount Constitution, cliffs and tower revealed, hovering above the lake.

Avoiding a side trail leading to Mount Pickett, continue by crossing Cascade Creek on

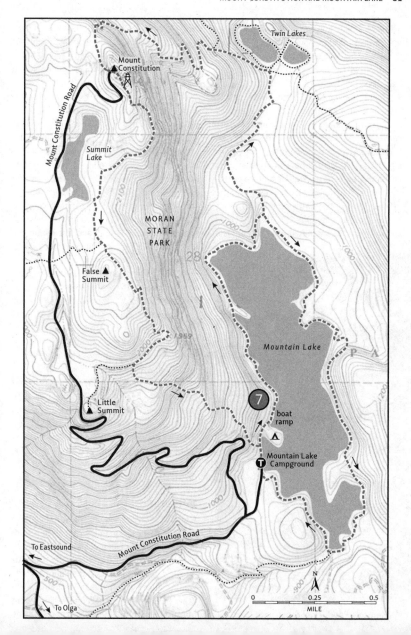

Twin Lakes

Mount
Constitution

Mount Constitution Road

Summit
Lake

MORAN
STATE
PARK

False ▲
Summit

1,959

Mountain Lake

Little ▲
Summit

7

boat
ramp

Mountain Lake
Campground

To Eastsound

Mount Constitution Road

To Olga

N

0   0.25   0.5
MILE

a bridge just below the dam. Here another trail diverges left, this one following Cascade Creek and leading to falls and lake of same name. Head right, hugging more Mountain Lake shoreline and closing the loop.

Mount Constitution–bound hikers should head left at 1.25 miles from the trailhead onto the Twin Lakes Trail, at the junction that comes along as you're hiking the lakeshore. Follow the well-trodden path for 1 mile, gaining an easy 200 feet of elevation to another junction (elev. 1100 ft). Trails leading to the little Twins and to Mount Pickett take off right.

You, however, are headed left. Take a break—you've got quite a climb ahead of you. In deep timber, begin your ascent. The

Moran State Park's eloquent signage

trail steepens, gaining 1000 feet in less than a mile as it works its way up Constitution. En route ignore a trail taking off right (North Trail), but consider the spurs leading left to nice viewpoints.

At 4 miles from your start, emerge on 2409-foot Mount Constitution's broad summit. Don't let gawking tourists who drove to the summit detract from your experience; well-earned views await. Head for Constitution's unique stone tower. Constructed by Civilian Conservation Corps crews in 1936, it's a facsimile of a twelfth-century Caucasus Mountains military fortification. From this roof top of the San Juan Islands, enjoy an unobstructed view of island, mountain, Sound, and strait from the Olympics to Rainier, Vancouver Island to British Columbia's Coast Range.

Now it's time to amend your views on Constitution, adding to the sights seen by continuing your hike. Leave the summit and crowds via the Little Summit Trail. Losing very little elevation, saunter for a mile on the summit plateau through stands of lodgepole pine and along the edge of sheer cliffs plummeting straight down to Mountain Lake.

After skirting frog-incubating Summit Lake, bear left at a junction (the trail right leads to Cold Springs and Cascade Lake), and in another mile reach another junction (elev. 1900 ft), bearing left once again. Begin your at times steep descent back to Mountain Lake, arriving at your vehicle and closing the loop in 0.75 mile.

EXTENDING YOUR TRIP

A myriad of trails interconnect with the above loops and allow for many extensive and/or additional hikes. Head to Mount Pickett to hike through one of the largest tracts of old-growth forest remaining in the Puget Trough. Want solitude? Venture down (or up) the North Trail. Looking for a challenge? Hike Mount Constitution from Cascade Lake, taking the

4.3-mile Cold Spring Trail to the Little Summit Trail. Of course, with all of these hiking opportunities, plan on spending a night or two camping in the park (reservations are necessary during the summer).

⑧ Obstruction Pass

RATING/ DIFFICULTY	ROUND-TRIP	ELEV GAIN/ HIGH POINT	SEASON
★★/1	1.2 miles	125 feet/ 125 feet	Year-round

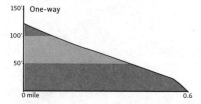

Map: USGS Blakely Island; **Contact:** Moran State Park, (360) 376-2326, *www.parks.wa.gov*; **Notes:** Dogs must be leashed; **GPS:** N 48 36.510, W 122 49.595

Hike an easy half mile under big firs, cedars, and madronas to a secluded beach on Obstruction Pass at the mouth of East Sound. While away time skipping stones, identifying birds, napping on polished driftwood logs, or just staring out at a backdrop of emerald islands and the snowy Olympic Mountains. Being an obstructionist never felt so positive!

GETTING THERE
Take the Washington State Ferry from Anacortes to Orcas Island. From the Orcas ferry landing follow Orcas Road (Horseshoe Highway) 9 miles north to the village of Eastsound. Continue east on Crescent Beach Drive for 1 mile to an intersection. Turn right (south) onto Olga Road and proceed 3.25 miles to Moran State Park, passing through the entrance

Quiet beach on Obstruction Pass

arch. Continue for another 3.25 miles to the small hamlet of Olga and an intersection. Turn left onto Point Lawrence Road, and follow it for 0.5 mile, bearing right onto Obstruction Pass Road. After 1 mile turn right onto dirt Trailhead Road and drive 0.8 mile to the road end at Obstruction Pass State Park (elev. 125 ft). Privy available.

ON THE TRAIL
Once a Washington State Department of Natural Resources tract, in 2002 this 80-acre prime piece of shoreline property fell under the auspices of the state parks department. Local

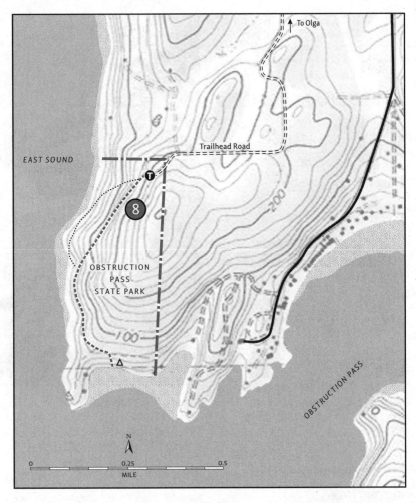

volunteers help maintain the park's trails and campsites and provide the proper attention this part of our natural heritage deserves.

From the parking lot, pass through a gate and immediately come to a junction with a new trail taking off right. A nice alternative for the return, this path loops back to the main trail after skirting along the shoreline, provid-

ing good views of Buck Bay and the village of Olga with Entrance Mountain rising behind it.

On a gently descending course, carry on down the main trail. Lined with ferns, salal, and Oregon grape, the way winds through attractive woods. In 0.3 mile the new trail reconnects. Soon come to a series of madrona-adorned bluffs hovering 75 feet above the surf. Keep children nearby and enjoy the view across East Sound.

At 0.5 mile from the parking lot, the trail ends at a forested bluff harboring a scattering of campsites. Two steep stairways lead down to the beach. Comb the cobbled coast or picnic on a polished driftwood log. Watch waterfowl wading in the pass and ferries plying outlying channels. Stay awhile. The park is peaceful, the scenery is beautiful, and the return hike is short and easy.

⑨ Mount Finlayson

RATING/ DIFFICULTY	LOOP	ELEV GAIN/ HIGH POINT	SEASON
★★★★/2	3.5 miles	285 feet/ 285 feet	Year-round

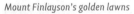

Maps: USGS False Bay, park map from American Camp Visitors Center; **Contact:** San Juan Island National Historical Park, (360) 378-2240, www.nps.gov/sajh; **Notes:** Dogs must be leashed; **GPS:** N 48 27.817, W 122 59.935

Mount Finlayson's golden lawns

Who said "War is hell"? Hell, if the Pig War never broke out we wouldn't have been left with the longest stretch of public beach in the San Juan Islands and some great hiking trails to boot. Once the site of an American military encampment, San Juan Island National Historical Park's American Camp offers plenty of natural splendors and historical relics. From Mount Finlayson, marvel at an undeveloped coastline spread out below you. Stare across the Strait of Juan de Fuca at a backdrop of snowy Olympic Mountain summits. Watch for eagles, plovers, sandpipers, and hawks. Enjoy one of the most spectacular settings in all of the San Juans.

GETTING THERE
Take the Washington State Ferry from Anacortes to Friday Harbor on San Juan Island. Follow Spring Street for 0.5 mile through town. Turn left (south) onto Mullis Road, which becomes Cattle Point Road, and follow it for just over 5 miles to American Camp in the San Juan Island National Historical Park. Continue on Cattle Point Road for 1.7 more miles to the trailhead, on the left and signed "Jakle's Lagoon" (elev. 100 ft).

ON THE TRAIL

Established as a national historical park to commemorate the Pig War—a confrontation between the United States and Britain over possession of the Oregon Country in which the only casualty was a Hudson's Bay Company hog—the 1750-acre park is divided into two sections, the American and English camps. Along with its historical importance, the park protects some important habitat, including at Mount Finlayson, one of the few surviving native grasslands along the Strait of Juan de Fuca.

From the Jakles Lagoon trailhead, head east on the wide Mount Finlayson Trail. Paralleling Cattle Point Road, the trail gradually climbs, cutting a swath across golden grasslands lined by a forested edge of wind-blasted, contorted firs. Maritime views grow with each step. At 0.3 mile ignore a trail to the left. Pass through a clump of trees and then begin to climb, cresting the long ridge of Mount Finlay-

son, which was named for one of the founders of Victoria, British Columbia. The provincial capital can easily be seen from along the trail.

Hike along the windswept ridge, mouth agape at the astonishing views. Stare across the Strait of Juan de Fuca to the Olympic Mountains and down Puget Sound to the bluffs of Whidbey Island. Scan the choppy waters for whales, the skies for eagles.

At 1.3 miles a trail leads left, near a group of large firs—this is your return route. But first continue straight for another 0.1 mile, reaching one of Finlayson's summits (elev. 285 ft) to take in a spectacular view of Cattle Point.

Head back down to take up the loop again, turning right and dropping steeply in a cool ravine shaded by big firs and cedars to reach a trail junction at Third Lagoon after 0.25 mile. Turn left and follow this trail, an old woods road, 1.75 miles back to the trailhead. Be sure to take the side trail to Jakles Lagoon for a nice view of Mount Constitution and Turtleback

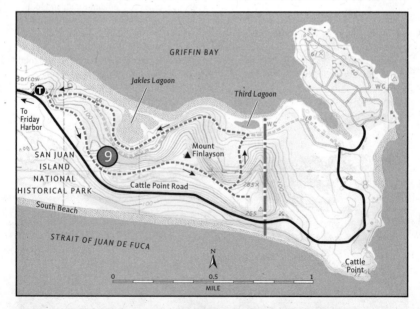

Mountain across Griffin Bay. Not a bad spoil of war all this natural beauty.

EXTENDING YOUR TRIP

Jakle's Lagoon and nearby Old Town Lagoon offer nice bayside beach walking. For the supreme San Juan shoreline stroll, head over to South Beach, a mere 0.5 mile away. Enjoy 2 miles of undeveloped coastline, the largest public beach in the San Juan Islands. Hike along bluffs, across prairie, or along the surf.

10 Young Hill and Bell Point

Young Hill

RATING/ DIFFICULTY	ROUND-TRIP	ELEV GAIN/ HIGH POINT	SEASON
★★★/2	2 miles	600 feet/ 650 feet	Year-round

Bell Point

RATING/ DIFFICULTY	ROUND-TRIP	ELEV GAIN/ HIGH POINT	SEASON
★★/1	1.5 miles	50 feet/ 50 feet	Year-round

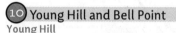

Maps: USGS Roche Harbor, park map from American Camp Visitor Center; **Contact:** San Juan Island National Historical Park, (360) 378-2240, www.nps.gov/sajh; **Notes:** Dogs must be leashed; **GPS:** N 48 35.202, W 123 08.810

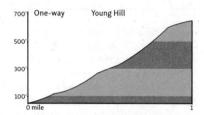 Stroll along the placid bay waters surrounding Bell Point, or peer down at them from the grassy and ledgy slopes of Young Hill. Better yet, combine these fine hikes that lie within San Juan Island Nation-

Garrison Bay from Young Hill

al Historical Park's English Camp. Once a British Royal Marine garrison, the grounds are now peacefully administered by the National Park Service for resource protection and heritage preservation. The United States and Great Britain nearly went to war over this piece of land, but sane heads prevailed, leaving you to enjoy a beautiful corner of the San Juans permanently protected from assaults from the modern world. Cheers.

GETTING THERE

Take the Washington State Ferry from Anacortes to Friday Harbor on San Juan Island. Follow Spring Street through town for 0.4 mile, turning right onto Blair Avenue. Continue for 0.2 mile, turning left onto Guard Street at the stop sign. Proceed another 0.2 mile to another stop sign and turn right onto Tucker Avenue. In 0.4 mile bear left at the Y intersection onto Roche Harbor Road. Continue for 7.4 miles to an intersection, where you turn left (south) onto West Valley Road. Drive 0.4 mile and turn right onto the dirt road for English Camp. In another 0.4 mile arrive at the parking area and trailhead (elev. 50 ft). Privy available.

ON THE TRAIL

Both hikes begin from the large English Camp parking area. For Young Hill, head east on a

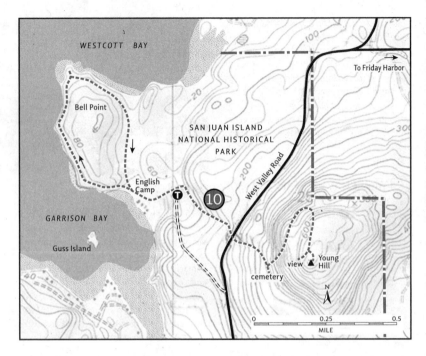

wide path that climbs gently through a forest of Doug-fir and madrona laced with salal and Oregon grape. Cross the West Valley Road and soon come to a junction. The spur right leads to the English Camp cemetery, a tranquil final resting spot enclosed by a white picket fence and shaded by big, old Garry oaks.

The main trail continues left to make a big switchback and emerge at the edge of a grassy ledge, granting sweeping views west over Garrison Bay and Bell Point out over finger coves and narrow straits to Victoria and the Gulf Islands. Continue another 0.25 mile, climbing and snaking around mossy ledges, and arrive at Young Hill's 650-foot summit for more views—the Olympics and San Juan Island's highest peak, 1015-foot Mount Dallas, are additions to the visual menu.

For Bell Point, return to the main parking area and head for the old garrison grounds, where a storehouse, blockhouse, old hospital, and barracks still stand. Locate the start of the trail at the northwest corner of the field.

Make a 1-mile loop around Bell Point under big madronas (arbutus if you're Canadian), taking in splendid coastal scenery. In particular, Westcott Bay, bearing a resemblance to coastal Maine, is strikingly beautiful. No need to hurry along this splendid loop. The resident eagles, ravens, and kingfishers don't mind if you linger.

EXTENDING YOUR TRIP

An extensive network of trails exist on the adjacent Washington State Department of Natural Resources' Mitchell Hill tract and the privately but open to the public Roche Harbor Highlands. Maps of both are available from the San Juan Island Trails Committee, an organization committed to preserving and enhancing hiking trails on the island.

Chuckanut Mountains

The only place where the Cascades meet the sea (okay, technically the foothills meet the Sound), the Chuckanuts offer a wonderful mix of mountain and coastal landscapes. Forming a greenbelt between expanding Mount Vernon and Bellingham, the Chuckanuts are growing in importance as wildlife habitat and for recreation. In response, state and county agencies continue to expand public land ownership and trails. In these gentle mountains, find small quiet lakes, panorama-providing ledges, secluded coastal coves, pockets of old growth, and miles of excellent trail. And in winter, find little snow, making the Chuckanuts a wonderful year-round hiking destination.

11 Fragrance Lake

RATING/ DIFFICULTY	LOOP	ELEV GAIN/ HIGH POINT	SEASON
★★/2	5.5 miles	1000 feet/ 1100 feet	Year-round

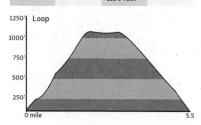

Maps: USGS Bellingham South; Chuckanut Mountain Recreation Map (Square One Maps); **Contact:** Larrabee State Park, (360) 676-2093, www.parks.wa.gov; **Notes:** Dogs must be leashed; **GPS:** N 48 39.203, W 122 29.411

👪 🐾 *A popular spot in the heart of the Chuckanut Mountains, little Fragrance Lake makes for a fine destination any time of year. On a well-built hiker-only trail through big timber, the way to Fragrance Lake includes a scenic lookout of Samish Bay and a glistening horizon dotted with islands. Loop back on a gentle old fire road and admire a crashing cascade. And if more exercise and exploration are desired, miles of interconnecting trails will more than satisfy. You won't be without company however—folks from Bellingham flock to this "backyard wilderness."*

GETTING THERE

From Mount Vernon head north on I-5 to exit 231. Follow State Route 11 (Chuckanut Drive) north for just shy of 15 miles. The trailhead is on right side of the road just after the campground entrance to Larrabee State Park. If you're coming from Bellingham follow SR 11 south for 7 miles to the trailhead (elev. 100 ft). Alternative parking is located near the campground entrance booth and 0.4 mile south at the Clayton Beach trailhead. Water and privy available at the nearby day-use beach area.

ON THE TRAIL

Waste no time warming up. The trail commences in a series of short, steep switchbacks. Upward mobility is quickly interrupted, however, upon intersecting the Interurban Trail. Once a trolley line that serviced Mount Vernon and Bellingham in the early twentieth century, the railbed was converted into a 6-mile trail in the late 1980s.

Cross the Interurban, regaining the Fragrance Lake Trail a few dozen feet to your right. Through a dark, dank forest of mature cedar and Doug-fir the trail winds its way upward. At 0.9 mile (elev. 600 ft) reach a well-marked junction. Take the fairly level side path 0.2 mile to a madrona-framed ledge that grants delightful views westward over Samish Bay to Lummi Island and the San Juans.

Soak up the scenery and perhaps some

sunshine, then resume your trek to Fragrance Lake. Back under a coniferous canopy, the trail briefly dips into a damp ravine before once again heading upward, occasionally at a steep pitch. At 1.9 miles pass through a bike barricade and arrive at another junction. The trail left heads to Fragrance Lake. The trail right leads to an old road (your return trip).

Head left first, slightly dropping into a muddy depression. Reach the small lake in about 0.1 mile and circumnavigate it on a 0.7-mile loop. Take a break at a pair of shoreline benches. Admire big cedars and babbling brooks along the eastern shore, and be impressed by a series of sandstone ledges along the western shore.

For your return, follow the old road for a gentle descent, pausing briefly about halfway to check out a pretty little cascade. The road ends in 2.2 miles, delivering you to the Clayton Beach parking lot. Return to your vehicle by following the Interurban Trail 0.5 mile north back to the Fragrance Lake Trail.

EXTENDING YOUR TRIP

There are several options to extend your hike. From the turnoff to Fragrance Lake, a trail heads 0.75 mile and climbs 700 feet to meet up with the dirt Fred Cleator Road. From there it's a short hike south (right) to a nice viewpoint overlooking Samish Bay. Or there's the Lost Lake Trail, which takes off from the old road just a couple hundred feet west of the trail to Fragrance Lake. Follow this trail (also an old road) 2.5 miles to a sliver of a lake wedged between ledges. You may also want to check out some of Larrabee State Park's fine beaches. Several short trails will lead you there. Consider the park's campground for a starry night out after all of your exploring.

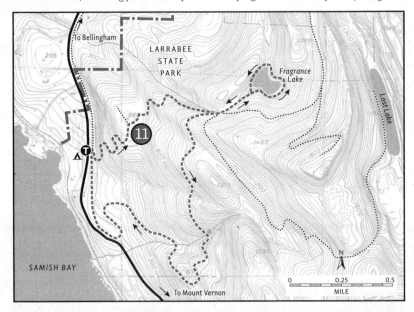

Opposite: The hike to Fragrance Lake is a treat for the four-footed hiker as well.

12 Oyster Dome

RATING/ DIFFICULTY	ROUND-TRIP	ELEV GAIN/ HIGH POINT	SEASON
★★★/3	6.5 miles	1900 feet/ 2025 feet	Year-round

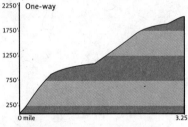

Maps: USGS Bow; Chuckanut Mountain Recreation Map (Square One Maps) **Contact:** Department of Natural Resources, Northwest Region (Sedro-Woolley), (360) 856-3500, *www.dnr.wa.gov*; **Notes:** Oyster Dome and Bat Caves can be hazardous in icy and wet conditions; **GPS:** N 48 36.518, W 122 26.002

⭐ A glacial-polished and fractured exposed hunk of sheer cliff on Blanchard Mountain, Oyster Dome is an intriguing and scenic natural landmark. Its base is littered with jumbled boulders, talus fields, and bat-breeding caves. And from atop, views abound of the Sound, mountains, and a smorgasbord of islands. A popular hiking destination

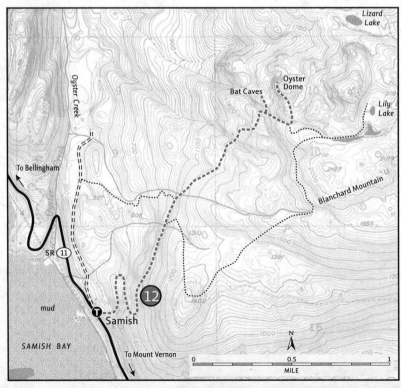

year-round, Oyster Dome is the pearl of the Chuckanut Mountains.

GETTING THERE

From Mount Vernon head north on I-5 to exit 231. Follow State Route 11 (Chuckanut Drive) north for 10.2 miles. The trailhead is on the right side of the road just after passing milepost 10. There is parking on the left (west) shoulder of the highway. If you're coming from Bellingham follow SR 11 south for 11.5 miles to the trailhead (elev. 100 ft).

ON THE TRAIL

Your route begins on the Pacific Northwest Trail, a 1200-mile long-distance trail-in-the-making from the Olympic Coast to Montana's Glacier National Park (see "North by Northwest" in this section). Through a uniform forest of second-growth conifers, gain elevation steadily. A few giant snags and remnant firs stand testament to the cathedral forests that once blanketed this region. The trail is well constructed and maintained, thanks not to the government but to dedicated volunteers.

Smell sweet maritime air as you ascend the verdant slopes of Blanchard Mountain. Rising from Samish Bay, Blanchard is the only place in the Cascades where mountain meets sea. A recreational and biological gem between Bellingham and Mount Vernon, much of this landmass was slated to be logged. But due to the work of Conservation Northwest and other local organizations, a consensus of sorts has been reached, with the Washington State Department of Natural Resources protecting Blanchard's trails and guaranteeing that its core will remain in a natural state.

In 1 mile reach a small ledge with big views out to the San Juan Islands and Olympic Mountains. In another 0.5 mile reach a signed junction (elev. 1100 ft). Head left on the Samish Bay Connection Trail. Now on rougher tread, make a gentle traverse across Blanchard's western

Oyster Dome's bat caves

slopes, hopping across a few streams in the process. In 0.5 mile from the junction, reach another junction, this one with the Oyster Dome Trail. The way left leads to a logging road. Head right for your objective. The grade once again steepens and you enter a damp, dark glen. Pass giant erratics, springboard-notched cedar stumps, and an ice-age interpretive sign before coming to a junction with the Talus Trail.

To reach the base of Oyster Dome, an area referred to as the Amphitheater Bat Caves, proceed left. After a tricky creek crossing, the short trail delivers you to a jumbled mess of talus beneath sheer cliffs. It's quite a sight. This rocky chaos contains numerous caves. Extremely hazardous to explore, they should be left for the resident bat colonies.

To get to the top of the dome, continue 0.1 mile on the main path, climbing steeply to yet another junction. Head left on the Rock Trail. Pass rusty old cable and other logging relics. Cross a small creek, then make one final push, breaking out of the forest onto the rim of the open promontory. Be careful. Keep children and dogs nearby. Oyster Dome's abrupt drop may lead you to clam up. Its views, however, are succulent. Spread out before you are the San Juan Islands, Fildalgo Island, Whidbey Island, Vancouver Island, the snow-capped Olympic Mountains, the Skagit River flats and a whole lot of saltwater. Count islands, watch boats, and soak up the sun's rays.

EXTENDING YOUR TRIP

For a round-trip hike that adds about 2 extra miles, continue on the Oyster Dome Trail to Lily Lake. Return to the trailhead via the Pacific Northwest Trail. Oyster Dome can also be reached from the east via the Lizard–Lily Lakes Trail, which is reached via a series of logging roads from exit 240 (Alger) off of I-5.

13 Pine and Cedar Lakes

RATING/ DIFFICULTY	ROUND-TRIP	ELEV GAIN/ HIGH POINT	SEASON
★★/3	5 miles	1400 feet/ 1600 feet	Year-round

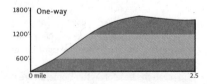

Maps: USGS Bellingham South; Chuckanut Mountain Recreation Map (Square One Maps); **Contact:** Whatcom County Parks, (360) 733-2900, *www.co.whatcom.wa.us/parks*; **Notes:** Dogs must be leashed; **GPS:** N 48 41.436, W 122 27.193

🦴 *Explore two little lakes high on Chuckanut Mountain. Despite the trailhead being just minutes from downtown Bellingham, you won't be rubbing packs with scores of hikers here. The initial steepness of this trail helps mitigate the crowds, sending the huddled masses instead to nearby Fragrance Lake. Pine and Cedar make wonderful destinations in their own right. But save some energy to push farther—to a hovering ledge with satisfying views of Mount Baker and the San Juan Islands.*

GETTING THERE

From Mount Vernon follow I-5 north to exit 246 (North Lake Samish). From Bellingham follow I-5 south to exit 246. Turn right (east), cross the freeway, and in 0.3 mile turn right onto Old Samish Road. Proceed 2.7 miles to the trailhead, on your left (elev. 300 ft). Privy available.

ON THE TRAIL

The way to Pine and Cedar lakes traverses a patchwork of public lands that host the sprawling Chuckanut Mountains Trail System—a weave of Whatcom County Parks, Washington State Parks, and State Department of Fish and Wildlife lands—but you'll hardly notice any change in ownership. The abutting agencies have agreed to manage these tracts in a like fashion—undeveloped and for recreation and wildlife enhancement.

The entire hike is through deep unbroken forest. And while the buzz of vehicles zipping along I-5 reminds you just how close civilization is, most of the hike feels remote. Starting at an elevation just below 300 feet, head up the steep trail under a canopy of maturing hemlock, cedar, and maple. The trail, an old skid road, passes rushing creeks, pocket wetlands, and a few patches of big old trees.

In 0.75 mile the trail angles left, leaving the old road and taking a more gradual approach toward its destinations. After another mile and upon cresting a slope at 1600 feet, reach a junction with the Hemlock Trail. Continue left on a former logging railroad grade, now a pleasant path. Entering a notched valley, lose the I-5 hum and begin concentrating instead on the melodies of thrushes, warblers, and flycatchers.

An easy 0.3 mile from the Hemlock junction, reach another trail junction. Choices. Continue straight for 0.25 mile, dropping a bit to reach shallow Pine Lake. Here a short boardwalked trail leads right to the lake's eastern shore, but it's often flooded. Firs and cedars grace the quiet shoreline, but you'll be hard-pressed to find a pine.

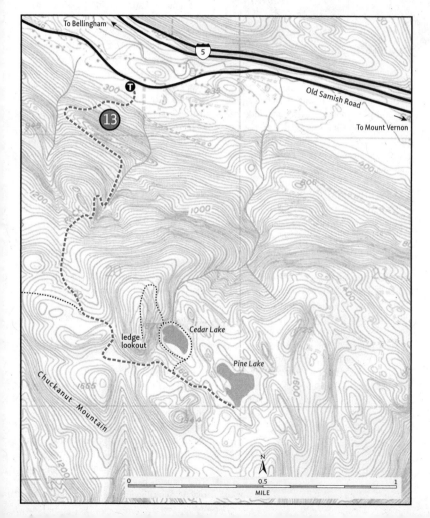

Solid trailhead sign

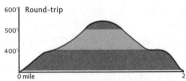

Map: USGS Lake Whatcom; **Contact:** What-com County Parks, (360) 733-2900, *www.co.whatcom.wa.us/parks.* Skagit County Parks, (360) 336-9414. Skagit Parks Foundation, *www.skagitparksfoundation.org;* **Notes:** Dogs must be leashed; **GPS:** N 48 38. 620, W 122 21.320

Deeper Cedar Lake, with its varied shore-line of big evergreen groves and sun-kissed clearings, is the more attractive of the two lakes. It's reached via the short trail (0.1 mile) that takes off left on your way up the main trail, dropping about 100 feet.

EXTENDING YOUR TRIP

A delightful loop trail of about 0.3 mile will take you around Cedar Lake. And at the north-west corner of Cedar, near an inviting bench, a side trail leads steeply and about 0.4 mile to a couple of lookout ledges. From these vistas, peer straight down to Cedar Lake, out to snowy Baker, and the jagged Twin Sisters, and across deep blue bays speckled with emerald islands. Pine and Cedar lakes can also be reached via the longer and more remote Hemlock Trail. It's about 4.5 miles one-way to the lakes from the trailhead at Bellingham's Arroyo Park. If you opt for this route, be sure to take the 0.4-mile side trip to Huckleberry Point for views north to Lake Padden and Seahome Hill.

Straddling the Whatcom-Skagit county line, Squires Lake is coop-eratively managed by both counties' parks departments. Opened to the public in 1997, this little park located just off of busy I-5 has become a popular place for area hikers, bird-watchers, trail runners, and hardcore trek-kers wishing to continue farther on the Pacific Northwest Trail. Comprised of land belonging to the Squires family since 1905, the little lake and its surroundings were acquired by Whatcom County Parks in 1995.

GETTING THERE

From Mount Vernon follow I-5 north to exit 242 (Lake Samish). From Bellingham follow I-5 south to exit 242. Head southeast onto Old Highway 99, reaching the trailhead in 0.8 mile on your left (elev. 300 ft). Privy available.

ON THE TRAIL

From the trailhead, a well-used and well-graded trail uses an old railroad bed, climb-ing 100 feet in 0.3 mile to the lake's outlet at a small dam built in the 1920s. Here you can sit and enjoy the view and admire resi-dent waterfowl, or set off to make a delightful 1.4-mile loop.

Take the well-worn Squires Lake Loop Trail right to begin your circuit. In 0.1 mile reach a junction for the more adventurous

14 Squires Lake

RATING/ DIFFICULTY	ROUND-TRIP	ELEV GAIN/ HIGH POINT	SEASON
★★/2	2 miles	250 feet/ 550 feet	Year-round

South Ridge Trail. This trail, part of the 1200-mile Pacific Northwest Trail (PNT) route that travels from the Olympic Coast to Montana's Glacier National Park, runs parallel to the main loop for a short distance, climbing to a series of so-so viewpoints. In 0.4 mile it reaches the park boundary, where a side trail takes off left heading back to the main loop trail. If you remain on the main loop trail you'll reach the second junction in 0.4 mile.

In another 0.2 mile come to another junction, this one for the Beaver Pond Loop. Take it, heading right to cross a small creek and venture through a forest of big old cedar stumps brandishing springboard notches. Loggers of yesteryear used bandsaws to cut the humongous trees while standing on boards notched into the trunks just above the trees' fluted bases.

After a short and easy climb, reach Beaver Pond. More of a marsh, the pond isn't exceptionally scenic, but the forest near its outlet is quite attractive. The trail continues a short distance along the shore before descending back to Squires Lake. But before reaching the Squires Lake Loop Trail the route comes to an old logging road, an alternative route back to the lake.

Through a tunnel of alders, the loop trail heads directly to Squires's northern shore. Under moss-draped maples and over boardwalks spanning bursting-with-birds wetlands, this section of trail is a pure delight. Benches along the placid pond invite lingering. Come to the old logging road and follow it left (west) a short distance back to the dam to close the loop. Head back down the railroad grade trail to return to your vehicle.

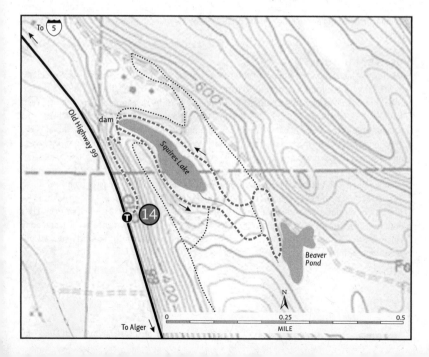

Well-groomed trail to Squires Lake

EXTENDING YOUR TRIP

Hikers looking for a long leg-stretcher can continue farther along South Ridge on the PNT. Most of the way is through cut-over timberlands, but there are views aplenty of the nearby Chuckanut Mountains and Skagit Valley.

NORTH BY NORTHWEST

Back during the backpacking boom of the 1970s, transplanted New Englander Ron Strickland was struck with a novel idea. How about adding another classic long-distance hiking trail to our country's stock? One to accompany and rival the likes of the Appalachian, Pacific Crest, and Colorado Divide trails. Such began the quest to build the Pacific Northwest Trail (PNT), a 1200-mile path from Cape Alava on the Olympic Peninsula to Montana's Glacier National Park.

Forming the Pacific Northwest Trail Association, Strickland and a good number of tireless volunteers set out promoting, constructing, and maintaining the new trail. Using existing trails along with new tread, the PNT weaves together a good portion of the North Cascades. And while parts of the trail still exist only on paper, much of the PNT is currently hikeable.

Good sections of the PNT exist in the Chuckanut Mountains (Hikes 12, 14), along Baker Lake (Hike 58), in Schriebers Meadow (Hike 56), and along Ross Lake (Hike 88). Much work still lies ahead for the association to complete the trail, and members hope that the PNT will someday be included in the National Trails System. In the meantime, give the trail a hike and visit *www.pnt.org* for more information.

Opposite: McIntosh Falls on Goat Lake Trail

mountain loop highway

Running for 50 miles between the towns of Granite Falls and Darrington, the Mountain Loop Highway, a National Scenic Byway, provides perhaps more hiking and camping choices per mile than any other road in the North Cascades. Easily accessible from Everett, the mostly paved road is the taking-off point for some of the region's most popular trails. Threading together the Sauk and Stillaguamish river valleys, the area contains great biological and scenic diversity. Its radiating trails run the full gamut too, from easy strolls to challenging scrambles. Explore primeval forest, open mountaintops, sparkling alpine lakes, historical mines and fire lookouts, sprawling meadows, thundering waterfalls, and wild rivers from this beloved outdoor destination.

15 Lime Kiln Trail

RATING/ DIFFICULTY	ROUND-TRIP	ELEV GAIN/ HIGH POINT	SEASON
★★/2	7 miles	625 feet/ 750 feet	Year-round

Map: Green Trails Granite Falls No. 109 (trail not shown); **Contact:** Snohomish County Parks, Ranger District No. 4, (360) 435-3441; **Notes:** Dogs must be leashed. Park open dawn to dusk. Parking lot gated when park closed. Please stay on trail through private property; **GPS:** N 48 04.642, W 121 55.948

The Lime Kiln Trail not only takes you deep into a lush and remote canyon carved by the South Fork Stillaguamish River, but also leads you deep back into history. Developed almost entirely by volunteers, this delightful trail serves up a unique journey into the heart of Snohomish County's 970-acre Robe Canyon Historical

Park. The fairly new park protects over 7 miles of frontage along the South Fork Stillaguamish, as well as preserving an old townsite and a century-old limekiln. The kiln, located 2.6 miles up the trail, is a 20-foot tall stone structure once used to cook limestone. The powdered lime was then transported by the Everett and Monte Cristo Railway to smelters and mills in Everett. Built in 1892 and abandoned in 1934, a section of this rail line has been resurrected as part of the Lime Kiln Trail.

GETTING THERE
Follow State Route 92 east to Granite Falls. At the blinking-light four-way stop in town, turn right onto Granite Avenue. Continue south for three blocks, turning left onto Pioneer Street and then reaching the city limits in 0.3 mile, where Pioneer Street becomes Menzel Lake Road. Continue another 0.9 mile and turn left onto Waite Mill Road. In 0.6 mile (just beyond a school bus turnaround sign), bear left at a Y intersection onto a gravel road. Reach the turnoff for Robe Canyon Historical Park in 500 feet and then turn left into the trailhead parking area (elev. 575 ft). Privy available.

ON THE TRAIL
Before embarking on this historical hike, take time to read the informative kiosk at the trailhead. It'll help you more fully appreciate the journey you are about to set off on. The wide and graveled trail takes off through a scrappy forest recovering from years of timber harvesting. The way temporarily leaves the park to traverse private land. Please stay on the path. Cross a small creek and emerge onto an old road. Continue on a slightly rolling course, following directional signs, and after 0.75 mile reenter the park, leave the road, and continue once again on real trail.

Pass Hubbard Pond, a shallow body of water surrounded by old cedars and thickets of salal. Cross its outlet creek on a sturdy bridge, then follow another old road a short distance to a well-marked junction. Here a sign directs you to head left and leave the roadway for a descent into a cool, lush, emerald ravine. Amid giant cottonwoods, Hubbard Creek provides a background score of tumbling tunes.

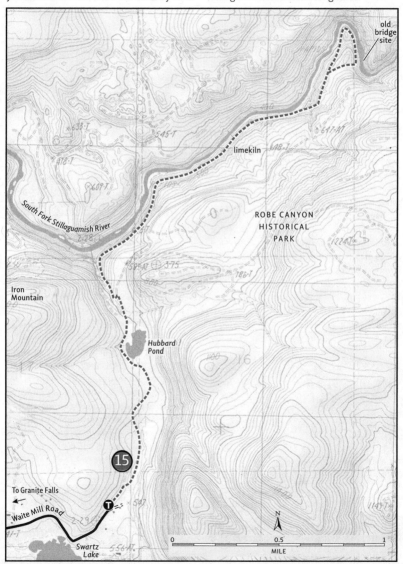

Emerge on a bench high above the roaring waters of the South Fork Stilly. Now using the former railbed of the old Everett and Monte Cristo Railway, the trail travels upriver through a narrow canyon. Under a canopy of towering moss-draped maples, the fern-lined trail continues on its way to the old limekiln.

En route you'll pass scores of historical relics literally littering the forest floor. Old saw blades, bricks, bottles, stove parts, and bed frames testify that this remote locale once supported a thriving community, Cut-Off Junction (please leave all artifacts in place for others to enjoy). Just up ahead (2.6 miles from your start) lies the source of this past activity, the limekiln, which remains remarkably intact (please stay off of it to ensure it stands another hundred years).

Beyond the old kiln, the trail continues for another 0.8 mile, ending at where a rail bridge once spanned the river. A short loop path takes off left, leading to a graveled bar on the river—a perfect spot to sit and reflect on the area's history and its natural beauty.

EXTENDING YOUR TRIP

Six miles east of Granite Falls on the Mountain Loop Highway is the trailhead for Robe Canyon. This 1.3-mile trail provides access to the eastern section of the historical park, delivering hikers to the old Robe townsite and a series of railroad tunnels. Perhaps in the near future the two trails will be connected.

16 Tin Can Gap

RATING/ DIFFICULTY	ROUND-TRIP	ELEV GAIN/ HIGH POINT	SEASON
★★★★★/4	12 miles	2800 feet/ 5800 feet	Mid-July– mid-Oct

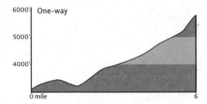

Maps: Green Trails Granite Falls No. 109, Silverton No. 110; **Contact:** Mount Baker–Snoqualmie National Forest, Darrington Ranger District, (360) 436-1155, or Verlot Public Service Center, (360) 691-7791, www.fs.fed.us/r6/mbs; **Notes:** NW Forest Pass required; **GPS:** N 48 11.624, W 121 46.296

⚙ *Venture to where the deer and the mountain goats play—to a precipitous ridge above a massive glacier on Three Fingers, one of the most prominently recognizable peaks in the Cascades. En route take in ancient forest, a pastoral mountain lake, and acres of amazing meadows and parklands punctuated with tarns. And did I mention the bountiful berry patches?*

GETTING THERE

From Granite Falls follow the Mountain Loop Highway east for 7 miles. Turn left onto paved Forest Road 41 (across from the Robe Canyon trailhead). In 2 miles the pavement ends at a junction. Bear left, continuing on FR 41 for 11.5

Historical relic along Lime Kiln Trail

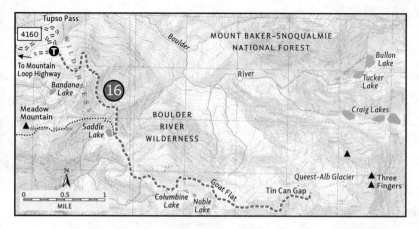

very rough and slow miles. Then bear right on FR 4160 for 4 more rough and slow miles to the trailhead (elev. 3000 ft). Park along the narrow road shoulders.

ON THE TRAIL

The first half of this hike entails a rough and tumble trek over roots, rocks, ledges, and other generally uneven and unpleasant ankle-twisting terrain. Immediately after entering the Boulder River Wilderness, the way commences to cut a route through an old-growth jungle of monster cedars and a near-impenetrable understory of lush greenery. Following along a rugged ridge high above Boulder River, the going is slow, with occasional peekaboo views of the valley's sprawling old-growth drapery—as well as sporadic but exhilarating shots of impressive Three Fingers looming above.

After a slight descent, the trail heads upward once again, clambering around and over ledges to reach a signed trail junction at shallow and serene Saddle Lake at 2.5 miles (elev. 3770 ft). The trail right leads to Meadow Mountain. Grown over, it's rapidly fading into history; yet another casualty of the U.S. Forest Service's lack of trail funding (ask your senator or rep why). The trail to Tin Can Gap, however,

improves from this point with smoother tread and gentler climbing. Grassy marshy meadows soon replace dark forest.

And tarns! Scores of them. Blueberries, huckleberries, bring out the barrel! Sweeping views of surrounding peaks and ridges—Pilchuck, Whitehorse, Baker, and plenty of others—grow with each step forward. At 4.5 miles, after some moderate climbing, enter Goat Flat (elev. 4800 ft), a heather and berry plateau wonderland splotched with tarns and clusters of contorted mountain hemlock and subalpine fir. For many hikers this is far enough, contentment has already set in. Please respect this delicate and fragile environment.

Adventurous souls continue. Climb a small forested knoll before breaking out to traverse steep slopes saturated with wildflowers. Good trail continues to just below the gap. Then ascend a short, steep, rocky way to the 5800-foot tight rocky notch. Guard your breath—the view is sure to take it away. Staring you right in the face is Three Finger's trio of awe-inspiring appendages. The Queest-Alb Glacier spreads its icy blanket beneath them.

Traveling beyond this point is strictly for experienced scramblers and resident mountain goats. Plop yourself down and enjoy.

17 Mount Pilchuck

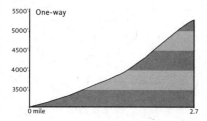

RATING/ DIFFICULTY	ROUND-TRIP	ELEV GAIN/ HIGH POINT	SEASON
★★★★/3	5.4 miles	2200 feet/ 5324 feet	Mid-July– early Nov

Map: Green Trails Granite Falls No. 109;
Contact: Mount Baker–Snoqualmie National
Forest, Darrington Ranger District, (360) 436-
1155, or Verlot Public Service Center, (360)
691-7791, *www.fs.fed.us/r6/mbs*; **Notes:** NW
Forest Pass required. Dogs must be leashed;
GPS: N 48 04.211, W 121 48.884

*Rising 1 mile above the surrounding
countryside and perched on the western edge of the Cascades, Pilchuck packs
some of the best panoramic viewing to be
found in these parts. From its historical and
restored fire lookout, scan the horizon—
from Rainier to Baker, Glacier Peak to the
Olympics, Seattle to the San Juans—and every jagged, rugged, and snow-capped peak
lining the Mountain Loop Highway. One of
the most popular hikes in Washington, Pilchuck is a "social mountain." Expect company and enjoy the camaraderie.*

GETTING THERE
From Granite Falls follow the Mountain Loop
Highway east. One mile beyond the Verlot
Public Service Center, turn right onto graveled
Forest Road 42 immediately after crossing the

Opposite: Three Fingers from Tin Can Gap

Fire lookout perched on Mount Pilchuck

"Blue Bridge." Drive 7 miles to the trailhead at
the road end (elev. 3100 ft). Privy available.

ON THE TRAIL
While not an overly difficult hike, scores of
hikers each year end up injuring themselves
or worse on this little mountain each season.
Why? Its easy accessibility and proximity to
the Greater Pugetopolis make it an attractive
destination for ill-prepared neophytes. Snow
often lingers late, making an easy hike in August potentially dangerous in June. And while

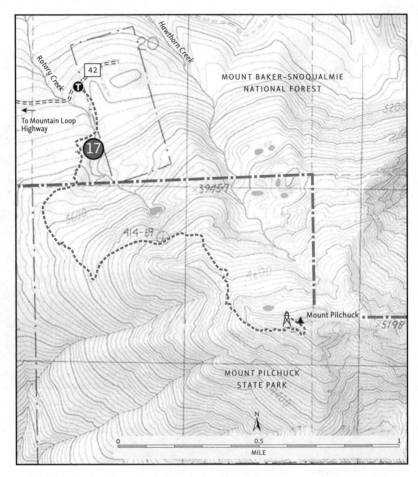

the distance isn't great, parts of the trail are rocky, muddy, and slippery—not a problem for experienced hikers, but potentially troublesome for others.

The hike starts on what was once a service road to ski slopes on the mountain. Skirt the base of the rapidly growing-in former ski area, entering mature forest of hemlock and yellow cedar. Hop across a small creek, and at 0.25 mile enter Mount Pilchuck State Park. Much

of the mountain, as well as Pinnacle Lake, are contained within a 1900-acre Washington State Parks property. The trail is jointly managed with the U.S. Forest Service. And thanks to the Washington Trails Association and its volunteers, a good portion of it has been recently reconstructed and reinforced with solid cribbing and steps.

At 0.7 mile briefly pass through a scree slope that offers a small scenic taste of what lies ahead. The trail rounds the mountain's northwest shoulder, breaks out into heather and granite gardens, and then ratchets up the climbing. The rocky summit comes into view—and so do scores of other summits. The way angles for a 4700-foot saddle between the summit and Little Pilchuck and then wraps around the mountain's south side. After a scenic traverse along the summit ridge, the trail heads back toward the summit block, ending with a boulder scramble for the final 100 feet to the attractive restored lookout.

You can easily while away time in the lookout, a virtual museum with its many historical exhibits. But no doubt the outside attraction—one of the finest views in the Cascades—has captured your attention. Peer north to Three Fingers, Baker, Shuksan, and the Stillaguamish Valley and east to Glacier, Big Four, Dickerman, Index, and the Spada Reservoir. Rainier dominates the southern sky. On the western front, it's Seattle, Everett, and Puget Sound with its myriad islands and inlets, all capped off by the Olympic Mountains. What a view!

18 Heather Lake

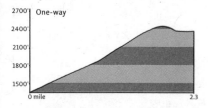

RATING/ DIFFICULTY	ROUND-TRIP	ELEV GAIN/ HIGH POINT	SEASON
★★/2	4.6 miles	1100 feet/ 2500 feet	Apr–Nov

One-way

2700'
2400'
2100'
1800'
1500'
0 mile   2.3

Map: Green Trails Granite Falls No. 109; **Contact:** Mount Baker–Snoqualmie National Forest, Darrington Ranger District, (360) 436-1155, or Verlot Public Service Center, (360) 691-7791,

www.*fs.fed.us/r6/mbs*; **Notes:** NW Forest Pass required; **GPS:** N 48 04.973, W 121 46.442

Don't expect to find much heather growing along the shores of this pretty little subalpine lake. That ubiquitous mountain shrub is pretty hard to find on this hike. But what you can expect to see along the way are some mighty fine old cedars. Expect, too, to be serenaded by babbling brooks, wooed by fine views of Mount Pilchuck's craggy, rocky north face, and charmed by Heather's placid waters. Don't plan on being alone here, however; this easy trail is one of the premier stomping grounds off of the Mountain Loop Highway. On a sunny summer weekend, you'll likely encounter the entire spectrum of the hiking world, from old-timers to neophytes and everyone in between.

Hiker at Heather Lake in November snow

GETTING THERE

From Granite Falls follow the Mountain Loop Highway east. One mile beyond the Verlot Public Service Center, turn right onto graveled Forest Road 42 immediately after crossing the "Blue Bridge." Drive 1.3 miles to the trailhead (elev. 1400 ft). Privy available.

ON THE TRAIL

Heather Lake Trail No. 701 takes off into a crowded forest of second-growth fir. Colossal cedar stumps punctuate the forest floor, testaments of the impressive ancient forest that graced these slopes not too long ago. On rocky but good tread, the trail winds its way through the dark woods. A few frothing streams help break the bleakness.

After a short burst of climbing, the trail merges onto an old woods road. The grade eases to round a ridge. Soon, however, it's once again up you go. The trail then enters a cool ravine—Heather Creek tumbles below, giant old-growth cedars tower above, and bountiful boughs of ferns grace the forest floor. Your new dynamic surroundings are quite a contrast to the woods you first entered.

Cross a few more creeklets and traverse a few openings in the primeval forest. After

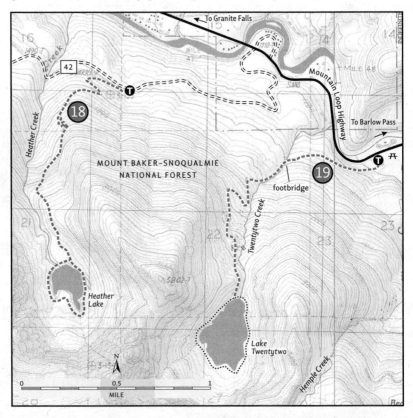

about 1.75 miles, climbing ceases and, on a slight descent through another impressive grove of ancient giants, the trail approaches Heather Lake. At 2 miles you'll find the tranquil backcountry lake tucked in a semi-open cirque beneath Mount Pilchuck. A loop of 0.6 mile circumnavigates it. Follow it to experience the many facets of this little lake, from its jumbled boulder fields to its marshy meadows. Notice, too, the presence of yellow cedar and mountain hemlock, trees usually more associated with higher climes.

Consider a visit in midfall, when tangles of vine maple add a crimson touch. Winter is also a delightful time to visit, but stay away from the lake's southern shores, where avalanches careen down from Pilchuck's steep upper reaches.

19 Lake Twentytwo

RATING/ DIFFICULTY	ROUND-TRIP	ELEV GAIN/ HIGH POINT	SEASON
★★★/3	5.4 miles	1350 feet/ 2400 feet	Mid-May– Nov

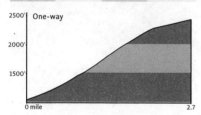

Maps: Green Trails Granite Falls No. 109, Silverton No. 110; **Contact:** Mount Baker–Snoqualmie National Forest, Darrington Ranger District, (360) 436-1155, or Verlot Public Service Center, (360) 691-7791, www.fs.fed.us/r6 /mbs; **Notes:** NW Forest Pass required; **GPS:** N 48 04.618, W 121 44.742

Perched in a spectacular basin at the base of Mount Pilchuck's sheer northern face, sparkling Lake Twentytwo is a stunning sight. But there's more to this popular hike than the picturesque lake and its backdrop of waterfalls and avalanche chutes. For much of the way the well-constructed trail follows cascading Twentytwo Creek through an exemplary ancient forest of gargantuan cedars. An excellent hike to acquaint children and neophytes with the natural world—just don't expect to be alone on this favorite of many a Puget Sound hiker.

GETTING THERE
From Granite Falls follow the Mountain Loop Highway east for 11 miles to the Verlot Public Service Center. Proceed 2 more miles to the trailhead, on your right (elev. 1050 ft). Privy available.

ON THE TRAIL
As delightful a destination as Lake Twentytwo may be, the real treat on this hike is the forest. Nearly 800 acres of pristine forest surrounding the lake and its outlet were set aside in 1947 as a Research Natural Area (RNA) to study the effects on water, wildlife, and timber of an area left in its virgin state compared to a similar area that has been intensively managed. Upon initial observation entering this primeval patch it doesn't take a forester, scientist, or naturalist to tell you that nature does a pretty darn good job of taking care of things when people aren't messing with it!

The surroundings are lush. Water appears to seep and bubble from the ground everywhere. Moss carpets boulders and rotting logs. Maidenhair, deer, and lady ferns form showy bouquets beneath the behemoth trees. Although western hemlock and silver fir are the predominant species, it's the western red cedars that'll garner most of your attention. Colonnades of the giants, some with trunks measuring almost 12 feet in diameter, hold up the sky.

The trail starts by gently traversing a side hill paralleling the road and the South Fork

Stilly. In 0.5 mile cross Twentytwo Creek on a little bridge and pause to admire cascades both up- and downstream. The trail then begins to climb, but never too harshly. Volunteers and Forest Service employees have worked hard over the years to crib much of this well-trampled trail, ensuring tread that'll stand the impact of thousands of boots.

At 2 miles enter a talus slope punctuated with vine and big-leaf maples. Exceptionally

Lake Twentytwo in late spring

pretty in the fall, the views of Green Mountain and the South Fork Stilly valley can still be enjoyed anytime. Upon reentering the cool cloak of ancient conifers, the climbing commences and you can glimpse a thundering waterfall through the thick timber.

Next, enjoy 0.25 mile of level walking following along Twentytwo Creek as you enter the cirque housing Lake Twentytwo. Break out of the trees and behold the lake set beneath an impressive vertical wall of rock. Waterfalls crash off of the sheer cliffs. In early season, so do avalanches—stay well away. By midsummer it's safe to circumnavigate the lake on a delightful 1.2-mile trail.

The lake, which is over 50 feet deep, supports a fair amount of fish. But the only thing you may be intent on catching here is the sun's rays shimmering off of the twinkling waters and a whole lot of gorgeous scenery.

EXTENDING YOUR TRIP
The nearby Gold Basin Campground, 0.5 mile from the trailhead toward Barlow Pass, provides a family-friendly base camp along the South Fork Stilly.

20 Pinnacle Lake

Pinnacle Lake in early summer

RATING/ DIFFICULTY	ROUND-TRIP	ELEV GAIN/ HIGH POINT	SEASON
★★★/3	3.8 miles	1100 feet/ 3800 feet	Late June– early Nov

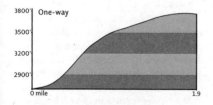

Maps: Green Trails Granite Falls No. 109, Silverton No. 110; **Contact:** Mount Baker–Snoqualmie National Forest, Darrington Ranger District, (360) 436-1155, or Verlot Public Service Center, (360) 691-7791, *www.fs.fed.us/r6/mbs*; **Notes:** NW Forest Pass required; **GPS:** N 48 03.521, W 121 44.160

Pinnacle is a delightfully beautiful alpine lake perched in a splendidly rugged basin on a shoulder of Mount Pilchuck. The hike is short, but not so sweet—unless you stop at Bear Lake, which is the kid-friendly part of this trip. The rest is rocky, rooty, muddy, and steep, and if it weren't for the big trees you'd swear you were hiking the Appalachians. But once upon

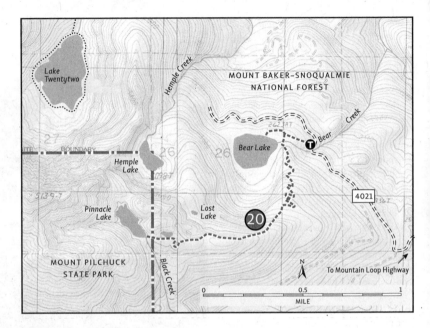

the tarn-tarnished ridge leading up to Pinnacle Lake, you're quickly reminded that this can only be the Northwest.

GETTING THERE

From Granite Falls follow the Mountain Loop Highway east for 11 miles to the Verlot Public Service Center. Drive 4.6 more miles, turning right onto Forest Road 4020 signed for Boardman Lake, Ashland Lakes, and Bear/Pinnacle lakes. Follow this gravel road for 2.7 miles to a junction. Bear right onto FR 4021 and continue for 3 miles to the trailhead (elev. 2700 ft).

ON THE TRAIL

Start by taking the very short Bear Lake Trail No. 661. On good trail pass through a gateway pair of massive cedars and in no time come to a junction. Take the level path right and be delivered to placid Bear Lake within minutes. Ringed with ancient forest and lined with skunk cabbage, horsetails, and huckleberries, when it comes to vegetation Bear is far from bare. It's a nice place for lounging around or introducing young children to the wilds.

The trail leading left from the junction, the one heading for Pinnacle Lake, offers quite a contrasting experience from the easy stroll to Bear. After crossing Bear Creek on a bridge that's seen better days, the way climbs steeply on an ankle-twisting entanglement of root and rock.

After 1 mile of difficult going, the climb eases and the tread becomes more agreeable. Now along a ridge crest, the trail heads due west for the lake. Gaps in the forest allow limited but good views north to Three Fingers, Liberty, Baker, and other impressive peaks.

At 1.8 miles reach a small tarn in marshy meadows. Then follow a muddy path along its outlet creek for 0.1 mile to Pinnacle Lake, which is sitting pretty beneath a prominent point on Mount Pilchuck. Soak sun and scenery from inviting rocks and a ledge near Pinnacle's cascading outlet creek.

21 Ashland Lakes

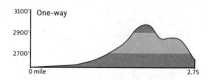

RATING/ DIFFICULTY	ROUND-TRIP	ELEV GAIN/ HIGH POINT	SEASON
★★★/2	5.5 miles	800 feet/ 3000 feet	Mid-May– early Nov

Map: Green Trails Silverton No. 110; **Contact:** Mount Baker–Snoqualmie National Forest, Darrington Ranger District, (360) 436-1155, www.fs.fed.us/r6/mbs. Department of Natural Resources, Northwest Region (Sedro-Woolley), (360) 856-3500, www.dnr.wa.gov; **GPS:** N 48 02.860, W 121 42.851

Surrounded by sphagnum bogs and primeval forest tucked in a quiet corner behind bustling Mount Pilchuck, the Ashland Lakes are the showpiece to the Washington State's Department of Natural Resources' 9600-acre Mount Pilchuck Natural Resource Conservation Area (NRCA). The placid lakes are an ideal destination for introducing children to the wonders of nature. Young hikers will especially delight in the numerous boardwalks traversing the saturated and stimulating landscape.

GETTING THERE
From Granite Falls follow the Mountain Loop Highway east for 11 miles to the Verlot Public Service Center. Proceed 4.6 more miles, turning right onto Forest Road 4020 signed for Boardman Lake, Ashland Lakes, and Bear/Pinnacle lakes. Follow this gravel road for 2.7 miles to a junction. Bear right onto FR 4021 and continue 1.4 miles to another junction. Turn left onto FR Spur 016, reaching the Ashland Lakes trailhead in 0.2 mile (elev. 2550 ft).

ON THE TRAIL
Begin your hike on an old logging road turned easy-to-walk hiking trail across bog and former ancient forest, now big stumps surrounded by dense new growth. In 0.5 mile cross a tannic creek on a sturdy bridge. After a slight climb, at 1.2 miles leave the old road for real trail, the old cut for real forest.

On boardwalks, puncheon, and circular cedar crosscuts, the trail traverses a forest floor

Upper Ashland Lake

full of running and stored water. The Mount Pilchuck NRCA is among the wettest regions in the Cascades, receiving between 100 and 180 inches of annual precipitation, including heavy snowfall. Consequently, the area supports an abundance of plants and ecological zones more common to nearby higher elevations. While the trail has been constructed well, take care on all planking. In rainy weather the boards can be slippery.

Work your way up a ledgy low ridge, pausing to admire a handful of humongous cedars among equally impressive big old hemlocks and silver firs. At 1.7 miles reach a signed junction. Take the trail on the left 0.1 mile to little Beaver Plant Lake (elev. 2840 ft) a sensitive wetland of sphagnum and peat bog. While appreciating this intricate ecosystem, contemplate what a Beaver Plant is (a factory that builds rodents or a tree that blossoms them?).

In 0.25 mile beyond the Beaver Plant spur, crest a 3000-foot divide and reach another junction. Left heads to the hinterlands of Bald Mountain. Head right instead for a gentle 0.25 mile to Upper Ashland Lake (elev. 2846 ft) and yet another junction. The trail left loops around the lake, meeting the main path at the outlet. It tends to be brushy, so stay right on nice boardwalks that offer great shoreline viewing. A couple of tent platforms along the way make sunny napping and lunch spots.

From where the lake loop rejoins it, the main trail continues to the right to Lower Ashland Lake, losing 200 feet of elevation in 0.25 mile. Less-visited than the upper lake, the lower cousin sits in a more rugged setting, flanked by cliffs and talus along its southern shores. Be sure to check out the elaborate bridge at the lake's outlet before heading back.

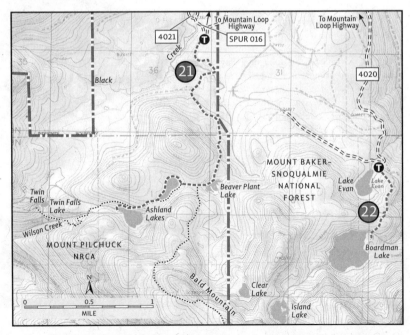

EXTENDING YOUR TRIP

The trail continues beyond the lower lake for another 1.5 miles, losing 400 feet to arrive at a pool between the awesome Twin Falls—a trip well worth the effort, but not suitable for children because of the rough and steep terrain. Lightly traveled Bald Mountain Trail is another option. It traverses a long ridge of meadow and old-growth forest for over 8 miles to the base of 4851-foot Bald Mountain. Expect lots of ups and downs, and the trail can be dry by late season.

22 Boardman Lake

RATING/ DIFFICULTY	ROUND-TRIP	ELEV GAIN/ HIGH POINT	SEASON
★★★/1	2 miles	300 feet/ 3000 feet	May– early Nov

Map: Green Trails Silverton No. 110; **Contact:** Mount Baker–Snoqualmie National Forest, Darrington Ranger District, (360) 436-1155, or Verlot Public Service Center, (360) 691-7791, www.fs.fed.us/r6/mbs; **Notes:** NW Forest Pass required; **GPS:** N 48 02.022, W 121 41.148

The hike to big, beautiful Boardman Lake is one of the easiest off of the Mountain Loop Highway. Just under a mile and gaining a mere 250 feet of elevation along the way (and 50 on the way back), this lovely backcountry body of water can be reached by just about every hiker—young and old, long-legged and short-breathed, and everyone else in between.

GETTING THERE

From Granite Falls follow the Mountain Loop Highway east for 11 miles to the Verlot Public Service Center. Proceed 4.6 more miles, turning right onto Forest Road 4020 signed for Boardman Lake, Ashland Lakes, and Bear/ Pinnacle lakes. Follow this gravel road for 2.7 miles to a junction. Bear left, continuing on FR 4020, and in 2.2 miles come to the trailhead, on your left (elev. 2750 ft).

ON THE TRAIL

While it'll take most hikers a mere thirty minutes to reach this delightful destination, allow yourself a good half day to fully enjoy and appreciate the lake and its environs. Boardman is an ideal place for acquainting children with the wonders of nature. Its shimmering waters invite lounging, feet soaking, and, during the dog days of summer, perhaps even a quick dip.

Even the trail itself will captivate young minds. Gargantuan ancient cedars lining the way will keep heads cocked upward in a constant state of bewilderment. But be sure to watch the trail! While generally well-groomed, a few roots and rocks may stagger your pace.

No more than two minutes into your hike, little Lake Evan greets you. While children may want to immediately loiter along the forested and marshy shore, Boardman promises much better diversions, so continue up the trail under an emerald canopy supported by massive trees as old as this country.

Negotiate one little climb around a ledgy area, then begin a short descent to the basin housing Boardman. Surrounded by timbered and rocky knolls, brushy talus slopes, and primeval forest, the lake feels like it's deep in the wilderness. There are plenty of good spots for sunning, soaking, and fishing.

You can cross the outlet creek on a logjam and explore a forested bluff on the lake's eastern shore. A handful of tidy campsites perfect for neophyte backpackers occupy the area. A primitive path continues but, like the one on the northern lakeshore, it peters out in brushy and marshy terrain.

Boardman Lake in late spring

While Boardman is a fairly popular place on a sunny weekend afternoon, it's a large enough locale to accommodate all guests. Please do treat the area with care. Visit on an overcast day for peace and quiet and surrealistic sauntering in a forest that has stood for centuries.

23 Bald Mountain via the Walt Bailey Trail

RATING/ DIFFICULTY	ROUND-TRIP	ELEV GAIN/ HIGH POINT	SEASON
★★★/3	10 miles	2300 feet/ 4700 feet	July– early Nov

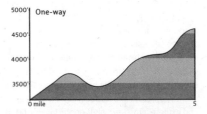

Maps: Green Trails Silverton No. 110, Index No. 142; **Contact:** Mount Baker–Snoqualmie National Forest, Darrington Ranger District, (360) 436-1155, or Verlot Public Service Center, (360) 691-7791, *www.fs.fed.us/r6/mbs*. Depart-

ment of Natural Resources, Northwest Region (Sedro-Woolley), (360) 856-3500, *www.dnr .wa.gov*; **Notes:** NW Forest Pass required; **GPS:** N 48 01.420, W 121 38.450

Good views, good fishing, good berry picking, good hiking—all on a trail without a good amount of use! This gem of a trail exists because of the goodwill of Walt Bailey and his Civilian Conservation Corps buddies. But we're not talking the 1930s, here. This trail was constructed in the 1990s, when Walt was in his seventies. A lifelong love for the area led Walt and his friends to construct this wonderful trail entirely with volunteer labor.

GETTING THERE
From Granite Falls follow the Mountain Loop Highway east for 11 miles to the Verlot Public Service Center. In 7 more miles turn right onto Forest Road 4030 (the turnoff is just before Red Bridge). Continue for 1.4 miles, turning right onto FR 4032. Drive 5.7 miles on FR 4032 (avoiding all side spurs) to the trailhead at the road end (elev. 3100 ft). Parking is limited—more space is available 0.25 mile back down the road.

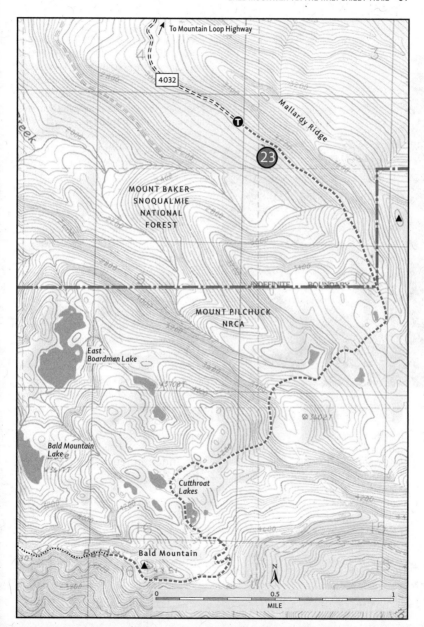

To Mountain Loop Highway

4032

Mallardy Ridge

T

23

MOUNT BAKER–
SNOQUALMIE
NATIONAL
FOREST

INDEFINITE   BOUNDARY

MOUNT PILCHUCK
NRCA

East
Boardman Lake

Bald Mountain
Lake

Cutthroat
Lakes

Bald Mountain

N

0   0.5   1
MILE

One of the Cutthroat Lakes

ON THE TRAIL

From the edge of an old cut on Mallardy Ridge, enter mature forest and begin an up-and-down, but always delightful journey through stands of impressive timber, bountiful berry patches, and bird- and bug-boasting bogs. At about 1 mile enter the Washington State Department of Natural Resources Mount Pilchuck Natural Resource Conservation Area, an area off-limits to logging and road building. After reaching a 3700-foot high point, the trail drops 200 feet to emerge in parkland meadows. Skirting a cliff and crossing a rocky avalanche slope, the trail drops another 200 feet.

Start climbing again, with an occasional dip, and at 3 miles arrive at the first of the Cutthroat Lakes (elev. 3800 ft), a series of small tarns surrounded by heather meadows tucked beneath the long ridge of Bald Mountain. Campsites dot the area, and despite the area's low usage the little lakes' fragile shorelines have been stressed. Treat the area with care.

After admiring the peaks reflected in the placid waters, carry on to higher ground—you'll carry on more quickly if the mosquitoes are intolerable. The trail continues another mile, climbing 700 more feet to connect with the Bald Mountain Trail. Turn right (west) and amble for 0.5 mile through gorgeous meadows with breathtaking views out over Puget Sound to Mount Rainer, and directly below to the Spada Reservoir and the Sultan Basin.

EXTENDING YOUR TRIP

Bald Mountain's 4851-foot summit requires scrambling that casual hikers will find difficult. Be content with the sweeping views from the trail. For a challenging hike, continue west along the Bald Mountain Trail for 8 miles to the Ashland Lakes Trail (and 2 more miles to the trailhead, where you'll need a ride back to your car). Parts of this trail are rough and overgrown. Expect a few ups and downs, plus more meadows, ancient forest, good views, and plenty of solitude.

24 Independence and North Lakes

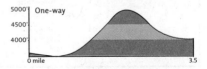

RATING/ DIFFICULTY	ROUND-TRIP	ELEV GAIN/ HIGH POINT	SEASON
★★★/4	7 miles	2200 feet/ 4950 feet	July– mid-Oct

Map: Green Trails Silverton No. 110; **Contact:** Mount Baker–Snoqualmie National Forest, Darrington Ranger District, (360) 436-1155, or Verlot Public Service Center, (360) 691-7791, *www.fs.fed.us/r6/mbs*; **Notes:** NW Forest Pass required; **GPS:** N 48 07.018, W 121 31.357

It's a tough trek up, over, and down a steep and rocky ridge to North Lake—a fair price to pay for the solitude you'll more than likely find. But if you prefer an easier adventure—one perfect for the kids and your dog—feel free to go no farther than Independence Lake. Either way, both lakes make fine destinations. Surrounded by a rugged topography cloaked in ancient forest, the setting is as wild as any along the Mountain Loop Highway, except for one noticeable difference. North and Independence lack the crowds that inundate nearby backcountry lakes.

GETTING THERE
From Granite Falls follow the Mountain Loop Highway east for 26 miles. At milepost 26, just beyond the entrance for the Big Four Picnic Area, turn left onto Forest Road 4060 (signed "Coal Creek Road"). Follow this gravel road for 4.8 miles to its terminus at the trailhead for Trail No. 712 (elev. 3600 ft).

ON THE TRAIL
The way begins in an old clear-cut. After a series of short switchbacks, primeval forest is soon encountered. Beneath giant hemlocks, the trail commences on a level to gently descending course toward Independence Lake. However, while the grade is easy the way is rough. Plenty of exposed roots and rocks will slow you down. After 0.5 mile, cross a rocky streambed and begin a short climb to regain the 200 feet you lost. Independence Lake (elev. 3700 ft) greets you 0.25 mile farther.

The lake sits in a rugged little basin, flanked

on the west by ancient trees and on the east by rocky slopes. It's a pleasing enough spot, but the wild country surrounding Independence Lake rings out to be explored. Continue onward along the western shore to the marshy and brushy north end of the lake.

Amid a myriad of social paths, locate the trail to North Lake taking off to the northeast. On narrow but defined tread, the trail steeply climbs—its direction at times baffling. Cross scree slopes

Massive Alaska yellow cedar

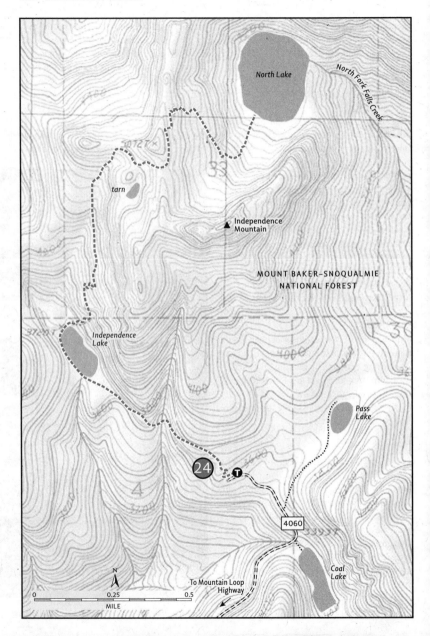

North Lake

North Fork Falls Creek

tarn

▲ Independence Mountain

MOUNT BAKER–SNOQUALMIE NATIONAL FOREST

Independence Lake

Pass Lake

24 **T**

4060

Coal Lake

N

0   0.25   0.5
MILE

To Mountain Loop Highway

streaked with wildflower regalia, and take time to admire a massive double-trunked Alaska yellow cedar, one of the largest this side of Ipsut Creek's record-holding specimen.

Continue clamoring on the rough and tumble ascent. Reenter old forest, drop a little to cross a small creek, then resume upward mobility. Pause for a moment at a small gap to take in views that include Devils Thumb. Then work your way through heather meadows, passing a small tarn. Just off to your right is a larger tarn. This picturesque body of water, often mistaken for North Lake by wishful hikers, is nevertheless worth exploring and is a good spot for those not inclined to continue the rough journey.

North Lake–bound trekkers must still climb another 200 feet to a narrow shoulder (elev. 4950 ft) on Independence Mountain. From here your objective lies 700 feet below in a basin of glacial-scoured ledges and fields of heather. Carefully make your way down the steep path, passing tarns, talus, and cascading creeks to the secluded lake (elev. 4150 ft). There's not much room to wander, but you shouldn't have to worry about sharing this spot with too many fellow hikers.

North Lake sits right dab in the middle of a 32,000-acre roadless area. Nearly pristine and supporting prime old-growth forest and wildlife habitat, this tract would make a nice addition to the adjacent Boulder River Wilderness.

EXTENDING YOUR TRIP

Two nearby small and fairly quiet lakes can be explored on your drive back. In 0.25 mile from the trailhead, an abandoned trail leads 0.3 mile to Pass Lake. Just 0.1 mile down the road beyond this trail is a large parking area for Coal Lake, a mere 0.1-mile walk from the road. Want more? Kalcema Lake makes a great kid-friendly hike. Accessed from FR 4052, this delightful lake in the Boulder River Wilderness is reached by a 0.5-mile trail through ancient forest.

25 Big Four Ice Caves

RATING/ DIFFICULTY	ROUND-TRIP	ELEV GAIN/ HIGH POINT	SEASON
★★★★/1	2.2 miles	200 feet/ 1900 feet	May–Nov

Map: Green Trails Silverton No. 110; **Contact:** Mount Baker–Snoqualmie National Forest, Darrington Ranger District, (360) 436-1155, or Verlot Public Service Center, (360) 691-7791, www.fs.fed.us/r6/mbs; **Notes:** NW Forest Pass required. Ice caves themselves are extremely dangerous—stay out of them and don't climb on them. **GPS:** N 48 03.955, W 121 30.644

Hikers have been marveling at these frozen spectacles of nature for over a century. Reached by one of the most manicured trails in the Cascades, Big Four's famed ice caves can be enjoyed by hikers of all walks. Formed from cascading water and warm winds hollowing out heaps of avalanche-deposited snow, the caves usually appear by midsummer.

GETTING THERE

From Granite Falls follow the Mountain Loop Highway east for 26 miles to the trailhead, on the right (elev. 1750 ft). Privy available. You can also hike from the Big Four Picnic Area, which is 0.5 mile before (west of) the caves trailhead off of the Mountain Loop Highway.

ON THE TRAIL

Instead of immediately heading for the caves, take a short diversion right, following a paved path 0.25 mile to the Big Four Picnic Area. This trail was once a rail line and was responsible for delivering thousands of tourists to a grand hotel where the picnic area now sits.

A hiker inspects the ice caves.

From 1921 to 1949, vacationers came to this spot to golf (the flats before you were once a green), paddle (the wetlands you just crossed were flooded), admire the inspiring view of Big Four Mountain (still in front of you), and hike to the base of the ice caves (just like you!). All that remains of the hotel is a chimney. The grounds have reverted to a semiwild state, and the trail has been upgraded to a top-notch walk in the woods.

From this trip back in time, follow the main trail toward the ice caves, crossing through bird-bursting wetlands. In 0.25 mile come to a junction. The trail left will return you to your vehicle. For now, continue straight, soon coming to a bridge crossing the South Fork

Stillaguamish River. Two hops and a skip beyond, cross Ice Creek by bridge as well.

Now on a very gentle grade, wind through open forest. Notice clumps of mountain hemlock, a tree that usually grows at eleva-tions above 3500 feet. Cross Ice Creek once more and emerge at the barren base beneath the north face of Big Four Mountain. Stare straight up sheer 4000-foot walls where ava-lanches careen down all winter and spring,

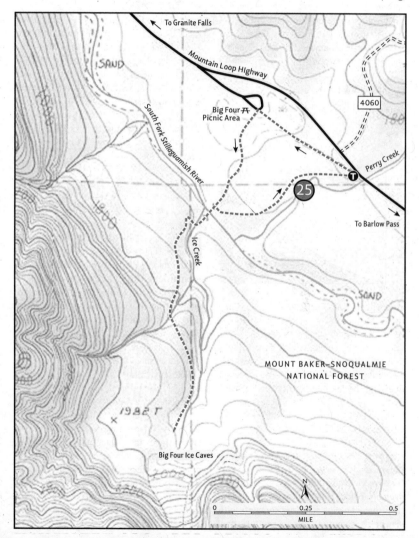

depositing tons of snow in the shadow of the mountain. Admire the cascades now crashing down those same walls, helping to hollow out the caves.

Walk across the fireweed-rimmed rocky flats to get a closer peek at the caves. But don't venture into or onto them—they can collapse at any time. If it's a hot summer's day, cherish the air-conditioned breezes funneling out of the icy catacombs.

26 Perry Creek

RATING/ DIFFICULTY	ROUND-TRIP	ELEV GAIN/ HIGH POINT	SEASON
★★★★/4	8 miles	3200 feet/ 5250 feet	July–Oct

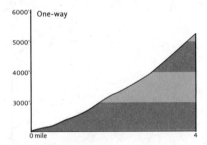

Map: Green Trails Sloan Peak No. 111; **Contact:** Mount Baker–Snoqualmie National Forest, Darrington Ranger District, (360) 436-1155, or Verlot Public Service Center, (360) 691-7791, *www.fs.fed.us/r6/mbs*; **Notes:** NW Forest Pass required. Forest Service prefers that dogs be leashed. Forest Service plans to close this trailhead. New access will be from Mount Dickerman trailhead; **GPS:** N 48 04.228, W 121 29.800

Venture up a wild basin beneath the towering cliffs of Mount Dickerman. Transition along the way from avalanche blast zones to forest primeval to tarn-topped alpine meadows complete with views of Washington's most elegant volcano, Glacier Peak. *And there's more: an awesome waterfall, a slew of rare plants, and an opportunity for experienced scramblers to subdue a duo of scenic summits.*

GETTING THERE
From Granite Falls follow the Mountain Loop Highway east for 26 miles, turning left onto Forest Road 4063 just 0.25 mile beyond (east of) the Big Four Ice Caves trailhead. Follow narrow FR 4063 1.1 miles to the road end and trailhead (elev. 2050 ft). The turnaround is tight and parking is limited—be careful of the steep drop-off. The Forest Service is planning on relocating the start of this hike to the Mount Dickerman trailhead (Hike 27), so check with them for updates.

ON THE TRAIL
A quieter and somewhat easier alternative to nearby Mount Dickerman (Hike 27), Perry Creek still attracts its legion of loyal fans. Rough in spots, the trail's rich variety offsets any inconvenience. Most of the way marches up the middle of the Perry Creek Research Natural Area (RNA), a 2066-acre protected tract. Established by the Forest Service after years of advocacy from noted botanist Art Kruckeberg and the Washington Native Plant Society, the RNA contains many rare plants, including male fern, leathery grape fern, and maidenhair spleenwort.

The trail immediately enters deep forest only to soon break out to cross an open avalanche slope. On rocky terrain but gentle grade, work your way up the valley, alternating between forested groves and brushy avalanche slopes. In fall, vine and Douglas maples add streaks of crimson to the surrounding greens and grays. Look across the valley to the long ridge of Stillaguamish Peak. Look over the valley to Big Four's imposing north face. And look straight up Mount Dickerman's frightening cliffs.

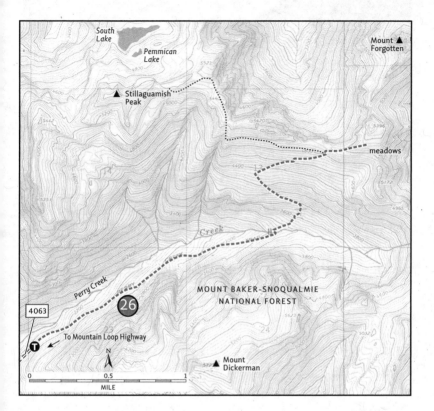

Hop across a creek, gentle in fall, testy in early summer. Soon afterward, at 1.9 miles, enter primeval forest. Showing off with magnificent falls in a deep, narrow cleft, Perry Creek finally greets you (elev. 3300 ft). Use caution appreciating the waters. Then cross Perry—tricky in high water—and begin working your way up steep slopes cloaked in ancient cedars and firs.

After some steep slogging on rooty terrain, the enveloping forest begins yielding to heather meadows. At 3.6 miles, come to an unmarked junction (elev. 4900 ft). The main trail continues right, steeply climbing another 300 feet to end on a meadowed bench (elev.

5250 ft) dabbed with delightful tarns and graced with splendid views out to Big Four, Glacier, Pugh, and Forgotten. And speaking of Forgotten, that 6005-foot peak is reached by continuing on an at times sketchy way trail that turns into a rocky scramble. Save it for the hardcore peak baggers. Enjoy the meadows.

EXTENDING YOUR TRIP

At that unmarked junction at 3.6 miles, the trail to the left is abandoned but well used. It travels 1.5 miles through magnificent meadows on its way to Stillaguamish Peak. Good tread ends on a high knoll offering spectacular viewing of remote and enchanting South Lake

Mount Forgotten and small tarn

(which has the distinction of being shaped like my home state, New Hampshire). Beyond this knoll the route is strictly for experienced scramblers seeking Stilly's summit.

27 Mount Dickerman

RATING/ DIFFICULTY	ROUND-TRIP	ELEV GAIN/ HIGH POINT	SEASON
★★★★/4	8.6 miles	3875 feet/ 5723 feet	Mid-July– Oct

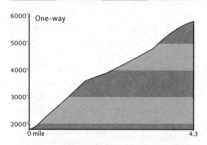

Map: Green Trails Sloan Peak No. 111; **Contact:** Mount Baker–Snoqualmie National Forest, Darrington Ranger District, (360) 436-1155, or Verlot Public Service Center, (360) 691-7791, *www.fs.fed.us/r6/mbs*; **Notes:** NW Forest Pass required; **GPS:** N 48 03.229, W 121 29.400

One of the most popular hikes off of the Mountain Loop Highway, the Mount Dickerman Trail delivers jaw-slacking views of a ring of rugged peaks near and far. Big Four and Del Campo practically leap out at you, while Glacier mesmerizes off in the distance. Though well-built and well-maintained, the trail is not easy. It starts low and heads high, wasting little time on the way to the 5723-foot summit. Come in September and Dickerman's legendary blueberry patches will slow your momentum even more than the steep trail. You'll likely end up looking like an "indigo girl" with all your picking and sampling.

GETTING THERE

From Granite Falls follow the Mountain Loop Highway east for 27 miles to the trailhead, 1.8 miles beyond (east of) the Big Four Picnic Area (elev. 1850 ft). Privy available.

ON THE TRAIL

Starting in thick timber, the way traverses the slope for a minute or two before commencing into switchback rhythm. The tread can be rocky at times, a result of erosion from when much of the mountain's lower slopes went up in flames nearly a century ago. Remnant old-growth giants displaying their fire survival scars stand proudly among scrappy successive growth.

After 2 miles of continuous clambering under a dark canopy and beside and around big mossy ledges, the grade eases at a small creek crossing (dry by late summer, pack plenty of water).

Big Four Mountain

Welcome daylight too as the way breaks out into boundless blue- and huckleberry-bursting flats as you near 3 miles (elev. 4400 ft). After vacil- lating through the vacciniums, resume upward momentum.

Cresting Dickerman's western shoulder, you'll

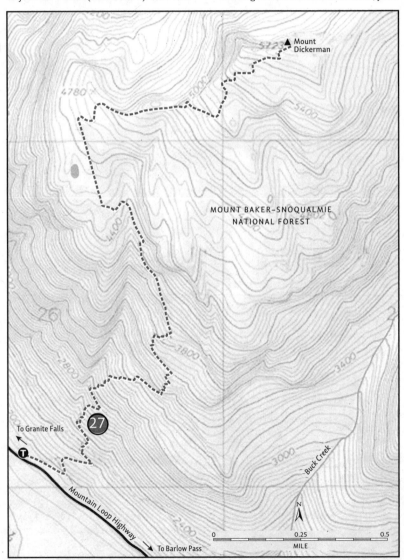

have the summit in view—1 mile away and 1000 feet above. Winding through hemlock groves and heather meadows, the way once again steepens. But the stunning view south to Big Four, Del Campo, and the countless Monte Cristo peaks will help keep your mind off the grind. Finally, after gaining almost 3900 feet in 4.3 miles, reach the open summit.

Sheer cliffs drop from the north face, so keep dogs, children, and the vertically phobic nearby. Securely seated, start savoring the scenery. Admire the Perry Creek basin below, flanked by Mount Forgotten and Stillaguamish Peak. Look at all the mountains! Prominent to the north are Baker and White Chuck. East, it's Pugh, Sloan, and Glacier. South, Rainier peeks above a wall of jagged summits. And west, Pilchuck and Three Fingers stand out. No wonder this hike is so darned popular!

EXTENDING YOUR TRIP
Noticeable from Dickerman is a small knoll, Barlow Point, rising above Barlow Pass. This 3200-foot bump makes for a nice destination when Dickerman is blanketed in snow. The view-granting former lookout site is reached by a 1.2-mile trail that climbs 800 vertical feet from Barlow Pass.

28 Headlee Pass and Vesper Lake

RATING/ DIFFICULTY	ROUND-TRIP	ELEV GAIN/ HIGH POINT	SEASON
★★★★/5	7 miles	2600 feet/ 4950 feet	Mid-July– Oct

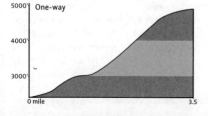

Maps: Green Trails Silverton No. 110, Sloan Peak No. 111; **Contact:** Mount Baker–Snoqualmie National Forest, Darrington Ranger District, (360) 436-1155, or Verlot Public Service Center, (360) 691-7791, www.fs.fed.us/r6/mbs; **Notes:** NW Forest Pass required; **GPS:** N 48 01.503, W 121 28.673

Huff and puff up a grueling old miners trail. Brave crashing creek crossings and a steep open hillside choked in jungle greenery before making an Achilles-aching ascent to Headlee Pass, an inconspicuous gap between towering and rocky Morning Star and Sperry peaks. From this portal to past riches, follow a scant path across jumbled talus to beautiful Vesper Lake, sparkling beneath the granite-graced slopes of Vesper Peak. Once the domain of hardscrabble prospectors, Vesper Lake now pays scenic dividends to tenacious trekkers.

GETTING THERE
From Granite Falls follow the Mountain Loop Highway east for 29 miles, turning right onto Forest Road 4065 about 3 miles beyond (east of) the Big Four Picnic Area. Follow this gravel road for 2.3 miles to its terminus at the trailhead for Trail No. 707 (elev. 2400 ft).

ON THE TRAIL
Built by miners over a century ago, nature has done its darndest to reclaim this trail. Rock slides, avalanches, washouts, and creeping greenery have kept modern-day trail crews busy assuring that the Sunrise Mine Trail No. 707 doesn't fade into history like its namesake.

The trail begins in scrappy forest. Plenty of exposed roots and rocks will help keep your pace in check. So will numerous creek crossings, especially the one at 0.5 mile, where the South Fork Stillaguamish crashes through a rocky draw. In early season and after heavy

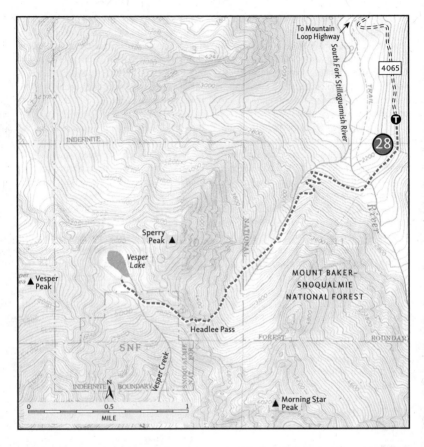

rainfall, it may have you seeking an alternative hike for the day.

Once past the gauntlet of roots and rivulets, break out of the forest to an open slope flush in thick tread-concealing vegetation. Work your way up the steep hillside, avoiding hidden obstacles like ankle-twisting holes and rocks. Stop and marvel at a huge and impressive landslide gully and contemplate the forces of nature that created it.

Push through more brushy terrain before entering an attractive grove of big yellow cedars. Soon afterward, the trail comes to a forbidden basin flanked by steep rocky walls—a stark corridor deprived of the sun's warming rays for much of the day. Scan the encompassing sheer slopes for Headlee Pass. Surely this passage must be up there somewhere.

Press on over rocky terrain and through cloisters of mountain hemlock spared from

Opposite: Red Mountain rises above tumbling Vesper Creek.

cavalcades of unforgiving avalanches, and toil into the high country so coveted by those who hastily built this trail. After a series of short switchbacks and a bit of scree hopping, the trail makes a sharp bend right, the passage out now revealed. The next 0.25 mile is extremely steep on tread periodically destroyed by heavy snows and tumbling rocks. Use caution to avoid threatening hikers below with dislodged rocks.

Between breaths, stop to take in newly emerging views of Mount Dickerman across the South Fork Stillaguamish valley and of Glacier Peak in the distance. At 2.7 miles and after 2400 feet of climbing, reach Headlee Pass (elev. 4600 ft), a small notch of a gap between Sperry and Morning Star peaks. There's not much here to compensate you for your effort, so carry on following good but unmaintained tread. After a slight drop, the way resumes climbing, crossing a large scree slope. Carefully traverse the open rock heap coming to Vesper Creek. Then turn upslope to follow the churning creek a short way until—voilà!—a stark but gorgeous upper valley is revealed.

Here beneath the snowfields and shiny granite slopes of Vesper Peak is sparkling Vesper Lake (elev. 4950 ft). Of course the miners weren't interested in any of this beauty, only in the precious gems and valuable ore that might have been hidden beneath it. And while the surrounding hills no longer carry the sounds of grunting prospectors, occasionally low murmurs can be heard emanating from the alpine tundra. Keep your eyes open for white-tailed ptarmigans, a member of the grouse family that makes this beautiful but harsh alpine environment its home.

EXTENDING YOUR TRIP

Experienced scramblers can follow a path through the heather slopes above the lake to Vesper Peak's 6214-foot summit. It's not technical, but steep snowfields and open ledges must be crossed. Routefinding skills are a must. From the pyramidal summit the view is amazing, especially down to azure Copper Lake, 2000 sheer feet below Vesper's north face.

29 Gothic Basin

RATING/ DIFFICULTY	ROUND-TRIP	ELEV GAIN/ HIGH POINT	SEASON
★★★★/4	9 miles	2840 feet/ 5200 feet	Mid-July– mid-Oct

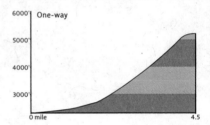

Maps: Green Trails Sloan Peak No. 111, Monte Cristo No. 143; **Contact:** Mount Baker–Snoqualmie National Forest, Darrington Ranger District, (360) 436-1155, or Verlot Public Service Center, (360) 691-7791, www.fs.fed.us/r6/mbs; **Notes:** NW Forest Pass required; **GPS:** N 48 01.567, W 121 26.550

Rugged and spectacular—yes. Gothic, perhaps, for this stark and mysterious basin harbors hidden tarns and disappearing waterways and is surrounded by spiraling peaks. A difficult hike on steep and rocky terrain, Gothic Basin with all its rich beauty can't keep hikers away; just as it couldn't keep miners away a century ago with its lure of riches. It was those hardy folk who built this path. It has been upgraded since—somewhat. The splendor of the basin, however, can't be improved one bit. Past glaciers and the agents of erosion have left it pretty darn near to perfect.

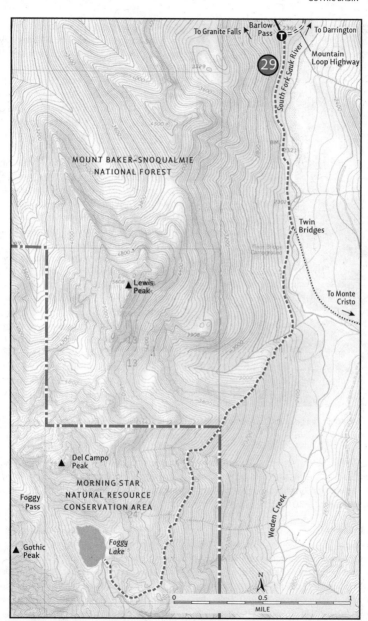

To Granite Falls

Barlow Pass

To Darrington

Mountain Loop Highway

South Fork Sauk River

29

BM 2321

MOUNT BAKER–SNOQUALMIE NATIONAL FOREST

2302

Twin Bridges

To Monte Cristo

5608 ▲ Lewis Peak

3908

Del Campo Peak ▲

MORNING STAR NATURAL RESOURCE CONSERVATION AREA

Foggy Pass

Weden Creek

Gothic Peak ▲

Foggy Lake

N

0   0.5   1

MILE

The views of Foggy Lake and Del Campo Peak are stunning.

GETTING THERE

From Granite Falls follow the Mountain Loop Highway east for 31 miles to Barlow Pass and park there (elev. 2360 ft). Privy available.

ON THE TRAIL

Start by hiking the Monte Cristo Road. This 4-mile connection to the now-defunct mining town of Monte Cristo has been permanently closed to vehicles (but for a few landowners and others) since December 1980, when the South Fork Sauk River severed it. Volunteers have since restored the road, making it at least passable to bicycles and pedestrians. But the river hasn't given up trying to put the road to rest.

After 1 mile of easy road rambling, reach the trailhead for Gothic Basin (Weden Creek Trail No. 724) just before the Twin Bridges (elev. 2350 ft). The trail takes off into old-growth timber paralleling the South Fork Sauk, coming to a tributary of Weden Creek (elev. 2450 ft) in about 0.6 mile. The crossing can be tricky in high water. From this point forward, the trail gets down to business, following much of the original miners route.

Climbing steeply up a slope shrouded in scrappy forest, you gain elevation rapidly. After 1 mile of serious ascending, the trail breaks out onto a spectacular ledge complete with waterfall crashing down a cleft (elev. 3900 ft). In early summer, lingering snow can make crossing this cleft dangerous.

With views opening up to the Monte Cristo mélange of mountains, continue upward. Cross two more clefts complete with cataracts—two more potentially dangerous areas if snow-covered. Encountering rockier and brushier terrain, the way grows more difficult. Pause to admire some impressive yellow cedars including a "four-trunked" monster.

More creek crossings and a few ledges requiring help from your hands stagger your pace. Pass ruins of the Consolidated Mine. Ore was transported to the valley floor via a tramway. Contemplate the tenacity of the hardscrabble folk who looked to this rugged environment for their paychecks.

Make the final push to the basin over scoured rocks and ledges and through heathered meadows. Be sure to look back at the jagged skyline with prominent Mount Pugh and Sloan Peak standing out. At about 4 miles from Barlow Pass, the trail ends at a small tarn (elev. 4900 ft). Explorations, however, have only just begun.

Following sketchy tread northwest to ledges and polished rock, you can make your way another 0.5 mile to Foggy Lake (elev. 5200 ft). Flanked by Gothic and Del Campo peaks and denuded of any shoreline vegetation, Foggy is a starkly beautiful alpine lake. Scout the nooks and knolls surrounding it. However, while this area is indeed a harsh environment, it is also fragile. Meadows can't withstand a constant onslaught of boots. Stick to ledge and rock in your wanderings as you're enjoying this wild landscape.

30 Silver Lake

RATING/ DIFFICULTY	ROUND-TRIP	ELEV GAIN/ HIGH POINT	SEASON
★★★★/4	12 miles	2100 feet/ 4350 feet	July–Oct

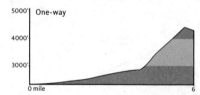

Maps: Green Trails Sloan Peak No. 111, Monte Cristo No. 143; **Contact:** Mount Baker–Snoqualmie National Forest, Darrington Ranger District, (360) 436-1155, or Verlot Public Service Center, (360) 691-7791, *www.fs.fed .us/r6/mbs*; **Notes:** NW Forest Pass required. Monte Cristo Road sustained severe damage, including major washout at the South Fork Sauk, in November 2006 floods. Ford is only safe in late summer. Road subject to closure if damage worsens. Check with Forest Service for current conditions; **GPS:** N 48 01.567, W 121 26.550

A wild river, historic mining town, magnificent old-growth forest, and a large sparkling alpine lake set in an open basin of heather and huckleberry—this hike has wide appeal. Hike through Monte Cristo and over Poodle Dog Pass in the heart of a once-bustling mining district that bore little resemblance to the ghost town and surrounding wilderness of today.

GETTING THERE
From Granite Falls follow the Mountain Loop Highway east for 31 miles to Barlow Pass and park there (elev. 2360 ft). Privy available.

Silver Lake beneath Silvertip Mountain

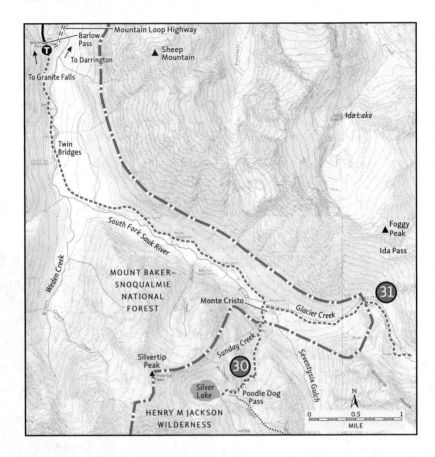

ON THE TRAIL

Start by hiking the 4-mile Monte Cristo Road. Closed to vehicular traffic since 1980 (except for a handful of permit owners), the road has become a popular hiking and biking destination for recreationists from all walks of life. At 1 mile is the trail for Gothic Basin (Hike 29) and the Twin Bridges over the South Fork Sauk (washed out in November 2006). Continue along the delightful road. Except for two short sections, the way is fairly level.

At 4 miles the road ends at a campground (privy available). Cross the South Fork Sauk on a good bridge, entering the Monte Cristo townsite (elev. 2800 ft) where about a dozen structures still stand. The trail starts at the east end of a grassy opening by a cabin. Linger around the old mining town (see "The Final Count of Monte Cristo" in this section), or get heading to the lake.

Cross Sunday Creek, passing through a white-picket fence welcoming you to the

"76" building. Start working your way toward Sunday Flats, following an old water line and passing the ruins of an old concentrator. At 0.25 mile from the townsite, reach a junction at the Sunday Falls overlook. The trail left circles back to Monte Cristo. Continue right on refurbished tread. The old trail was a curse-inducing steep rocky bed—not very enjoyable. The new trail will be music to your boots.

Entering the Henry M. Jackson Wilderness, the trail winds through groves of big old trees, crossing Sunday Creek at 1.1 miles from Monte Cristo. The way now steepens as it approaches Poodle Dog Pass. After crossing a small scree gully, pleasurable walking returns. At 1.75 miles from Monte Cristo, reach a junction with the Twin Lakes Trail in the huckleberry-enhanced pass (elev. 4350 ft).

Head right for 0.25 mile, dropping an easy 100 feet through tarn-dotted heather flats to glistening Silver Lake in a cirque beneath Silvertip Peak. The setting, like the metals that were extracted from the surrounding slopes, is precious.

EXTENDING YOUR TRIP

Extremely strong day hikers can continue on the trail 2.7 miles to the dazzling Twin Lakes in the shadows of 7172-foot Columbia Peak. It's not an easy hike, though, and is perhaps best left for backpackers with time on their side.

THE FINAL COUNT OF MONTE CRISTO

Trips to Silver Lake (Hike 30) and Glacier Basin (Hike 31) will take you through the old townsite of Monte Cristo. Only a few structures remain of what was once a booming gold- and silver-mining town of nearly 2000 people. Five hotels, a school, a store, rows of homes, and a huge concentrator lined the streets of this now-deserted locale. Ore was transported to the town from the steep surrounding peaks via tramways. It was then sent to Everett by rail. The Lime Kiln Trail (Hike 15) follows along a section of this long-defunct rail line.

And while Monte Cristo was the result of perhaps the biggest gold rush in the Cascades, like all rushes it was short-lived. By the 1930s the town was abandoned and rapidly decaying. A county road connected the townsite to the outside world in the 1940s, and several attempts were made to convert a couple of the old hotels into mountain resorts. But these ultimately failed, and by 1980 a flood had destroyed sections of the road and the county abandoned it.

In 1983 the Monte Cristo Preservation Association (MCPA) was formed to help preserve and protect the town's remaining structures and relics. The association also restored the road, but only members and property owners are allowed to drive it; others can walk it or use bicycles. The road continues to wash out, though, and as of the fall of 2006 it was once again inaccessible to motor vehicles. Most hikers and mountain bikers will also find the route inaccessible at the South Fork Sauk River crossing, which now requires a ford that is treacherous in high water.

When hiking in the region, take time to visit the historic townsite. But respect private property. Many of the structures are privately owned and there are still active mining claims in the valley. Respect, too, all relics in the valley, leaving them for others to enjoy. For more information on the history and preservation of the area, visit the MCPA website (www.whidbey.com/mcpa).

31 Glacier Basin

RATING/ DIFFICULTY	ROUND-TRIP	ELEV GAIN/ HIGH POINT	SEASON
★★★★/5	12.5 miles	2040 feet/ 4400 feet	July–Oct

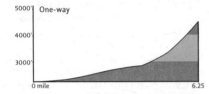

Maps: Green Trails Sloan Peak No. 111, Monte Cristo No. 143; **Contact:** Mount Baker–Snoqualmie National Forest, Darrington Ranger District, (360) 436-1155, or Verlot Public Service Center, (360) 691-7791, *www.fs.fed.us/r6/mbs*; **Notes:** NW Forest Pass required. Monte Cristo Road sustained severe damage, including major washout at the South Fork Sauk, in November 2006 floods. Ford is only safe in late summer. Road subject to closure if damage worsens. Check with Forest Service for current conditions; **GPS:** N 48 01.567, W 121 26.550

Follow an abandoned road along the wild and temperamental South Fork Sauk River to the once-booming mining town of Monte Cristo. Head up "main street" past relics of a bygone era, following an old miners path high into the barren country beneath the stark and imposing walls and spires of the Monte Cristo peaks. With snow-fed braided creeks cascading through mounds of talus ringed with wildflowers, the scenery of Glacier Basin is simply breathtaking. And so is the climb—one of the roughest, rockiest, and steepest around.

GETTING THERE
From Granite Falls follow the Mountain Loop Highway east for 31 miles to Barlow Pass and park there (elev. 2360 ft). Privy available.

ON THE TRAIL
Start by hiking 4 miles on the Monte Cristo road, closed to vehicles (except for a few pass holders). There's plenty of good river and mountain viewing along the way. At 1 mile is the trail for Gothic Basin (Hike 29) and the Twin Bridges over the South Fork Sauk (washed out in November 2006).

After the 4 fairly easy miles, come to a campground at the edge of the historic townsite. Cross the South Fork Sauk on a good

Monkey flowers add color to barren Glacier Basin.

bridge where a handful of have-seen-better-days structures, remnants of a boomtown, greet you. Walk across a grassy flat (once a rail yard) to the trailhead (elev. 2800 ft) located near a Forest Service cabin.

Cross Seventysix Creek on a good bridge and head up what was once Dumas Street, the commercial artery of Monte Cristo where hotels, brothels, a mercantile, and residences once stood (see "The Final Count of Monte Cristo" in this section). Little of the old town remains. The forest has reclaimed its territory.

At 0.2 mile from the trailhead, come to a four-way junction. The trail to the right heads uphill, joining the Silver Lake Trail at Sunday Flats. The trail left leads a short distance to where the five-story United Companies Concentrator once stood and processed ore. Continue straight on old roadway through dark forest. Daylight returns 0.25 mile farther thanks to the work of hundreds of past avalanches.

Continuing on the old road, head up an increasingly tighter and wilder valley and say goodbye to easy strolling. The trail turns downright mean, heading straight up a worn-to-bedrock gully. It's the same type of rocky, steep trail you'd find in New York's Adirondacks or New Hampshire's Whites. East Coast transplants may wax nostalgic. Or not—this is one tough stretch of trail. There are even two sections with rope to aid your ascent (and descent) up smooth ledges (no exposure). Avoid this trail in the rain.

At 0.75 mile from Monte Cristo, take a break at a waterfall's edge (elev. 3600 ft), only to resume your toil. Thankfully, it's short. Sanity returns at about 1.5 miles with good tread and grade, the way rounding a ridge. Glacier Basin's guardian peaks come into view, and Glacier Creek crashes below through rock and snow and then disappears under mounds of talus. As you follow the now near-level course, the creek appears once again snaking through willow flats.

If the creek allows, continue alongside it on grassy bottomlands. If it's flooded, pick your way through talus. The original miners road can still be followed too. Locate it just to the left of a huge tailings pile. A small cascade marks the entrance to Glacier Basin (elev. 4400 ft), a wide expanse of boulder, moraine, snowfields, bubbling creeks, and wildflowers beneath a cluster of jagged ice-adorned peaks.

Wander the basin, taking care not to step on fragile vegetation. Stay to the left of Glacier Creek and work your way up higher in the basin to a hemlocked hump. Visit in August when monkey flowers streak the rocky creek beds in resplendent yellows and pinks.

32 Goat Lake

RATING/ DIFFICULTY	ROUND-TRIP	ELEV GAIN/ HIGH POINT	SEASON
★★★/3	10.4 miles	1400 feet/ 3161 feet	Late May– early Nov

Map: Green Trails Sloan Peak No. 111; **Contact:** Mount Baker–Snoqualmie National Forest, Darrington Ranger District, (360) 436-1155, or Verlot Public Service Center, (360) 691-7791, *www.fs.fed.us/r6/mbs;* **Notes:** NW Forest Pass required; **GPS:** N 48 03.220, W 121 24.680

A spectacular backcountry lake—one of the largest in the area—awaits those who walk this way. Once the site of a bustling mining operation, complete with company town and lakeside hotel, Goat Lake boasts plenty of history along with its fine views. Waterfalls too! So grand is Goat that the Washington Department of Transportation chose it to grace its official road maps in the early 1990s. But you can't

Cadet Peak above Goat Lake

drive there, so millions of map admirers never got any closer than a dusty road. You, however, are on your way.

GETTING THERE

From Granite Falls follow the Mountain Loop Highway east for 31 miles to Barlow Pass and the end of the pavement. Continue for 3.5 miles, turning right onto Forest Road 4080. (From Darrington the turnoff is 19.5 miles along the Mountain Loop Highway.) Follow FR 4080 for 0.8 mile to the road end and trailhead for Elliott Creek Trail No. 647 (elev. 1900 ft).

ON THE TRAIL

From the noisy trailhead thanks to roaring Elliott Creek, two trails heading for Goat Lake

diverge. The lower trail offers a slightly shorter more interesting route along the creek and through old growth than the upper trail, which follows an old logging road lined with alders. The upper trail, however, is easier to travel and offers some nice views. The lower trail is prone to slides. The upper trail is the safer bet.

Follow this good, at times slightly rocky, path as it moderately gains elevation. In 1 mile (elev. 2200 ft), the Chokwich Creek Trail takes off left to reach the Bedal Creek Trail (Hike 33) in 2.5 miles. Continue to the right through thinning forest with good glimpses of the Elliott Creek valley and out to Sheep Mountain. Cross numerous cascading streams and at about 3 miles begin a slight descent, meeting up with the lower trail at 3.5 miles (elev. 2650 ft). The old logging road the trail has been using soon ends, and you enter a cool, mature forest of humongous cedars.

At 4.5 miles cross a braided stream and enter the Henry M. Jackson Wilderness. The trail now climbs, hugging a high bank of Elliott Creek and heading along a washed-out streambed. Plenty of notched cedar stumps stand testament to the human activity that once flourished in this area. Where the trail makes a sharp left turn, look right to see cedar puncheon (planking) of the original wagon road that serviced the area. The old mining town was located across the creek from this spot. Nothing remains of the bridge, however, so exploring the townsite may not be feasible.

Continue up the trail to explore Goat Lake. As you near the lake, magnificent McIntosh Falls forces you to take a break. After marveling at the cascading waters, reach the lake. Pass the camping area and head straight for the day-use area located just beyond a brushy meadow. Cast your eyes across the rippling waters to snow-capped Cadet Peak hovering above. A primitive path continues a short way along the lake's eastern shore,

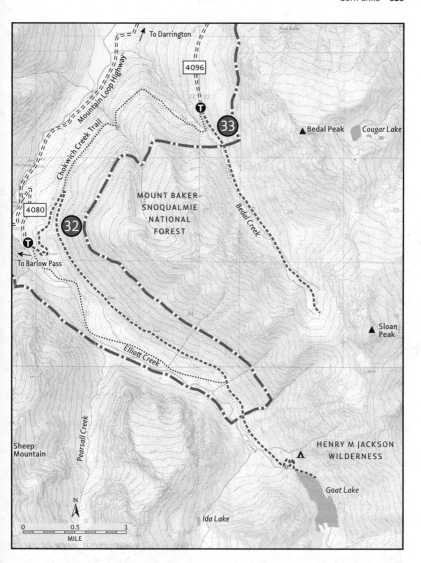

offering better views of that prominent peak that lured more than its fair share of past fortune seekers.

EXTENDING YOUR TRIP

Venture an easy mile up the Chokwich Creek Trail (another logging road turned hiking path) to where it crosses the creek at the base of an impressive waterfall—a refreshing destination on a hot afternoon.

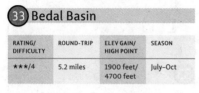

33 Bedal Basin

RATING/ DIFFICULTY	ROUND-TRIP	ELEV GAIN/ HIGH POINT	SEASON
★★★/4	5.2 miles	1900 feet/ 4700 feet	July–Oct

Map: Green Trails Sloan Peak No. 111; **Contact:** Mount Baker–Snoqualmie National Forest, Darrington Ranger District, (360) 436-1155, or Verlot Public Service Center, (360) 691-7791, www.fs.fed.us/r6/mbs; **Notes:** NW Forest Pass required; **GPS:** N 48 04.395, W 121 22.600

❌ ⚙ 🏠 *One of the loneliest trails off of the Mountain Loop Highway, that is, if you don't count the resident marmots. Follow an old mining trail deep into magnificent primeval forest to a boulder-strewn basin beneath Sloan Peak's sheer southern face. Roam heather meadows and admire painted slopes of wildflowers. While the first half of this trail makes for a nice walk, the second half can be tricky, requiring a 0.25-mile slog up a steep rocky creek bed. Such is the price of solitude.*

GETTING THERE

Take exit 208 off of I-5 and drive 4 miles east on State Route 530 to Arlington. Continue east on SR 530 for 28 more miles to Darrington. At a three-way stop, turn right (south) onto the Mountain Loop Highway and proceed 17.2 miles (the pavement ends at 9 miles), turning left onto Forest Road 4096 (0.8 mile past Bedal Campground). Follow FR 4096 for 3 rough miles to the trailhead at the road end (elev. 2800 ft).

ON THE TRAIL

Forester Harry Bedal helped build this trail back in the 1920s to access his mine claim on Sloan Peak. He built a cabin in the high basin beneath the peak. Nature claimed it twenty years later and has continuously taken swipes at the trail. The Forest Service doesn't get out as much these days to maintain trails, especially obscure ones likes Bedal Creek. Fortunately, climbers have helped keep this interesting route open over the years. In the summer of 2007 it was in very good shape, avalanche chutes brushed out and major windfall cleared. Nature may change all of that, of course.

Start by following the trail left signed for Bedal. The trail right, marked Chokwich, follows an old road 2.5 miles to the Elliott Creek Trail (Hike 32). The Bedal Creek Trail immediately enters a magnificent stand of old growth. In about 0.4 mile enter the Henry M. Jackson Wilderness. Continuing on a gentle grade, the trail undulates between ancient groves of towering trees and avalanche swaths of towering brush. If a trail crew hasn't been through in some time, expect to encounter head-high brackens, calf-zapping nettles, and thigh-scratching raspberries.

While audible for some time, Bedal Creek finally becomes visible after about 1 mile. Hugging the soothing waterway, the trail continues on its gentle course, coming to a side creek in about 1.5 miles (elev. 3600 ft). This is the end of "good trail." Following the now rougher, steeper track, cross a rocky channel of Bedal Creek (difficult in early season), and then work your way up a forested wedge between creek flows. In 2 miles the trail apparently ends at the base of a huge rocky outwash (elev. 4050 ft).

The going gets interesting here. Head straight up the steep rocky creek bed. At a

Site of Harry Bedal's cabin

lone big yellow cedar, cross the creek to the right bank. Now work your way along the bank. After 0.25 mile, where a monkey flower–lined side creek flows into the main channel (elev. 4450 ft), locate the trail that heads to the right into the woods. You're almost there. Follow tread through thinning forest, arriving at the lip of Bedal Basin (elev. 4700 ft) after 0.3 mile.

Rugged and beautiful, the basin is strewn with big boulders, and wildflowers adorn the rocky outwashes. Sloan Peak is most imposing. Stare straight up 2700 feet of sheer rock wall. More modest Bedal Peak rises to the left. Mount Forgotten is seen in the distance. The remains of Harry's cabin are hidden between some boulders—whimsical whistlers look after it. Roam the basin or just sit and listen to the voices in the wind.

EXTENDING YOUR TRIP
The Bedal Campground, 4 miles from the trailhead, is an excellent place to prolong your stay in the area. It's my favorite campground on the Mountain Loop Highway. Choose a Sauk-side site or one under a colossal cedar.

34 Round Lake

RATING/ DIFFICULTY	ROUND-TRIP	ELEV GAIN/ HIGH POINT	SEASON
★★★★/5	11 miles	4300 feet/ 5600 feet	Mid-July–Oct

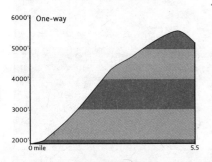

Map: Green Trails Sloan Peak No. 111; **Contact:** Mount Baker–Snoqualmie National Forest, Darrington Ranger District, (360) 436-1155, or Verlot Public Service Center, (360) 691-7791, *www.fs.fed.us/r6/mbs*; **GPS:** N 48 05.617, W 121 20.208

While Round Lake, tucked securely in a hidden basin on Lost Creek Ridge, is a wonderful locale, this hike is definitely more about the journey than the destination. After a demanding initial grunt, amble along a mile-high, flower-swaying, peak-packed, view-granting ridge. Savor one of the finest vantages for admiring spiraling Sloan Peak's sprawling sparkling glacier. And if you can ever move your eyes away from this mesmerizing mountain, a multitude of others demand your attention as well.

GETTING THERE
Take exit 208 off of I-5 and drive 4 miles east on State Route 530 to Arlington. Continue east on SR 530 for 28 more miles to Darrington. At a three-way stop, turn right (south) onto the Mountain Loop Highway and proceed 16 miles (the pavement ends at 9 miles), coming to a junction with Forest Road 49 (signed for the North Fork Sauk Trail). Turn left (east) and follow FR 49 for 3 miles to the trailhead (elev. 1850 ft).

ON THE TRAIL
Start off easily enough on an old roadbed through lush cedar bottomlands. After a pleasant 0.5 mile, get down to business. Climbing steeply, the trail furiously works its way up Lost Creek Ridge. Under a canopy of magnificent old growth, you're at least sheltered from the sun on this south-facing slope. However, the way is dry, so be sure to pack plenty of water.

Cross several small avalanche chutes that give teaser views of Red Mountain and the North Fork Sauk Valley before resuming your arduous ascent up tight, steep switchbacks. At 3.25 miles reach Bingley Gap (elev. 4400 ft), a small forested saddle on Lost Creek Ridge. The trail now heads eastward along the ridge, and though you're still climbing, emerging views assuage your pain. Pugh, White Chuck, and Baker greet you first. Sloan and Bedal soon steal the show. As difficult as it may be to lift thine eyes away from them, hundreds of other summits are yelling out to be recognized: Stuart, Daniel, Del Campo, Morning Star, Sperry, and Vesper among them.

After 1.5 miles of spectacular ridge running, come to an unmarked junction. The main trail continues right for miles and miles of amazing alpine wanderings. Take the trail left to a small gap (elev. 5600 ft) and a great view down to Round Lake twinkling in an open basin. The lake looks like a trek to get to, and it is. If you're spent, there's no shame in not continuing—kick back and enjoy the view.

If you're enticed to soak your feet in that sparkling gem and the trail is free of steep snow patches, proceed, dropping 550 feet in 0.75 mile. Bugs can be a nuisance lakeside when the air is calm. But they're nothing the resident frogs and swallows won't eventually take care of.

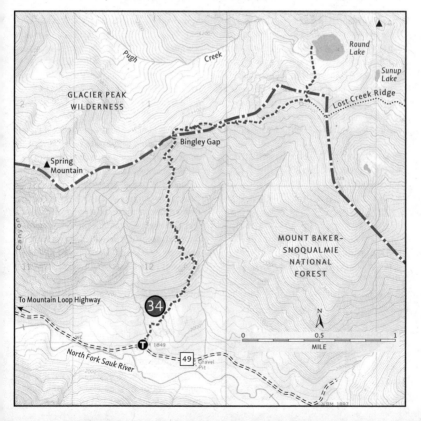

Sloan Peak and Bedal Peak from Lost Creek Ridge

EXTENDING YOUR TRIP

There are two very short but excellent trails nearby, ideal for loosening tight legs after your trip back (and down, down, down) from Round Lake. Thundering North Fork Sauk Falls is reached by a 0.25-mile trail 2 miles west of the Round Lake trailhead. The Engles Grove of giant ancient cedars can be enjoyed on a 0.5-mile trail that lies 0.5 mile east of the trailhead.

35 North Fork Sauk River and Red Mountain

North Fork Sauk

RATING/ DIFFICULTY	ROUND-TRIP	ELEV GAIN/ HIGH POINT	SEASON
★★★/2	10 miles	800 feet/ 2800 feet	May– early Nov

Red Mountain

RATING/ DIFFICULTY	ROUND-TRIP	ELEV GAIN/ HIGH POINT	SEASON
★★★/3	2 miles	700 feet/ 2775 feet	May– early Nov

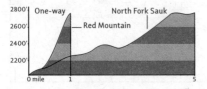

Maps: Green Trails Sloan Peak No. 111, Glacier Peak No. 112; **Contact:** Mount Baker–Snoqualmie National Forest, Darrington Ranger District, (360) 436-1155, or Verlot Public Service Center, (360) 691-7791, www.fs.fed.us/r6/mbs; **Notes:** NW Forest Pass required; **GPS:** N 48 03.515, W 121 17.285

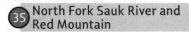

Choose between a leisurely jaunt up a wilderness valley harboring some of the biggest and oldest trees this side of Glacier Peak, or a short, steep stint to an old lookout site with a grand view of Sloan Peak's glistening glacier. Or combine destinations for a most satisfying day in the woods. Whether you aim for Red Mountain or head deep up the valley, the tumbling, churning, glacial-fed North Fork Sauk River is always present in sight or in sound.

GETTING THERE

Take exit 208 off of I-5 and drive 4 miles east on State Route 530 to Arlington. Continue east on SR 530 for 28 more miles to Darrington. At a three-way stop, turn right (south) onto the Mountain Loop Highway and proceed 16 miles (the pavement ends at 9 miles), coming to a junction with Forest Road 49 (signed for the North Fork Sauk Trail). Turn left (east) and follow FR 49 for 6.4 miles to a junction signed for Sloan Creek Trail. Turn left and reach the trailhead in 0.1 mile (elev. 2075 ft). Privy and primitive camping available.

ON THE TRAIL

The trail immediately begins in the company of a contingent of giant cedars. Trail No. 651 for Red Mountain parts from the main path after a couple of hundred feet. If Red is your objective, head left on the lightly traveled, likely to be abandoned, but still decent trail. Pass an old sign for the Mount Baker National Forest (the Mount Baker and the Snoqualmie national forests were combined in 1974). Enter the Glacier Peak Wilderness and up you go. Under a thick canopy of fir and cedar the trail climbs 700 feet, reaching the site of the Red Mountain Lookout (elev. 2775 ft) in 1 mile.

The lookout was removed in 1967, but the site still provides excellent looking out. Directly below is the confluence of the North Fork Sauk and Sloan Creek. Look south to the Cadets and north to Spring Mountain, with Pugh peeking out from behind it. But it's Sloan Peak directly west that will dominate your attention. Don't forget your sunglasses—Sloan's massive glacier and snowfields glisten in the afternoon sun. Beyond the lookout site, a primitive path continues higher up Red Mountain and should only be attempted by experienced scramblers.

Meanwhile, back in the valley the North Fork Sauk Trail No. 649 marches upstream, entering the Glacier Peak Wilderness in about 0.3 mile. The way is fairly gentle, but you may find yourself frequently stumbling as your eyes are averted upward to admire the ancient giants surrounding you. Some of the cedars along the trail measure over 9 feet in diameter.

In about 1 mile, cross a creek in a swath of brush. Look back over your shoulder for a glimpse of Sloan Peak hovering above, and continue along in primeval forest. The North Fork Sauk, while always audible, reveals itself

only occasionally. When it does, stare into its silvery flow and let its songs serenade you. At 2 miles reach a junction with the Pilot Ridge Trail that heads right to a series of glorious high-country meadows—a strenuous journey that begins with fording the river.

The North Fork Sauk Trail marches on through yet more impressive groves of cedar, Douglas-fir, and some silver fir to boot. In late spring the forest floor is lined with yellow violets, purple bleeding hearts, and white and pink trilliums. At 5 miles reach a backcountry

Towering ancient cedars

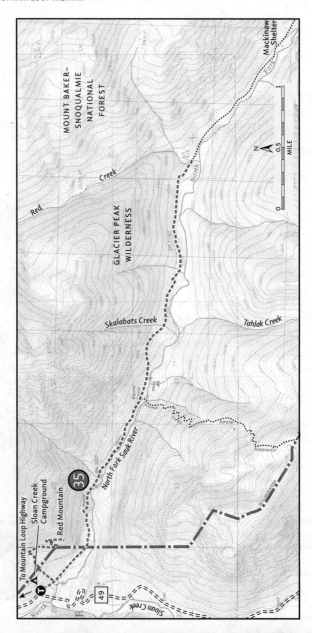

camping area and crashing Red Creek (elev. 2800 ft). This is a logical spot to turn around. However, with a new bridge now in place, feel free to carry on. Otherwise, recall favorite groves and river viewing spots for return rest stops.

EXTENDING YOUR TRIP
After crossing Red Creek continue upvalley for another 1.7 miles through forest and avalanche chutes to the Mackinaw Shelter. Beyond that, the trail climbs 3000 feet in 3.5 miles to reach the Pacific Crest Trail between Red and White passes.

36 Mount Pugh

RATING/ DIFFICULTY	ROUND-TRIP	ELEV GAIN/ HIGH POINT	SEASON
★★★★★/5	11 miles	5300 feet/ 7201 feet	July–Oct

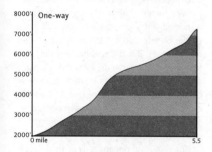

Map: Green Trails Sloan Peak No. 111; **Contact:** Mount Baker–Snoqualmie National Forest, Darrington Ranger District, (360) 436-1155, or Verlot Public Service Center, (360) 691-7791, www.fs.fed.us/r6/mbs; **Notes:** Last 1.5 miles cross a knife-edge ridge with considerable exposure. Only confident hikers with scrambling experience should attempt it; **GPS:** N 48 08.713, W 121 25.004

The view from Pugh seems too good to be true! The Olympics, Three Fingers, Baker, Shuksan, Rainier, Stu- *art, the Monte Cristo massif, and nearly every peak ringing the Mountain Loop Highway are in full view from this cloud-piercing peak. Rising over 7000 feet, this lofty summit provides one of the best alpine showings in all of western Washington. And even with its crowded field of summit stars, Glacier Peak dominating the eastern horizon steals the show. Snowy, showy Sloan Peak makes a stellar appearance as well.*

GETTING THERE
Take exit 208 off of I-5 and drive 4 miles east on State Route 530 to Arlington. Continue east on SR 530 for 28 more miles to Darrington. At a three-way stop, turn right (south) onto the Mountain Loop Highway and proceed 12.4 miles (the pavement ends at 9 miles). Turn left onto Forest Road 2095 and continue 1.5 miles to the trailhead (elev. 1900 ft).

ON THE TRAIL
Before beginning, let's make one thing perfectly clear. This is an extremely difficult and taxing hike. From trailhead to summit, over 1 vertical mile is gained. Parts of the trail, blasted into rock ledges to provide access to a long-gone lookout, are exposed and can be downright frightening (and dangerous in bad conditions and for inexperienced hikers). But a hiker in good physical shape, conditioned for scrambling, and setting off in ideal weather conditions can expect to return home both beat and content—glowing from completing one of the most exhilarating and satisfying hikes in all of the Cascades.

The trail starts off easily enough. On good tread and under a magnificent canopy of old growth, the trail nonchalantly travels 1.5 miles to Lake Metan, gaining a modest 1300 feet along the way. Not much of a lake, the small pool provides the last reliable water and a good view up massive Mount Pugh. The trail goes up that?!

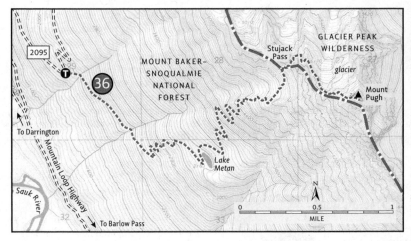

Still on good tread and still under majestic ancient trees, the route steepens. Switchbacks shorten. Up. Up. Up. At 3.1 miles break out of forest to a jumble of boulders at the base of steep talus and avalanche slopes (elev. 4900 ft). The trail gets even steeper, now on rocky tread as it works its way up the harsh slope. Emerging views distract you from your toil. So too do a myriad of wildflowers painting the rough terrain. At 3.8 miles reach 5750-foot Stujack Pass, a notch of a gap on Pugh's northwest shoulder. Admire White Chuck Mountain to the north, while cool air from permanent snowfields below refreshes you.

Start working your way eastward, entering the Glacier Peak Wilderness (how about expanding it to protect all of that old growth below?) and climbing higher. Up steep heather slopes, but still on fairly decent tread, the way soon rounds a bend to reveal Pugh's intimidating summit block and an impressive glacier wedged beneath it. At 4.2 miles reach the remnants of an old tram (elev. 6200 ft) once used to levitate supplies to the summit look-

out. Most hikers will want to stop here, fully content with their 4300 feet of climbing and amazing views spread out before them.

Sure-footed scramblers may proceed along a knife edge that precipitously drops off to the glacier on one side and the Sauk River valley on the other. But the real heart-racing section is next. Using hands, ascend a steep and exposed "cleft" that was blasted into a vertical ledge above the glacial trough. Carefully cross a short section of trail that has slid off—always difficult, and extremely dangerous when snow-covered.

But if you can negotiate all of this, the remaining route is relatively smooth sailing, albeit steep. At 5.5 linear miles and 1 vertical mile, arrive at the glorious 7201-foot summit of Mount Pugh. Plop yourself down on one of its massive shiny granite shards and soak up as much scenery as possible before your head explodes from taking in so many summits. Don't forget to bring a map—one for the entire national forest—to help you fully appreciate everything spread out before and below you.

Opposite: A nap is in order after summiting Mount Pugh.

37 Peek-a-boo Lake

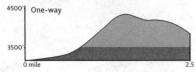

RATING/ DIFFICULTY	ROUND-TRIP	ELEV GAIN/ HIGH POINT	SEASON
★★★/3	5 miles	1500 feet/ 4350 feet	July–Oct

Map: Green Trails Sloan Peak No. 111; **Contact:** Mount Baker–Snoqualmie National Forest, Darrington Ranger District, (360) 436-1155, or Verlot Public Service Center, (360) 691-7791, www.fs.fed.us/r6/mbs; **GPS:** N 48 09.462, W 121 29.437

An emerging tarn stops a hiker in her tracks.

Peek-a-boo Lake sits in a peaceful little cirque on a ridge high above the Sauk River. And while this backcountry lake certainly makes for a delightful destination, it's the journey that really ranks supreme. En route be mystified by primeval forest and marvel at marshy meadows. Best of all, find more than just peekaboo views out to the prominent peaks White Chuck and Pugh.

GETTING THERE

Take exit 208 off of I-5 and drive 4 miles east on State Route 530 to Arlington. Continue east on SR 530 for 28 more miles to Darrington. At a three-way stop, turn right (south) onto the Mountain Loop Highway and proceed 8.5 miles, turning right onto Forest Road 2080 (the turnoff is just before the Sauk River bridge). Continue on FR 2080 for 1.1 miles and turn right onto FR 2081. Follow this narrow, alder- and hemlock-lined road 3.5 miles. Bear left onto FR 2086, and after 1 mile reach the trailhead at the road end (elev. 3200 ft). Assess vehicle for new body-job estimate.

ON THE TRAIL

Begin on an old logging road in scrappy forest, and after 0.3 mile pick up true trail in impressive old growth. Side-sloping, switchbacking, and with occasional direct attacks straight uphill, the rough-at-times trail makes its way up a thickly forested 4350-foot ridge. All the while, massive hemlocks, firs, and cedars as well as babbling brooks and a lush understory of greenery draw your attention away from the climb.

The trail then gently begins to lose elevation and after 0.5 mile emerges from the emerald canopy into a picturesque parkland meadow. Pass by a small tarn and continue along more magnificent meadows. Using care not to trounce delicate vegetation, leave the trail for the eastern edge of the meadow to be wooed by a breathtaking view of White Chuck Mountain and Mount Pugh hovering over the Sauk River valley.

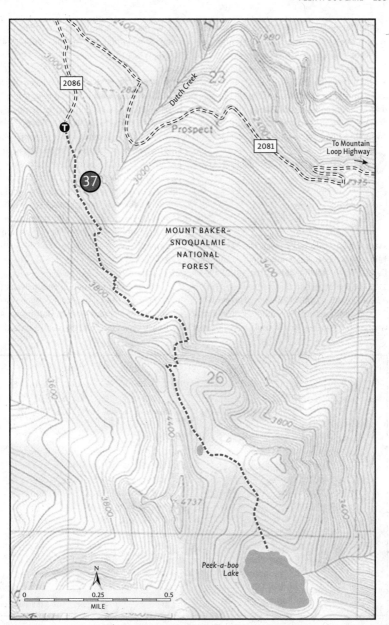

After taking in the peaks, head back toward Peek-a-boo Lake. The trail returns to the forest, dropping about 300 feet on rocky and rooty tread to the placid lake perched in an emerald bowl (elev. 3900 ft) of stately hemlocks and shaggy-barked Alaska yellow cedars. A boot path leads 0.25 mile to a logjam and cascading creek at the lake's outlet. Good swimming, lounging, and napping await.

38 Beaver Lake

RATING/ DIFFICULTY	ROUND-TRIP	ELEV GAIN/ HIGH POINT	SEASON
**/1	4 miles	100 feet/ 1000 feet	Year-round

Map: Green Trails Sloan Peak No. 111; **Contact:** Mount Baker–Snoqualmie National Forest, Darrington Ranger District, (360) 436-1155, or Verlot Public Service Center, (360) 691-7791, *www.fs.fed.us/r6/mbs*; **Notes:** NW Forest Pass required. November 2006 floods washed out two sections of trail, a small area

at 0.75 mile and a larger one at 1 mile. Until tread is restored, use caution; **GPS:** N 48 10.236, W 121 28.329

An easy hike on an old railroad bed, this oft-overlooked trail serves up plenty of surprises. Travel alongside the Wild and Scenic Sauk River, admiring eagles, mergansers, and kingfishers. Watch dippers flit on river rocks. Listen to thrushes bring the surrounding forest alive in song. Pause on open banks to take in sweeping views of surrounding peaks. Marvel at ancient giant cedars. Locate relics of past logging and railroading activity. And of course enjoy the wildlife-rich wetland known as Beaver Lake.

GETTING THERE

Take exit 208 off of I-5 and drive 4 miles east on State Route 530 to Arlington. Continue east on SR 530 for 28 more miles to Darrington. At a three-way stop, turn right (south) onto the

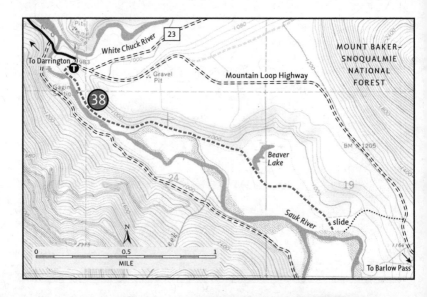

A row of ancient cedars

Mountain Loop Highway and proceed 9 miles to the trailhead, on the right just after you cross the Sauk River.

ON THE TRAIL

Starting just above the confluence of the Sauk and White Chuck rivers, the trail dips slightly from the parking lot onto an old logging railway grade. Rotting trestles can be seen just to the right. On a near straightaway, the trail cuts through a thick stand of second-growth hemlocks. In 0.5 mile the trail swings left on a high bank, and the Sauk churns and roars below. Enjoy a good view out to Mount Pugh and the Monte Cristo peaks.

The mighty river has continuously pounded the gravel-layered riverbank, causing portions to slump. Use caution crossing a small section that was battered in the November 2006 storms. Continuing alongside the mighty river, feel its pulse and vibrancy. Pass through a tunnel of alders, their glaucous trunks lighting the way. At 1 mile arrive at a large washout. If tread has been restored, proceed. Otherwise, carefully work your way around the 500-foot storm-ravaged area (on the gravel riverbed if the water level is low or through brush if the water is high), or call it a day and return to your vehicle.

Once beyond the damaged area, the trail resumes its easy course on the old railbed. After passing through skunk-cabbage patches you'll come to a delightful bridge crossing Beaver Lake. Look underneath the span; the bridge was built upon some of the original railroad trestles. The lake, actually an old channel of the river, is a good place to observe wildlife. And while its namesake isn't in abundance here, plenty of aviary residents are.

Beyond Beaver Lake the trail enters an impressive old-growth cedar grove. The trees are remarkable in size and girth, but also in that they were spared the ax. The trail continues for a short way, terminating at an impassable slide on the Sauk. Enjoy lunch at this often sunny spot before retracing your steps on this delightful trail.

EXTENDING YOUR TRIP

Beyond the slide, the last 0.75 mile of the original Beaver Lake Trail still exists. This section—now called the Lookout Tree Trail—can be accessed from the Mountain Loop Highway 2.3 miles south of the Beaver Lake trailhead. The short trail drops 200 feet to the site of the old Sauk Ranger Station and a big cedar that once served as a lookout. Also nearby, the White Chuck Bench Trail runs 6.5 miles along the White Chuck River, providing excellent year-round hiking—when you can reach it. Unfortunately, storms in 2003 and 2006 caused many washouts. The first 2 miles of this wonderful trail have been restored. Write to Congress asking for funding to restore the rest of this recreational asset.

39 Old Sauk River Trail

RATING/ DIFFICULTY	ROUND-TRIP	ELEV GAIN/ HIGH POINT	SEASON
★★★/1	6 miles	150 feet/ 800 feet	Year-round

Map: Green Trails Silverton No. 110; **Contact:** Mount Baker–Snoqualmie National Forest, Darrington Ranger District, (360) 436-1155, or Verlot Public Service Center, (360) 691-7791, *www.fs.fed.us/r6/mbs*; **Notes:** NW Forest Pass required; **GPS:** N 48 12.926, W 121 33.530

Sauk River

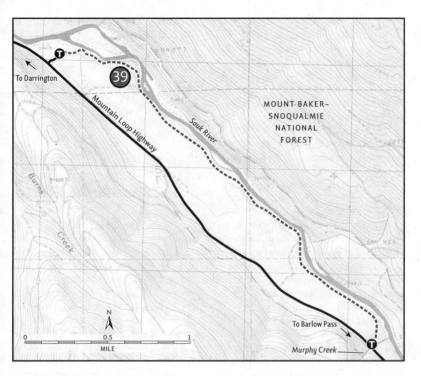

 A major tributary to the Skagit, the federally protected Wild and Scenic Sauk River supports a wide array of wildlife and provides critical habitat for Puget Sound salmon. And like the Skagit, this mighty river is also winter habitat for hundreds of bald eagles. The Old Sauk River Trail hugs the riverbank of this ecologically important and strikingly beautiful waterway for 3 virtually flat miles. And with an elevation below 1000 feet, the trail rarely sees snow, making it one of the few winter hiking choices along the Mountain Loop Highway. But any time of year is ideal for this delightful and easy trail.

GETTING THERE

Take exit 208 off of I-5 and drive 4 miles east on State Route 530 to Arlington. Continue east on SR 530 for 28 more miles to Darrington. At a three-way stop, turn right (south) onto the Mountain Loop Highway and drive 3.5 miles to trailhead. Alternatively, you can begin at the southern trailhead 2.8 miles farther down the road.

ON THE TRAIL

Within sound but not sight of the river, the trail begins in a thick stand of mature forest. Despite logging in the 1930s, many old-growth Douglas-firs still boldly stand. In 0.75 mile, after skirting a periodically dry channel, reach the mighty river. Behold its beauty and ever-changing mood. In the wet fall months, the river's volume and current increases. On more than a few occasions the Sauk has jumped its bed, taking a piece of the trail with it. But this trail is too admired to let go of—determined volunteers continuously restore lost tread.

At 1.25 miles cross a bridge over a small creek, and continue alongside the churning Sauk through attractive woods. Walk this way in springtime and be treated to brilliant displays of wildflowers. Thousands of trilliums, dwarf dogwoods, wood violets, twinflowers, and starflowers carpet the forest floor.

At 2 miles the trail was swallowed by the river in the November 2006 floods. But thankfully, trail builders restored tread by skirting around the unstable riverbank. Comprised of layers of glacial till and moraine, the Sauk's banks easily erode when assaulted with intense hydrological force.

The trail now briefly leaves the river to follow a quiet channel. Look for sign of active beaver. In late summer to early fall, chances are good for spotting spawning steelhead. The trail crosses an old road and then makes its way back to the riverbank. Silt deposits on and along the trail provide ample evidence of frequent past flooding.

At 2.75 miles the trail leaves the Sauk and its raucous bellowing behind. Briefly following Murphy Creek through a tunnel of moss-draped maples and under a canopy of towering cottonwoods, the trail reaches its southern terminus on the Mountain Loop Highway. Turn around and enjoy this trail downriver.

EXTENDING YOUR TRIP

The 1-mile Frog Lake Trail makes for a nice winter leg stretcher. The "lake" isn't much, but the forest is attractive and so is nearby Clear Creek. The trail starts nearby at the Clear Creek bridge on the Mountain Loop Highway, near Clear Creek Campground.

40 Crystal Lake

RATING/ DIFFICULTY	ROUND-TRIP	ELEV GAIN/ HIGH POINT	SEASON
★★★/4	9 miles	2300 feet/ 4485 feet	July–Oct

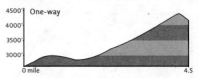

Map: Green Trails Sloan Peak No. 111; **Contact:** Mount Baker–Snoqualmie National Forest, Darrington Ranger District, (360) 436-1155, or Verlot Public Service Center, (360) 691-7791, *www.fs.fed.us/r6/mbs*; **Notes:** NW Forest Pass required. No road access—FR 23 (White Chuck River Road) washed out in several areas in fall of 2003, when and if it will be restored is uncertain. FR 27 via Rat Trap Pass also accesses this trail, but that road is closed because of washouts too. Consult Forest Service about road status before setting out. Mountain biking 6.7 miles to trailhead is possible, but requires difficult river fording; **GPS:** N 48 11.270, W 121 22.180

 A tranquil lake at the edge of the Glacier Peak Wilderness, chances are you'll have this place to yourself. The trail can be rough, overgrown, and at times steep—three good reasons for the crowd control. Kick back and harvest berries at the lake or, if you're feeling energetic, head off for Circle Peak on a rehabilitated trail to an old lookout site with mouthwatering views.

GETTING THERE

Take exit 208 off of I-5 and drive 4 miles east on State Route 530 to Arlington. Continue east

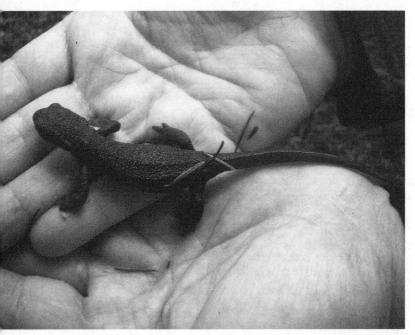

Resident newt of Crystal Lake

on SR 530 for 28 more miles to Darrington. At a three-way stop, turn right (south) onto the Mountain Loop Highway and proceed 9 miles, turning left onto Forest Road 23. Drive 6 miles and turn left onto FR 27. Continue another 2.4 miles to the trailhead, on your right (elev. 2550 ft).

ON THE TRAIL

Much of this hike uses old logging roads. While this assures an easy grade, look forward to a hot slog when the sun is beating down—there's no shade. When trees do begin to reclaim the roadbed and fringes, alders are the colonizers. If not cut back on a regular basis, the way can quickly take on a jungle ambience. Be forewarned. Bring loppers or an easy disposition.

Begin by following an old roadbed, climbing a few hundred feet and then losing most of it. Limited views of surrounding peaks break the scrappy alder monotony. At 1.5 miles (elev. 2800 ft), reach a junction. Crystal Creek Trail No. 638 departs left—take it. Now on a secondary old logging roadbed, follow Crystal Creek. With trail access closed for years, expect a route clogged with vegetation.

The grade is fairly easy for a mile or so, but then it's time to get serious. Leaving the creek behind, the trail works its way up a steep slope choked in thick regenerating growth. Traverse an old cut, and then head steeply straight up an old fire line. Yep, this area is a mess, the legacy of an era of intensive timber harvesting (ancient-forest slaughter). At the edge of the cut, come to a trail junction (elev. 4300 ft) that may or may not be signed. The trail left leads 4 miles on rehabilitated tread to Circle Peak.

For Crystal Lake continue to the right on real trail now, climbing more sanely and entering the Glacier Peak Wilderness, refuge from old clear-cuts and roads. In another 0.25 mile, Crystal Lake and its meadowy shores greet you. Enjoy—you deserve it.

EXTENDING YOUR TRIP

Follow the Circle Peak Trail on a sane course through forest and meadow to just below the 5983-foot peak (the actual summit is a sketchy scramble). From the old lookout site, enjoy sweeping views of forests "managed" and wild and of peaks near and far. Especially striking are the "three Matterhorns": White Chuck, Pugh, and Sloan.

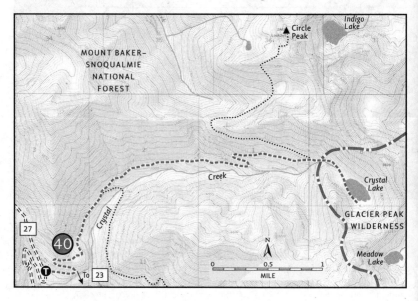

Opposite: Mount Baker from Sauk Mountain

west slope

North Fork Stillaguamish River

Slicing through steep folded ridges and rocky ice-capped peaks, the North Fork Stillaguamish River valley is dramatic indeed. While a handful of trails lead into the rugged surroundings, most of them are as rough as the terrain. The Squires Creek Pass Trail has been deemed unsafe by the Forest Service because of rock and landslide probability. Lone Tree Pass Trail is better suited for climbers and mountain goats. Two trails emanating from the valley, however, make excellent day-hiking choices. One offers an easy portal into the Boulder Creek Wilderness and traverses one of the largest remaining stands of low-country old growth in the North Cascades (Hike 42). The other travels into the elusive Finney Block, a wedge of little-hiked mountains and lost trails between the North Fork Stilly and the Skagit River (Hike 41).

41 Mount Higgins

RATING/ DIFFICULTY	ROUND-TRIP	ELEV GAIN/ HIGH POINT	SEASON
★★★/4	9 miles	3400 feet/ 4849 feet	Mid-June– early Nov

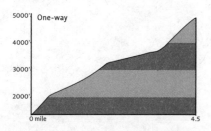

Map: Green Trails Oso No. 77; **Contact:** Mount Baker–Snoqualmie National Forest, Darrington Ranger District, (360) 436-1155, www.fs.fed.us /r6/mbs; **GPS:** N 48 18.636, W 121 51.035

 Rising above the pastoral farmlands of the North Fork Stillaguamish River valley between Arlington and Darrington is impressive Mount Higgins, with its folded strata of metamorphosed sandstone and shale. It's as if Atlas himself crunched this landscape into a giant accordion. Hum a Cajun tune or two and two-step up the steep trail to the vertigo-inducing former lookout site, where you can· peer straight down to the Stilly or out across to rows of jagged and glacier-clad peaks. Chances are you'll have this airy outpost all to yourself.

GETTING THERE

Take exit 208 off of I-5 and drive 4 miles east on State Route 530 to Arlington, and then continue east on SR 530 for 17 more miles. Just before milepost 38, turn left onto the easy-to-miss dirt "C Post Road." Proceed north, crossing the North Fork Stillaguamish in 0.5 mile and coming to an unmarked junction. Turn left, following a semirough road for 2.4 miles to its end at a berm. The trail, marked by a shot-up sign, begins on the east side of the road (elev. 1450 ft).

ON THE TRAIL

The trail begins on a decommissioned logging road through heavily harvested Washington State Department of Natural Resources land. Real trail is reached in 0.6 mile and after steeply gaining 500 feet. First, traverse a brushy steep slope scarred by clear-cutting, with good views of the valley below to help keep your mind off of this mangled management of our state land.

In 1 mile enter the Mount Baker–Snoqualmie National Forest (elev. 2400 ft). No longer side-sloping, the trail now heads up in a more direct fashion—steep at times through a luxuriant stand of mature Douglas-fir. Big, beautiful

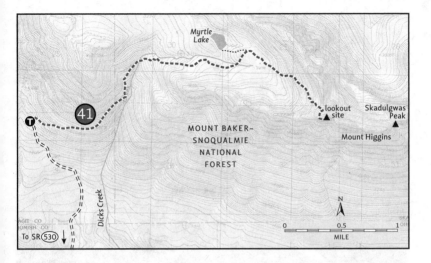

ancient cedars soon begin to line the way. How this board-footage escaped the chain saw is nothing short of miraculous.

These 100,000 acres of rugged national forest land between the Sauk, Skagit, and North Fork Stilly rivers—known as the Finney Block—have been intensively logged in the last several decades, resulting in miles of prime hiking trails obliterated, acres of primeval forest ravaged, and some of the best spotted-owl habitat in the state compromised. Only two small areas, just 25 percent of the Finney Block, remain roadless. The Mount Higgins area consists of 13,000 acres and has some of the last miles of maintained trail in the Finney Block. The area surely would have been logged too if not for legal actions taken by conservationists in the 1990s. This tract should be wilderness and its obliterated and abandoned trails should be resurrected.

Continue through magnificent forest. Use caution on the old puncheon (cedar planks) frequently encountered along the way; much of it is rotting, slippery, and contorted. At about 2 miles cross Dicks Creek, which can be difficult during times of heavy runoff. Now on rougher tread and parallel to the cascading creek, the trail once again climbs steeply.

Reaching a marshy area at 3 miles, the grade eases. At 3.5 miles, just after recrossing Dicks Creek, come to an easy-to-miss junction in a hardy huckleberry patch (elev. 3650 ft). The trail left drops to Myrtle Lake.

The way to Higgins continues right, along marshy meadows and mosquito-incubating pothole ponds. Then it's back into impressive old growth before once again steeply climbing, traversing scree and heather slopes and arriving at the 4849-foot former lookout site at 4.5 miles. Catch your breath and watch your step—it's one heck of a drop. To the north, snuggled in a blanket of old growth, is Myrtle Lake. The giants Whitehorse and Three Fingers vie for your attention to the south. In the west, Puget Sound sparkles against a backdrop of Olympic peaks. And to the east, follow the folded strata of peaks making up the Mount Higgins massif. The true summit is

Swirling clouds cloak Mount Higgins's jagged summits.

the farther peak at 5176 feet. The closer one, Skadulgwas, honors a legendary princess of the Sauk-Suiattle people.

EXTENDING YOUR TRIP

The trail to tranquil Myrtle Lake drops 150 feet in 0.5 mile. It's a brushy route badly in need of clearing and in danger of permanently disappearing.

42 Boulder River

RATING/ DIFFICULTY	ROUND-TRIP	ELEV GAIN/ HIGH POINT	SEASON
★★★/2	8.6 miles	700 feet/ 1550 feet	Year-round

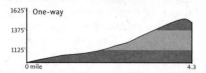

Maps: Green Trails Oso No. 77, Granite Falls No. 109; **Contact:** Mount Baker–Snoqualmie National Forest, Darrington Ranger District, (360) 436-1155, *www.fs.fed.us/r6/mbs*; **GPS:** N 48 15.053, W 121 49.031

A good hike any time of year, the trail is perfect for beating summer heat, enjoying winter rain, savoring autumn color, or being wooed by waterfalls that are swollen with spring rain. One thing about this trail remains constant: the trees. Whatever the season, you'll travel through a forest that has defied time. Boulder River's moss-draped giants represent one of the last remaining large, low-country old-growth forests in the Cascades. Protected within the nearly 49,000-acre Boulder River Wilderness, these ancient trees are as impressive as the wild river they embrace.

GETTING THERE

Take exit 208 off of I-5 and drive 4 miles east on State Route 530 to Arlington, and then continue east on SR 530 for 20 more miles. At milepost 41, near a subdivision, turn right onto Forest Road 2010 (French Creek Road) and continue for 3.7 miles to the trailhead (elev. 950 ft). Privy available at the Washington State Department of Natural Resources campground 2.8 miles east.

ON THE TRAIL

Start in an old cut on a logging railroad grade. Don't despair, though, virgin forest appears soon enough. Crashing Boulder Falls can be heard through the dense forest and becomes fully visible just ahead. At about 1 mile pass the wilderness boundary, and soon afterward encounter a spectacular yet unnamed twin waterfall tumbling down the canyon walls into the river. This is a good turnaround spot for young children and hikers who just want a quick wilderness dose.

For those intent on carrying on, the trail continues up the moisture-laden emerald valley. While the river's incessant gurgling and belching is continuously heard along the way, the raucous waterway is often hidden from

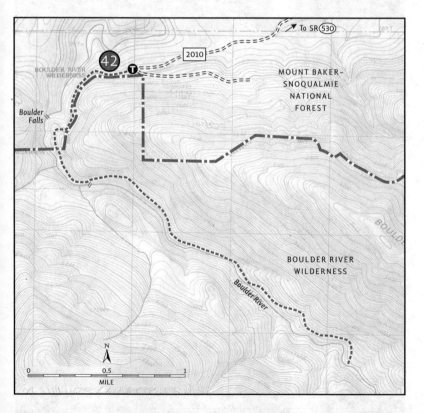

sight. Farther upstream the trail pulls a little ways from the river, climbing a couple hundred feet above it. At 4 miles the trail heads back down to the wild waterway, terminating at a damp riverside flat (elev. 1450 ft). Grab the granola and let the river serenade you with its timeless ballads.

EXTENDING YOUR TRIP

The trail once crossed the river, continuing all the way to Tupso Pass and down to the South Fork Stillaguamish River. Long-abandoned, the tread has been reclaimed by primeval forest. Very few trails traverse the Boulder River Wilderness, making it a wild place indeed. For further explorations, consider the trails to Lone Tree Pass (3500 ft elevation gain in 3.5 miles) and Squire Creek Pass via Eightmile Creek (2700 ft elevation gain in 3 miles). Both these trails are nearby, and both are primitive and difficult, for experienced hikers only.

Waterfall crashing into Boulder River

WHO WHO CARES ABOUT OLD GROWTH?

Perhaps no creature is more synonymous with the ancient forests of the Pacific Northwest than the northern spotted owl. Your view on how these centuries-old forests should be managed will dictate your response to this small bird of prey: warm and fuzzy for the owl's role in preserving huge tracts of virgin timber, or incredulous at how it was used to stop old-growth logging in the Northwest.

The spotted owl's 1990 listing as threatened under the Endangered Species Act was as much about protecting the bird as it was about protecting a threatened ecosystem—an ecosystem reduced to 10 percent of its size since European settlement. The owl needs old growth to survive, and its listing as threatened forced the federal government to provide for its recovery by protecting large areas of virgin forest.

Even without the spotted owl listing, the logging of old growth wouldn't have lasted much longer. The companies that logged the huge trees were on course to put themselves out of business within a decade or two because of the frenzied, unsustainable harvesting they had begun in the 1970s.

With old-growth forests on federal lands off-limits to harvesting, many in the timber industry blamed the spotted owl and the conservation community. But the real culprits of the industry's hard times were sawmills failing to adapt to smaller-diameter logs, the rising role of mechanization that reduced the need for labor, and the increased role of world trade favoring cheaper imports from Canada, Chile, and Russia.

Meanwhile, though much of the spotted owl's habitat has been protected, the bird's numbers continue to dwindle, with an estimated population of 500 pairs living in western Washington. Many former timber towns in the region remain depressed and devastated, and the old-growth forests of Siberia and British Columbia are rapidly being liquidated.

Suiattle River Valley

Born from ice and snow adorning 10,541-foot Glacier Peak, Washington's fourth-highest summit, the milky Suiattle River cuts through some of the wildest country in the entire Pacific Northwest. Surrounded by thousands of acres of deep forest and flanked by snow-capped peaks whose lower arms radiate in emerald ridges bursting with wildflowers, the Suiattle Valley is breathtaking country—and is mostly the domain of multiday backpackers. Still, the Suiattle offers day hikers some grand high-country exploring. Just beware the fickle river: it's known to periodically put the *Not Welcome* sign up when it jumps its banks and washes out the road, severing access to these trails.

43 Huckleberry Mountain

RATING/ DIFFICULTY	ROUND-TRIP	ELEV GAIN/ HIGH POINT	SEASON
★★★★/5	12 miles	4600 feet/ 5483 feet	July–Oct

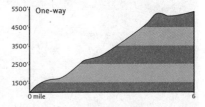

Map: Green Trails Snowking Mountain No. 79;
Contact: Mount Baker–Snoqualmie National

Forest, Darrington Ranger District, (360) 436-1155, *www.fs.fed.us/r6/mbs*; **Notes:** NW Forest Pass required; **GPS:** N 48 16.180, W 121 20.980

⊗ 🔦 *You want lonely? You got it on the Huckleberry Mountain Trail. But there's a price to pay in vertical gain, 5800 feet worth if you want to go all the way to the old lookout site. Settle instead for a 5483-foot knoll, saving yourself 1200 feet and 2 very difficult miles. The views are just as grand from this locale, encompassing the deep, dark emerald valleys and countless craggy, snow-capped peaks and ridges of the Glacier Peak Wilderness, one of the wildest corners in the Lower 48.*

GETTING THERE

From Darrington travel north on State Route 530 for 7.5 miles, turning right immediately after the Sauk River bridge onto Forest Road 26 (Suiattle River Road). (From Rockport drive south on SR 530 for 11 miles to FR 26.) Follow FR 26 first on pavement, then on gravel for 14.5 miles to the unobtrusive trailhead (elev. 1000 ft). The flood of 2006 washed out FR 26, requiring a 2-mile walk or bike ride to the trailhead. Check with Forest Service for current status of road.

ON THE TRAIL

Starting from valley bottom, the Huckleberry Mountain Trail is one of the last "complete" trails left in the North Cascades. A half century of aggressive logging severed many of our trails from their valley roots (or worse, obliterated them). Miraculously, Huckleberry Mountain's trail and more importantly its forests were spared this fate. On this trail you can propel yourself back in time to when it took time to reach coveted summits and high ridges. But more than mere time is required for this trek: you'll also need excellent endurance and a good cardiovascular system.

Starting under a glorious canopy of ancient Douglas-fir, the trail begins its long and winding way up the mountain. While the grade is good and the tread intact, undergrowth is

White Chuck Mountain in the distance

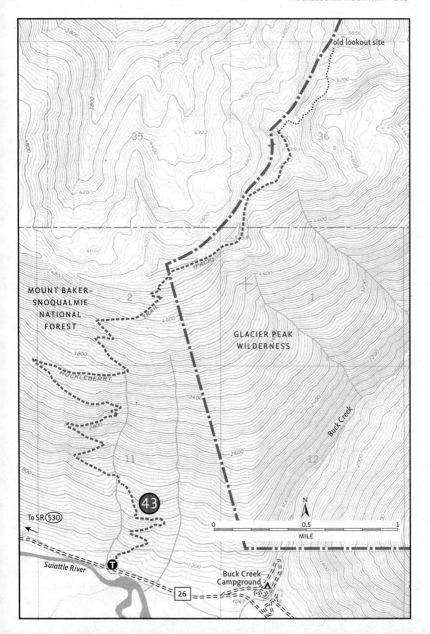

old lookout site

MOUNT BAKER–
SNOQUALMIE
NATIONAL
FOREST

GLACIER PEAK
WILDERNESS

HUCKLEBERRY

(PACT)

TRAIL

Buck Creek

43

To SR 530

Suiattle River

Buck Creek
Campground

26

N

0   0.5   1
MILE

encroaching upon this trail that receives little maintenance. (Actually, in these days of budgetary neglect, most of our trails receive little maintenance—a national shame.)

The trail alternates between short switchbacks and long traverses as it works its way up the broad mile-high peak. Well-shaded and near water for much of the way, this part of the strenuous hike at least won't threaten you with overheating. Finally, at about 4.5 miles and 4500 feet above the Suiattle River valley, the grade eases as you attain the ridge crest. By late summer you're looking at a dry run along the ridge, so be sure water bottles are adequately filled.

Through thinning forest and expanding meadows, enjoy expansive views east over the Suiattle to Glacier Peak, south to Whitehorse and White Chuck, and west to the Finney Block. Continue along the ridge, straddling the Glacier Peak Wilderness boundary—old growth to the east protected, old growth to the west fate unknown.

At about 6 miles, on fading tread, attain a 5483-foot knoll and a logical and sane post for calling it a day and savoring views. To the west, Tenas Creek roars below, draining Boulder Lake beneath Hurricane Peak. To the east, Buck Creek flows through an emerald valley. A scene little changed through the centuries.

EXTENDING YOUR TRIP

To reach the old lookout site, continue another mile on increasingly hard-to-follow tread, dropping to a 5000-foot saddle and then hoofing up to a 5800-plus-foot knoll. Huckleberry's true summit is another mile to the north. Don't even think about it—there's no trail and you've come far enough. Back in the lowlands and not far from the trailhead, Buck Creek Campground is set in deep old growth and is one of the finest car camps in the Cascades. A short, albeit primitive trail follows along the crashing creek for about 0.75 mile.

44 Green Mountain

RATING/ DIFFICULTY	ROUND-TRIP	ELEV GAIN/ HIGH POINT	SEASON
★★★★★/4	8 miles	3100 feet/ 6500 feet	July–Oct

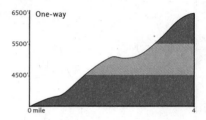

Map: Green Trails Cascade Pass No. 80; **Contact:** Mount Baker–Snoqualmie National Forest, Darrington Ranger District, (360) 436-1155, *www.fs.fed.us/r6/mbs*; **Notes:** NW Forest Pass required; **GPS:** N 48 15.970, W 121 14.740

The meadows alone make the trek to the top of 6500-foot Green Mountain worth the sweat and energy expended. Acres upon acres of emerald slopes burst with a dazzling display of wildflowers. But it's hard to stay focused on Green Mountain's brilliant floral arrangements when its jaw-dropping scenic sideshow is dominated by the gargantuan snow cone of Glacier Peak. Green Mountain offers one of the finest views in the North Cascades, and did I fail to mention the historical fire lookout to boot?

GETTING THERE

From Darrington travel north on State Route 530 for 7.5 miles, turning right immediately after the Sauk River bridge onto Forest Road 26 (Suiattle River Road). (From Rockport drive south on SR 530 for 11 miles to FR 26.) Follow FR 26 first on pavement, then on gravel for 19 miles, turning left onto FR 2680. Continue 6 miles to the trailhead, near the road end (elev. 3500 ft).

Glacier Peak backdrop

ON THE TRAIL

The route to the summit is fairly straightforward and occasionally straight up. Beginning in forest interrupted by teaser views, work your way up a southern shoulder of the peak. After 1.5 miles or so, enter the Glacier Peak Wilderness. Subalpine forest punctuated by meadows and berry patches that warrant a return in September leads to a small ridge, after which you drop 100 feet to a pair of small ponds (elev. 5200 ft).

Not long afterward, lose the trees for good and enter a big, verdant (after all, this is "Green" Mountain) basin. Steeply traversing the basin at first, the trail then heads for a ridge crest above the emerald slopes. Be sure not to veer off the trail. The Forest Service is

working hard trying to restore these loved-to-death meadows. Views expand exponentially as you march toward the summit. Be sure to take time to smell the myriad of flowers along the way. You may even spot a playful marmot or two.

At 4 well-deserved miles, Green's attractive 1933 fire lookout signals that you've reached the top. Wipe the sweat from your brow and

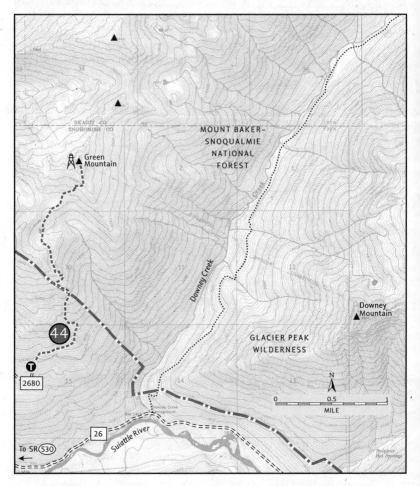

gaze out over a sea of green forest capped by waves of white summits. The Suiattle River valley, a deep U-shaped gorge, spreads out below you. Trace the wild waterway from its icy origins on Glacier Peak all the way to its confluence with the Sauk River.

EXTENDING YOUR TRIP

Many of the deep valleys visible from Green Mountain host throngs of backpackers each season on their way to points far into the Glacier Peak Wilderness, and day hikers may want to probe a few of these trails. Consider the Downey Creek, Milk Creek, and Suiattle River trails for excellent low-country roaming though prime forest and pristine waterways.

45 Sulphur Mountain

RATING/ DIFFICULTY	ROUND-TRIP	ELEV GAIN/ HIGH POINT	SEASON
★★★★/5	10 miles	4200 feet/ 6000 feet	July– mid-Oct

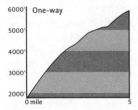

Map: Green Trails Glacier Peak No. 112; **Contact:** Mount Baker–Snoqualmie National Forest, Darrington Ranger District, (360) 436-1155, *www.fs.fed.us/r6/mbs*; **Notes:** NW Forest Pass required; **GPS:** N 48 14.680, W 121 11.330

❌ ⚙️ *This is an arduous climb, mostly through dense forest, to an old lookout site with stunning views over the unbroken virgin forests of the Suiattle River valley and to the icy north face of Glacier Peak. One of the closest vantages to the 10,541-foot volcano without actually being*

A hiker heading up Sulphur Mountain

on that mountain, you'll have to work hard to get it. As reward, you'll get flower-flowing meadows and the more-than-likely chance of having all this beauty all to yourself— aside from an inquisitive marmot or two.

GETTING THERE

From Darrington travel north on State Route 530 for 7.5 miles, turning right immediately after the Sauk River bridge onto Forest Road 26 (Suiattle River Road). (From Rockport drive

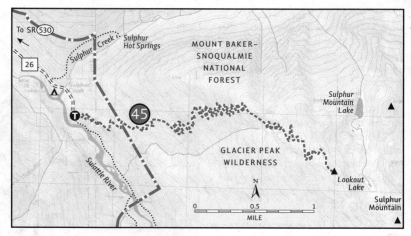

south on SR 530 for 11 miles to FR 26.) Follow FR 26 first on pavement, then on gravel for 22.5 miles all the way to its end at a large parking area for the Suiattle River trailhead (elev. 1800 ft). Privy and primitive campground available.

ON THE TRAIL

Of Washington's five grand volcanoes—Adams, Saint Helens, Rainier, Glacier, and Baker—Glacier remains the most remote, and to many hikers the most beautiful. Because of this seclusion, Glacier firmly remains in the backpacking realm. Day hikers must content themselves with distant portraits of the handsome peak. Sulphur Mountain, however, offers a rare up-close and personal showing of the snowy summit. The price is pretty steep, but worth every ounce of energy spent.

Head down the Suiattle River "hiker expressway" a couple of hundred feet to the Sulphur Mountain Trail that takes off left—for the time being, anyway. The tread is good but light, and without maintenance this trail could disappear.

Take this way less traveled and immediately start heading for the sky. In 0.25 mile

come to a small creek, the only water source (except for a lingering snowfield or two in early summer) on this hike. Make sure you carry adequate water.

The climb is relentless. Up, up, up—no rest for the weary. At about 3.5 miles and with 3200 vertical feet subdued, the grade eases a little. The forest thins, meadows begin, and the wild surrounding countryside is unveiled as the trail attains the lofty ridge crest.

At 5 miles—5 of the hardest miles you've ever hiked—rejoice! You've reached the 6000-foot knoll on Sulphur Mountain that was used as a fire lookout back in the 1930s (but probably never housed a structure). Amid flowering meadows, seize your scenic rewards. Directly east lie the craggy conglomerate of peaks of Sulphur Mountain, including the 6735-foot summit (an objective for experienced scramblers). Directly north is Sulphur Mountain Lake, snug in a tight basin 800 feet below (an objective for crazy scramblers). To the west, Lime Ridge and its lake-cradling cirques warrant attention. But big beautiful Glacier Peak breathes its icy breath upon you, leaving you in a frozen trance face-to-face with the majestic volcano.

EXTENDING YOUR TRIP

Sulphur Creek and Buck Creek campgrounds offer nice if primitive accommodations (bring drinking water) in the Suiattle River valley. After your arduous ascent of Sulphur Mountain, hike the 1.6-mile Sulphur Creek Trail for a quiet leg stretcher. There's minimal elevation gain and lots of gorgeous old growth, but don't bother looking for Sulphur Hot Springs—they're difficult to locate and not very hot. A soak in the cold creek, however, does wonders for aching muscles.

Skagit River Valley

Born in the northernmost reaches of the North Cascades in southern British Columbia and the third-largest watershed on the American West Coast, the Skagit River drains a diverse area of glaciated peaks, deeply forested ridges, and floodplains of productive farmland. The Skagit has long been an important transportation corridor and salmon-supporting river. A series of dams powering Seattle, however, were built in its gorge, forever robbing the upper reaches of spawning salmon and destroying one of the regions most dramatic set of rapids. Fortunately, though, large parts of the river are still free flowing and much of it below the Gorge Dam has been classified as a Wild and Scenic River, offering some protection from further development. One of the great "eagle rivers" of the West, the Skagit offers superb hiking from British Columbia to the delta at its mouth on Puget Sound.

46 Padilla Bay

RATING/ DIFFICULTY	ROUND-TRIP	ELEV GAIN/ HIGH POINT	SEASON
★★/1	4.8 miles	30 feet/ 30 feet	Year-round

Map: USGS La Conner; **Contact:** Skagit County Parks, (360) 336-9414. Skagit Parks Foundation,

www.skagitparksfoundation.org. Padilla Bay National Estuarine Research Reserve, (360) 428-1558, www.padillabay.gov; **Notes:** Dogs must be leashed; **GPS:** N 48 28.818, W 122 28.383

Hike on a snaking dike built by tenacious twentieth-century settlers and farmers through the Padilla Bay National Estuarine Research Reserve. Established in 1980 to protect extensive mudflats of eel grass, the 11,000-acre preserve is a bird-watcher's paradise. The trail twists and turns along sloughs, tidal flats, and salt marshes, allowing you to scope out herons, eagles, falcons, dunlins, brants, and scores of other winged residents. And in addition to the profuse birdlife, you'll be treated to unhindered views of surrounding mountains, islands, and farmland from this delightful and level path.

GETTING THERE

From Burlington (exit 230 on I-5), head west on State Route 20 for about 7 miles, turning right onto Bay View–Edison Road (the turnoff is approximately 1.75 miles west of the SR 20/SR 536 junction). Continue north on Bay View–Edison Road for 3 miles to the trailhead, on your left. Parking is located a little farther ahead. Turn right onto Second Street, and within 200 feet turn left into the Skagit County Historical Society's large parking area. Privy available.

ON THE TRAIL

Begin by walking back down Second Street and then Bay View–Edison Road for 0.15 mile to the Padilla Bay shore trailhead. Roads are lightly traveled, but keep children and dogs close by. The short drop in elevation from parking lot to trailhead is the only elevation change you'll experience on this hike. Relax and enjoy this perfectly level trail for the next 2.25 miles.

Developed in 1990 by a consortium of public agencies, the Padilla Bay Shore Trail allows the best pedestrian viewings of the estuarine reserve. Established for research, education, and stewardship, Padilla is one of only twenty-seven such reserves in the country. Padilla harbors some of the best remaining eelgrass flats north of Willapa Bay, but the area has been heavily influenced by agriculture and industry. Farmers have reclaimed thousands of acres of tideflats for cropland, and a large oil refinery sits across the bay at March Point.

But the area still remains ecologically viable and incredibly scenic, especially during low tide, when nearly the entire 8-by-3-mile bay is transformed into glistening mudflats and slithering sloughs. Hordes of herons harvesting succulent appetizers can often be observed. Be sure to cast your attention to the neighboring "drier" grounds for songbird and raptor sightings.

If bird-watching doesn't ruffle your feathers, the surrounding scenery should still tickle your fancy. Islands dot the bay, with Lummi and the San Juans guarding its northern waters. Across Padilla, the conifer-cloaked knolls of Sugarloaf and Mount Erie crown Fildalgo Island. Mount Baker rises above the countryside to the east, and to the south Mount Rainier hovers in the distance over the Skagit Flats.

In 1.8 miles you'll approach a lone cedar and a slough-side barn, a favorite among photographers casual and serious alike. The trail then turns away from the mudflats, following a snaking Indian Slough for a final 0.5 mile and terminating at its southern trailhead. From this alternative starting area (where parking is limited), begin your return, enjoying a new phase of the bay.

EXTENDING YOUR TRIP

Visit the reserve's Breazeale Interpretive Center about 1.5 miles north on the Bay View–Edison Road, where you'll also find a kid-friendly 0.8-mile nature trail through preserve uplands and an observation deck on the bay. Nearby Bay View State Park with its cozy campsites and cabins makes for a great excuse to stay overnight.

Familiar landmark on Padilla Bay Shore Trail

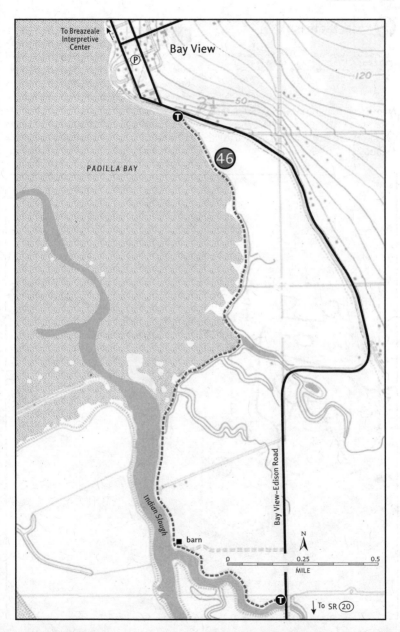

To Breazeale
Interpretive
Center

Ⓟ

Bay View

120

PADILLA BAY

Ⓣ

④⑥

Indian Slough

■ barn

Bay View–Edison Road

N

0   0.25   0.5
MILE

Ⓣ

↓ To SR ㉚

47 Rasar State Park

RATING/ DIFFICULTY	ROUND-TRIP	ELEV GAIN/ HIGH POINT	SEASON
★★★/1	Up to 3 miles	20 feet/ 125 feet	Year-round

Map: Green Trails Hamilton No. 45; **Contact:** Rasar State Park, (360) 826-3942, *www.parks .wa.gov*; **Notes:** Dogs must be leashed; **GPS:** N 48 30.881, W 121 54.245

Saunter along the mighty Skagit River under a verdant canopy supported by blotchy-barked alders and moss-wrapped maples. Observe eagles perched majestically on tall firs above the swirling turquoise river waters. Wander across fields set against a backdrop of valley-guarding peaks. Reflect upon a pioneer family that settled here in the Skagit Valley, and be grateful to their

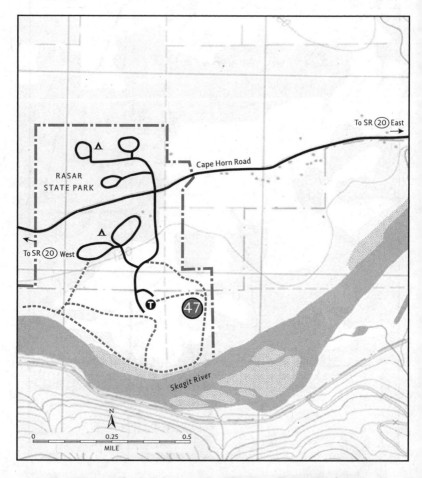

*enlightened heir who protected part of it
for all of us to enjoy today.*

GETTING THERE

From Burlington (exit 230 on I-5), head east
on the North Cascades Highway (State Route
20) for 21 miles. Just beyond milepost 80, turn
right onto Lusk Road. Continue 0.7 mile, turning left onto Cape Horn Road. Reach the Rasar
State Park entrance in 0.8 mile. Turn right and
proceed 0.25 mile to the day-use parking area
and trailhead. Water and restrooms available.

ON THE TRAIL

Donated to Washington State Parks by Dan
Rasar, grandson of Daniel and Sarah Peters
Rasar who migrated to Skagit County from
Tennessee in the 1880s, this top-notch park
celebrates both the pioneer spirit and natural
beauty of the Skagit Valley. Opened to the public in 1997, this 169-acre state park is rapidly
becoming one of the state's most popular.

Rasar State Park's natural beauty is comple-
mented with aesthetically appealing camping
and picnic grounds, complete with dwellings
constructed of fieldstone that echo the simple
beauty of earlier Civilian Conservation Corps
structures. The park sits on over 4000 feet of
shoreline along the Skagit River, allowing visitors to become better acquainted with the largest river emptying into Puget Sound.

A series of well-groomed trails, including a
paved wheelchair-accommodating one, depart
from the day-use parking lot. Walk them in any
fashion—straight to the river, big loop, small
loop, or figure-eight—for up to 3 miles worth
of carefree ambling. Walk through or around
a sprawling field still actively hayed by area
farmers. Enjoy views out to Sauk Mountain.

Stroll along the Skagit, occasionally breaking on sunny sandbars. Keep binoculars at
hand, ready to zoom in on eagles, osprey,
woodpeckers, geese, or a myriad of other
avian park residents. Lumber through thick

*Basking in the evening light on
the Skagit River*

forests of maple, alder, fir, and cedar. Spend
the night at the park campground and set out
on these trails for an owl watch or a moonlit
stroll across dew-catching grasses.

EXTENDING YOUR TRIP

Less than 2 miles away, at the junction of SR
20 and Baker Lake Road, is a trailhead for the
22.5-mile Cascade Trail. This unpaved rail trail
runs from Concrete to Sedro-Woolley through
farms, wetlands, and woodlots, offering no
shortage of outstanding Skagit Valley scenery.

48 Rockport State Park

RATING/ DIFFICULTY	LOOP	ELEV GAIN/ HIGH POINT	SEASON
★★/2	3 miles	250 feet/ 750 feet	Year-round

Maps: Green Trails Darrington No. 78, park map at trailhead kiosk; **Contact:** Rockport State Park, (360) 853-8461, www.parks.wa.gov; **Notes:** Dogs must be leashed; **GPS:** N 48 29.270, W 121 36.866

Take a leisurely stroll through an easily accessible low-country, old-growth forest. Big cedars, big firs, and if you visit in spring, big showy bouquets of flowering Pacific dogwood brightening the dark green groves.

Old-growth forest

GETTING THERE

From Burlington (exit 230 on I-5), head east on the North Cascades Highway (State Route 20) for 37 miles to Rockport State Park (7.5 miles east of Concrete and 1 mile west of the junction with SR 530). Turn left into the park, and then immediately turn right into the day-use parking area (elev. 500 ft). Water and restrooms available.

ON THE TRAIL

Rockport is one of my personal favorites in the Washington State Parks system, and I never tire of wandering its peaceful and well-manicured trails or camping beneath its towering timber. The Evergreen Trail makes a nice 3-mile loop around the 670-acre park. Before heading out, take a few minutes to read the interpretive displays about the park, the old-growth forests, and David Douglas (for whom the ubiquitous Douglas-fir is named).

The trail takes off east from behind the restrooms. In 0.1 mile intersect a service road, which can be used for more looping options. The trail winds through stately fir groves, under tunnels of vine maple draped in moss, along shoulder-high boughs of ferns, and over chattering creeks. Wrens, woodpeckers, and chickarees provide the background score.

The way dips and curves as it makes its way to the park's eastern boundary by an old logged area. Sauk Mountain can be seen rising above. The trail then turns west, and at 0.6 mile is the Broken Fir, which graced this forest as a healthy tree from 1660 to 1974. Gradually gaining elevation, you'll reach an intersection at 1 mile. Left heads to the service road, and right continues following alongside tumbling Fern Creek for 0.25 mile before crossing it in a cool ravine.

Now in quiet woods, enjoy the forest primeval. Gradually descending, at 1.75 miles once again reach the service road. The trail now follows alongside a delightful creek, crossing it several times. At 2.1 miles the Evergreen

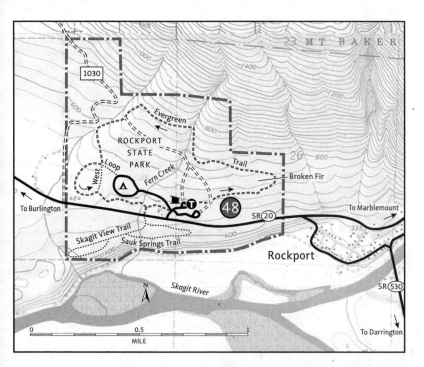

Trail merges with the wheelchair-accessible
West Loop Trail. Head right, traveling through
stately hemlocks, and after 0.4 mile veer right
and leave the West Loop. Continue for 0.5 mile,
skirting the campground and passing a junction
with the Skagit View Trail and a monster fir before returning to the day-use area to complete
your loop. Nice park, huh? Return often.

EXTENDING YOUR TRIP
Extend your hike by including the 0.7-mile
Skagit View Trail and 0.4-mile Sauk Springs
Trail. Consider spending the night at Rockport.
Aside from RV-friendly hookup campsites, the
park has a separate area of quiet walk-in sites
and Adirondack shelters. Note: As of early
2008, camping area is closed due to falling
tree danger; inquire about stats.

49 Sauk Mountain

RATING/ DIFFICULTY	ROUND-TRIP	ELEV GAIN/ HIGH POINT	SEASON
★★★★/3	4.2 miles	1190 feet/ 5537 feet	July– mid-Oct

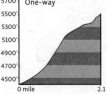

Map: Green Trails Lake Shannon No. 46;
Contact: Mount Baker–Snoqualmie National
Forest, Mount Baker Ranger District, (360) 856-
5700, www.fs.fed.us/r6/mbs; **GPS:** N 48 31.277,
W 121 36.429

Enjoy amazing views of the Sauk and Skagit river basins, and that's just from the trailhead parking lot! From the summit of this former fire lookout the views are beyond amazing. They're superlatively stupendous! And the wildflowers. Tread this way in mid-July for a floral show second to none. Short and sweet and just a tad bit steep, a score-plus set of switchbacks sets you on your way to this scenic summit.

GETTING THERE

From Burlington (exit 230 on I-5), head east on the North Cascades Highway (State Route 20) for 36.5 miles to the Rockport State Park boundary at milepost 96 (7 miles east of Concrete and 1.5 miles west of the junction with SR 530). Turn left onto Forest Road 1030 (signed "Sauk Mountain Road"). Follow this

steep, washboard-prone road for 7.5 miles to a fork. Bear right and continue 0.25 mile to the trailhead (elev. 4350 ft). Privy available.

ON THE TRAIL

A familiar landmark in the Skagit Valley, with its hogback summit and verdant meadow-draped western slopes, Sauk Mountain is recognizable from I-5. It's a popular hike, best avoided on sunny summer weekends.

Starting at the edge of a meadow, views begin immediately and never let up. Virtually the entire way is in the open—great if there's a refreshing breeze, stifling on hot afternoons. And because the first half of the hike is entirely within meadows, biting, buzzing, driving-you-crazy bugs are legion. Hey, somebody has to pollinate all those pretty blossoms.

Pass by an A-frame privy, one of my favor-

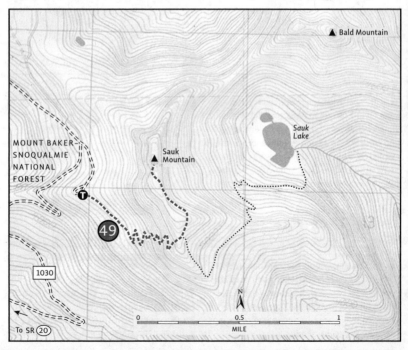

Sauk River from Sauk Mountain

ite outback outhouses in the Cascades. Enjoy a short stretch to warm up and then commence switching and backing up Sauk's steep west face. Harebell, lupine, daisy, parsley, thimbleberry, paintbrush, thistle, columbine, fireweed—how many different blossoms can you spot?

The way steadily gains elevation up the herbaceous hillside flush with scads of scurrying grasshoppers. Brushy at times, the trail sports hidden marmot holes and other potential ankle twisters. And be careful not to kick rocks below onto other Sauk summit seekers. You'll occasionally and briefly dip into cool forest groves, escaping the sun. Then it's back into the open.

After 1.3 miles of steady climbing, crest the hogback ridge (elev. 5200 ft). Pause and take in the amazing views south to the confluence of the Sauk and Skagit, the Finney Block, Glacier Peak, and Whitehorse. Look east to the Helen Buttes, the Pickets, Teebone Ridge, and the big green valley cut by the Cascade River.

Now skirting below crags, the trail turns north to head for the summit. At 1.5 miles, come to a junction. The trail right loses 1200 feet on its way to Sauk Lake. Stay left and soon you'll be able to see Sauk Lake twinkling below in an emerald bowl between Sauk and Bald mountains.

The final stretch traverses a somewhat rocky area where lingering snowfields may warrant some caution. Once on the 5537-foot summit, the same summit that beatnik poet Philip Whalen worked on in 1953, find a nook and grab your journal. Scan the horizons and let inspiration fly. Take in Mounts Baker, Blum, Shuksan, and Tomyhoi, the Pickets, the Olympics, even Mount Constitution on Orcas Island. Too many more to count, but plenty to enjoy.

EXTENDING YOUR TRIP

The trip to Sauk Lake is a worthy endeavor, but it's no easy pursuit. The 1.5-mile trail dropping from Sauk's ridge to the secluded lake loses more elevation than you climbed getting to the turnoff. This makes for a good people filter, though—expect to see few visitors sharing the shores with you.

50 Slide Lake

RATING/ DIFFICULTY	ROUND-TRIP	ELEV GAIN/ HIGH POINT	SEASON
★★★/1	2.5 miles	300 feet/ 3100 feet	June–Oct

3200' One-way

3000'

0 mile   1.25

Map: Green Trails Snowking Mountain No. 79; **Contact:** Mount Baker–Snoqualmie National Forest, Darrington Ranger District, (360) 436-1155, www.fs.fed.us/r6/mbs; **Notes:** FR 16 washed out at milepost 8.8 in 2009. Consult Forest Service on current road status; **GPS:** N 48 25.590, W 121 22.149

 *One of several big, gorgeous backcountry lakes in the northern hinterlands of the Glacier Peak Wilderness, Slide Lake is the only one accessed by maintained trail. It's a short and easy hike to the boulder- and old-growth-rimmed lake, and you may wonder whether it's worth the drive in on the long logging road. But, despite this hike's brevity, you can easily spend the day here— fishing, wading, berry picking, or just staring at Snowking Mountain from a sun-kissed shoreline boulder. Yep, it's worth it!*

GETTING THERE

From Burlington (exit 230 on I-5), travel 38 miles east on the North Cascades Highway (State Route 20) to the town of Rockport. Turn right (south) onto SR 530 and drive 2.5 miles, turning left onto Forest Road 16 (signed "Illabot Creek Road"). (From Darrington the turnoff is in 16 miles.) Follow this generally good gravel road for 20.5 miles to the trailhead, near Otter Creek Bridge (elev. 2800 ft). **Note:** At 6.2 miles on FR 16 is a confusing, unmarked junction—bear left.

ON THE TRAIL

Starting alongside babbling Otter Creek, the trail immediately enters one of the finest stands of old-growth forest to be found anywhere. The creek is soon lost—flowing secretly through a cavernous world of granite boulders carpeted in moss. Languidly continue up the rocky but gentle trail, admiring hundreds of years of arboreal artistry. In late summer treat your jowls to huckleberries galore.

In 1 mile enter the Glacier Peak Wilderness,

where a pair of ponds (somewhat) greets you. The trail now works it way over a jumble of boulders adorned in moss and old conifers. Hundreds of years ago they came crashing down from above, barricading Otter Creek and forming Slide Lake, hence its name. The beautiful lake lies just ahead. Go stake out a prime lakeside boulder; then take the snacks

Slide Lake and Snowking Mountain

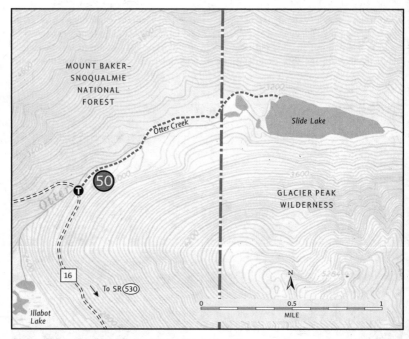

out and gaze across the sparkling waters to Snowking Mountain rising in the background. Feel free to snoop around the lake at any time. Take some garbage out with you left behind by unenlightened and inconsiderate visitors. This special area deserves better.

EXTENDING YOUR TRIP

Tenacious, experienced hikers may want to follow a trail of sorts that continues up the valley 2.5 miles and 1200 vertical feet to Enjar Lake. It's a brushy, buggy, difficult trip, but also wild, scenic, and rewarding.

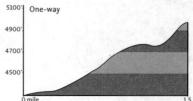

One-way

Map: Green Trails Oso No. 77; **Contact:** Mount Baker–Snoqualmie National Forest, Mount Baker Ranger District, (360) 856-5700, *www.fs.fed.us/r6/mbs;* **GPS:** N 48 25.014, W 121 49.149

51 Gee Point

RATING/ DIFFICULTY	ROUND-TRIP	ELEV GAIN/ HIGH POINT	SEASON
★★★/4	3 miles	700 feet/ 4974 feet	July–Oct

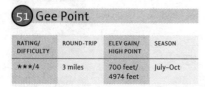

The first part is brushy and the last part is a bit of a scramble, but what a trail. Hike this remnant of what used to be an extensive network of trails traversing the elusive Finney Block of the Mount–Baker Snoqualmie National Forest.

From this old lookout site enjoy knockout views of the Skagit Valley—the Suiattle and Stillaguamish too. Stare out at Glacier, Baker, and the Olympics across a shimmering Puget Sound. Scan the little-known peaks of the Finney Block—Round, Finney, Little Deer—and pockets of old growth spared from the mill.

GETTING THERE

From Burlington (exit 230 on I-5), head east 28 miles on the North Cascades Highway (State Route 20) toward Concrete. Just after milepost 88 and just shy of the city limits, turn right onto the Concrete-Sauk Road. In 1 mile cross the Skagit River and bear left, proceeding another 8.8 miles. Turn right onto Forest Road 17 (Finney Creek Road). (From Darrington follow SR 530 north for 12 miles, turn left onto the Concrete-Sauk Road, and reach FR 17 in 7 miles.) Follow FR 17 10.5 miles (the first 6 miles are paved, the next 4.5 miles semipaved), and then turn right onto FR 1720. Follow this narrow and brushy-at-times road for 2.1 miles, bearing right onto FR 1722. Continue 5.4 miles to the road end at the edge of an old cut, where the trail starts on a decommissioned road (elev. 4300 ft).

ON THE TRAIL

Start by walking west on the decommissioned logging road. Willows and other herbaceous plants choke the way. But look carefully— tread exists. After a bushwhacking 0.25 mile, locate tread that heads right, steeply up the side of an old cut. A few cairns help keep you on track. Don't get discouraged—it gets better, much better. At about 0.4 mile, reach the ridge crest in beautiful old-growth forest and finally find good tread. The trail lives!

Now enjoy pleasant strolling through ancient fir and hemlock along a ridge loggers weren't allowed to access, thanks to the Timber Summit of 1993 and an economy now favoring old growth from Canada and Siberia instead. At 0.7 mile, rocky Gee Point can be viewed from an opening in the forest.

Soon afterward the trail breaks out onto a near perfectly level grassy lawn reminiscent of Mount Rainer's famed Grand Park, only in miniature. Drop slightly off the ridge into a marshy swale where a cabin once stood, and head left to avoid talus slopes. Climbing steeply, reattain the ridge crest. Then work your way up the summit block on blueberry-draped ledges. You'll need to use your hands in a few spots, which some hikers may be uncomfortable with even though the way is not overly difficult or exposed. For those that

Remnant tread and old growth on Gee Point

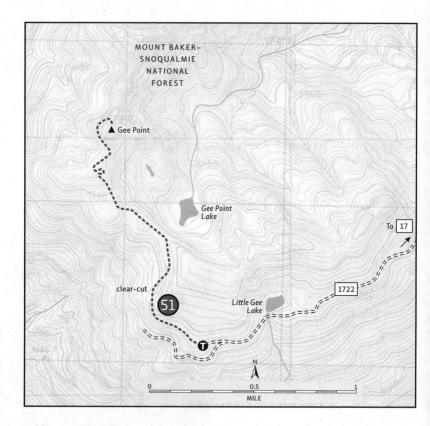

push on to the 4974-foot rocky knoll that once housed a fire lookout, spectacular panoramic viewing is your payoff.

Cupped in a hidden cirque directly below to the south is Gee Point Lake. Directly below to the north are the uncut old-growth forests of the Pressentin Creek valley. The Skagit Valley, Mount Baker, Sauk Mountain, Glacier Peak, and an entire eastern sky of rock and ice are yours to enjoy.

EXTENDING YOUR TRIP
Little Gee Lake is 0.3 mile east of the trailhead and is a good place to cast a lure after

your hike. Nearby Finney Mountain and Round Mountain also contain remnant trail that can still be hiked. However, expect difficulty locating their "trailheads." Use Green Trails map no. 78 (Darrington) to help find them. Once you do, decent tread can be followed. Both provide excellent views.

52 Cow Heaven

RATING/ DIFFICULTY	ROUND-TRIP	ELEV GAIN/ HIGH POINT	SEASON
★★★/4	10 miles	4000 feet/ 4400 feet	Late June– Oct

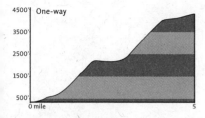

Map: Green Trails Marblemount No. 47;
Contact: Mount Baker–Snoqualmie National
Forest, Mount Baker Ranger District, (360)
856-5700, www.fs.fed.us/r6/mbs; **GPS:** N 48
32.498, W 121 26.873

*Here's the beef on Cow Heaven. It's a
steep and demanding climb through
thick forest culminating in lonely alpine*

meadows. The cows are long gone from this
*former summer grazing area high above the
Skagit Valley, but you can feast to your
heart's content on splendid views of snowy
North Cascades summits. A great conditioner
and good choice for solitude, if you're feeling
energetic, follow this steer-way to heaven all
the way to the rocky Helen Buttes for even
grander views.*

GETTING THERE
From Rockport follow the North Cascades
Highway (State Route 20) 8 miles east toward
Marblemount. Shortly before reaching town,
turn left onto Ranger Station Road (signed
"Ranger Station, one mile"). Proceed 0.7 mile
to the national park ranger station, and then
bear right onto Olson Creek Road, continuing

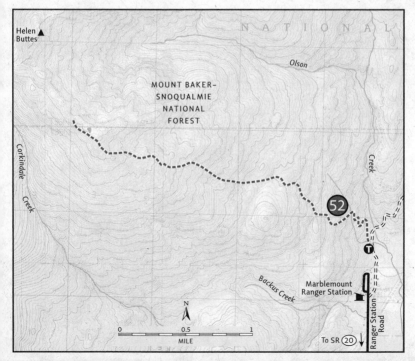

for another 0.3 mile to the trailhead, on your left (elev. 400 ft).

ON THE TRAIL

Trail No. 763 starts low, but aims high. From its valley-bottom beginning to its alpine destination, 4000 feet of elevation is gained—in less than 5 miles. These stats keep more than a handful of aerobically challenged hikers away. But despite this trail's lonely state, it's in fine shape. The tread is fairly smooth and the way is well defined.

Begin in cool cedar forest on new trail rerouted around private land. Soon after crossing a creek in a mossy grotto, the trail gets down to business. Following tight switchbacks, the way vigorously climbs up a near-vertical slope. The forest canopy is dense, mostly a uniform stand of second-growth conifers. A handful of vine maples punctuate it, lightening the dark understory during the autumn months.

After 1 mile recross the creek you hopped over earlier. Now in scrappy forest and alongside the cascading creek, continue climbing. Cross the creek yet again. The forest soon thins, offering glimpses to the jumbled array of peaks across the Skagit Valley.

Just after 2 miles the trail briefly drops to traverse a dank mossy hollow supporting a handful of mammoth cedars, and then the trail picks up the pace again. Lighter tread and a few gullied sections help keep your pace in check. After passing a series of boulders and overhanging ledges, the trail enters a grove of impressive old growth.

Eventually the forest thins, yellow cedars and subalpine firs indicating that much elevation has thus far been gained. After 4 miles and at about 4000 feet, finally break out of the canopy. Views begin to unravel across huckleberry-choked slopes that were scorched many decades ago by wildfire. Continue across the brushy terrain, coming to a small meadow with a small tarn.

For better panoramic viewing, find a faint path heading northwest up an open rib. Here in the heart of Cow Heaven, steak your viewing spot! The deep U-shaped Skagit Valley unfurls below you. Craggy Colonial Peak and the Teebone Ridge (seriously) tower above it. Jack is the big guy on the western horizon. The Newhalem powerhouse is the big structure below. Turn south to take in a sweeping view of the Cascade River valley. Snowking Mountain, the Illabot Peaks, Whitehorse Mountain, and the Finney Block area fill the southern horizon.

The Helen Buttes obstruct views northward and eastward. But if your scrambling and orientation skills are good, continue toward the buttes, where you can graze on more mouthwatering views. Contemplate, too, just how tenacious those cows must have been to hoof it all the way to this lonely and heavenly range.

53 Hozomeen Lake

RATING/ DIFFICULTY	ROUND-TRIP	ELEV GAIN/ HIGH POINT	SEASON
★★★/2	7.4 miles	1200 feet/ 2850 feet	May–Nov

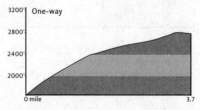

Map: Green Trails Ross Lake No. 16; **Contact:** North Cascades National Park Visitors Center (Newhalem), (206) 386-4495, ext. 11 (summer only), or Headquarters Information Station (Sedro-Woolley), (360) 856-5700, ext. 515, www .nps.gov/noca; **Notes:** Vehicle access to trailhead

Opposite: Berry heaven on Cow Heaven

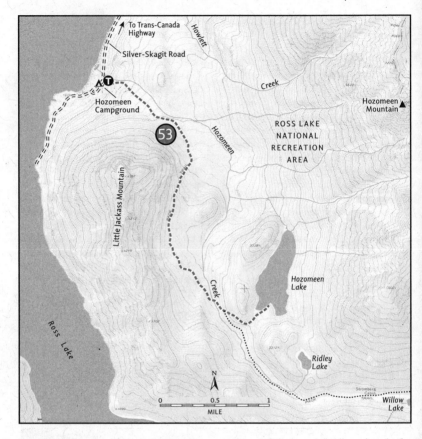

is via British Columbia. After June 1, 2009, passports are required for cross-border travel. Dogs must have proof of recent vaccination for rabies; **GPS: N 48 59.13, W 121 04.104**

Hozomeen is a placid body of water in the shadow of one of the fiercest-looking landmarks in the Cascades. Sit on a sunny shoreline rock staring at the twin sheer-vertical spires of Hozomeen Peak reflected in the lake's waters. Find soothing comfort in the soft breezes whistling through the surrounding old-growth forest, and let the *eerie cry of the loon enthrall you here in the northernmost reaches of the North Cascades, at the upper limit of the Skagit's watershed.*

GETTING THERE

From Sumas on the Canadian border, head north, going through customs and following BC 11 for 2 short miles to the Trans-Canada Highway (Highway 1). Follow the Trans-Canada east for 50 miles (80 km), exiting on the Silver-Skagit Road just before reaching the town of Hope. Follow this at times rough and slow-going road for 39 miles, reentering the United States and arriving at the Ross Lake National Recreation Area's Hozomeen Campground, where the trail begins (elev. 1650 ft). Water and privy available.

ON THE TRAIL

If it weren't such an expedition to get here, no doubt this hike would be one of the busiest in the North Cascades National Park Complex. The distance is perfect for most day trippers, the trail is well maintained, and the grade is easy. And the destination? A lovely large backcountry lake at the base of one of the Cascades' most dramatic mountains.

From the campground, the Hozomeen Lake Trail sets out eastward into open old-growth timber. Paralleling the trail for roughly 1 mile, the tumbling Hozomeen Creek provides a backdrop of mood music. The trail then climbs gently and skirts Little Jackass Mountain. Although not very high, the mountain's cliffs and steep rise make it a prominent landmark along Ross Lake. Now traversing a bench, enjoy easy wandering. At 3 miles cross Hozomeen Creek, and reach a junction shortly afterward.

The trail right continues 4.7 miles to Lightning Creek, passing Willow Lake at 2 miles—a worthy side trip. Hozomeen Lake is reached by heading left 0.7 mile. After cresting a small rise, the trail beelines for a small point protruding from the lake's southern shore. Soak your feet in the soothing waters and stare out at the dueling summits of Hozomeen Mountain. "Hozomeen, Hozomeen, most beautiful mountain I've ever seen," mused beatnik poet Jack Kerouac while observing the 8000-plus-foot mountain from nearby Desolation Peak. Meaning "twin peaks with a rocky depression between" in the dialect of Fraser River Native peoples, Hozomeen actually consists of three spiraling towers, better seen from Manning Provincial Park in British Columbia.

Complementing Hozomeen Lake's stunning backdrop are its resident loons. A common denizen in North America's northern woods, the common loon is uncommon in the North Cascades. For this guidebook writer raised in New Hampshire, home of Katharine Hepburn's Golden Pond, there's no sweeter sound in the wild than the loon's call.

EXTENDING YOUR TRIP

Since you drove this far, plan on spending a few nights in the wonderful 122-site Hozomeen Campground. There are some excellent hiking trails just a couple of miles north in British Columbia's adjacent Skagit Valley Provincial Park. Explore spectacular old-growth forest along a free-flowing section of the Skagit River, or climb high on the Skyline Trail for stunning views of Hozomeen Mountain and surrounding summits.

A hiker listens for loons on Hozomeen Lake.

LET FREEDOM FLY

After Alaska, the best place in America for observing our majestic national symbol is here in the Pacific Northwest. And there's no place better for bald-eagle watching than along the Skagit River during the winter months. One of the largest winter gathering spots for eagles in the Lower 48, the Skagit is lined each January with hundreds of the royal birds perched high in cedar snags and defoliated cottonwoods. Lured to the river by its spawning chum runs, the eagles dine on the salmon carcasses until the last of the carrion has been picked clean.

All along the Skagit River are great places to see these beautiful birds. Rasar and Rockport state parks (Hikes 47 and 48) are good starts. Pressentin County Park in Marblemount is a choice place too, and its Birding Trail makes a pleasant leg stretcher. The Washington Nature Conservancy manages nearly 8000 acres of land along the Skagit between Rockport and Marblemount as a bald-eagle natural area. Pullouts and information kiosks can be found along State Route 20 abutting the preserve. And in late January the little city of Concrete holds its annual Upper Skagit Bald Eagle Festival.

Baker Lake and River

A major tributary of the Skagit, a good portion of the Baker River is now a lake because of damming for hydroelectric power. The river valley is popular for camping and boating, and many fine hiking trails roam the area too. Some lead into the high country of Mount Baker's southern slopes. Others hug Boulder and Rainbow ridges and are crude paths, favored primarily by climbers. Still other trails, like those at Schriebers Meadow, are well groomed and well hiked. And the gentle rambles along Baker River and Baker Lake can often be hiked year-round.

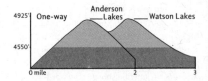

Map: Green Trails Lake Shannon No. 46; **Contact:** Mount Baker–Snoqualmie National Forest, Mount Baker Ranger District, (360) 856-5700, www.fs.fed.us/r6/mbs; **Notes:** NW Forest Pass required; **GPS:** N 48 40.480, W 121 36.100

54 Anderson and Watson Lakes

Anderson Lakes

RATING/ DIFFICULTY	ROUND-TRIP	ELEV GAIN/ HIGH POINT	SEASON
★★★★/3	4 miles	1100 feet/ 4900 feet	Mid-July– Oct

Watson Lakes

RATING/ DIFFICULTY	ROUND-TRIP	ELEV GAIN/ HIGH POINT	SEASON
★★★★/3	6 miles	1400 feet/ 4900 feet	Mid-July– Oct

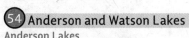

Beautiful backcountry lakes, bountiful berry patches, glimpses of glaciers, and the option of hoofing to an old lookout site overlooking Baker and peaks and valleys north and south—no wonder this area is darn popular. The trails are short and wonderful for introducing young'uns to the great outdoors, but there's a fair amount of elevation to be gained to and fro, so be sure to bring the kid harness or at least extra chocolate bars.

GETTING THERE

From Burlington (exit 230 on I-5), head east on the North Cascades Highway (State Route 20) for 23 miles, turning left (north) onto Baker Lake Road (between mileposts 82 and 83). Continue for 13.8 miles and turn right onto Forest Road 1106 (Baker Lake Dam Road). Proceed 2 miles (crossing dam), and then turn left onto FR 1107. Continue 9 miles and bear left onto FR Spur 022. In 1.1 miles find the trailhead at the road end (elev. 4300 ft).

ON THE TRAIL

When I first hiked this trail back in 1991 it looked like they were going to log right to the lakes. A beautiful mile of trail through old growth was permanently removed from the inventory. The Noisy-Diobsud Wilderness, which the Watson Lakes lie in, but not the Andersons, must be expanded to protect this trail and surrounding forests from further fragmentation.

Begin hiking in handsome hemlocks hedged with heather. In a quick 0.9 mile come to a junction (elev. 4800 ft). The trail left climbs to the shoulder of Anderson Butte. Continuing on the main trail, be sure to occasionally look back as you gently ascend through marshy meadows—Mount Baker hovers in the distance.

After rounding a 4900-foot rise, the trail reenters forest and drops, coming to another junction at 1.5 miles (elev. 4700 ft). The trail right drops 300 feet in a rough 0.5 mile, arriving at the lower of the three Anderson Lakes (elev. 4400 ft). Cradled in a semi-open basin beneath glacial-capped Mount Watson, it's a pretty scene. But, if you have to choose between Anderson and the Watson lakes, go for the latter.

The trail for the Watsons climbs 200 feet to a small notch, enters wilderness, and then drops 500 feet to arrive at the western lake

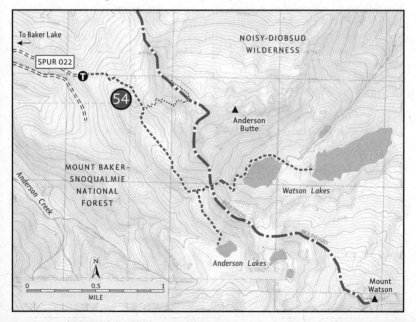

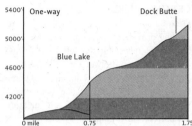

Glacier-covered Bacon Peak rises behind the Watson Lakes.

(elev. 4400 ft). Follow a boot-beaten path to the larger and more open eastern lake. Glacier-clad Bacon Peak rising behind the two lakes hogs the show. For all three lakes, the bugs can be bad, and the berries can be good!

EXTENDING YOUR TRIP

The trail to the shoulder of Anderson Butte rockets up 600 feet in 0.5 mile to an old lookout site. Take it only if you desire stunning views of Mount Baker, the Baker River valley, and a skyline pierced with rocky and icy peaks.

55 Blue Lake and Dock Butte

Blue Lake

RATING/ DIFFICULTY	ROUND-TRIP	ELEV GAIN/ HIGH POINT	SEASON
★★/1	1.5 miles	200 feet/ 4000 feet	Mid-June–Oct

Dock Butte

RATING/ DIFFICULTY	ROUND-TRIP	ELEV GAIN/ HIGH POINT	SEASON
★★★★/3	3.5 miles	1300 feet/ 5210 feet	July–mid-Oct

Map: Green Trails Hamilton No. 45; **Contact:** Mount Baker–Snoqualmie National Forest, Mount Baker Ranger District, (360) 856-5700, *www.fs.fed.us/r6/mbs*; **GPS:** N 48 39.240, W 121 47.077

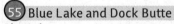 *Two short hikes that can be served together or enjoyed à la carte. The azure waters of Blue Lake sitting pretty in a talus- and meadow-ringed cirque will wash your blues away. Or see what's up, Dock. From this former lookout site, bask in the beauty of Mount Baker. One of the best viewing points from the south of the colossal volcano, Dock Butte packs the same meadow magic and alpine splendor as Park Butte (Hike 56), but with a fraction of the crowds.*

GETTING THERE

From Burlington (exit 230 on I-5), head east on the North Cascades Highway (State Route 20) for 23 miles, turning left (north) onto Baker Lake Road (between mileposts 82 and 83). Continue 12 miles and turn left on Forest Road 12 (the turnoff is 0.2 mile after you enter the Mount Baker–Snoqualmie National Forest). Drive 7 miles and turn left onto FR 1230, following it for 3.8 miles to its terminus and the trailhead (elev. 3900 ft).

ON THE TRAIL

Both hikes begin from the same trailhead at the edge of an old clear-cut. You soon come to majestic old growth spared from the frenzied timber felling of the late twentieth century. In 0.25 mile reach a junction.

For Blue Lake, veer left on a nearly level wide and well-constructed path passing by muddy seeps in an ancient forest of hemlock. After 0.5 mile drop about 50 feet to the pretty little lake. A small peninsula near its outlet is an especially inviting area for feet soaking, fish catching, and afternoon napping. The lake has seen its share of visitors over the years. Be kind to this fragile environment by not tramping through the heather meadows and cutting new paths.

For Dock Butte, head to the right at the junction on a less-traveled path. Climbing steadily and at times steeply, the trail emerges on a ridge high above Blue Lake. Views of Mount Baker grow from fleeting glimpses to knock your wool socks off, becoming outrageously beautiful, full-blown, and in your face. Continue up the ridge through heather and blueberry

patches, around knolls and tarns, and across wide-open meadows with wide-open views.

At about 1.4 miles reach a junction of sorts. The less-obvious trail leading right is the original tread. It attacks the summit knoll of Dock Butte by way of a long switchback across an open steep side slope. Quite scenic. But a lingering snowfield makes this route dangerous until mid-August.

Continue instead on the boot-beaten path heading straight up the ridge. Some difficult footing and a narrow ledge make this a less than ideal route for young children.

The two paths come together just below the 5210-foot summit, where often scores of swallows sail above on warm thermals. And the views. Wow! If you can take your eyes off of the blinding snow mass known as Baker, rotate your viewfinder clockwise to take in Shuksan, Blum, Watson, Sauk, Glacier, Whitehorse, Twin

Mount Baker from Dock Butte

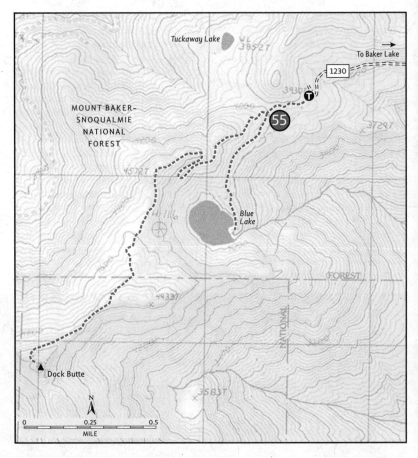

Sisters, and nearby Loomis Mountain. There's Park Butte, too, with its happy hordes. But not as happy as you, for chances are there's not much crowding on this butte.

56 Park Butte

RATING/ DIFFICULTY	ROUND-TRIP	ELEV GAIN/ HIGH POINT	SEASON
★★★★★/3	7.5 miles	2200 feet/ 5450 feet	July–Oct

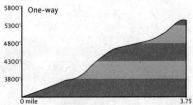

Map: Green Trails Hamilton No. 45; **Contact:** Mount Baker–Snoqualmie National Forest, Mount Baker Ranger District, (360) 856-5700, www.*fs.fed.us/r6/mbs*; **Notes:** NW Forest Pass required; **GPS:** N 48 42.404, W 121 48.734

One of the most spectacular settings in the entire North Cascades, Park Butte provides unsurpassed views of the snowy volcano Baker as well as inviting and outstanding high country that begs to be explored. The historical fire lookout, one of the few remaining in these parts, teeters on the edge of a craggy knoll offering Imax-like showings of Washington's third-highest summit. Come here in summer and play in fields of snow. Come in autumn and roam through fields scorched in crimson. But try to come on a weekday, for the crowds are legion at Park Butte, one of the top hiking destinations in the Northwest.

GETTING THERE

From Burlington (exit 230 on I-5), head east on the North Cascades Highway (State Route 20) for 23 miles, turning left (north) onto Baker Lake Road (between mileposts 82 and 83). Continue 12 miles and turn left on Forest Road 12 (the turnoff is 0.2 mile after you enter the Mount Baker–Snoqualmie National Forest). Drive 3.5 miles, turn right onto FR 13 (signed "Mt Baker National Recreation Area"), and follow it for 5.2 miles to its terminus at the large trailhead parking area (elev. 3300 ft). Primitive camping and privy available.

ON THE TRAIL

The trail immediately enters the 8000-acre Mount Baker National Recreation Area (NRA). Created through the 1984 Washington Wilderness Act, the NRA allows for snowmobile use in this otherwise nonmotorized protected area. Cross-country skiers and snowshoers would do better visiting a quieter corner of Mount Baker during winter months.

In 500 feet, come to a junction with the Scott Paul Trail (Hike 57), an alternative return route for strong hikers. Butte-bound hikers proceed left, crossing Sulphur Creek on a sturdy

Tarn on Park Butte reflects Mount Baker.

bridge. Enjoy easy walking for the first mile or so through pool-pocked Schriebers Meadow. In early summer, masses of mosquitoes prevent any dawdling.

Continue across flats of heather and hemlock, coming to Rocky Creek and its large outwashes. Fed by the Easton Glacier, this temperamental stream frequently changes course. Consequently, trail maintainers must constantly reconfigure crossings as bridges are often rendered useless.

Once across the silty waterway the trail enters stately old timber and begins swiftly climbing, reaching the upper junction of the Scott Paul Trail at 2 miles (elev. 4500 ft). Now through a thinning forest of yellow cedar and mountain hemlock, the trail gently climbs, breaking out into hopping-with-heather and bursting-with-blueberries Moritz Meadow.

At 2.4 miles the Railroad Grade Trail, a worthy side trip along the lateral moraine of the Easton Glacier, takes off right, reaching High Camp (elev. 5500 ft) in 1 mile. Park Butte lies left and soon comes into view. So too does giant snow cone Mount Baker, dwarfing its surroundings.

Frolic across alpine lawns and beside snowmelt ponds that reflect puffy white clouds and Baker's frozen face before making a steep little climb to yet another junction (elev. 4800 ft). Right heads down to Mazama Park, popular with equestrians and crowd-shunning hikers. Take the trail left for 1 mile of glorious ridge roaming through open parklands above shimmering tarns. Shortly after entering the Mount Baker Wilderness Area, reach Park Butte with its restored 1933 fire lookout.

By now Baker has dominated most of your

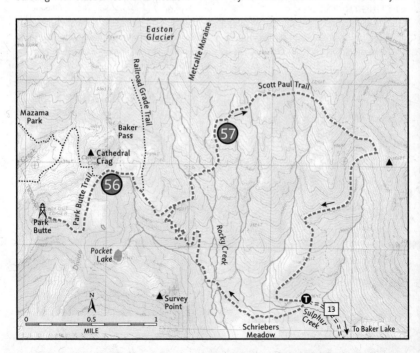

attention. Views west to the Twin Sisters, down the Nooksack Valley, and all the way out to Boundary Bay are equally impressive. Linger awhile reading lookout journals, soaking sunrays from the lookout's wraparound deck, or just looking out to some of the most spectacular alpine scenery on the planet.

EXTENDING YOUR TRIP
The high country surrounding Park Butte invites further exploration, but go easy on the land. The area's meadows have been badly trampled. Respect closed-off areas and restrict off-trail travel to snow and hard surfaces. The 1-mile Railroad Grade Trail offers stunning up-close views of the Easton Glacier. Consider quiet alternative routes to Park Butte for future visits: From the west side, follow the Ridley Creek Trail for a 6.5-mile journey to the lookout. The 5-mile Bell Pass Trail to Mazama Park traverses a lonely ridge through beautiful old-growth forest. Access this trail by following the Elbow Lake Trail either 3.5 miles from the east, off of FR 12, or 4.4 miles from its western trailhead off of FR 38.

57 Scott Paul Trail

RATING/ DIFFICULTY	LOOP	ELEV GAIN/ HIGH POINT	SEASON
★★★★/3	8 miles	2000 feet/ 5200 feet	Mid-July– Oct

Map: Green Trails Hamilton No. 45; **Contact:** Mount Baker–Snoqualmie National Forest, Mount Baker Ranger District, (360) 856-5700, www.fs.fed.us/r6/mbs; **Notes:** NW Forest Pass required; **GPS:** N 48 42.404, W 121 48.734

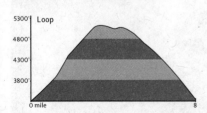 *An excellent loop that doesn't really go anywhere, unless you count miles of brilliant alpine meadows and rugged glacial moraine slopes as worthy destinations. Enjoy a scenic journey at the base of Mount Baker, complete with breathtaking close-ups of the hulking volcano as well as sweeping views of the surrounding sea of North Cascades peaks.*

GETTING THERE
From Burlington (exit 230 on I-5), head east on the North Cascades Highway (State Route 20) for 23 miles, turning left (north) onto Baker Lake Road (between mileposts 82 and 83). Continue 12 miles and turn left on Forest Road 12 (the turnoff is 0.2 mile after you enter the Mount Baker–Snoqualmie National Forest). Drive 3.5 miles, turn right onto FR 13 (signed "Mt Baker National Recreation Area"), and follow it for 5.2 miles to its terminus at the large trailhead parking area (elev. 3300 ft). Primitive camping and privy available.

ON THE TRAIL
Start your hike on the Park Butte Trail (Hike 56), entering the 8000-acre Mount Baker National Recreation Area (a sort of wilderness-light). Soon come to a junction with Scott Paul Trail No. 603.1. Combined with the first 2 miles of the Park Butte Trail, one of the finest day-hiking loops in the North Cascades can be made. For maximum viewing pleasure and minimum descent discomfort, it's best to loop clockwise.

So, follow the Park Butte Trail left through Schriebers Meadow, across the gravelly outwash of Rocky Creek, and then up a forested ridge to the upper junction with the Scott Paul Trail (elev. 4500 ft). The trail is named in honor of a national forest trails and wilderness coordinator who died in an accident in 1993; it was Paul who conceived of and helped build this trail.

Heading northeast, the trail skirts the

Glacial melt creek

Railroad Grade, glacial moraine deposited by the receding Easton Glacier. The impressive fluted heap of tilled rock and soil looks like a train trestle marching up the mountain. Chugging under the Railroad Grade the trail makes a slight descent to Rocky Creek where a suspension bridge from July through September safely transports you across (crossing can be dangerous without the bridge—check with the Forest Service to make sure it's in place).

Now begin climbing. On the way up Metcalfe Moraine, on a slow and sometimes rocky route, the snout of Easton Glacier and Baker's Black Buttes come into view. Gray gives way to green as moraine yields to meadow. Views! Baker breathes down upon you. Look back at the Railroad Grade, Park Butte, and the Twin Sisters.

Reaching a high point of 5200 feet, the trail contours the glacier-clad volcano. For the next 2 miles, undulate between moraine and meadow, rock gardens and parklands. Hovering at an elevation of around 5000 feet, it's pure alpine splendor. Gaze out to Sloan, Glacier, Pugh, Whitehorse, and Three Fingers—all distinguishable peaks on the southern horizon. You'll encounter several creeks along the way—easy rock hops or tricky boot soakers, depending on recent rainfall and snowmelt.

Eventually begin losing elevation to arrive at a meadowed saddle (elev. 4600 ft) offering outstanding views of Baker's "pointy peak," Sherman and Mount Shuksan looming in the distance. Now on excellent tread, commence an easy on the knees descent through huckleberry patches and giant hemlock groves to close the loop and arrive at the trailhead in 2.5 miles.

58 Baker Lake

RATING/ DIFFICULTY	ROUND-TRIP	ELEV GAIN/ HIGH POINT	SEASON
**/2	9 miles	500 feet/ 1000 feet	Year-round

Maps: Green Trails Mount Shuksan No. 14, Lake Shannon No. 46; **Contact:** Mount Baker–Snoqualmie National Forest, Mount Baker Ranger District, (360) 856-5700, www.fs.fed.us/r6/mbs; **Notes:** NW Forest Pass required; **GPS:** N 48 45.039, W 121 33.361

Man-made Baker Lake, with its stump flats, isn't anything spectacular. But that's not the real draw of this trail. The free-flowing Baker River, cascading tributaries, groves of old-growth giants, views of Mounts Baker and Shuksan, and a cool little suspension bridge—those are what will bring you here. And one more thing: this trail can be hiked in any season by just about anyone.

GETTING THERE
From Burlington (exit 230 on I-5), head east on the North Cascades Highway (State Route 20) for 23 miles, turning left (north) onto Baker Lake Road (between mileposts 82 and 83). Continue on Baker Lake Road for 26 miles (it becomes Forest Road 11, and the pavement ends after 23 miles), reaching the road end and trailhead (elev. 750 ft). Privy available.

ON THE TRAIL
Judging from the size of the parking lot, your hunch that this trail is a popular one is correct. Try it on a rainy weekday or during the winter months for more peaceful plodding. Sharing its start with the Baker River Trail No. 606 (Hike 59), the way heads up a wide and smooth path, brushing alongside the Baker River for an easy 0.5 mile. Here, the two trails diverge. The Baker River Trail continues straight ahead. Your hike hangs a right, crossing the pristine waterway on a neat suspension bridge built in the late 1990s.

No doubt children will want to linger here,

Sturdy suspension bridge spans Baker River.

crossing and recrossing the suspended span several times. Once the novelty wears off, continue down the trail. Immediately cross another bridge, this one stationary, over Blum Creek's rocky bed. Shortly after crossing the river, traverse a huge washout, another reminder of the incredible carnage that was inflicted on our trails in the November 2006 deluge.

In another 0.5 mile the trail comes right up to the river. In the floods of 2006 the river took away with it 1000 feet of perfectly good tread. At about 1.25 miles come to a ledge overlooking the sweeping gravel banks of the river Baker. Peaking in the distance, the mountain Baker can finally be seen. But still no Baker the lake. The trail now turns away from the watercourse, making a short and steep climb of about 200 feet to a high bridge crossing Hidden Creek. Pause to admire the fully revealed creek careening down a rocky cleft.

With slight ups and downs, the trail continues. Passing through old burns (set by a volcanic eruption in the 1840s) and impressive old growth and crossing several creeks, the way finally comes within sight of Baker Lake. But the lake is mostly obscured by thick timber. That's okay—the forest is much prettier. Created in 1959 by the Upper Baker River Dam, the lake is the byproduct of flood control and flicking on the lights. It provides recreation for boaters and paddlers too, but its cost was great for salmon, riparian forest, and the greater North Cascades ecosystem.

At 4.5 miles come to a junction. The spur right leads a short way to Noisy Creek Campground on a small peninsula on the lake. This is a good spot for turning around, but not before first enjoying lunch, a snooze, views of Mount Baker, and perhaps a little shoreline exploration.

EXTENDING YOUR TRIP

If intent on continuing your hike, consider the somewhat primitive path traveling left from the junction. This trail climbs 700 feet along Noisy Creek to a spectacular stand of old growth that was saved from the chopping block in 1991, including one of the largest Doug-firs in the state. If transportation can be arranged, you can also continue on the Baker Lake Trail for another 10 miles to its southern terminus on FR 1107 near the dam. Or start out from the southern trailhead and head 2 miles to Anderson Point or 4.5 miles to Maple Grove. Extend your stay in the area by pitching a tent in one of the pleasant car campgrounds on the lake, and take the time to walk the 0.5-mile Shadow of the Sentinels Nature Trail off of FR 11 during your visit.

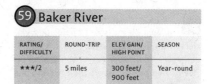

59 Baker River

RATING/ DIFFICULTY	ROUND-TRIP	ELEV GAIN/ HIGH POINT	SEASON
★★★/2	5 miles	300 feet/ 900 feet	Year-round

Map: Green Trails Mount Shuksan No. 14; **Contact:** Mount Baker–Snoqualmie National Forest, Mount Baker Ranger District, (360) 856-5700, *www.fs.fed.us/r6/mbs*; **Notes:** NW Forest Pass required. Dogs prohibited at park boundary, last 0.5 mile of trail; **GPS:** N 48 45.039, W 121 33.361

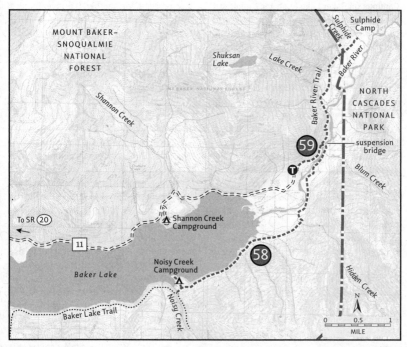

Saunter along a pristine waterway birthed by massive icefields and glaciers in the heart of the North Cascades wilderness. Explore wide gravel banks ideal for siestas and peering up at the towering and rugged summits surrounding you. Marvel at massive cedars and their adaptive growing techniques, from hugging boulders to sprouting in riparian zones. With its mere probe into the mostly roadless North Cascades National Park, this trail will make you feel like you're miles away from civilization.

GETTING THERE
From Burlington (exit 230 on I-5), head east on the North Cascades Highway (State Route 20) for 23 miles, turning left (north) onto Baker Lake Road (between mileposts 82 and 83). Continue on Baker Lake Road for 26 miles (it becomes Forest Road 11, and the pavement ends after 23 miles), reaching the road end and trailhead (elev. 750 ft). Privy available.

ON THE TRAIL
Sharing the first 0.5 mile with the Baker Lake Trail No. 610, enjoy an easy amble through cedar groves, mossy rock gardens, and alongside the pristine river—a preview of what lies ahead. The two trails diverge at an aesthetically appealing suspension bridge. Honor poet Robert Frost and take the path least traveled, continuing straight up the river valley.

Baker River Trail No. 606 makes a quick maneuver through a boulder strait before emerging onto a alder flat. Enjoy views across the river up to the crags and snowfields of Hagan Mountain. Savor sweeping views of the river, with its wide graveled banks and snaking, ever-changing channel. It's very Alaska-esque.

Leaving the flats, the trail climbs a bit to round a slope. Stare down into turquoise pools and captivating currents. Take note of the enveloping forest too. Monstrous cedars humble your presence. At 1.2 miles cross Lake Creek and its series of converging creeklets. Expect to get your feet wet negotiating the wily waterways. The deluge of 2006 left a sturdy footlog half submerged in silt and gravel.

A short distance farther, the trail returns to the river on a high open bluff—quite beautiful. Continuing upvalley, the trail crosses more outwashes—compliments of the flood of '06—before brushing up against a beaver pond (doubling as a springtime symphony hall for crooning frogs). Shortly after passing the base of a cliff (doubling as a springtime cataract tract), the trail reaches the North Cascades National Park boundary. Four-legged hikers must stop here. Two-legged hikers may proceed for another 0.5 mile through quiet forest, reaching hike's end at Baker River tributary, Sulphide Creek (elev. 900 ft). If water level permits, make your way out onto the creek's rocky bed for an awesome look at Mount Shuksan breathing down upon you. Pretty impressive, huh?

EXTENDING YOUR TRIP
If Sulphide Creek can be safely forded, it's possible to continue up the Baker River valley for another 2 miles of primitive path to Crystal Creek. Expect plenty of solitude, perhaps a tenacious climber. For more wild river-valley hiking, consider the nearby Swift Creek Trail No. 607 off of FR 1130. The first 0.5 mile to Rainbow Creek makes good walking for all ages through majestic old growth. Beyond the raging waterway, which must be forded and is potentially dangerous, it's strictly a hike for minimalists. The path, difficult to follow at times, makes another tough creek crossing and continues for 8 miles to the Lake Ann Trail and SR 542 at Austin Pass.

Opposite: Sulphide Creek

KLAHOWYA TILLICUM

Many place names in the North Cascades, like in much of the Pacific Northwest, come from the Chinook jargon. Not an actual language, Chinook is a collection of several hundred words drawn from various Native American tribal languages as well as from English and French. It was used as a trade language among Native peoples, Europeans, and American settlers in the Pacific Northwest throughout the nineteenth century. A unique part of our Northwest cultural heritage, Chinook names are sprinkled throughout the landscape. Below are some Chinook words you may encounter in the North Cascades.

chuck	water, river, stream
cultus	bad or worthless
elip	first, in front of
hyas	big, powerful, mighty
ipsoot	hidden
kimtah	behind, after
klahowya	hello, greetings, how are you?
klip	deep, sunken
lemolo	wild, crazy
memaloose	dead
mesachie	bad, evil, dangerous
moolock	elk
muckamuck	food
ollalie	berries
pil	red, therefore Pilchuck means "red stream"
saghalie	above, high, on top, sacred
sitkum	half of something, part of something
skookum	big, strong, mighty
tenas	small, weak, children
tillicum	friend, people
tupso	pasture, grass
tyee	chief, leader

Opposite: Mount Shuksan viewed from Goat Mountain

mount baker highway

With its easy access to the magnificent high country surrounding 10,778-foot Mount Baker, Washington's third-highest summit, it's no wonder that many Northwest hikers list trails in this region among their favorites. Connecting Bellingham to the base of the snowy volcano, this National Scenic Byway cuts through ancient forests, hugs the banks of the glacier-fed North Fork Nooksack River, and meanders through high alpine meadows. Trails range from easy wheelchair-accessible jaunts to family-friendly strolls to all-out, all-day, get-out-your-ice-ax adventures. From the Mount Baker Highway, hike across resplendent meadows, along raging rivers, to sparkling lakes, above glistening glaciers, and to lofty summits that open out to jaw-slacking horizons.

60 Horseshoe Bend

RATING/ DIFFICULTY	ROUND-TRIP	ELEV GAIN/ HIGH POINT	SEASON
★★/1	2.4 miles	250 feet/ 1200 feet	Year-round

One-way
1300'
1050'
0 mile   1.2

Map: Green Trails Mount Baker No. 13; **Contact:** Mount Baker–Snoqualmie National Forest, Glacier Public Service Center, (360) 599-2714 (summer only), or Mount Baker Ranger District, (360) 856-5700, www.fs.fed.us/r6/mbs; **GPS:** N 48 54.135, W 121 54.705

Hike a gentle trail along a raging river. Perfect for evening and early morning strolls. Perfect for introducing children to the wonders of nature. Perfect for stretching your legs out on the way to Heather Meadows. Perfect for watching diving dippers and daring river kayakers. And perfect for staring into tumultuous rapids. But a terrible place for carrying on a conversation— the river's roar is deafening, its allure oh-so intoxicating.

GETTING THERE
From Bellingham follow the Mount Baker Highway (State Route 542) east for 34 miles to the Glacier Public Service Center. Continue east for another 1.8 miles to the trailhead (elev. 980 ft), on your right directly across from the entrance to the Douglas-Fir Campground and just after crossing the North Fork Nooksack River.

ON THE TRAIL
Despite being easy to walk, near a popular campground, and offering access to a spectacular wild river, Horseshoe Bend surprisingly is not a terribly busy trail. Don't be stunned to find a handful of vehicles at the trailhead, however; the trail may be deserted, but the river may not be. This is a popular launch and take-out for river runners. And don't expect peace and quiet either. As the river plunges over boulders and ledges and squeezes through chasms it lets out thunderous roars.

Head upstream, first on a wide and well-groomed path, then up a nice stairway to more standard tread. Cross a big rocky draw that may or may not be harboring water. Then drop down to a bench perched on a riverfront ledge granting fine viewing of big boulders being bashed by a furious river. Continue upstream, meandering around big firs, big cedars, and big boulders, to big views of big rapids. Look for dippers, robin-sized birds who dig the rapids, looking for morsels in the milky glacial waters.

After about 1 mile the trail briefly climbs, coming to an old road beneath a powerline. This is far enough for most visitors. But if you want go to the actual Horseshoe Bend, continue on rougher tread another 0.2 mile to a point high

Opposite: The North Fork Nooksack River is mesmerizing.

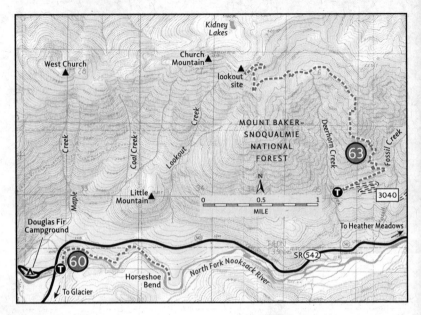

above the raucous river. Turn around and enjoy the river show one more time.

61 Canyon Ridge

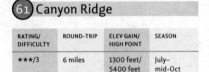

RATING/ DIFFICULTY	ROUND-TRIP	ELEV GAIN/ HIGH POINT	SEASON
★★★/3	6 miles	1300 feet/ 5400 feet	July– mid-Oct

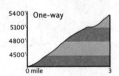

Map: Green Trails Mount Baker No. 13; **Contact:** Mount Baker–Snoqualmie National Forest, Glacier Public Service Center, (360) 599-2714 (summer only), or Mount Baker Ranger District, (360) 856-5700 (winter), *www.fs.fed.us/r6/mbs*; **Notes:** NW Forest Pass required; **GPS:** N 48 57.546, W 121 48.421

⊗ 👪 ✎ ⚙ *Wander on a high and lonely ridge just south of the 49th parallel. Stare out at a seemingly infinite array of imposing peaks—snow-capped and stone-faced, both here in America and over there in Canada. Meander through meadows that in summer burst in a kaleido-scope of colors, then two months later brush the ridge in streaks of crimson and gold. The route starts high, so sweat loss is minimal.*

GETTING THERE

From Bellingham follow the Mount Baker Highway (State Route 542) east for 34 miles to the Glacier Public Service Center. Continue east for another 2 miles, turning left onto Forest Road 31 (Canyon Creek Road) just after passing the entrance to the Douglas-Fir Campground. Follow FR 31 for 15.1 miles to the trailhead (elev. 4250 ft)—the pavement ends at 7.8 miles, bear left at 9.9 miles, and bear left again at 14.5 miles. Privy available.

ON THE TRAIL

Don't let the packed parking lot put a damper on your plans. You can bet your Northwest Forest Pass that nearly all of those vehicles belong to hikers heading for Damfino Lakes and Excelsior Pass (Hike 62). Beginning on the same trail as those popular destinations, hike an easy 0.7 mile through fine hemlock and fir forest to a signed junction (elev. 4600 ft).

Head left on less-trodden tread—that I can't understand why the Forest Service allows motorcycles on! In 0.4 mile come to a junction with the Boundary Way Trail (elev. 4800 ft), an excellent side trip. Continue left, sidehilling

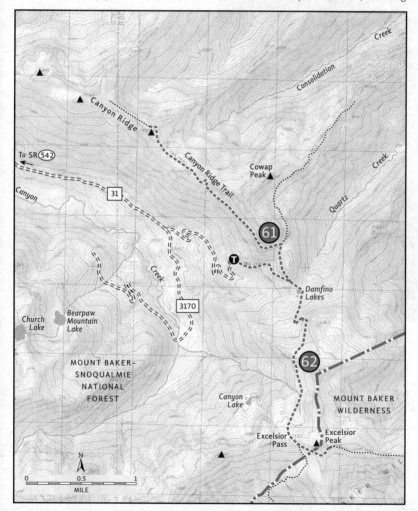

Canadian Border and American Border peaks from Canyon Ridge

a little into a forested notch (elev. 5075 ft) before making a short and steep climb to a 5400-foot knoll that demands that you stop, have lunch, and feast on incredible views of the amazing landscapes straddling the international boundary. Look south and east to Tomyhoi, Baker, Shuksan, and Excelsior and the High Divide. Peer north and east to Slesse, Cheam, and McGuire—that big white-faced behemoth staring you in the face. Contemplate the concept of a North Cascades International Park. This would be the logical place for one.

EXTENDING YOUR TRIP

While maps show the Canyon Ridge Trail continuing for another 6 miles or so, much of that route barely exists. It will make a nice extended hike once trail crews work their magic. But be aware that this trail is open to motorcycles (though currently barely used by them), and a longer improved route may attract more. Let the Forest Service know what you think about motorcycles in this fragile environment. In the meanwhile, extend your hike by heading up the lightly used Boundary Way Trail for 1 mile to a 5300-foot ridge. From here, follow a well-defined way path left for 0.5 mile to the 5650-foot summit of Cowap Peak. Views from this obscure peak are incredible—from Baker's snowy neighbors to the pastoral farms of the Fraser Valley.

first through forest, then meadows with good views out to Bald and Bearpaw mountains. Reenter forest and start climbing, steeply at times. Break out into more meadows. Heather, blueberries, views! Notice, too, junipers and manzanita, indicating a little rainshadow effect here thanks to that big mountain Baker just to the south.

Round a knoll and enjoy a wide-open stroll through yet more meadows. The trail then drops

62 Excelsior Peak

RATING/ DIFFICULTY	ROUND-TRIP	ELEV GAIN/ HIGH POINT	SEASON
★★★★/3	6.5 miles	1500 feet/ 5699 feet	July– mid-Oct

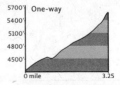

Map: Green Trails Mount Baker No. 13; **Contact:** Mount Baker–Snoqualmie National Forest, Glacier Public Service Center, (360) 599-2714 (summer only), or Mount Baker Ranger District, (360) 856-5700, www.fs.fed.us/r6/mbs; **Notes:** NW Forest Pass required; **GPS:** N 48 57.546, W 121 48.421

Excelsior! Always upward! And certainly that would be true if you tackled this former lookout site on the High Divide from the North Fork Nooksack Valley. That access would cost you nearly 4000 vertical feet of sweat and toil. But by hiking to this expansive-view-granting promontory via the Damfino Lakes Trail, all of that alpine glory can be yours for a mere song—and only 1500 feet of elevation gain.

GETTING THERE
From Bellingham follow the Mount Baker Highway (State Route 542) east for 34 miles to the Glacier Public Service Center. Continue east for another 2 miles, turning left onto Forest Road 31 (Canyon Creek Road) just after passing the entrance to the Douglas-Fir Campground. Follow FR 31 for 15.1 miles to the trailhead (elev. 4250 ft)—the pavement ends at 7.8 miles, bear left at 9.9 miles, and bear left again at 14.5 miles. Privy available.

ON THE TRAIL
Despite the long forest-road access to this trail, don't expect to be alone. With spectacular North Cascades views and resplendent alpine meadows so easily attained, half the hikers in Bellingham and Vancouver, British Columbia, head this way on sunny summer weekends. Oh well—that's the price you pay for convenience. Put on your happy face and enjoy the hike.

After an easy 0.7 mile through pleasant forest, come to a junction (elev. 4600 ft). Save the trail left (Hike 61) for when you want to be

alone, and instead head right, dropping 100 feet in 0.2 mile to the tiny Damfino Lakes. The lakes purportedly received their name many moons ago from a ranger's response to a query as to what they were called. His answer: "Damn if I know." Damn if I know why they're called lakes! In berry season, however, they make a damn fine destination.

Pass the small water holes and continue for another mile or so, a little bit of climbing required, through more pleasant forest. At 2 miles the countryside begins to open up. Soon

Meadows carpet Excelsior Peak.

find yourself on a verdant rolling carpet sprinkled with dazzling blossoms. Continue upward through magnificent meadows, reaching 5375-foot Excelsior Pass and a trail junction at 2.8 miles. Views! But they get even better. Head left up the High Divide Trail for about 0.3 mile, locating the short spur heading straight for 5699-foot Excelsior Peak.

From this little knoll at the edge of the Mount Baker Wilderness, views reign supreme. Mount Baker breathes down upon you. Scan the emerald lawns of the High Divide. Locate Church, Bearpaw, Cowap, and the Border Peaks. Stare straight down into the North Fork Nooksack Valley and be grateful you didn't start this hike from there.

EXTENDING YOUR TRIP
Do all of those marvelous meadows spread out below have you itching for more wandering? Continue along the High Divide for 2 more miles to a 5930-foot knoll, or hike 4.5 up-and-down miles to Welcome Pass (elev. 5200 ft). There's good wandering, too, west along the divide on way paths to more knockout view knolls. If you can arrange a car shuttle, descend via the Excelsior Pass Trail for 4.5 knee-knocking, ever-switchbacking, ever-downward miles to the Mount Baker Highway.

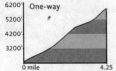

63 Church Mountain

RATING/ DIFFICULTY	ROUND-TRIP	ELEV GAIN/ HIGH POINT	SEASON
★★★★/5	8.5 miles	3750 feet/ 6100 feet	Mid-July– mid-Oct

Map: Green Trails Mount Baker No. 13; **Contact:** Mount Baker–Snoqualmie National Forest,

Glacier Public Service Center, (360) 599-2714 (summer only), or Mount Baker Ranger District, (360) 856-5700, www.fs.fed.us/r6/mbs; **Notes:** NW Forest Pass required; **GPS:** N 48 54.738, W 121 51.468

All congregants of nature are invited to attend this Church. But hallelujah, it's a tough calling! While the trail is built well, it switchbacks like there's no tomorrow. The scenery is heavenly, but with over 3700 vertical feet to climb there's a little hell to pay on the way. It's worth the sacrifice, though. From the old lookout site just beneath Church Mountain's impressive steeple-like summit, a promised land of North Cascades beauty abounds.

GETTING THERE
From Bellingham follow the Mount Baker Highway (State Route 542) east for 34 miles to the Glacier Public Service Center. Continue east for another 5.4 miles, turning left onto Forest Road 3040 (East Church Mountain Road). Follow FR 3040 for 2.7 miles to the road end and trailhead (elev. 2350 ft).

ON THE TRAIL
Start off easy enough on an old road turned delightful trail. But after an easy 0.5 mile of minimal elevation gain, ascending begins with a vengeance. At least the old-growth canopy makes prospects for overheating minimal. Occasional holes in the green cloak reveal the North Fork Nooksack River roaring below.

Traversing southern slopes, the lower half of this trail often melts out by late spring. By late summer however, it can be quite dry—pack plenty of water. At 2.5 miles, after seemingly endless climbing, the grade eases up and the forest cover thins. At 3 miles emerge into an open basin (elev. 4800 ft) beneath Church's spires. Meadows! Wildflowers! Look at them all—paintbrush, buttercup, columbine, violets, louse-

Resplendent alpine meadows

wort, saxifrage, stonecrop, cinquefoil, lupine, penstemon, lilies, asters, bistort, and valerian.

Soon the trail crosses Deer Horn Creek in a boggy orchid-strewn swale. Then it's back to business. In heather parklands and steep meadowy slopes, the trail works its way out of the basin. Be careful here, as the trail is subject to slumping. Making a long switchback, the trail enters a small rocky upper basin where snow often lingers into August.

Just beneath the craggy ridge crest, the trail heads west to angle under and up and over some rocky sections. Pass the ruins of a shed and an old precariously placed privy before making the final push to a 6100-foot knoll. Just beneath Church's summit spires (reserved for climbers and angels), this airy point (keep children, dogs, and the vertigo-inclined nearby) was once blessed with a fire lookout. The views, however, remain—and they're divine.

Look south to Shuksan, Baker and the Skyline Divide, the Twin Sisters, and all the way to Rainier; west to the San Juans; and east across the verdant and craggy High Divide. North it's Canyon Ridge, big beautiful British Columbia, and straight below, in a snowbound basin, the Kidney Lakes.

64 Welcome Pass and the High Divide

RATING/ DIFFICULTY	ROUND-TRIP	ELEV GAIN/ HIGH POINT	SEASON
★★★★/5	8 miles	3400 feet/ 5850 feet	July– mid-Oct

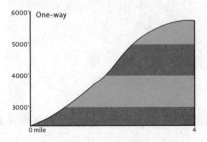

Map: Green Trails Mount Shuksan No. 14; **Contact:** Mount Baker–Snoqualmie National Forest, Glacier Public Service Center, (360) 599-2714 (summer only), or Mount Baker Ranger District, (360) 856-5700, *www.fs.fed .us/r6/mbs*; **Notes:** NW Forest Pass required; **GPS:** N 48 54.813, W 121 42.038

Welcome to the High Divide, an emerald carpet laden with dazzling bouquets draped over a rolling mile-high ridge. Only one problem with this invitation—delivering your reply will be downright demanding. The hike to Welcome Pass is a doozy: 2800 feet of elevation gain in 2.5 miles. And talk about switchbacks. There are more than sixty— count 'em! But once you make the grade, Welcome Pass extends a warm benvenuti and a sincere invite to poke around on the wide-open slopes of the divide, drinking fine views and savoring precious alpine moments.

GETTING THERE

From Bellingham follow the Mount Baker Highway (State Route 542) east for 34 miles to the Glacier Public Service Center. Continue east for another 12.5 miles, turning left onto easy-to-miss Forest Road 3060 (the turn-off is 0.3 mile west of the Department of Transportation's Shuksan garage). Continue 0.7 mile to the road end and trailhead (elev. 2450 ft).

ON THE TRAIL

Consider the first mile a mere warm-up. Using an old logging road, the trail gently wanders out of the valley, gaining a leisurely 400 feet. Real trail then brings real work. Under a cool canopy of old growth, the way steeply switches and backs, gaining over 2300 feet in 1.5 miles. Talk about steep! But once the daunting march is complete, daylight, spectacular alpine views, and a dazzling floral show greet you at Welcome Pass (elev. 5200 ft).

After such a grueling ascent you may be

Opposite: Wildflowers and wide-ranging views from High Divide

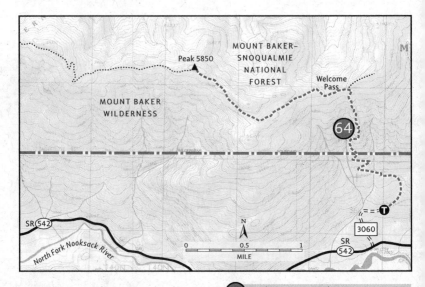

inclined to call it a day here, completely mesmerized by Baker and Shuksan's glistening beauty. But miles of supreme alpine wandering through magnificent meadows await. And because this approach to the High Divide is so tough (unlike the western approach via Damfino Lakes, Hike 62), chances are you'll have all this high country to roam alone.

Continue west for 1.5 miles to a 5850-foot knoll. Now take your well-deserved nap. Awake refreshed to take in more incredible views from Baker to British Columbia, Tomyhoi, Yellow Aster, Goat, Icy, and all those other impressive summits gracing the horizon.

EXTENDING YOUR TRIP

Continue west along the High Divide for 3 more miles to Excelsior Pass. It's one of the finest ridge walks in the North Cascades. From Welcome Pass you can explore the divide east too, following a way path of sorts all the way to the tarns beneath Yellow Aster Butte (off-trail travel experience necessary).

65 Heliotrope Ridge

RATING/ DIFFICULTY	ROUND-TRIP	ELEV GAIN/ HIGH POINT	SEASON
★★★★★/3	5.5 miles	1800 feet/ 5550 feet	Late July– mid-Oct

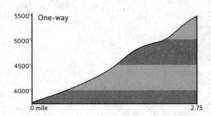

Map: Green Trails Mount Baker No. 13; **Contact:** Mount Baker–Snoqualmie National Forest, Glacier Public Service Center, (360) 599-2714 (summer only), or Mount Baker Ranger District, (360) 856-5700, www.fs.fed.us/r6/mbs; **Notes:** NW Forest Pass required; **GPS:** N 48 48.125, W 121 53.740

Intimate ice is what this hike is all about. Follow a well-trodden path to the scoured world of the Coleman Glacier, the largest of Baker's dozen-plus glaciers. From along a steep heap of lateral moraine, stare down into a cavernous abyss of ice and compacted snow. Locate blue grottos in the crevasses of Baker's frozen icing. Come in July for the lilies, September for the berries, October for the quiet, but don't try this hike early in the season. The creeks are unbridged and are difficult enough to negotiate in dry periods.

GETTING THERE

From Bellingham follow the Mount Baker Highway (State Route 542) east for 34 miles to the Glacier Public Service Center. Continue east for another 0.8 mile, turning right onto Forest Road 39 (Glacier Creek Road). After 8 mostly paved miles, bear left at a junction and reach the trailhead in another 0.3 mile (elev. 3750 ft). Privy available.

ON THE TRAIL

After your initial shock at the size of the parking lot (this trail is the beginning of a popular climbing route too), enter cool hemlock forest and immediately drop to cross Grouse Creek, on a bridge thankfully. Now in the Mount Baker Wilderness (how many party-size violations can you spot?), the well-beaten path steadily climbs a bit before easing off.

Encounter the first of three cascading creeks that must be crossed, all *sans pont*. The second one is the most difficult. Trekking poles come in handy. The trail picks up the pace, once more steeply climbing, now alongside Kulshan Creek. The forest thins, revealing teaser views.

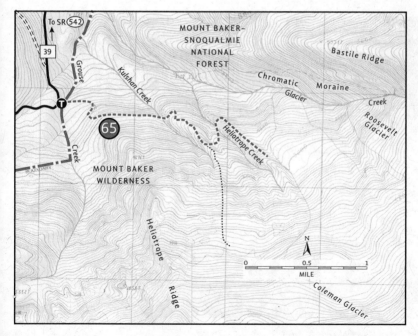

At 2 miles pass a backcountry campsite (elev. 4700 ft), the former site of the Kulshan Cabin, a structure built in 1925 by the Mount Baker Club and used until the 1980s. Soon afterward, come to a junction.

Take the trail left; the trail right is a climbers route. As you travel through stunted evergreens, the incredible hulking Baker makes its presence known. Soon encounter the first of two challenging (potentially dangerous) crossings of braided Heliotrope Creek. Plan on getting your feet wet in icy-cold, rapidly moving waters. Be aware, too, that if it's a hot day your return will be even more difficult because of melting snows from above.

Once safely across, proceed through marmot-enhanced meadows to the hemlock-lined edge of Coleman's lateral moraine. Wow! Right below you, snaked out like an oversized ice-cream cone on its side, a massive glacier! Continue on scant path, climbing alongside the glacier up the moraine—using care and staying away from the edge—to a 5550-foot ledgy knoll.

Sit here in awe, gazing at the icy intricacies of the glacier. Rippled crevasses. Blue pools. Frozen portals. Be sure to look out at the alpine world around you too: Bastile Ridge just across the glacier, Golden Ears Mountain just across the border. And if you're wondering just what the heck a heliotrope is—it's a flower, one not native to the area. But early surveyors thought the native valerians looked awfully close.

EXTENDING YOUR TRIP

Late in the season, experienced hikers can follow the climbers route about 0.75 mile to a 6000-foot knoll for excellent viewing of the Coleman

Baker's Coleman Glacier

and Roosevelt ice masses. If interested, stick to the trail on solid ledge. Do not hike on the glacier or adjacent snowfields. More than a couple of hikers have died here venturing off-trail.

66 Skyline Divide

RATING/ DIFFICULTY	ROUND-TRIP	ELEV GAIN/ HIGH POINT	SEASON
★★★★★/3	9 miles	2500 feet/ 6563 feet	Mid-July– Oct

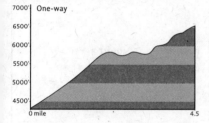

Map: Green Trails Mount Baker No. 13; **Contact:** Mount Baker–Snoqualmie National Forest, Glacier Public Service Center, (360) 599-2714 (summer only), or Mount Baker Ranger District, (360) 856-5700, www.fs.fed.us/r6/mbs; **Notes:** NW Forest Pass required; **GPS:** N 48 52.857, W 121 51.877

With miles of flower-saturated meadows along a rolling lofty ridge radiating from the big volcano itself, Skyline Divide is one of Baker's best offerings to the hiking community. While the views are supreme—from the snowy peaks of British Columbia to the salty waters of Puget Sound—you'll struggle keeping your eyes off of what the area's first peoples called Koma Kulshan, "the Great White One." A popular place on a summer weekend, Skyline provides enough nooks and crannies to spread out. And while this hike is 4.5 miles long, feel free to quit anytime after 2 miles—there's no shortage of views along the way.

GETTING THERE

From Bellingham follow the Mount Baker Highway (State Route 542) east for 34 miles to the Glacier Public Service Center. Continue east another 0.8 mile, turning right onto Forest Road 39 (Glacier Creek Road). Then immediately turn left onto FR 37 (signed "Skyline Trail 12"), following this rough, at times gravel road 12.8 miles to its terminus and the trailhead (elev. 4300 ft). Privy available.

ON THE TRAIL

Without delay, begin climbing in a beautiful stand of mature silver fir. The trail is wide and firm; many a boot has walked this way. As you toil up and up, steeply at times, let the anticipation of alpine rapture carry you to the ridge crest. Approaching timberline, the trail passes into the Mount Baker Wilderness. At 2 miles clutch your heart and prepare for visual attack as the trail emerges onto a grassy knoll (elev. 5900 ft), unfurling a backdrop of the Great White One, surrounded by some pretty darn nice ones.

Roam the knoll. Look out to Shuksan, Ruth, Table, Goat, Winchester, and of course, Koma Kulshan. Be sure to smell the flowers too. Lupine, harebell, bistort, valerian, daisy, and aster make bountiful bouquets beside your boots. But it gets better, so carry on. Drop a little into a small saddle, a little up and down, and then sidehill around the next knoll, coming to a flat where Baker poses ever so majestically for your memory card to capture. Climb the 6215-foot knoll or continue on the ridge.

With Baker now breathing upon you and bearing a slight resemblance to Rainier from this angle, come to an unmarked junction at 3.5 miles in a small saddle (elev. 6000 ft). The trail left continues for 1 mile, dropping a couple hundred feet into a wild peaceful basin. The trail right continues on a rougher route along the divide, climbing higher. Over ledge and through krummholz and heather, work

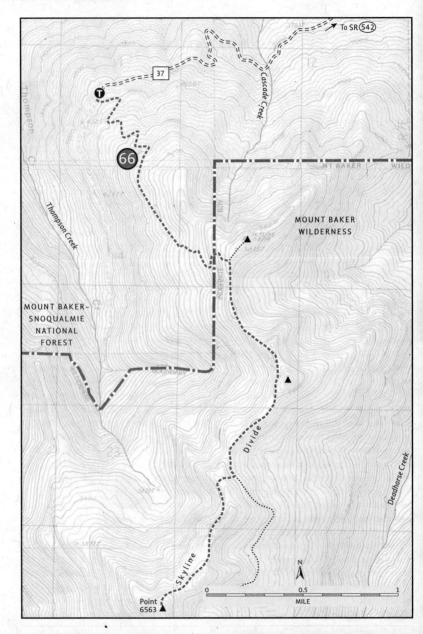

Skyline Divide

your way up to yet another knoll, number six if you're keeping track, and call it quits upon this 6563-foot gem. Beyond to Chowder Ridge is strictly for climbers and goats.

Look at all those mountains! The Cheam Range, Golden Ears, and McGuire in Canada, the High Divide and company in front of them. East is Yellow Aster Butte, Shuksan, and a slew of craggy goliaths. The Black Buttes and Twin Sisters are to the south, and the Olympics and San Juan Islands lie to the west. Simply amazing!

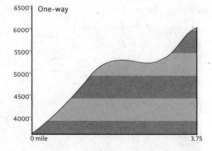

67 Yellow Aster Butte

RATING/ DIFFICULTY	ROUND-TRIP	ELEV GAIN/ HIGH POINT	SEASON
★★★★★/4	7.5 miles	2550 feet/ 6150 feet	July– mid-Oct

Map: Green Trails Mount Shuksan No. 14; **Contact:** Mount Baker–Snoqualmie National Forest, Glacier Public Service Center, (360) 599-2714 (summer only), or Mount Baker Ranger District, (360) 856-5700, *www.fs.fed .us/r6/mbs*; **Notes:** NW Forest Pass required.

Forest Service discourages dogs on this popular hike; **GPS:** N 48 56.611, W 121 39.747

⚙ *Find supreme wildflower gardens and a high-country plateau speckled with shimmering tarns—but that's not all. Spectacular alpine vistas abound too—of Baker, Shuksan, and all those rugged and craggy peaks straddling the 49th parallel. Yellow Aster Butte may be a misnomer (those yellow-petaled delights are actually daisies), but you definitely don't want to miss hiking here.*

GETTING THERE

From Bellingham follow the Mount Baker Highway (State Route 542) east for 34 miles to the Glacier Public Service Center. Continue east another 13 miles, turning left onto Forest Road 3065 (signed "Twin Lakes Road"; the turnoff is just beyond the Department of Transportation's Shuksan garage). Immediately bear left at an unmarked junction and continue on FR 3065 for 4.5 miles to the trailhead located at a sharp switchback with tight parking (elev. 3600 ft). Privy available.

ON THE TRAIL

Sharing a start with the Tomyhoi Lake Trail, begin on a steep course alternating between cool old-growth forest and warm brushy avalanche slopes. Views out to Goat Mountain and big ol' Baker aren't bad from the brushy openings. Shortly after entering the Mount Baker Wilderness, the grade thankfully eases up. The tread remains excellent, the result of a lot of volunteer work over the years on this heavily traveled trail.

The way soon breaks out into a basin bursting with berry patches. Do this hike in September and you're sure to be caught red handed (and mouthed) partaking in gluttonous behavior. But these antioxidants sure make a better choice than chips! In 1.4 miles come to a junction (elev. 5150 ft) with the Tomyhoi Lake Trail. Head left for Yellow Aster on trail constructed in the 1990s that replaced the deeply eroded (but beloved by many) Keep Kool Trail.

Slab around the basin on a fairly level course, flushing rodents, birds, and perhaps a weary hiker or two out of the bountiful berry patches. As you round the basin, Mount

A pair of hikers peer at Tomyhoi Peak from Yellow Aster Butte.

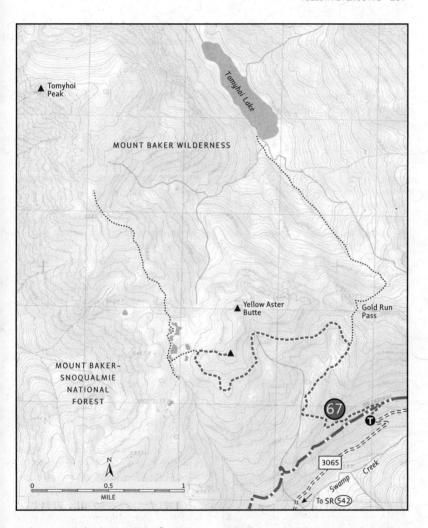

Shuksan reveals her beauty. Baker flaunts his as well from across Austin Pass. After moderate climbing across boulder-strewn heather meadows, the trail drops about 100 feet into a snow-harboring basin. Showy penstemon and monkey flowers spruce up the stark gulch with touches of purple and gold.

Climb more steeply, now, rounding Yellow Aster's south shoulder. Catch your breath—not from altitude, but from multitude—a beautiful multitude of peaks, ridges, and tarns spread out before you. At 3.5 miles reach a junction on a ledge overlooking the glacier-scoured tarnished plateau below. Head left, dropping about

200 feet to explore this water-pocked pocket; or take the way trail right, steeply climbing 400 feet in 0.25 mile to ascend the butte.

From this 6150-foot promontory, look out over an amazing landscape of emerald ridges, verdant valleys, snow-capped spires, and glacier-clad giants. Winchester, Larrabee, American Border, and Canadian Border peaks are particularly striking. So too is Tomyhoi, the big broad behemoth dominating the north viewscape.

EXTENDING YOUR TRIP

Yellow Aster's true summit lies about 0.3 mile north and is reached by scrambling a narrow and slightly exposed ridge. It's best left for experienced peak baggers. There is a good way path for quite a distance up 7451-foot Tomyhoi Peak, though, beginning from the tarn basin. The summit block is strictly for climbers. Mile-long Tomyhoi Lake is reached by a 2-mile trail that leaves the Yellow Aster Butte Trail 1.4 miles from the trailhead. After climbing to 5400-foot Gold Run Pass, the trail drops 1700 insanely steep feet to the forested lake. It's a grueling return.

68 Winchester Mountain

RATING/ DIFFICULTY	ROUND-TRIP	ELEV GAIN/ HIGH POINT	SEASON
★★★★/3	3.5 miles	1320 feet/ 6521 feet	Mid-July– mid-Oct

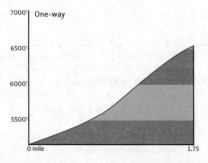

Map: Green Trails Mount Shuksan No. 14; **Contact:** Mount Baker–Snoqualmie National Forest, Glacier Public Service Center, (360) 599-2714 (summer only), or Mount Baker Ranger District, (360) 856-5700, *www.fs.fed .us/r6/mbs*; **Notes:** NW Forest Pass required. Final stretch of access road not suitable for many vehicles, adding 5 miles round-trip and 1600 feet elevation gain; **GPS:** N 48 57.158, W 121 38.147

England may have Winchester Cathedral, but here in Washington State we have Winchester Mountain, in the natural cathedral of the North Cascades. From the restored lookout perched atop this heavenly peak, praise boundless beauty beaming before you. Sparkling lakes, shining snowfields, and rows of mountain spires separated by deep emerald valleys—simply divine. And best of all, just a little physical sacrifice is required on this moderate hike.

GETTING THERE

From Bellingham follow the Mount Baker Highway (State Route 542) east for 34 miles to the Glacier Public Service Center. Continue east another 13 miles, turning left onto Forest Road 3065 (signed "Twin Lakes Road"; the turnoff is just beyond the Department of Transportation's Shuksan garage). Immediately bear left at an unmarked junction and continue on FR 3065 for 4.5 miles to the trailhead for Yellow Aster Butte. The road beyond this point is extremely rough, suitable only for four-wheel-drive vehicles. Either park here and walk the road, or continue driving 2.5 very rugged miles to the trailhead at Twin Lakes (elev. 5200 ft). Primitive camping and privy available.

ON THE TRAIL

Beauty begins immediately. The trail takes off from between the Twin Lakes, a deep blue, icy-cold pair of subalpine aquatic gems.

Despite the area's rugged appearance, the heather-lined lakeshores are quite fragile and have been trampled by gold- and view-seekers alike. Treat these lakes like the precious jewels they are.

Begin climbing through a "stand" of false hellebore, soon entering the Mount Baker Wilderness. Continue through stately hemlocks, and at about 0.25 mile come to a junction with the High Pass Trail (Hike 69). Bear left through blueberry patches, marmot playgrounds, and parklands carpeted in heather and garnished with anemones. Views grow. At about 1 mile come to a gully that harbors a dangerous snowfield well into summer. Cross with an ice ax or bypass it below if possible, otherwise return later in the season and go explore the lake basin instead.

The trail then traverses a steep slope high above the west Twin Lake before wrapping around the mountain to commence a short switchback shuffle to the 6521-foot summit. Old glory is usually flying in front of the restored lookout perched on the peak. Built in 1935, the lookout was scheduled for demolition in the early 1980s until the Mount Baker Club saved and restored it. Now the elegant structure is a popular place to spend the night.

Okay, enough about the lookout: how about those views? They're amazing! Look west to Baker and Yellow Aster Butte, north to Tomyhoi, Larrabee, American Border Peak, Canadian Border Peak, and into the snowy abyss known as British Columbia. East, pick out the Pickets among a prominent pack of North Cascades pinnacles. To the south Shuksan pokes its icy head up between the twin peaks of Goat Mountain. The Twin Lakes twinkle directly below.

EXTENDING YOUR TRIP
Consider camping at Twin Lakes and further explore the region. The area is littered with old mining relics and shafts. A tent-city

West Twin Lake, Goat Mountain, and Mount Shuksan

boomtown once sat on these shores. Hike over Skagway Pass and down, down, down to Silesia Creek on a primitive and little-traveled path. It's about a 3.5-mile journey with 2600 feet of elevation change.

69 High Pass

RATING/ DIFFICULTY	ROUND-TRIP	ELEV GAIN/ HIGH POINT	SEASON
★★★★/3	4 miles	1350 feet/ 5950 feet	Mid-July– mid-Oct

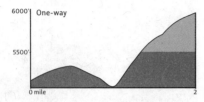

Map: Green Trails Mount Shuksan No. 14; **Contact:** Mount Baker–Snoqualmie National Forest, Glacier Public Service Center, (360) 599-2714 (summer only), or Mount Baker Ranger District, (360) 856-5700, www.fs.fed .us/r6/mbs; **Notes:** NW Forest Pass required.

Mount Larrabee towers over High Pass.

Final stretch of access road not suitable for many vehicles, adding 5 miles round-trip and 1600 feet elevation gain; **GPS:** N 48 57.158, W 121 38.147

Follow a no-nonsense trail to a high shoulder (hence, High Pass) on 7868-foot Mount Larrabee. Once the domain of clambering miners, now clambering climbers, High Pass offers a quieter alternative to nearby Winchester Mountain. The views are just as grand, the wildflowers just as splendid, and the opportunities for exploring old mines and talking to spirits from the past are better.

GETTING THERE

From Bellingham follow the Mount Baker Highway (State Route 542) east for 34 miles to the Glacier Public Service Center. Continue east another 13 miles, turning left onto Forest Road 3065 (signed "Twin Lakes Road"; the turnoff is just beyond the Department of Transportation's Shuksan garage). Immediately bear left at an unmarked junction and continue on FR 3065 for 4.5 miles to the trailhead for Yellow Aster Butte. The road beyond this point is extremely rough, suitable only for four-wheel-drive vehicles. Either park here and walk the road, or continue driving 2.5 very rugged miles to the trailhead at Twin Lakes (elev. 5200 ft). Primitive camping and privy available.

ON THE TRAIL

Find the Winchester Mountain Trail wedged between the delightful lake duo, and take to it, entering the Mount Baker Wilderness. After 0.25 mile reach the junction for High Pass Trail No. 676 and head right. Crest a small ridge, and wham—Mount Larrabee and the saw-toothed Pleiades get right in your face.

The way now drops 300 feet to skirt under cliffs and ledges, and it traverses steep slopes awash in an array of dazzling wildflowers. Enjoy good views into the deep, dark Silesia Creek valley, once a bustling byway for prospectors and bootleggers. Sunlight struggles to kiss these abrupt north-facing slopes. Consequently, snow lingers long here, creating potentially hazardous conditions for hikers unskilled with an ice ax. If the way is covered in snow, return later in the season (for an added bonus of ripe berries), and opt for explorations around Twin Lakes.

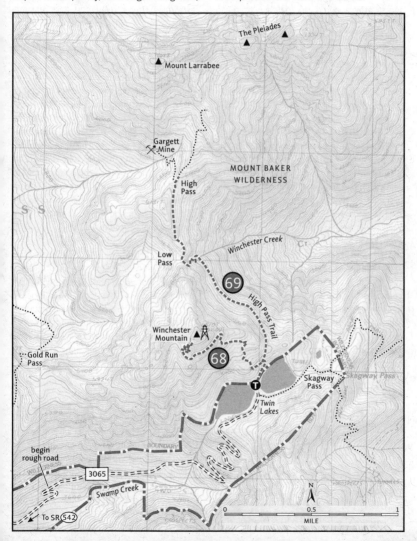

Reaching Winchester Creek, the trail turns westward and steeply climbs on taut switchbacks to the tight little notch, 5600-foot Low Pass. Take in a good view of Tomyhoi Peak, and then continue climbing steeply through forest groves and berry patches to reach 5950-foot High Pass shortly after slabbing a little knoll. From this broad gap 2000 feet beneath the rusted summit of Mount Larrabee, sit back and enjoy splendid views near and far. Tomyhoi Lake, the Skagit Range, Hannegan Peak, and Ruth Mountain are among the scenic attractions.

EXTENDING YOUR TRIP

A few hundred feet below High Pass to the northwest lie the ruins of the Gargett Mine. It's easily reached by still-decent tread. The real adventure, however, lies above. If the way is snow free, follow a steep and aerie path 0.7 mile to 6700-feet "Even Higher Pass" (or as we'd say in New England, Wicked High Pass). From this slightly exposed gap just beneath the Pleiades, brace yourself for an amazing view that includes just about every corner of the Mount Baker Wilderness, seldom-seen corners of the North Cascades National Park, and glimpses to far-off locales like Whitehorse Mountain and the Olympics. There are a few old mines up here too, but you'll need the fearlessness and fortitude of a mountain goat to find them.

70 Nooksack Cirque

RATING/ DIFFICULTY	ROUND-TRIP	ELEV GAIN/ HIGH POINT	SEASON
★★★/3	7 miles	600 feet/ 2700 feet	June–Oct

Map: Green Trails Mount Shuksan No. 14; **Contact:** Mount Baker–Snoqualmie National Forest, Glacier Public Service Center, (360) 599-2714 (summer only), or Mount Baker Ranger District, (360) 856-5700, www.fs.fed.us/r6/mbs; **Notes:** NW Forest Pass required. River crossing required. Summer 2007 logjam may shift, requiring a difficult and at times dangerous ford; **GPS:** N 48 53.634, W 121 39.144

Guidebook pioneers Ira Spring and Harvey Manning described the Nooksack Cirque as one of the most dramatic spots in the North Cascades. I can't argue with that. One of the region's largest cirques (a glacially carved amphitheater), it's shadowed by snow-shrouded 9127-foot Mount Shuksan and flanked by sheer cliffs that have been polished by eons of ice and cascading runoff. These are the headwaters of the North Fork Nooksack, and the wild river makes a dramatic departure from its icy spawning grounds.

GETTING THERE

From Bellingham follow the Mount Baker Highway (State Route 542) east for 34 miles to the Glacier Public Service Center. Proceed another 13 miles, turning left onto Forest Road 32 (Hannegan Pass Road) just before a bridge over the North Fork Nooksack River. Follow FR 32 for 1.3 miles, bearing right onto FR 34. Continue for 0.9 mile to the road end and trailhead (elev. 2200 ft).

ON THE TRAIL

While the hike to the edge of the cirque isn't overly difficult, beginning your adventure may be. From the trailhead, drop onto the broad gravel bed of Ruth Creek. The cold and swiftly moving waterway must be crossed, and the bridge is long gone. A logjam usually forms just to the south of the old bridge site, sometimes requiring slight acrobatic maneuvers to cross it. Call in the Cirque de Soleil for the

Icy Peak and icy-cold North Fork Nooksack River

Cirque de Nooksack! You'll be in a jam with no jam, in which case consider returning in late summer to ford the creek when the water level is lower.

Once across, follow boot-beaten tread left and up to an old logging road now serving as trail. The way marches on through maturing hemlock forest, ascending ever so slightly. After crossing a creek (on a log bridge no less)

that tumbles down from Mount Sefrit, begin an ever so slight descent. At about 3 miles enter the Mount Baker Wilderness with its accompanying impressive primeval forest.

You'll also finally catch glimpses of the North Fork Nooksack and hear its roar loud and clear. Under an ancient canopy and through brushy and marshy patches, work your way closer to the source of all that racket. Not long

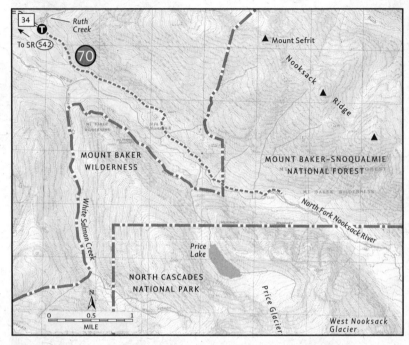

after crossing a small creek in a deep gully, reach the river. After paralleling the mighty watercourse for a short ways, the path pretty much putters out on a wide gravel bar. The view here up the glacier-fed river to glacier-dipped Icy Peak—the eastern end of the massive cirque—is absolutely stunning. Soak your feet if you dare while savoring the wild beauty surrounding you.

EXTENDING YOUR TRIP

Adventurous souls who want to push farther into the cirque can follow rude and interrupted way paths another 0.5 mile or so, and then take to the wide gravel bars. Travel on the rocky bars is slow and arduous and only possible during late summer when the river is running low. It should only be considered by experienced off-trail travelers.

71 Goat Mountain

RATING/ DIFFICULTY	ROUND-TRIP	ELEV GAIN/ HIGH POINT	SEASON
★★★★/5	11 miles	4100 feet/ 6650 feet	Late June– Oct

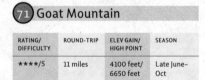

One-way

Map: Green Trails Mount Shuksan No. 14; **Contact:** Mount Baker–Snoqualmie National Forest, Glacier Public Service Center, (360) 599-2714 (summer only), or Mount Baker Ranger District, (360) 856-5700, www.fs.fed.us/r6/mbs; **Notes:**

NW Forest Pass required; **GPS:** N 48 53.857, W 121 38.761

This is a long, steep climb to a prominent peak perched smack-dab in the middle of some of the finest mountain scenery in North America. Mounts Baker and Shuksan breathe their frosty breaths upon you. A choppy sea of jagged peaks from British Columbia to the Picket Range washes up upon your boots. Gaze out to salty waters or deep into the heart of the

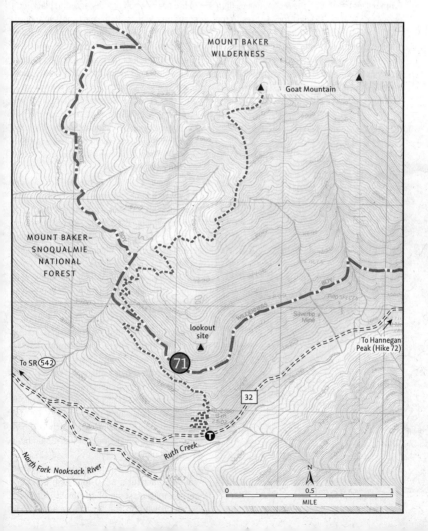

North Cascades wilderness. And best of all, you won't be competing for space on the summit. The crowds are over at nearby Hannegan Peak (Hike 72).

GETTING THERE
From Bellingham follow the Mount Baker Highway (State Route 542) east for 34 miles to the Glacier Public Service Center. Proceed another 13 miles, turning left onto Forest Road 32 (Hannegan Pass Road) just before a bridge over the North Fork Nooksack River. Follow FR 32 for 2.4 miles to the trailhead (elev. 2550 ft). More parking is available just beyond the trailhead.

Mount Shuksan from high on Goat Mountain

ON THE TRAIL
Starting in thick forest decorated with mossy boulders, the way immediately winds upward. On excellent tread the grade is mostly moderate—but trust me, it'll get steeper. Much of Goat Mountain succumbed to fire nearly a half century ago, and blackened snags bear witness to the past conflagration.

At about 1.75 miles enter the Mount Baker Wilderness. Shortly afterward pass an unmarked side trail (elev. 3900 ft) that heads right. It leads 0.5 mile to an old lookout site. The view is good, but the ones waiting for you along the main trail are better. Far better. So continue climbing. Thick forest cover soon thins, replaced by a jungle of mountain ash, maple, alder, and willow. Then the surrounding walls of shrubbery begin to dissipate, yielding to low-lying blueberry bushes and expanding views.

At about 3.75 miles arrive on a 5100-foot knoll with a knockout view of glacier-harboring Mounts Sefrit and Shuksan. From this good early turnaround option (or early season objective), you'll also find an excellent shot of glistening Price Lake tucked in a high cirque on Shuksan's northern face of ice and rock.

The trail continues along the spine of a ridge, officially terminating at 5600 feet at the base of expansive meadows high on Goat's south-facing slopes. From here follow a rough but well-defined route, first across, then straight up those flower-studded steep slopes. Cross a couple of spring-fed creeks adorned with showy bouquets. The way here is prone to slumping, so travel carefully. After a long traverse the trail insanely heads straight up the verdant slope, reaching a 6250-foot shoulder and an amazing view north to Tomyhoi, the High Divide, and British Columbia's infinite summits.

Now turn right and follow a ridgeline course, reaching a 6650-foot high point after 0.5 mile of some of the most incredible alpine viewing in the North Cascades. Look at all those peaks: Redoubt, Jack, Ruth, Blum, Triumph, and Whitehorse among them, and Slesse, Rexford, and Silver Tip among their Canadian cousins.

Don't forget to admire your immediate surroundings too, like the small glacier directly below wedged between Goat's two prominent summits. And speaking of summits, the peak's actual high point is just to the north of you. Only 100 feet higher, it requires crossing a dangerous snowfield and scrambling exposed rock. Leave it for the peak's namesake.

72 Hannegan Peak

RATING/ DIFFICULTY	ROUND-TRIP	ELEV GAIN/ HIGH POINT	SEASON
★★★★★/4	10.4 miles	3100 feet/ 6187 feet	July–Oct

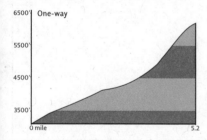

Map: Green Trails Mount Shuksan No. 14; **Contact:** Mount Baker–Snoqualmie National Forest, Glacier Public Service Center, (360) 599-2714 (summer only), or Mount Baker Ranger District, (360) 856-5700, www.fs.fed.us/r6/mbs; **Notes:** NW Forest Pass required; **GPS:** N 48 54.608, W 121 35.502

March up a wide-open valley resplendent in wildflowers, flanked by snowy crags, and reverberating with the sounds of crashing water. Under the ever-watchful eye of snow- and ice-heaped Ruth Mountain, make your way to a high pass—

Ruth Mountain's snowy north face

one of the few portals into the deep, dark wilderness of the North Cascades National Park. But that's for backpackers: your objective is nearby Hannegan Peak, with its dizzying views of that sylvan landscape and nearby Ruth, Shuksan, and Baker draped in layers of glistening ice.

GETTING THERE
From Bellingham follow the Mount Baker Highway (State Route 542) east for 34 miles

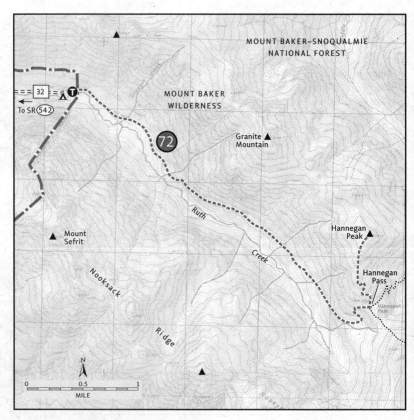

to the Glacier Public Service Center. Proceed another 13 miles, turning left onto Forest Road 32 (Hannegan Pass Road) just before a bridge over the North Fork Nooksack River. Follow rough-at-times FR 32 for 5.3 miles to the road end and trailhead (elev. 3100 ft). Primitive camping and privy available.

ON THE TRAIL

Keep sunglasses and sunscreen at the ready, for much of this hike is in the open. Keep bug dope nearby too, for swarms of voracious bloodsuckers are as fond of the flowering veg-etation as you are. Starting on a wide groomed path that's loath to gain elevation, head up the valley. Sensory overload immediately begins. Sparkling waters glide off towering polished walls. Tenacious snowfields cling to dark clefts in spiraling crags.

Alternate between cool evergreen groves and steamy avalanche fans choked in head-high greenery. Beware the nettles. At 0.6 mile cross the first of many crashing creeks. In early season be aware of crumbling snowbridges. In hot weather be aware of raging torrents.

The magnificently snow-capped Ruth Mountain soon comes into view, keeping a lock on your attention. At 2.5 miles the trail decides to gain some elevation, making its way to a ledge above the valley floor. Stare out at snaking, silvery Ruth Creek slicing through a jungle of greenery of varying shades. Cross rock slides and gullies, young and old. Ruth Mountain continues to hold its mesmerizing spell over you. At 3 miles cross a creek beneath a refreshing cascade (elev. 4200 ft), before entering thick forest for a respite from the sun.

The trail finally gets serious about climbing, switchbacking steadily toward Hannegan Pass. At 3.5 miles a spur trail leads to the right across lovely meadows to backcountry campsites. Continue left through forest, meadow, then forest again to reach the 5050-foot pass at 4 miles. You worked too hard to settle just for the okay view down into the forested Chilliwack Valley. Head left on the trail for Hannegan Peak. Climbing over 1000 feet in 1.2 miles, it's a steep grunt. But once you break out onto the talus and tundra top of the 6187-foot peak, there'll be no doubt in your mind that it was worth it.

From one of the best viewing posts in these parts, start scanning the horizons. West down the valley you come to Goat, the High Divide, and the long serrated Nooksack Ridge. Look north down the remote Silesia Creek valley to British Columbia's Slesse Mountain and others. East, follow Copper Ridge out to massive Mount Redoubt in the distance. But by far, your eyes will spend the most time fixed south on Baker, Ruth, and Shuksan—particularly Shuksan, with its East Nooksack Glacier and Nooksack Tower so prominently displayed.

EXTENDING YOUR TRIP

From Hannegan Pass a steep climbers trail travels almost 2 miles along Ruth's northern shoulder. When free of snow it is generally okay for experienced hikers. Stop when the going gets tough, and don't venture on any glaciers unless equipped and trained. The views rival those from Hannegan Peak.

73 Chain Lakes

RATING/ DIFFICULTY	LOOP	ELEV GAIN/ HIGH POINT	SEASON
★★★★★/3	8 miles	1600 feet/ 5400 feet	Late July– mid-Oct

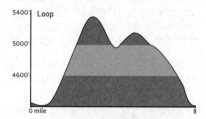

Map: Green Trails Mount Shuksan No. 14; **Contact:** Mount Baker–Snoqualmie National Forest, Glacier Public Service Center, (360) 599-2714 (summer only), or Mount Baker Ranger District, (360) 856-5700, www.fs.fed.us/r6/mbs; **Notes:** NW Forest Pass required; **GPS:** N 48 51.830, W 121 40.780

Set against a backdrop of plateau-topped Table Mountain's rock and ice are a half-dozen alpine lakes, each with its own flavor. Enjoy them on an amazing loop through talus slopes, deep forest, berry meadows, and windswept ridges. Take in breathtaking views of the frosty bookend giants, Baker and Shuksan. The beauty of Chain Lakes is unsurpassed. So too are the crowds that flock to this Heather Meadows highlight during its short hiking season.

GETTING THERE

From Bellingham follow the Mount Baker Highway (State Route 542) east for 34 miles to the Glacier Public Service Center. Drive another 22 miles to Heather Meadows, turning right into a large parking area signed for Bagley Lakes (elev. 4250 ft). The trailhead is located just after the Picture Lake Trail and just before the Mount Baker Ski Area lodge. Privy available.

ON THE TRAIL

Folks in epic numbers have been descending on Heather Meadows since 1927, when the Mount Baker Highway made its way here. Six years later the Civilian Conservation Corps constructed trails, bridges, and cabins in the area, inviting more visitors. Anniversaries, weddings, and reunions are common, and even a few movies have been filmed here (*Call of the Wild, Deer Hunter*).

All of this activity has taken its toll on this fragile alpine environment that's free from

Table Mountain hovers over the Bagley Lakes.

snow three months a year at best. The Forest Service has been rehabilitating the social trails that have scarred the area. You can do your part by staying on established trails and helping enlighten others who don't understand that the plants here grow by the inch and die by the foot.

That said, this is truly one of the most spectacular places in the Northwest. The loop outlined here can be shortened or altered to your taste. There are no bad variations.

Begin by dropping a little to lower Bagley Lake, a sliver of a lake in a narrow draw. Turn right to cross its outlet near a small old power-generating plant. Then enjoy near-level walking. At 0.7 mile reach a junction at an arched stone bridge. The trail left goes to the Heather Meadows Visitors Center and to the Fire and Ice and Wild Goose trails that can be used for shorter loops.

For the Chain Lakes, continue right, passing along the rocky shores of upper Bagley Lake twinkling beneath Table Mountain's columnar cliffs of ancient lava. Perpetual snowfields send continuous streams of meltwater cascading down them. Now on open and rocky slopes, start climbing—steeply at times—reaching 5400-foot Herman Saddle with knock-your-sunglasses-off views of Baker in the west and Shuksan in the east.

The trail now drops 600 feet on steep meadows that frequently harbor snowfields all summer long. At 3.5 miles arrive at Iceberg Lake, the first and largest of the Galena Chain Lakes. As tempted as you may be to take a plunge, recall this lake's name—spot its namesake floating—and reconsider! Warmer Hayes and Arbuthnet lakes make better wading choices and they're easily reached by a side trail taking off right.

Beyond Iceberg, continue the loop through forest and berry patches along gurgling Mazama Creek to tiny Mazama Lake (elev. 4750 ft) set in parkland meadows teeming with wildflowers and

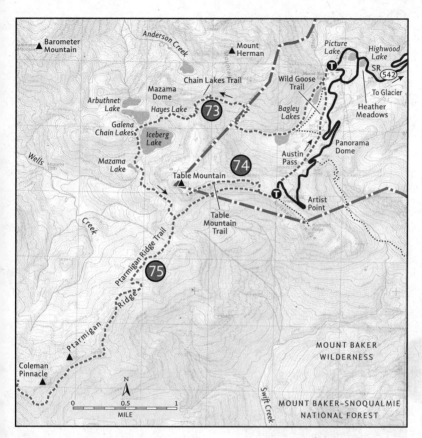

wildlife. Now begin climbing again over rock and snow to a 5200-foot gap between Table Mountain and Ptarmigan Ridge, views expanding with each step. Here you'll intersect the Ptarmigan Ridge Trail (Hike 75) and enjoy a stunning view of that snow and tundra appendage of Baker.

Head left for a pleasant mile, crossing sunny southern slopes. Gaze out over the expansive greenery of the Swift Creek valley and waves upon waves of peaks sinking into the horizon. At 6.5 miles arrive at 5140-foot Artist Point (an alternative start) and its municipal-sized parking lot. Close the loop by taking the

Wild Goose Trail 1.5 miles back to the trailhead, dropping about 850 feet. If steep snow blocks the way (which it often does), carefully walk the Mount Baker Highway back. Expect more fine views of the Bagleys and Table on your return.

EXTENDING YOUR TRIP

The nearby paved 0.5-mile Picture Lake loop is a must. Capture on film or pixels the same shot of Shuksan that graces more calendars, postcards, and placemats than—dare I say?—Elvis.

74 Table Mountain

RATING/ DIFFICULTY	ROUND-TRIP	ELEV GAIN/ HIGH POINT	SEASON
★★★★★/2	3 miles	560 feet/ 5700 feet	Aug– mid-Oct

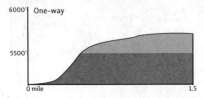

Map: Green Trails Mount Shuksan No. 14; **Contact:** Mount Baker–Snoqualmie National Forest, Glacier Public Service Center, (360) 599-2714 (summer only), or Mount Baker Ranger District, (360) 856-5700, *www.fs.fed .us/r6/mbs*; **Notes:** NW Forest Pass required. Dogs prohibited. Road from Picture Lake to trailhead often remains snowbound into August, sometimes year-round. Check with Forest Service; **GPS:** N 48 50.780, W 121 41.560

From this high, barren, snow-blotched plateau that resembles a giant anvil wedged between "the great white one" (Baker) and "the rocky and precipitous one" (Shuksan), savor some of the finest horizon-spanning views this side of the Mississippi. And while room at the Table is often at a premium on late summer weekends, beware: this hike can be dangerous if snow-covered, and parts are steep and somewhat exposed. If the route looks unnerving, turn around and enjoy the much mellower nearby Artist Point Trail instead.

GETTING THERE

From Bellingham follow the Mount Baker Highway (State Route 542) east for 34 miles to the Glacier Public Service Center. Drive another 25

Mount Shuksan provides a dramatic backdrop to Table Mountain.

miles to the road end at the mega parking lot for Artist Point (elev. 5140 ft). Privy available.

ON THE TRAIL

Starting at nearly a mile high, follow the Chain Lakes Trail (Hike 73) about 50 feet to the Table Mountain Trail that diverges right. Heading straight up the near-vertical east wall of the nearest thing to a mesa in the North Cascades, the trail climbs rock steps and snakes up ledges on a steep and some-what exposed route. Children should be kept close by.

After 500 feet of either exhilarating or nerve-wracking ascent, emerge on the wind-blasted exposed-to-the-elements Table top. The trail continues along the plateau, pass-ing clumps of tenacious trees and small pools perfect for catching reflections of surround-ing mountains. And speaking of those peaks, 10,778-foot Baker and 9127-foot Shuksan dominate the show. But give the others their due. The Canadian Border Peak, Ruth, Goat, the High Divide, Blum, Glacier, the Pickets, the list goes on. Enjoy, too, the Bagley Lakes twinkling directly below, but don't venture too close to the edge.

The trail ends at 1.5 miles on the west end of the Table top, a perfect spot for admir-ing the patterns of glacier and snow etched into Ptarmigan Ridge. Once this trail made a loop, but it involved traversing a treacherous snowfield that claimed more than a couple of hikers. Return the way you came, spellbound by Shuksan's looming presence.

EXTENDING YOUR TRIP

While you're in the neighborhood, by all means saunter along the easy 0.5-mile Artist Ridge Trail to Huntoon Point. Continue soaking up spectacular North Cascades scenery, this time with Table Mountain in the lineup. Try not to knock into anyone's tripod. A jaunt here during sunset is unforgettable.

75 Ptarmigan Ridge

RATING/ DIFFICULTY	ROUND-TRIP	ELEV GAIN/ HIGH POINT	SEASON
★★★★/4	10 miles	1300 feet/ 6200 feet	Aug– mid-Oct

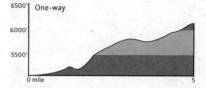

Map: Green Trails Mount Shuksan No. 14; **Contact:** Mount Baker–Snoqualmie National Forest, Glacier Public Service Center, (360) 599-2714 (summer only), or Mount Baker Ranger District, (360) 856-5700, www.fs.fed.us/r6/mbs; **Notes:** NW Forest Pass required. Road from Picture Lake to trailhead often remains snowbound into August, sometimes year-round. Ptarmigan Ridge often retains snow all season. Only hikers experienced and comfortable with snow travel should make this trip. Check with Forest Service on road and trail status; **GPS:** N 48 50.780, W 121 41.560

Travel along a rugged knolled snowy and rocky spine above glaciers and barren slopes to almost within embracing distance of majestic Baker. Across alpine tundra, and snowfields that never retreat in summer's heat, feel the pulse of the frozen volcano on this hike. But be forewarned: this trail is more of a climbers path, rough and sketchy in spots, buried beneath snow in others. Take ice ax and map and turn around when the going gets spooky. If you're prepared and conditions are good, however, your journey across Ptarmigan Ridge will be one of the most stimulating and exhilarating in your life.

Glacier-draped Mount Baker

GETTING THERE

From Bellingham follow the Mount Baker High-way (State Route 542) east for 34 miles to the Glacier Public Service Center. Drive another 25 miles to the road end at the mega parking lot for Artist Point (elev. 5140 ft). Privy available.

ON THE TRAIL

Starting on the Chain Lakes Trail, head west toward Mount Baker—ever present, ever hovering, and ever impressive, unless shrouded in fog and mist. In 0.2 mile pass the Table Mountain Trail (Hike 74) and leave some people behind. Now enjoy a near-level mile across Table's open southern slopes, admiring the snowy ridge before you and the verdant Swift Creek and Rainbow valleys below you.

At 1.2 miles reach a junction (elev. 5200 ft). The Chain Lakes Trail diverges right, along with most of the folks trailing behind you. Now off into the tundra you go, straight ahead. Drop a little, skirting beneath a snow-draped 5600-foot knoll. Soon the way heads upward again, and chances are good it'll be on fairly steep snowfields. Crest the ridgeline and continue on your way toward the North Cascades' mightiest peak. Scan the slopes below for mountain goats. Carefully inspect the wind-blasted, frost-burned ridge for its namesake, ptarmigans—chickenlike birds that live in the alpine tundra. They spend most of their lives on the ground foraging on buds, berries, and seeds.

Continue across rock, snow, the occasional meadow, every step taking you closer to the 10,778-foot volcano. Climbing higher, round a 5800-foot knoll. A mile farther, round the prominent 6414-foot Coleman Pinnacle. A popular scrambling destination, no need to go all the way to the top for good views—you've already got them!

At about 5 miles from the trailhead arrive at a flat known as Camp Kiser that sports hemlocks and colorful tents. This is the turnaround for most day hikers. Admire Rainbow Glacier in all its crevassed beauty right before you. Turn your attention southward down into a lonely basin to a beautiful sparkling tarn, just recently revealed to the world.

EXTENDING YOUR TRIP

If Ptarmigan's snowpack is low it may be possible to continue along the ridge on a sketchy track for another mile to a 6450-foot steep bluff above the Sholes Glacier and beneath the Portals. Feel the mountain breathe and catch your breath as well, it doesn't get much better than this.

76 Lake Ann

RATING/ DIFFICULTY	ROUND-TRIP	ELEV GAIN/ HIGH POINT	SEASON
★★★★/4	8.2 miles	1900 feet/ 4900 feet	Aug– mid-Oct

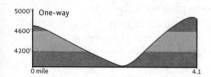

One-way

Map: Green Trails Mount Shuksan No. 14;
Contact: Mount Baker–Snoqualmie National
Forest, Glacier Public Service Center, (360)
599-2714 (summer only), or Mount Baker
Ranger District, (360) 856-5700, *www.fs.fed
.us/r6/mbs*; **Notes:** NW Forest Pass required.
Road from Picture Lake to trailhead often
remains snowbound well into August, some-
times year-round. Check with Forest Service;
GPS: N 48 51.010, W 121 41.090

*Mount Shuksan is the star on this
glorious hike. Traverse forest and
meadow, bogs and talus, all while anticipat-
ing the hidden gem of Lake Ann. And once
she's revealed—dark blue-green waters oft-
ringed in snow—her charm is enhanced
hundredfold by the awesome backdrop of
craggy, glacier-clad, 9127-foot Shuksan
hovering above.*

GETTING THERE
From Bellingham follow the Mount Baker Highway (State Route 542) east for 34 miles to the
Glacier Public Service Center. Drive another 23
miles (about 1.5 miles beyond the Mount Baker
Ski Area lodge) to Austin Pass. The trailhead is
on the left (elev. 4700 ft). Privy available.

ON THE TRAIL
This trail is living proof that statistics lie. Consider: Start at an elevation of 4700 feet. Finish

at an elevation of 4800 feet. Total elevation
gain, 100 feet? Yeah, you wish! Lake Ann will
cost you 1900 feet in gradient change, and
quite a bit of that is on the return. So keep that
in mind when toting along the little ones.

Starting in attractive forest, begin a long
descent into the Swift Creek valley. Tree cover
soon thins, revealing Shuksan looking down
on you. At 2.3 miles your downward drive bot-
toms out at a trail junction (elev. 3900 ft) set in
a lush parkland of showy flowers and babbling
creeks. The trail right heads down the Swift
Creek valley toward Baker Lake. It's obscure
and brushy, requires some difficult creek
fords, and is definitely for the adventurous.

Summer comes late at Lake Ann.

For Lake Ann continue left, climbing 1000 feet through forest, then meadow, then rock, and then on slopes that often harbor stubborn snowfields. Reach a small saddle and rejoice that your climb is finished. Rejoice, too, when you look down into the rocky and snowy basin housing Lake Ann. Descend 100 feet to the sparkling jewel and savor its beauty. Gaze across its toe-numbing waters to a row of hemlocks dwarfed by Mount Shuksan behind them. Admire Shuksan's numerous hanging glaciers, which are deeply crevassed by late summer.

Linger long enough to hear blocks of glacial ice crashing down valley floors and echoing through the wilderness. The Skagit people gave Shuksan its name, meaning "roaring mountain." A fitting name indeed.

EXTENDING YOUR TRIP

A climbers path, generally suitable for hikers continues beyond Lake Ann about 0.75 mile to pretty near the base of the Lower Curtis Glacier (elev. 5200 ft). With Baker in view, it's quite a dramatic scene.

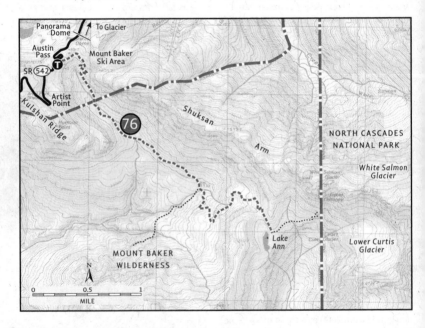

Opposite: Crater Mountain

north cascades

Cascade River

One of the great rivers of the North Cascades, the Cascade River drains an amazing array of glacier-clad craggy summits in the North Cascades National Park and adjacent Glacier Peak Wilderness. Its dramatic U-shaped glaciated valley has long been used by Native peoples, explorers, traders, and settlers as a transportation corridor across the mountains. Now a good Forest Service road winds alongside a good portion of the pristine river, allowing the only drive-in access to the North Cascades National Park.

77 Lookout Mountain and Monogram Lake

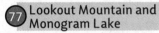

Lookout Mountain

RATING/ DIFFICULTY	ROUND-TRIP	ELEV GAIN/ HIGH POINT	SEASON
★★★★/5	9.4 miles	4470 feet/ 5719 feet	July–Oct

Monogram Lake

RATING/ DIFFICULTY	ROUND-TRIP	ELEV GAIN/ HIGH POINT	SEASON
★★★★/5	9.8 miles	4675 feet/ 5400 feet	July–Oct

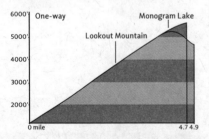

Map: Green Trails Marblemount No. 47; **Contact:** Lookout Mountain: Mount Baker–Snoqualmie National Forest, Mount Baker Ranger District, (360) 856-5700, www.fs.fed.us/r6/mbs. Monogram Lake: North Cascades National Park Visitors Center (Newhalem), (206) 386-4495, ext. 11 (summer only), or Headquarters Information Station (Sedro-Woolley), (360) 856-5700, ext. 515, www.nps.gov/noca; **Notes:** Dogs prohibited at Monogram Lake; **GPS:** N 48 32.219, W 121 17.639

⚙️ *Enjoy a spectacular view of jagged and icy peaks from a lookout on a mile-high ridge above the confluence of the Skagit and Cascade rivers. Or venture to a large alpine lake tucked in an open cirque beneath glacial Little Devil Peak on the western edge of the North Cascades National Park. Whichever destination you choose, prepare for some serious climbing. It's an arduous ascent to these awesome destinations, but worth every ounce of sweat expended.*

GETTING THERE

From Marblemount head east on the Cascade River Road for 7 miles to the trailhead, 0.5 mile beyond the national forest boundary (elev. 1250 ft). The trail begins on the north side of the road. Park in the small lot on the road's south side.

ON THE TRAIL

From the relatively low trailhead elevation of 1250 feet, waste no time reaching for the clouds. In thick timber the trail switchbacks relentlessly up a steep spine between Lookout and Monogram creeks. And while the rush of water can often be heard, the way is fairly dry—barring the sweat beading on your brow.

After incessantly climbing for 2.5 miles and 2400 vertical feet, reach a reliable creek where more than a fair number of bandanas and water bottles have been dipped. In another 0.3 mile and a few hundred feet higher, reach a junction (elev. 4000 ft). Decision time. Lake or Lookout? For most hikers, combining them is too much, warranting a return trip for the destination not chosen.

To reach Lookout Mountain, continue left. Still furiously climbing, the grade eases a little

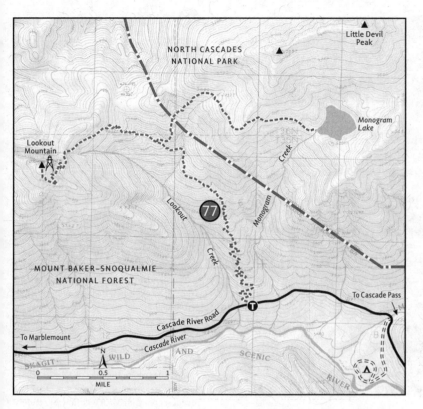

after about 0.5 mile. It's then a traverse across a steep open slope flush in brushy and flowering vegetation before making one final grunt, reaching the fire lookout on the meadowy crest of aptly named Lookout Mountain (elev. 5719 ft).

Okay, one more climb—short and sweet up the steps of the 1962 lookout to the balcony for much-deserved sun worshipping and scenery ogling. Gaze west down the Skagit Valley and up to the verdant slopes of Sauk and Bald mountains. To the south, Snowking dominates. To the east it's Teebone Ridge, Big Devil and Little Devil peaks, and Eldorado Peak stealing the show. The Pickets and a plethora of pointy peaks are what you'll see northward.

To reach Monogram Lake turn right at the junction. Continuous climbing is part of the repertoire on this route as well. Enter the national park (pooches prohibited) and, after about 1 mile and 1000 feet of climbing, cross a creek. Replenish. In another 0.3 mile or so through subalpine meadows, reach a ridge crest (elev. 5400 ft) blessed with views, including one straight down into the cirque housing Monogram Lake. Now lose a bit more than 500 feet (you'll find them on the return), reaching the lovely lake in 0.7 mile (elev. 4873 ft).

Lookout Mountain's namesake

EXTENDING YOUR TRIP

At Monogram Lake, if the shimmering waters aren't enough to satisfy your wanderlust, it's possible to scramble a ridge to the southeast, where you'll be greeted with a spectacular view of the near 9000-foot giant Eldorado. Continue higher along that ridge if you like to the 6844-foot south summit of Little Devil Peak for up-close observing of its glacial cloak. Back in the lowlands, not far from the trailhead, is the Marble Creek Campground. Set in a lush flat on the Cascade River, it makes a great base camp for exploring area trails.

78 Hidden Lake Lookout

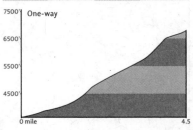

RATING/ DIFFICULTY	ROUND-TRIP	ELEV GAIN/ HIGH POINT	SEASON
★★★★★/4	9 miles	3290 feet/ 6890 feet	Late July– mid-Oct

Maps: Green Trails Diablo No. 48, Cascade Pass No. 80; **Contact:** Mount Baker–Snoqualmie National Forest, Mount Baker Ranger District, (360) 856-5700, www.*fs.fed.us/r6/mbs*; **Notes:** NW Forest Pass required. Trail can be extremely dangerous in early season, requiring ice ax and snow-travel skills; **GPS:** N 48 30.890, W 121 12.910

Simply spectacular! One of the finest hikes on the face of the planet, the trail to Hidden Lake Peaks grants continuous sensory overload. Sprawling meadows bursting with wildflowers, granite slabs and boulders laced with heather, glistening snowfields birthing tumbling waters, alpine nooks providing refuge to ptarmigans and pipits, a historical fire lookout, and views—stunning, mouth-gaping views of a serrated skyline of snow, ice, and rock. It doesn't get any better than this.

GETTING THERE

From Marblemount head east on the Cascade River Road for 9.7 miles, turning left onto Forest Road 1540 (Sibley Creek Road), 1.5 miles beyond the Marble Creek Campground entrance. Follow rough-at-times FR 1540 for 4.7 miles to its terminus and the trailhead (elev. 3600 ft).

ON THE TRAIL

After starting in a clear-cut predating common sense, the trail soon enters unmolested forest where it begins to climb steeply. At about 1 mile leave the forested canopy behind for an avalanche chute filled with alder. Cross East Fork Sibley Creek and recommence climbing. While you're traversing the steep side slope that's often brushy and overgrown, showy flowers give some consolation as you slog. Biting flies, however, may diminish the blossom bonus.

At 2.5 miles the trail recrosses the creek (elev. 5200 ft) and begins angling south. Stop to admire Mount Baker hovering in the western sky. Now across heather slopes punctuated with shiny granite slabs funneling cascading snowmelt, enjoy increasing views and an alpine wonderland intensifying in beauty.

At 3 miles a potential hazard may exist. Early season, or some years all summer, a treacherously steep snow gully may be present. Extremely dangerous to cross without ice ax and appropriate skills, it may be necessary to call it quits, taking solace in prudence and a decent hike even to this point. If the coast is clear, proceed, enjoying heather meadows,

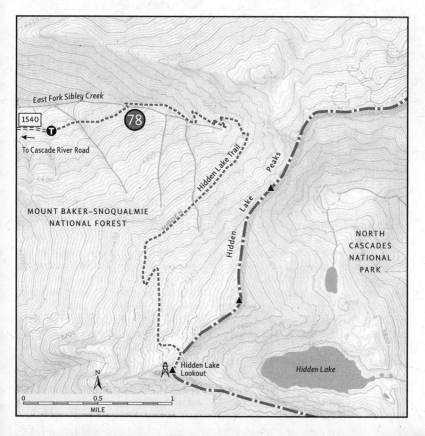

Frozen Hidden Lake

glacier lily fields, snowfields dyed red (thanks to an algae), unhindered Cascade mountain views west and south, and territorial views of Hidden Lake Peaks to the east.

At 4.2 miles attain a 6600-foot saddle (and the North Cascades National Park boundary) between the 7088-foot true summit of Hidden Lake Peaks (to the left and a fairly easy scramble) and the 6890-foot knoll with the lookout (to the right). Hidden Lake is just below, a glorious backcountry body of water, its azure waters shimmering in the sun. It's a rough-and-tumble drop of 800 feet through talus to reach it. Instead, enjoy its beauty from above and the framing backdrop of impressive North Cascades summits—Eldorado, Forbidden, and Boston among them.

To reach the lookout, follow the trail right for 0.3 mile, climbing 300 feet over ledge and rock and possibly snow (use caution). Wow! Drink in views from Rainier to Baker and every peak, valley, and ridge between. Take time to appreciate the lookout too. Built in 1931, it was restored by Fred T. Darvill of the Skagit Alpine Club back in 1961. A tireless advocate for the North Cascades National Park, Darvill, who passed away in 2007, was the writer of an early guidebook that introduced me to this region back in 1985.

79 Middle and South Fork Cascade River

Middle Fork

RATING/ DIFFICULTY	ROUND-TRIP	ELEV GAIN/ HIGH POINT	SEASON
★★/3	10 miles	1500 feet/ 3200 feet	Late May– early Nov

South Fork

RATING/ DIFFICULTY	ROUND-TRIP	ELEV GAIN/ HIGH POINT	SEASON
★★/3	9 miles	500 feet/ 2200 feet	Aug–Oct

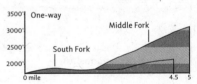

Map: Green Trails Cascade Pass No. 80; **Contact:** Mount Baker–Snoqualmie National Forest, Mount Baker Ranger District, (360) 856-5700, *www.fs.fed.us/r6/mbs*; **Notes:** NW Forest Pass required. Bridge out on South Fork Trail, requiring difficult ford of the Middle Fork, dangerous in early season and during heavy rains; **GPS:** N 48 27.907, W 121 09.365

 Glacier-fed, free-flowing, and surrounded by a fortress of jagged peaks glistening with snow and ice, the forks of the Cascade are classic North Cas-

cades rivers. *The Cascade River Road keeps the North Fork company, but the South and Middle Forks remain wild and lonely. The trails up these wilderness valleys are rough, neglected by land managers and hammered by nature. If it's solitude you seek, you'll find it here—but you'll have to work a little for it.*

GETTING THERE

From Marblemount head east on the Cascade River Road for 16 miles to the Mineral Park Campground (the pavement ends after 10 miles). Continue for 0.7 mile to where the road makes a sharp turn left at gated FR 1590. Park here. The hike starts out along FR 1590 (elev. 1700 ft).

ON THE TRAIL

Nature is constantly in flux. Along the South and Middle Forks of the Cascade River the forces of nature are evident. Primeval forests grace most of the region. But a forest fire ravaged the confluence area in 2003. Even here along the wet and saturated west slope of the Cascades, fire plays an important role in succession. While lovers of nature may not exactly find the charred, denuded, and befallen giants aesthetically pleasing, they should still stand in awe at the aftermath of such a landscape-altering event. The forest will come back. It already has in part. Whether the trail comes back, however, is another matter. Before the fire, these two trails received very little maintenance and were in danger of disappearing. That would be a shame. We've already lost plenty of miles of trail in the adjacent valleys and on nearby ridges.

Start your hike by heading up FR 1590. Before 2003 this road was on its way to becoming a trail. The Forest Service "reopened" it for fire crews. Surely the Forest Service can help "reopen" the trails too. After 0.5 mile of easy walking, come to Pincer Creek, which in early

season may be difficult to cross. Shortly afterward enter the burn area.

At 1.4 miles reach the end of the road (elev. 1800 ft). The trail takes off into a stand of old cedars that miraculously survived the wildfire. High above the roaring river, the way winds across a steep forested ridge. Soon enough, the burn zone is reentered. Until this trail is rehabilitated, expect rough going. Lots of big downed trees and slumped tread make travel extremely difficult in spots.

The trail drops down to river level near the confluence of the forks and once again enters spared forest. At 2 miles reach a signed junction. Left (Trail No. 767) leads back into the burn, climbing a steep hillside to follow the

Fire-spared trail sign

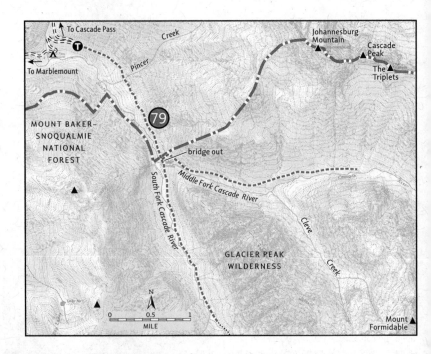

Middle Fork. The way involves very difficult routefinding until old growth is once again reached. From there the trail continues about 3 miles, ending in a tangle of brush in a series of avalanche slopes at the base of 7428-foot Cascade Peak.

The better choice is to continue straight on the South Fork Trail (No. 769), but you'll need to ford the Middle Fork, near impossible in high water. Scout around for a strategically fallen tree. Once across, enjoy 2.5 miles of splendid riverside rambling under a magnificent canopy of ancient timber. Enjoy, too, occasional glimpses of the majestic peaks and ridges lining the valley. Decent tread ends 2.5 miles from the confluence. Beyond, a path of sorts exists for 6 miles, used primarily by climbers, loners, and critters on their way to South Cascade Lake.

EXTENDING YOUR TRIP

The nearby Kindy Creek Trail is another spectacularly beautiful hike through a lonely valley that the Forest Service has stopped maintaining. You can still follow this path for about 2 miles through some of the most spectacular old growth around. However, to reach the trail a very difficult ford of Kindy Creek is first required. Just down the road is the Mineral Park Campground, a great place for bedding down for the night in scenic riverside sites.

80 Cascade Pass and Sahale Arm

RATING/ DIFFICULTY	ROUND-TRIP	ELEV GAIN/ HIGH POINT	SEASON
★★★★★/4	12 miles	3600 feet/ 7200 feet	July– mid-Oct

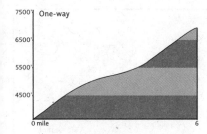

Map: Green Trails Cascade Pass No. 80; **Contact:** North Cascades National Park Visitors Center (Newhalem), (206) 386-4495, ext. 11 (summer only), or Headquarters Information Station (Sedro-Woolley), (360) 856-5700, ext. 515, *www.nps.gov/noca*; **Notes:** Dogs prohibited; **GPS:** N 48 28.490, W 121 04.410

This is one of the most scenic, most accessible (including for kids, at least to the pass), and not surprisingly the most crowded high-country romps in the North Cascades—and the only trailhead in the 684,000-acre North Cascades National Park that you can drive to. Mixed in with the throngs of Puget Sound hikers are folks from Munich, Tokyo, and Kalamazoo. And none of them return disappointed after frolicking among fields of flowers, peaks of ice, and boulders bearing basking marmots— some of the most outstanding alpine landscapes to be found anywhere in the world.

GETTING THERE
From Marblemount head east on the Cascade River Road for 23 miles all the way to its end at the trailhead (elevation 3600 ft). Privy available.

ON THE TRAIL
Long used by Native Americans, explorers, prospectors, and surveyors, this relatively low pass was a wise choice for passage through the North Cascades. And it was once considered by railroad and highway planners too. Thank-

fully it will remain trail, protected as wilderness within a national park. But despite its wilderness status, this special place needs your care. Stay on established trails, or when you choose to veer off keep your boots on snow and rock, not fragile heather and alpine vegetation.

Pelton Creek valley

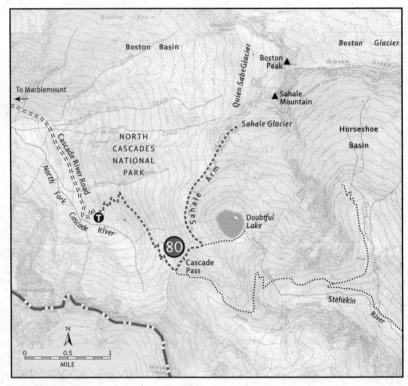

The views are amazing before you even hit the trail. To the south, the fierce face of Johannesburg Mountain peers down at you as you lace up, periodically shedding shards of ice to the valley floor from its hanging glaciers. Stop staring and hit the trail—it gets better. The trail starts by switchbacking some thirty times on a forested rib to propel you high above the avalanche-debris-littered valley floor.

After climbing 1400 feet in the first 2 miles or so, the grade eases, making a long traverse toward the pass, breezing by meadows, talus, and the occasional lingering snowfield en route. Johannesburg's equally fierce neighbors introduce themselves: Cascade Peak, Mix-up Peak, and The Triplets. At 3.7 miles

reach the heather parklands of Cascade Pass (elev. 5400 ft), a perfectly fine place to call it a day. But if the prospects of going higher and farther tempt you, carry on.

Locate the trail for Sahale Arm that takes off north just a short way east of the pass. Prepare to get down to business. Beat to the ground by climbers, the trail wastes no time, gaining about 800 feet in 1 rocky and steep mile. Reach a junction (elev. 6200 ft) with a trail heading right, bound for Doubtful Lake and losing all of that hard-earned elevation gain.

The trail left to Sahale Arm, however, is nothing but pure delight from this point. Follow the path upward through rolling meadow and alpine tundra while peeping pipits and whistling pigs (marmots) announce your arrival. Hike all the way to the toe of Sahale Glacier at 7200 feet (but not on it—that's for equipped climbers) or until snowfields block passage. You may have to overcome panorama paralysis, a condition known to stop hikers dead in their tracks when barraged by boundless beauty.

Don't fight it. Look north to 8484-foot Sahale Mountain's glistening glacier; south to the sheer vertical walls of Johannesburg and company clad in hanging glaciers; east down the lush Stehekin River valley, with McGregor Mountain standing proud and Doubtful Lake below; and west to Hidden Lake Peaks, Eldorado Peak, and Mount Torment.

EXTENDING YOUR TRIP

The 1-mile hike down to Doubtful Lake is definitely worth the effort. The trail drops 800 feet to a deep waterfall-streaked cirque housing the sparkling lake. Look for old mine shafts and debris. Doubtful you'll have any company here. Nearby Boston Basin makes for a worthy return trip to the area. Find the "trailhead" (an old mining road) 0.5 mile west from the Cascade Pass trailhead. Primarily a climbers path, the trail to beautiful-beyond-words Boston Basin travels 4 very difficult miles and gains 3200 feet of elevation. Raging creeks need to be crossed and a few vegetation belays (using trees to hoist yourself up) are required along the way.

PRESERVING AMERICA'S ALPS

On October 2, 1968, President Lyndon B. Johnson signed into law a bill establishing the North Cascades National Park and adjacent Lake Chelan and Ross Lake National Recreation Areas. Today, nearly 93 percent of the North Cascades National Park Complex is comprised of federal wilderness, to be managed in an untrammeled state. A cause for celebration among the conservation and hiking communities, establishment of America's thirty-fourth national park was no slam dunk.

Though the park was originally proposed by the Portland, Oregon–based Mazama hiking club in 1906, there was little threat to the greater North Cascades ecosystem at that time. In 1937 the U.S. Department of Interior (which administers the Park Service) agreed that the North Cascades were of national park caliber. However, no action was taken. By this time the region's great river, the Skagit, sported two dams with another on the way—it was wild no more.

By the 1950s and '60s, mining and timber interests, especially the latter, were well entrenched in the region, and roads pushed deep into the wilderness. One of America's largest remaining roadless areas was in danger of being seriously and irreparably destroyed.

In 1956 a group of concerned citizens, including guidebook pioneers Harvey Manning and Ira Spring, formed the North Cascades Conservation Council intent on finally establishing a national park in the region. Republican congressman Thomas Pelly of Washington introduced a bill that year that failed. The council, however, continuously campaigned and lobbied for a park, partly through books intended to make people aware of what was at stake. The group's tireless efforts came to fruition in 1968 when the state's Democratic senator Henry "Scoop" Jackson and Democratic congressman Lloyd Meeds successfully pushed through bills for establishing the park. Forty years later we continue to enjoy that legacy.

North Cascades Highway

Completed in 1972, the North Cascades Highway (State Route 20) is not only one of the most scenic stretches of pavement ever laid in America, but is also the only road to cross the rugged North Cascades—and that's for only half the year. Usually closed from late November to early April because of heavy avalanche activity, the road when open provides easy access to a wide range of trails. The entire highway from Sedro-Woolley to Winthrop (132 miles) is classified as a National Scenic Byway, and the corridor from the company town of Newhalem to just outside the berg of Mazama (60 miles) is administered by the Park Service and the Forest Service as a scenic corridor. Within this stretch of highway, other than a couple of campgrounds, scenic overlooks, and more than a dozen trailheads, there are no services or development. It's as wild as a highway can be.

81 Thornton Lakes and Trappers Peak

Thornton Lakes

RATING/ DIFFICULTY	ROUND-TRIP	ELEV GAIN/ HIGH POINT	SEASON
★★★★★/5	10.2 miles	2900 feet/ 5000 feet	Mid-July– Oct

Trappers Peak

RATING/ DIFFICULTY	ROUND-TRIP	ELEV GAIN/ HIGH POINT	SEASON
★★★★★/5	10.6 miles	3300 feet/ 5964 feet	Mid-July– Oct

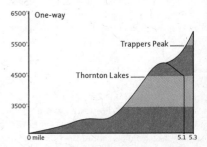

The Picket Range

Map: Green Trails Marblemount No. 47; **Contact:** North Cascades National Park Visitors Center (Newhalem), (206) 386-4495, ext. 11 (summer only), or Headquarters Information Station (Sedro-Woolley), (360) 856-5700, ext. 515, *www.nps.gov/noca*; **Notes:** Dogs prohibited; **GPS:** N 48 39.220, W 121 19.450

Hike to the largest of three gorgeous backcountry lakes set in deep scoured cirques, or

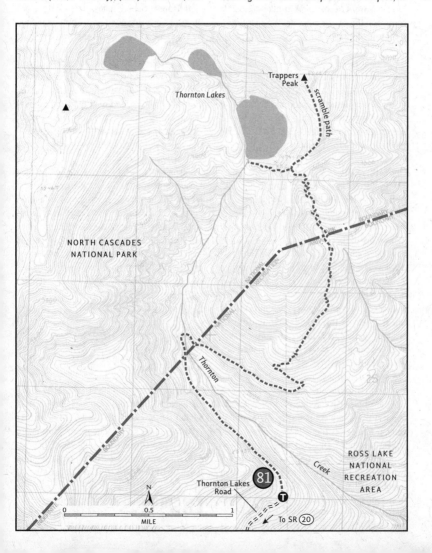

scramble up a narrow spine to Trappers Peak to snag some of the best alpine viewing this side of the Continental Divide. Both destinations will cost you dearly in caloric output. Lots of elevation gain over steep and rough terrain is what keeps this day-hike-accessible corner of the North Cascades National Park from being overrun.

GETTING THERE

From Marblemount follow the North Cascades Highway (State Route 20) east for 11 miles, turning left onto Thornton Lakes Road between mileposts 117 and 118. Continue on this rough-at-times gravel road 5 miles to the trailhead at the road end (elev. 2600 ft).

ON THE TRAIL

The trail starts at the edge of a huge clear-cut from the early 1960s. If the North Cascades National Park hadn't been created in 1968, you could bet your weight in sawdust that many more of these surrounding slopes would have been severely scarred. Begin on decommissioned logging road-turned-trail and hike 2.3 easy miles, crossing Thornton and a few minor creeks en route.

After gaining only a couple of hundred feet, the trail leaves the old roadbed and heads straight up deeply forested and mucky-at-times slopes. Never commissioned by the Parks Service, this trail was beaten into the ground long ago by anglers lured in by the three Thornton gems.

Enter the North Cascades National Park at about 4 miles and continue steeply climbing, coming to a 5000-foot saddle and trail junction at 4.5 miles. Decision time. Should you head left to the lake basin, dropping 500 feet (which you'll need to regain on the return) in 0.6 mile, or climb another 900 feet in 0.8 mile to the peak? Either way, you have to climb some more.

The lake trail ends at the rocky outlet of the largest and lowest of the Thorntons (elev. 4500 ft), in a cirque that doesn't leave much room for spreading out. The other two lakes require challenging cross-country travel, so break out the snacks and be content at the first lake.

If Trapper bound, follow the trail right, another never-sanctioned path, this one beaten by climbers up, up, and away. The going gets steep along a narrow ridge, and at times requires the help of hands. It's not exposed, though, and not particularly difficult for seasoned hikers. From the 5964-foot summit, find yourself a nice rock to rest upon and prepare for an onslaught of sensory overload. One of the most awesome ranges in the Cascades—the sheer and jagged Pickets—charge across the northern horizon.

Shimmering directly below are the Thornton Lakes. Directly above them, glacier-decorated Mount Triumph stands victoriously. To the south 1 vertical mile below, the Skagit River slices through steep verdant slopes, the little company town of Newhalem perched quaintly upon its banks. Get the topo maps out as you twirl round and round. There's a whole lot of gorgeous country screaming out at you.

82 Skagit River

RATING/ DIFFICULTY	ROUND-TRIP	ELEV GAIN/ HIGH POINT	SEASON
★★/1	1.8 miles	100 feet/ 575 feet	Year-round

Map: Green Trails Marblemount No. 47; **Contact:** North Cascades National Park Visitors Center (Newhalem), (206) 386-4495, ext. 11 (summer only), or Headquarters Information Station (Sedro-Woolley), (360) 856-5700, ext. 515, www.nps.gov/noca; **Notes:** Dogs must be leashed; **GPS:** N 48 39.951, W 121 16.011

Enjoy a carefree saunter under big timber along a mighty river on this easy and delightful trail. Perfect for

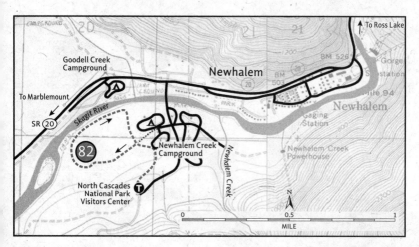

lazy summer evenings or quiet winter days, the Skagit River Loop can be enjoyed by all hikers, from the very young to the young at heart. While away the time on a sunny gravel bar or hike all day on the adjoining paths of Newhalem's network of nature trails.

GETTING THERE

From Marblemount follow the North Cascades Highway (State Route 20) east for 14 miles to Newhalem. Turn right on the access road to the Newhalem Creek Campground and the national park visitors center. Cross the Skagit River, pass the campground booth, and in 0.25 mile come to a four-way stop. Continue straight ahead for 0.6 mile, reaching a large parking area for the visitors center. The trail begins behind the northeast corner of the center. Water and restrooms available.

ON THE TRAIL

Leave the hubbub of the visitors center for the peaceful allure of forest. On a wide and well-tended path, begin a slow descent of 75 feet or so to a nearly level bottomland flush with cedars, firs, ferns, and salal. In 0.25 mile pass a side trail leading to one of

the Newhalem Creek Campground's attractive loops.

If you pass by in summer, the air will be filled with the sounds of joyous campers banging tent stakes, rattling tin pans, and chopping firewood. If you're here during winter, the soothing sounds of water take over, from the Skagit's distant roar to a procession of raindrops dripping on leathery and decaying leaves.

Soon reach a major junction. Right heads to the campground, and you'll be returning from straight ahead. Head left on the straight path, cutting through a pine barren. Notice remnant logging roads along the way, evidence of the Forest Service's stewardship before the Park Service inherited these lands in 1968.

The trail soon drops a little more. After you cross a moist flat of mossy maples and yews, the Skagit River finally comes into view (poetic, huh?). Now enjoy a riverside ramble. Sun kissed gravel bars invite lingering. Look for otters, eagle, dippers, and salmon. Marvel at the towering ancient firs and cedars gracing the riverbanks. When it's time to return, continue the loop, avoiding all side trails left— unless you happen to be camping here for the night, in which case linger a little longer.

EXTENDING YOUR TRIP
The adjacent Newhalem Creek Campground makes a wonderful place to explore from. Be sure to allot time for the visitors center exhibits too. Consider sampling some of the nearby nature trails connecting the campground to Newhalem village. Some are wheelchair accessible. Looking for something longer and wilder? The Newhalem Creek Trail south of the visitors center follows an old road for more than 4 miles into the North Cascades National Park wilds. The way can be rough going and very brushy. A better choice is the Stetattle Creek Trail from Diablo Village (6 miles east of Newhalem). This semimaintained and slightly less brushy trail heads 4 miles into the northern half of the national park, solitude guaranteed.

83 Sourdough Mountain

RATING/ DIFFICULTY	ROUND-TRIP	ELEV GAIN/ HIGH POINT	SEASON
★★★★★/5	11 miles	5085 feet/ 5985 feet	Late June–Oct

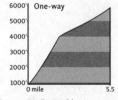

Map: Green Trails Diablo No. 48; **Contact:** North Cascades National Park Visitors Center (Newhalem), (206) 386-4495, ext. 11 (summer only), or Headquarters Information Station (Sedro-Woolley), (360) 856-5700, ext. 515, www.nps.gov/noca; **Notes:** Dogs prohibited; **GPS:** N 48 43.072, W 121 08.730

Grueling is the hike. Awesome are the views. Supreme is the experience. One of the most challenging trails in the North Cascades, the arduous haul to the historical lookout atop Sourdough Mountain is worth every ounce of sweat you'll expend. And you'll expend plenty. A mile straight up and 5.5 on the ground—can you say steep? But a priceless panorama of craggy, spiraling, glacier-hugging, cloud-piercing, unbelievably breathtaking peaks are the payoff. And directly below is an added dividend—Diablo Lake's surreally turquoise-tinted waters.

GETTING THERE
From Marblemount follow the North Cascades Highway (State Route 20) east for 20 miles. Turn left onto Diablo Road (just before the bridge over Gorge Lake) and proceed 0.7 mile, crossing an iron bridge that spans Stetattle Creek. Bear right and reach the trailhead in 0.25 mile (elev. 900 ft). Park on the right side of the road. The trail begins on the opposite side, near the tennis courts.

ON THE TRAIL
From the lowly trailhead elevation, waste no time heading for the heavens. In thick timber switchback relentlessly, gaining 3000 feet in the first 2 miles. As you approach the North Cascades National Park, the grade eases somewhat, but it's still a bear. Thinning forest provides sneak peeks of surrounding peaks, a much needed enticement to push on.

At 4 miles (elev. 5000 ft) Sourdough Creek's cascading waters are a welcome sight, as more than likely your water supply is nearly spent. Hop across the energy-recharging creek and begin reaping the long-anticipated rewards of this hike. Traversing subalpine forest groves and sprawling meadows bursting with wildflowers, finally start enjoying your journey.

In-your-face views of Ruby Mountain, Pyramid Peak, and Colonial Peak and its massive

Opposite: Skagit River

glacier knock what little breath you have left right out of you. Diablo Lake's turquoise waters twinkle 1 mile directly below. One last set of switchbacks is all that's left between you and the lookout.

Reach the broad summit ridge of Sourdough Mountain and dart across lingering snowfields. Behold nearly the entire North Cascades kingdom before you. To the north are Mount Prophet, Hozomeen Mountain, Ross Lake, and the wilds of British Columbia. At nearly 9000 feet, Jack Mountain dominates the eastern horizon. To the south it's Colonial Peak and company, while the Picket Range commands your attention to the west.

The fire lookout was constructed in 1933 and is listed on the National Historical Lookout Register. It's still staffed in the summer. With Old Glory flapping defiantly in the mountain breezes, it is a sentry post bordering America's wild backcountry. Beatnik poet Philip Whalen worked a couple of summers on Sourdough as a lookout back in the 1950s (see "Poem on the Range" in this section). Talk about the ideal work environment! Linger long and rest up for the knee-jarring descent.

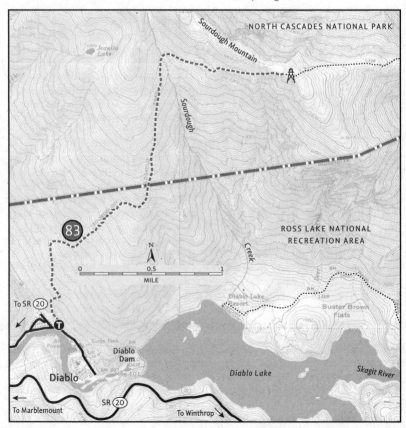

Diablo Lake is one mile below.

EXTENDING YOUR TRIP

A lightly used trail descends Sourdough's eastern slopes to reach the Big Beaver Trail at Ross Lake in 5 miles. A loop of about 19 miles can be made by following Big Beaver Trail to Ross Dam and then taking the Diablo Lake Trail back to the trailhead. Routefinding skills are necessary for the descent. Experienced off-trail travelers may want to roam northwest along Sourdough's broad summit ridge. Enjoy views down to Sourdough Lake set in a lonely basin.

84 Diablo Lake

RATING/ DIFFICULTY	ROUND-TRIP	ELEV GAIN/ HIGH POINT	SEASON
★★★/2	7.5 miles	1400 feet/ 1950 feet	Apr–Nov

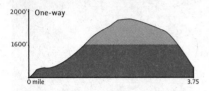

Map: Green Trails Diablo No. 48; **Contact:** North Cascades National Park Visitors Center (Newhalem), (206) 386-4495, ext. 11 (summer only), or Headquarters Information Station (Sedro-Woolley), (360) 856-5700, ext. 515, www.nps.gov/noca; **Notes:** Dogs must be leashed. Access road gated at 4:15 PM during winter; **GPS:** N 48 43.172, W 121 07.191

Okay, it's not a natural lake. Formed when the waters of the mighty Skagit were dammed back in the 1920s to power the ever-growing city of Seattle, Diablo Lake is still a hell of a beautiful body of water. Filled with glacial flour from Thunder Creek, the lake becomes turquoise when the sun's rays glance off the suspended particles. But even more impressive than the lake's greenish-blue waters are the mighty mountains it reflects and the deep canyon hidden at its eastern end. The trip overlooking Diablo Lake is full of surprises and it's no devil of a hike.

GETTING THERE

From Marblemount follow the North Cascades Highway (State Route 20) east for 20 miles to Gorge Lake Bridge (just after the intersection with Diablo Road). Continue for another 1.5 miles, turning left onto the Diablo Dam Road (signed for the North Cascades

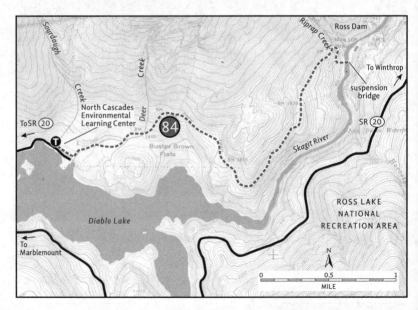

Environmental Learning Center). Proceed on this narrow road, crossing the Diablo Dam, and in 1.2 miles come to the trailhead at the road end (elev. 1200 ft).

ON THE TRAIL

Leave the scenic lakeside parking area, briefly following alongside tumbling Sourdough Creek. You'll traverse dry Douglas-fir forest (Diablo lies in a mini rain shadow) and cross former creek beds as the trail skirts the North Cascades Environmental Learning Center (www.ncascades.org). The center opened in 2005 and is a nonprofit educational institute serving learners of all ages.

Come to Deer Creek in an alder flat in 0.3 mile. Follow alongside the gentle waterway in a cool glen and cross the creek several times before beginning to climb up a salal-saturated slope. More former creek beds and old slides are encountered. At 1 mile traverse the first of several talus slopes. Good tread and a fairly easy grade ensure enjoyable walking.

At 1.5 miles a short spur leads to the right to a viewing area in a powerline clearing (elev. 1750 ft). The view is better in another 0.25 mile along the main trail. Gaze south to the prominent peaks Pyramid, Snowfield, and Colonial and east to Davis Peak hovering above Diablo Lake. From here the trail gains a couple of hundred feet more and then teeters on the edge of a spectacular gorge. Keep children and pooches nearby. Stare down the forbidding canyon walls and marvel at the waterfalls plummeting 700-plus feet down them.

Directly across the gorge, cars whirl by on the North Cascades Highway. See what they're missing? Hike this way in early spring when the highway is closed to cross-Cascades traffic and enjoy only the sounds of crashing water.

At 2.5 miles the way begins to descend. Pause at a clearing thanks to transmission lines and take in a fine view of Ross Dam and majestic Jack Mountain rising behind it. This

Ross Lake Dam

is a good spot to turn around if you want to avoid a climb on the return; otherwise, begin losing 650 feet. Cross a series of creeks, one at the foot of an avalanche slope (dangerous in winter), and a side trail with a close-up view of Ross Dam before coming to a neat suspension bridge spanning the Skagit.

Have lunch with the Canada geese on the grassy lawn before heading back. You may even find that you also have some human company. During the summer months a passenger ferry run by Seattle City Light journeys up the lake to this point from docks near the trailhead. A nice option is to take the scenic cruise one-way (departs at 8:30 and 3:00 AM PM) then hike back to your vehicle.

85 Pyramid Lake

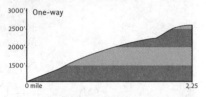

RATING/ DIFFICULTY	ROUND-TRIP	ELEV GAIN/ HIGH POINT	SEASON
★/2	4.5 miles	1500 feet/ 2600 feet	Late Apr– Nov

Giant ancient cedar

Map: Green Trails Diablo No. 48; **Contact:** North Cascades National Park Visitors Center (Newhalem), (206) 386-4495, ext. 11 (summer only), or Headquarters Information Station (Sedro-Woolley), (360) 856-5700, ext. 515, *www.nps.gov/noca*; **Notes:** Dogs must be leashed; **GPS:** N 48 42.590, W 121 08.710

Do this hike not for the destination, but for the journey. "Lake" is an overstatement. Pond, maybe, but Pyramid Puddle is more like it. Still, this easily accessible trail gets a fair amount of traffic, as it makes for a good spring conditioner or late-fall snow prober. And while Pyramid Lake is tiny, some of the trees along the way are anything but small. The real allure of this trail is the impressive old-growth forest it traverses, compensating for any lake letdown.

GETTING THERE

From Marblemount follow the North Cascades Highway (State Route 20) east for 20 miles to Gorge Lake Bridge (just after the intersection with Diablo Road). Continue for another 0.75 mile to the trailhead, on your right (elev. 1100 ft). Park on the left side of the road just beyond.

ON THE TRAIL

The trail starts right beside Pyramid Creek. Catch its cool breezes, and then immediately get to work climbing. Under a thin canopy of lodgepole pine, work your way up a ledge. It's slow going, with roots, loose rocks, and tread-choking salal. Hang in there—it gets better.

Marching up a rib above the crashing creek, periodically peer over your shoulder through the sparse forest cover for glimpses of Davis Peak and Sourdough Mountain across the Skagit Valley. After about 1 mile the pine and fir forest transitions to mature hemlocks. Come to a branch of Pyramid Creek (elev. 1700 ft) and hop across it to a beautiful cedar grove.

Now alongside the babbling waterway,

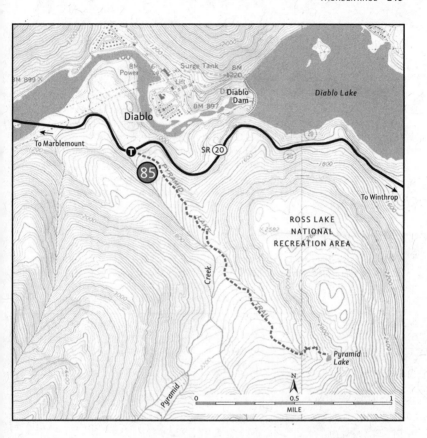

continue climbing. Towering ancient cedars and Douglas-fir soon humble your stature. Make one final grunt, crossing the babbling creek once more to arrive at puny Pyramid Lake shortly afterward. Not much, huh? Actually, there is if you look at this body of water through ecological instead of aesthetic eyes. Rough-skinned newts, those adorable amphibians of the Northwest, thrive here. Look for them floating near the surface and hiding in the detritus. And those big ol' logs floating in the lake harbor scads of sundew, a carnivorous plant. No need for you or the newts to worry, though—they prefer insects.

If after observing some of nature's fascinating creations, you still desire a view, try wiggling around the lakeshore a bit and you may catch a glimpse or two of not-so-puny Pyramid Peak poking out above.

86 Thunder Knob

RATING/ DIFFICULTY	ROUND-TRIP	ELEV GAIN/ HIGH POINT	SEASON
★★/2	3.8 miles	635 feet/ 1875 feet	Year-round

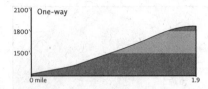

One-way

2100'
1800'
1500'

0 mile — 1.9

Map: Green Trails Diablo No. 48; **Contact:** North Cascades National Park Visitors Center (Newhalem), (206) 386-4495, ext. 11 (summer only), or Headquarters Information Station (Sedro-Woolley), (360) 856-5700, ext. 515, *www.nps.gov/noca*; **Notes:** Dogs must be leashed; **GPS:** N 48 41.430, W 121 05.878

From popular Colonial Creek Campground in the Ross Lake National Recreation Area, this short and easy hike takes off for a promontory high above manmade Diablo Lake. A series of

overlooks along the way allows you to admire the surrounding majestic North Cascades summits hovering above, or to marvel at the blue-green waters of the glacier-fed lake twinkling below. Thunder Knob makes a perfect family-friendly hike if you're camping below, or a great leg stretcher if you're traveling through on the North Cascades Highway. The trail is all accessible too, meaning outdoor lovers confined to wheelchairs can also enjoy this hike. And due to its low elevation, it rarely snows on the knob, allowing for winter rambling in the heart of the North Cascades National Park Complex.

GETTING THERE

From Marblemount follow the North Cascades Highway (State Route 20) east for 24 miles. Just past milepost 130, turn left at the Colonial Creek Campground, but don't pull

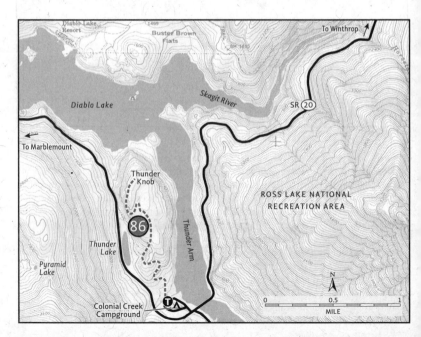

Snow-capped Davis Peak and Diablo Lake

into the campground. Trailhead parking is just to the right of the entrance (elev. 1240 ft). Water and restrooms available.

ON THE TRAIL

Begin by walking up the campground road to the trailhead. Via log bridges cross a series of channels cut by Colonial Creek when it jumped its banks in 2003, slicing through the campground and destroying several of my personal favorite car-camping sites in the state. On my very first trip to the North Cascades—back in the summer of 1985, traveling all the way from the East Coast—I camped here. I lament the destruction in one of my favorite retreats, but admire the power and fury of nature. The creek will undoubtedly change course again—nature is dynamic, ever changing, ever in flux.

After crossing the braided creek come to a wide, dry rocky channel. This is the former creek bed, the one I used to camp by. Now enter a forest of mature hemlocks. Weaving around moss-covered ledges and parting a sea of salal, the wide and well-groomed trail gently works its way up Thunder Knob. Watch the forest transition to one dominated by lodgepole pine. If the terrain surrounding you suddenly seems drier—it is. You're in a small rain shadow. The towering cloud-piercing peaks help catch and wring out passing rain clouds, providing a little reprieve from precipitation.

In about 1 mile come to the first of several lookout spots complete with resting benches. Gaze south to Colonial Peak with its large alpine glacier, the source for the campsite-consuming Colonial Creek. Continue easy climbing before dropping slightly into a marshy depression. In ten more minutes reach the broad apex of the knob. A short spur path leads left to an impressive view out over Diablo Lake to Davis Peak, the McMillan Spires, and the narrow Stetattle Creek valley. Sourdough Mountain sticks its west end into the frame.

Continue a couple of hundred feet to the end of the main trail to yet another viewpoint, this one offering a glimpse of massive Jack Mountain, the supreme summit of the Skagit Valley.

EXTENDING YOUR TRIP

Colonial Creek Campground is an excellent base for exploring area trails. The Thunder Creek Trail (Hike 87) begins at the south end of the campground.

87 Thunder Creek

RATING/ DIFFICULTY	ROUND-TRIP	ELEV GAIN/ HIGH POINT	SEASON
★★★/3	12 miles	650 feet/ 1900 feet	Apr–Nov

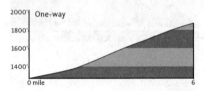

One-way

Map: Green Trails Diablo No. 48; **Contact:** North Cascades National Park Visitors Center (Newhalem), (206) 386-4495, ext. 11 (summer only), or Headquarters Information Station (Sedro-Woolley), (360) 856-5700, ext. 515, www.nps.gov/noca; **Notes:** Dogs must be leashed; **GPS:** N 48 41.131, W 121 05.550

Hike one of the deepest, wildest, and most accessible wilderness valleys in the North Cascades National Park Complex. Let Thunder Creek's incessant bellowing woo you into this primeval pocket. Enjoy scenic creekside resting posts perfect for whiling away the afternoon. Admire ancient cedars and towering firs and, from holes in the thick forest canopy, gaze out to jagged peaks cloaked in glacial ice. And while the surrounding high country is blanketed in white, enjoy this hike early or late in the season thanks to its low elevation.

GETTING THERE

From Marblemount follow the North Cascades Highway (State Route 20) east for 24 miles. Just past milepost 130, turn right into the Colonial Creek Campground and proceed 0.5 mile to the trailhead, near the amphitheater at the day-use area (elev. 1250 ft). Water and restrooms available.

ON THE TRAIL

A large information board greets you at the trailhead and it's worth a gander before setting out up the valley. Yes, this is cougar country and necessary precautions should be exercised (see "This Is Cougar Country" in the introduction). But for your first mile or two, you'll probably need to be more concerned with saying hello to the throngs of people who venture out from the campground.

The wide, smooth trail immediately enters an impressive stand of old-growth forest. Hugging the thickly forested shore of Thunder Arm, an aquatic protrusion of Diablo Lake, the trail passes the Thunder Woods Nature Trail, a recommended diversion. On still mornings and evenings, catch glimpses of emerald ridges reflected in the placid turquoise waters of Thunder Arm.

Continue on a near-level course under giant firs and cedars and past big boughs of ferns, reaching Thunder Creek in about 1 mile. Soon new tread is encountered where the trail was rerouted in 2004. The old steel suspension bridge that once crossed Thunder Creek and that many hikers thought was sturdy and reliable evidently wasn't. The destructive floods of 2003 claimed this span along with many others throughout the Cascades and Olympic Mountains.

Continue alongside the west side of the creek, passing several inviting gravel bars. At 2 miles the trail comes to a new bridge, one that I and many others hope is sturdier and more reliable than the old one. Pass through

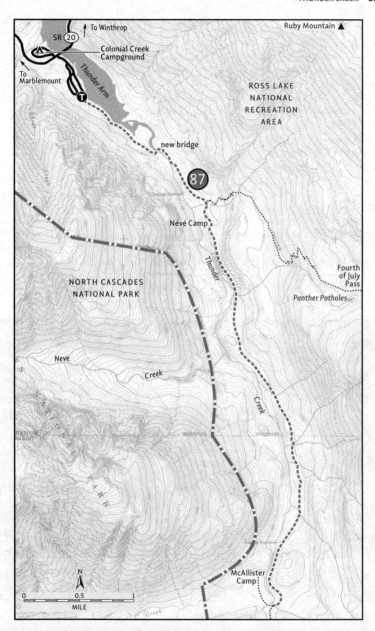

Thunder Camp, set in a centuries-old grove of behemoth firs.

Leaving the riverside, the trail now travels through a much younger forest and at 2.5 miles comes to a junction with the Fourth of July Pass Trail. Proceed right, cross a creek, and in 2.8 miles come to a junction with a short side trail that drops back to the river, landing in Névé Camp—a nice place to call it quits if you're content not to carry on.

Those inclined to experience more of the Thunder Creek valley can continue following the trail deeper into the wilderness. The thundering waterway is nearby the trail, always audible but not seen. Undulate between old-growth groves and younger forests that are replacing stands scorched by fires over the last few decades. Enjoy periodic openings in the dense canopy and impressive views of the array of towering peaks that line the valley. Their extensive glacial systems help feed the roaring creek beside you.

At 6 miles and only 1900 feet elevation, come to the junction with the side trail to McAllister Camp. This is a good place to call it a day, though you may still want to push the 0.5 mile to the camp to get a good glimpse of the narrow gorge where McAllister Creek roars into Thunder Creek. Savor the wildness. Return when you must.

EXTENDING YOUR TRIP

Strong hikers can continue farther up Thunder Creek Trail into the North Cascades National Park. But if you're traveling with Rover you'll have to stop at the park boundary. The hike up Fourth of July Pass is a good conditioner. You'll gain 2200 feet in 2.5 miles. The 3600-foot pass usually melts out by mid-June. The hike is nice enough, but don't expect any sweeping views—just a few teaser glimpses of the surrounding high country are visible from this low forested gap.

"New and improved" bridge over Thunder Creek

88 Happy-Panther Trail

RATING/ DIFFICULTY	ROUND-TRIP	ELEV GAIN/ HIGH POINT	SEASON
★★/2	12.4 miles	550 feet/ 2100 feet	Mar–Nov

One-way elevation profile: 2200', 2000', 1800' from 0 mile to 6.2.

Maps: Green Trails Diablo No. 48, Mount Logan No. 49 (trail not shown); **Contact:** North Cascades National Park Visitors Center (Newhalem), (206) 386-4495, ext. 11 (summer only), or Headquarters Information Station (Sedro-Woolley), (360) 856-5700, ext. 515, www.nps.gov/noca; **Notes:** Dogs must be leashed; **GPS:** N 48 43.670, W 121 03.778

An old pack trail reincarnated, Happy-Panther is both one of the oldest and newest trails in the North Cascades National Park Complex. It connects the Ross Dam Trail near Happy Creek with the East Bank Trail near Panther Creek, hence its colorful name. Panthers are also known to periodically prowl these grounds. Their emotional state leans more toward subdued than jubilant. Hikers, however, should be quite happy with this trail's lakeside views, quiet forest, and enchanting waterfalls.

GETTING THERE
From Marblemount follow the North Cascades Highway (State Route 20) east for 29 miles. Just beyond milepost 134, locate a large parking area on your left for the Ross Dam Trail (elev. 2100 ft). Privy available.

ON THE TRAIL
In the summer months a showcase of vehicles fills the parking lot. This is a popular trail for

Jack Mountain watches over Ross Lake.

day trippers to the dam, Ross Lake Resort vacationers, and backpackers heading for the Big Beaver Valley—expect lots of company for your first mile.

Begin descending to Ross Lake on the Ross Dam Trail. Through a thin veil of forest catch nice glimpses of surrounding peaks. At 0.25 mile cross Happy Creek. Let its captivating cascades inspire a smile. At 0.6 mile come to a dirt road. Left leads 0.25 mile to Ross Dam, a good objective for children and those seeking a short trip. Happy-Panther pursuers should head right, coming to the trail in another 0.3 mile (elev. 1650 ft), just before the dock for the Ross Lake Resort.

Now leave your fellow hikers. The Happy-Panther Trail sets out hugging the shore of man-made Ross Lake. In 0.25 mile you'll come to a scree slope that gives a breathtaking view of Jack Mountain, one of the most prominent peaks in these parts. The trail then works its way on ledges, under ledges, and through mossy carpets fringed with lichen. Undulating between fir, pine, and hemlock forest, the path pulls away from water's edge. It's hard to believe that the state

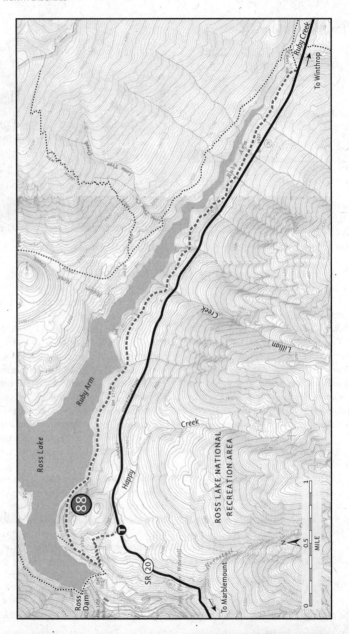

highway is just a short distance away—the surrounding forest is so peaceful.

Much of the Happy-Panther route follows what was once a bustling pack trail for prospectors and miners in the late 1800s and early 1900s. Today, backpackers hiking from Olympic National Park to Montana's Glacier National Park use this resurrected pathway as part of the Pacific Northwest Trail.

At 2.5 miles cross the first of several cascading creeks. The trail continues through a landscape shrouded in green, crossing crashing creeks on sturdy bridges from time to time. At 5 miles Ruby Creek makes its presence seen and heard. The last mile of trail brushes up against SR 20 and may lose its appeal for some. Turn around at any time. But for trail purists, follow the Happy-Panther to its happy end, reaching the East Bank trailhead at 6.25 miles (elev. 1800 ft).

A quiet hike year-round, Happy-Panther is especially peaceful during the early spring when the North Cascades Highway is still closed beyond the Ross Dam trailhead, affording serenity at the trail's eastern end.

EXTENDING YOUR TRIP

The Panther Creek Trail begins 0.3 mile east (across the bridge) from the East Bank Trail. Wander 6 miles along this wild waterway, climbing 2000 feet to reach the Panther Potholes at forested Fourth of July Pass. From the western trailhead you can arrange a trip on the Ross Lake Resort Water Taxi (206-386-4437) to Big Beaver Creek. Hike back along Ross Lake on the Big Beaver Trail, returning to your vehicle in 7 miles.

89 Ruby Creek

RATING/ DIFFICULTY	ROUND-TRIP	ELEV GAIN/ HIGH POINT	SEASON
★★/2	6.5 miles	400 feet/ 1900 feet	Apr– mid-Nov

Map: Green Trails Mount Logan No. 49; **Contact:** North Cascades National Park Visitors Center (Newhalem), (206) 386-4495, ext. 11 (summer only), or Headquarters Information Station (Sedro-Woolley), (360) 856-5700, ext. 515, www.nps.gov/noca; **Notes:** Dogs must be leashed; **GPS:** N 48 42.484, W 120 58.686

Lightly traveled, the Ruby Creek Trail is a real gem, taking hikers back into history along a mesmerizing waterway. The area once bustled with a fury of mining activity, and old digs, dilapidated structures, and rusting equipment can still be seen along this delightful trail. The hardscrabble prospectors left long ago, but their presence can still be felt in the

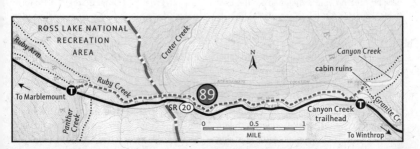

Ruby Creek rapids

creek's crashing waters and breezes rushing down the narrow valley walls.

GETTING THERE

From Marblemount follow the North Cascades Highway (State Route 20) east for 33 miles. Just beyond milepost 138, locate a large parking area on your left signed for the East Bank Trail (elev. 1800 ft). Privy available.

ON THE TRAIL

The trail begins by a handsome log-cabin privy, dropping 100 some feet to reach Ruby Creek in 0.25 mile. Here, just below the confluence with Panther Creek, a sturdy bridge spans the churning waterway to immediately reach a junction. The well-trodden path left, the East Bank Trail, is a popular backpacking route along Ross Lake. Take the path less traveled, the trail leading right.

Long before the state highway cut through these parts, the tranquil Ruby Creek Trail saw its share of travelers, especially ones intent on striking it rich. Claims, mines, and cabins lined the way. Life was tough along this pretty creek, and many a doughty fortune seeker left empty-handed after a short stint. One hardy soul, George Holmes, a former slave, stayed for over thirty years; his pits are still visible along the trail.

Traveling upstream the trail almost always keeps the creek in sight. Most of the way is fairly level, but expect a few ups and downs that circumvent some ledges and steep banks. A couple of times the creek practically kisses the trail, and during heavy rains it often plants a wet one on the tread. And while SR 20 parallels the trail on the opposite side of Ruby Creek, its presence is barely noticed.

At 1.2 miles cross crashing Crater Creek on a good bridge, leaving national park land for national forest. Follow the creek as it slices through a narrow chasm, then climb a steep bluff with a commanding view of the waterway (keep children close by). Keep your eyes peeled for old sluice ways and decaying cabins. Walk beneath towering cottonwood and through cedar flats and mini pockets of rainshadow forest.

At 3.25 miles reach a large, fairly intact cedar-shingled structure on a flat where Canyon Creek and Granite Creek join to form Ruby. Soak your feet, let your mind wander, and then retrace your steps.

EXTENDING YOUR TRIP

While day hiking certainly is possible along the East Bank Trail, you don't reach the lakeshore until 5 miles. Strong day hikers looking for some excellent views of Ross Lake and the Ruby Creek valley can set off for the Jack Mountain Trail, reached 3 miles up the East

Bank Trail. Be warned, however, that this is a tough and waterless trail, climbing 4800 feet in 6 miles to a 6745-foot knoll on Jack Mountain. But what a view!

90 Crater Mountain

RATING/ DIFFICULTY	ROUND-TRIP	ELEV GAIN/ HIGH POINT	SEASON
★★★★★/5	14 miles	5150 feet/ 7054 feet	July– mid-Oct

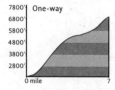

Map: Green Trails Mount Logan No. 49; **Contact:** Okanogan National Forest, Methow Valley Ranger District, (509) 996-4003, www.fs.fed.us/r6/oka; **Notes:** NW Forest Pass required; **GPS:** N 48 42.376, W 120 55.113

❌ ⚙ 🏠 *Hike to one of the finest viewpoints in the entire North Cascades. Yes, the entire North Cascades. From an old lookout site 7000 feet into the troposphere, scan all four horizons. Waves of peaks, familiar and obscure, overload your vision. Hundreds of them, from the sun-baked, cloud-piercing peaks of the east side to the jagged, ice-cloaked, spiraling summits of the west side. But all of this natural beauty has a price. The trek to Crater Mountain is among the most challenging hikes in this book. Are you up for it? All 5150 vertical feet?*

GETTING THERE
From Marblemount follow the North Cascades Highway (State Route 20) east for 35 miles. Just past milepost 141, locate the Canyon Creek trailhead on your left (elev. 1900 ft). Privy available.

ON THE TRAIL
Start by easily sauntering through a wooded bottomland at the confluence of two mighty creeks, Granite and Canyon. Cross Granite on a big sturdy bridge and immediately reach a junction. Head left on the Jackita Ridge Trail. The way right heads up the Canyon Creek valley (Hike 91), a wise choice for a future hike.

Just before crossing Canyon Creek on another sturdy bridge, pass a deteriorating old cabin that once served as a ranger guard station. Then come to an intersection. The trail left leads along Ruby Creek, tying in with the East Bank Trail (Hike 89)—a nice and easy stroll. Take the tough way instead, and go

Glacier-fed lake with Jack Mountain in distance

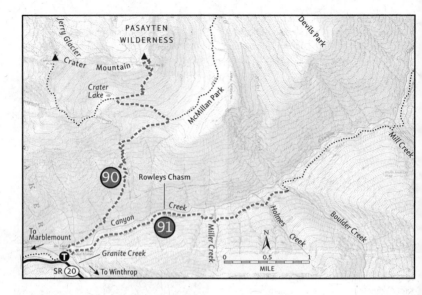

right. Begin ascending, first by gradually skirting a slope above crashing Canyon Creek, then straight up a slope via tight switchbacks.

The forest is scrappy and the trail may be brushy. After a slight reprieve from steep slogging, the incline once again intensifies. At about 2 miles, touch upon the Pasayten Wilderness (elev. 3600 ft). "Brutal" best describes the next mile as the trail straddles the wilderness boundary and subdues 1200 vertical feet. Emerging views help ease the pain.

The insanity eventually ends at a creek crossing. Soak your head and refill water bottles. Now heading east, the trail continues on a more gradual grade. About 0.5 mile from the creek crossing and just before another crossing, locate a somewhat obscure side trail heading left (elev. 5300 ft). Follow it.

Though overgrown with yellow cedar and huckleberry, the tread is well defined. After a little over 1 mile of easy ambling, pop out of subalpine forest to find yourself beneath the massive southern face of Crater Mountain.

Wow. A small cairn denotes a faint path leading to the right through heather 1.7 miles to the lookout site. That's your route. But first proceed a few hundred feet farther toward the mountain to shallow Crater Lake. If mosquitoes haven't set up shop, it's a lovely spot for taking a break. Make it a short one—the lookout site awaits.

Following fading but distinguishable tread, the spur trail makes a long sweep east through meadows and over ledges, revealing breathtaking views. Next come a few twists and turns before a long sweep west takes you through alpine tundra. Look for ptarmigans. The trail ends on a 7054-foot knoll.

From this former lookout site, prepare for one of the most satiating alpine views this side of the Continental Divide. Directly below, between massive 8128-foot Crater Mountain and jumbo 9065-foot Jack Mountain, the Jerry Glacier hangs in a high cirque above polished and striated rock, and an emerald lake sparkles in the afternoon sunlight. Now gaze outward to the horizons. Mountains! Look at them all! Devils Dome and a plethora of Pasayten pinnacles to the north. Slate Peak and another slew of Pasayten summits to the east. Ballard, Azurite, Tower, and tons of other majestic mountains to the south. And to the west, Ruby, Colonial, Eldorado, and enough glacial ice to make a penguin happy.

EXTENDING YOUR TRIP

From Crater Lake a rough trail leads nearly 2 miles to the 8128-foot summit of Crater Mountain. The last stretch is exposed and requires a Class 3 scramble—more suitable for climbers than hikers. A lookout once graced this lofty location, but was abandoned for the more agreeable lower site in the late 1950s. The glorious parklands of McMillan Park make for a satisfying destination. To reach them, continue on the main trail instead of turning off for Crater Mountain. Roam this mile-high meadowed wonderland to your heart's content.

91 Canyon Creek

RATING/ DIFFICULTY	ROUND-TRIP	ELEV GAIN/ HIGH POINT	SEASON
★★★/3	7 miles	800 feet/ 2500 feet	May– early Nov

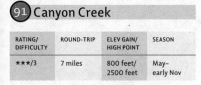

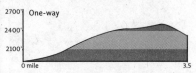

Map: Green Trails Mount Logan No. 49; **Contact:** Okanogan National Forest, Methow Valley Ranger District, (509) 996-4003, *www.fs.fed .us/r6/oka*; **Notes:** NW Forest Pass required; **GPS:** N 48 42.376, W 120 55.113

Long before State Route 20 delivered throngs of tourists to the Methow Valley, the Chancellor Road provided passage to the Okanogan. Up the deep and forbidding Canyon Creek valley, prospectors and profiteers pushed on to Harts Pass and its fields of gold and other minerals and to the boomtowns of Chancellor and Barron. But alas, most of the mines went bust along with the miners. Towns vanished and the Chancellor Road transformed into peaceful trail, traversing a once-again wild corner of the North Cascades.

GETTING THERE

From Marblemount follow the North Cascades Highway (State Route 20) east for 35 miles. Just past milepost 141, locate the Canyon Creek trailhead on your left (elev. 1900 ft). Privy available.

ON THE TRAIL

Sharing a start with the Jackita Ridge Trail, head into noisy forest, thanks to the thundering of crashing creeks. At 0.2 mile, just after crossing Granite Creek on a durable bridge, come to a junction. The trail left heads to Ruby Creek (Hike 89) and Crater Mountain (Hike 90). Head right on the Chancellor Trail for your journey up the deep and lonely Canyon Creek.

The trail starts by steeply switchbacking over lateral moraine left behind long ago by receding glaciers (global warming in its infancy!). Be sure to catch a glimpse of Canyon Creek crashing below; for most of this hike it'll remain hidden in a narrow and inaccessible chasm. Through dark forest, continue climbing. In late spring thousands of calypso orchids help perk up the forest floor in purple.

While Canyon Creek is now firmly out of view, its raucous bellowing never leaves you. Enjoy occasional glimpses through the trees of cascading creeks careening down Crater Mountain across the valley. The way soon levels off and even begins to head a little downward. At about 2 miles reach a signed short side trail to

Rowleys Chasm (elev. 2400 ft). Exercising extreme caution, check out this vertigo-inducing cleft in the canyon wall, named after an early prospector. The rugged side trail continues, heading down to still-active claims.

Back on the Chancellor Trail, pass a nice view upvalley, and then cross a trio of cascading creeks before swinging around a ledge (elev. 2500 ft) high above Canyon Creek. Pause here to take in an excellent view down the canyon and out to Ruby Mountain. Beyond, the trail crosses Holmes Creek before steeply dropping 200 feet to Boulder Creek, 3.5 miles from your start and a good turnaround spot.

Looking down Canyon Creek

Enjoy the surrounding solitude—quite a contrast from the fury of human activity that once echoed off these canyon walls.

EXTENDING YOUR TRIP
If Boulder Creek's footlog is in place, strong hikers can continue farther upvalley 2 more miles to Mill Creek, once the site of—imagine this—a saw mill. Beyond Mill Creek the trail is subject to frequent washouts, and Canyon Creek must be forded if the bridge is out. But if all is well and you're feeling exceptionally energetic, follow the trail another 3.5 miles to the former townsite of Chancellor.

92 East Creek

RATING/ DIFFICULTY	ROUND-TRIP	ELEV GAIN/ HIGH POINT	SEASON
★★/3	8 miles	2300 feet/ 4800 feet	Late June– Oct

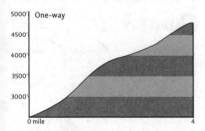

Map: Green Trails Mount Logan No. 49; **Contact:** Okanogan National Forest, Methow Valley Ranger District, (509) 996-4003, www .fs.fed.us/r6/oka; **Notes:** NW Forest Pass required. East Creek at 2.2 miles requires a ford, may be dangerous in high water; **GPS:** N 48 40.036, W 120 52.389

Looking for a quiet retreat off of the busy North Cascades Highway? East Creek Trail should do the trick. You won't find killer views, alpine lakes, or cathedral forests, but you probably won't

Old mining ruins

find another vehicle in the parking lot either. If you want solitude, it's here. There are some fair views along the way, and nice unbroken pine forests, too. And who needs a lake when you have a soothing creek tumbling by your side? One other enticement—an old mine to set your prospects on.

GETTING THERE
From Marblemount follow the North Cascades Highway (State Route 20) east for 39 miles. Just past milepost 144, locate the trailhead on your left (elev. 2500 ft). Privy available.

ON THE TRAIL
Start by crossing Granite Creek on a solid bridge. Just below, East Creek's rapidly flowing waters careen into Granite's furious flow. The trail then makes a few gradual switchbacks before climbing more steadily up a pine-cloaked slope above East Creek. Limited views across the Granite Creek valley can be had through the thin lodgepole pine canopy. At 1 mile good views are granted, especially of Beebe Mountain, as the trail traverses a small boulder field.

The ascent eases as the trail moves in closer to the creek. Sunny pine groves yield to cool glades of fir and hemlock. Finally, come to East Creek at 2.2 miles (elev. 4400 ft), where it must

be forded. Though easy in late summer, during periods of high runoff you may have to call it quits here. If you can safely cross, carry on farther up the valley.

The way continues to climb, but easily and away from the creek. The wild waterway fades from view and the surroundings grow quieter. At 4 miles, after crossing several side creeks, come to an unsigned junction with the abandoned Boulder Creek Trail (elev. 4800 ft). Ruins of the Gold Hill Mine lie just a few minutes farther on the main trail. Founded by Charles and Hazard Ballard in 1916, operations ceased years ago. Nearby Mount Ballard, however, helps keep the prospecting brothers' name from fading into history.

The old mine makes a good spot for calling it a day. Locate old timbers and rusting equipment. Enjoy snooping around, but please leave all artifacts for others to enjoy. Savor the solitude, sharing it only with deer, grouse, and the voices of yesteryear blowing in the wind.

EXTENDING YOUR TRIP

You can continue for another 4 miles on the East Creek Trail, climbing to 6500-foot Mebee Pass and the site of an old fire lookout. Maintenance beyond Gold Hill tends to be sporadic, so prepare for brush and faded tread in places.

The Boulder Creek Trail can be followed for a couple of miles to open slopes on McKay Ridge, where views are good from a 6400-foot high point. Beyond, travel is extremely difficult and not recommended. En route you'll pass some active mine claims. Respect private property.

93 Easy Pass

RATING/ DIFFICULTY	ROUND-TRIP	ELEV GAIN/ HIGH POINT	SEASON
★★★★/5	7 miles	2800 feet/ 6500 feet	Mid-July– mid-Oct

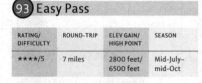

Map: Green Trails Mount Logan No. 49; **Contact:** Okanogan National Forest, Methow Valley Ranger District, (509) 996-4003, *www.fs.fed.us/r6/oka*; **Notes:** NW Forest Pass required; **GPS:** N 48 35.275, W 120 48.172

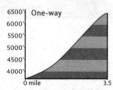

Savor spectacular views of glistening glaciers gracing massive Mount Logan. Peer straight down into a valley of jungle

greenery embracing Fisher Creek, or up to rock, crag, and ice adorning Fisher Basin. Come in midsummer for a cornucopia of wildflowers, or early autumn when larches set the high ridges aglow. Despite its name, this hike will cost you some sweat. But it's easily one of the prettiest hikes in the North Cascades.

GETTING THERE

From Marblemount follow the North Cascades Highway (State Route 20) east for 45 miles. Between mileposts 151 and 152, turn right onto a spur road signed for Easy Pass and drive 0.1 mile to the trailhead (elev. 3700 ft). Privy available.

ON THE TRAIL

Starting in thick forest, the trail wastes no time arriving at thundering Granite Creek. Blessed are the bridge builders; for many years hikers were met here with a treacherous ford. Once across, the trail begins climbing—and never stops until reaching the pass.

Heading toward Easy Pass Creek, then paralleling it, the way ascends through lush cedar and hemlock groves. Highway noise fades, replaced by tumbling waters. After 1 mile or so, greet daylight as the forest succumbs to brushy avalanche slopes. Work your way up increasingly open and more difficult terrain. Hop across creeks and steady your foot strikes on rocky tread.

Across a big basin under the pass, traverse heather slopes, fanned rock slides, snowfields, and talus. "Easy" Pass? It was the easiest way across Ragged Ridge for early prospectors. Think what the other passes on the ridge must be like. Pass through a small patch of forest before heading back into the open.

Tight switchbacks soon begin. Break for blueberries. Under cliffs and on rocky tread that frequently requires retreading, make the final steep push to the pass. Fireweed and yellow asters (daisies, actually) line the way. At 3.5 miles arrive at the larch- and heather-graced 6500-foot pass and the boundary of the North Cascades National Park. Wow! The view west

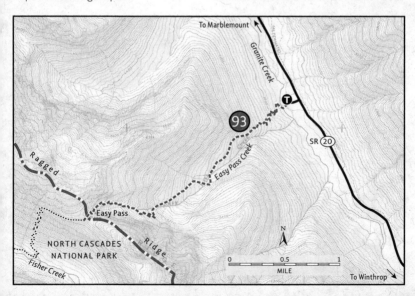

of massive 9087-foot glacier-covered Mount Logan, hovering over the emerald U-shaped Fisher Creek valley, is a North Cascades classic. The view east to Mount Hardy and the Golden Horn ain't too bad either. Even better views can be had by scrambling slopes north and south of the pass. Take care not to trample fragile heather meadows in your explorations.

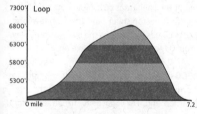

94 Maple Pass

RATING/ DIFFICULTY	LOOP	ELEV GAIN/ HIGH POINT	SEASON
★★★★★/3	7.2 miles	2000 feet/ 6850 feet	Mid-July– mid-Oct

Maps: Green Trails Mount Logan No. 49, Washington Pass No. 50; **Contact:** Okanogan National Forest, Methow Valley Ranger District, (509) 996-4003, www.fs.fed.us/r6/oka; **Notes:** NW Forest Pass required; **GPS:** N 48 30.973, W 120 44.124

Among the many supreme North Cascades Highway hikes, the Maple Pass loop is perhaps the most exalted. More than a few hikers have been caught humming Julie Andrews tunes while sauntering on this scenic sojourn. In just 7 nonrepeating miles you'll be treated to majestic old-growth forests, a sparkling alpine lake, resplendent alpine meadows, enticing open ridges, and stunning North Cascades vistas. And if you love wildflowers, Maple Pass's annual floral show is a bloomin' spectacle.

GETTING THERE
From Marblemount follow the North Cascades Highway (State Route 20) east for 51 miles to

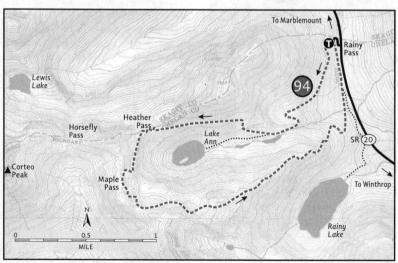

Opposite: Looking east from Easy Pass

Whistler Mountain and Lake Ann

Rainy Pass near milepost 158. Turn right into the Rainy Pass Picnic Area for the trailhead (elev. 4850 ft). Water and privy available.

ON THE TRAIL

On loops I normally prefer to ascend the steeper direction, giving my knees a respite from pain on the descent, but I deviate here. By hiking to Maple Pass counterclockwise, the gentle ascent allows slow passage through the various life zones this trail traverses, giving the opportunity to note the diverse fauna that flourishes here.

From the trailhead immediately leave the paved path that heads to Rainy Lake. Veering right on a well-beaten and well-maintained trail, begin a quick ascent through a stately ancient forest of fir, spruce, and hemlock. Huckleberry bushes crowd the understory, warranting a return trip in September. In early summer, twinflower, spring beauty, and vanilla leaf bring life to the forest floor.

Continuing through deep timber you'll pass several marshy areas. In midsummer they're saturated with columbine and marigold. At 1.3 miles reach a junction with the trail to Lake Ann (elev. 5300 ft). The loop continues right—upward—gradually gaining elevation. Breaking out of the coniferous cover, enter the subalpine world. An astonishing landscape of towering peaks comes into view as the trail works its way around the cirque cradling Lake Ann.

At 2.3 miles reach Heather Pass (elev. 6200 ft), where a way trail branches right to Lewis and Wing lakes. Continue left through heather and rock gardens to an amazing array of alpine plants abloom. Melting snowfields unveil dazzling displays of glacier lilies, while creek beds, rocky nooks, and sun-kissed meadows present monkey flower, paintbrush, penstemon, arnica, cinquefoil, lupine, gentian, aster, partridgefoot, valerian, harebell, spiraea, anemone, lousewort, and bistort.

Meandering along the cirque rim, Lake Ann glistening 1000 feet below, the trail approaches Maple Pass (elev. 6600 ft) at 3.5 miles. Climbing doesn't cease, however. Continue upward for another mile, topping out on a 6850-foot shoulder of Frisco Mountain. Respect the fragile meadows, leaving off-trail trampling to the marmots. Savor the sublime views before beginning your descent. Imposing peaks—Corteo, Black, Frisco, Whistler, and Tower—ring the immediate surroundings. Glacier Peak and its icy entourage dominate the southwestern skyline.

The loop rapidly plunges off the ridge to a hanging valley, but not without traversing yet more glorious meadows and flower gardens. Rainy Lake, 1700 feet below, soon comes into view. So do Frisco's glaciers. It's then a quick descent through hemlock, heather, and huckleberry back to the paved Rainy Lake Trail. Follow it left for 0.5 mile back to your start. Now wasn't that supreme?

EXTENDING YOUR TRIP

Lake Ann, tucked in an open cirque beneath towering rock walls laced with cascades, makes a worthy 1-mile round-trip addition to the loop. Experienced hikers can set off on the primitive path from Heather Pass to the backcountry gems of Lewis and Wing lakes. Routefinding and off-trail experience is necessary; you'll need to navigate a nasty boulder field and a potentially dangerous gully. Back in the lowlands, don't neglect the easy and nearly level 0.9-mile paved trail to Rainy Lake, fed by waterfalls and in a cirque beneath 7760-foot

Frisco Mountain—a perfect trip for introducing nonhikers to the world of trails.

95 Cutthroat Pass

RATING/ DIFFICULTY	ROUND-TRIP	ELEV GAIN/ HIGH POINT	SEASON
★★★★/3	10 miles	2000 feet/ 6800 feet	July–Oct

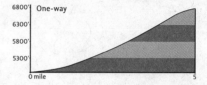

Map: Green Trails Washington Pass No. 50; **Contact:** Okanogan National Forest, Methow Valley Ranger District, (509) 996-4003, www.fs.fed.us/r6/oka; **Notes:** NW Forest Pass required; **GPS:** N 48 31.084, W 120 43.988

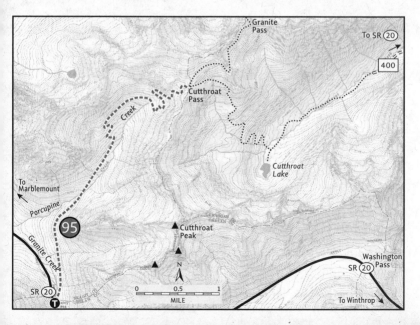

Hikers at Granite Pass admire Tower Mountain.

Stroll first through deep forest, then up, up, and away to an alpine world flush in meadows, larches, and delectable views of stark craggy mountains spiraling to the heavens. From the pass, a broad saddle teetering on the demarcation zone between the wet west and the dry east, there are exploratory side-trip options. And while this section of the Pacific Crest Trail usually teems with fellow hikers, it's never shy of wild critters. With everything from frantic ground squirrels, to lumbering bears, to wallowing mountain goats, you'll feel like you've walked onto the set of Wild America.

GETTING THERE

From Marblemount follow the North Cascades Highway (State Route 20) east for 51 miles to Rainy Pass near milepost 158. Turn left onto the spur road and drive 0.3 mile to the Pacific Crest Trail parking area (elev. 4800 ft). Privy available.

ON THE TRAIL

Your trek to Cutthroat Pass is by way of the Pacific Crest Trail, a 2600-mile National Scenic Trail following the Sierra and Cascade crests from the Mexican to the Canadian border. Veteran PCT hikers rank this section of trail from Rainy Pass to the Pasayten Wilderness among its most scenic stretches. You'll probably agree.

From a lofty start at 4800 feet, the way starts gentle enough in cool forest, skirting the base of Cutthroat Peak. At 1.5 miles cross tumbling Porcupine Creek (elev. 5200 ft). Now following alongside the mountain stream, elevation gain accelerates. A thinning forest cover begins to reveal imposing neighbors. Look west to Corteo, Black, and Fisher peaks peeking above the North Cascades Highway.

Negotiate a series of switchbacks, angle across a high slope, and then begin another set of switchbacks. Make the final grunt to the pass across meadows speckled with boulders and spliced with granite slabs. Whistling marmots and shrilling ground squirrels announce your passing. At 5 miles reach Cutthroat Pass and relish its sweeping views. Jagged giants encircle you. Look east out to the sunny Methow Valley and the 8876-foot behemoth, Silver Star Mountain, dominating the horizon. Cutthroat Pass was my very first hike in the Washington Cascades back in 1985. What a place to begin!

EXTENDING YOUR TRIP

Feel free to roam this wide gap for better viewing. Just south of the pass is a small knoll easily attained by way path. Granite Pass is north along the PCT another 1.25 miles, and from this tight notch you can climb a little way on the ridge west to feast on a mouth-widening view of Tower, Azurite, and the Golden Horn.

If you can arrange to get picked up, consider a one-way hike descending east via Cutthroat Pass Trail No. 483. The trailhead is 1 mile up FR 400, whose turnoff is near milepost 167 on SR 20. This trail also makes a good alternative approach to the pass. Starting slightly lower (elev. 4500 ft), the trail first travels 2 easy miles along Cutthroat Creek to Cutthroat Lake (elev. 4900 ft), an ideal destination for children and for those wanting an easy leg stretcher. Beyond, the trail climbs 1900 feet in 3.8 miles, traversing blueberry patches, larch groves, and wide-open slopes. It's an exceptionally appealing jaunt in autumn.

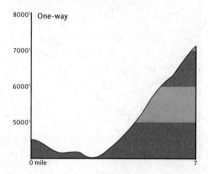

96 Stiletto Peak

RATING/ DIFFICULTY	ROUND-TRIP	ELEV GAIN/ HIGH POINT	SEASON
★★★★★/5	14 miles	3720 feet/ 7223 feet	July– mid-Oct

Maps: Green Trails Washington Pass No. 50, Stehekin No. 82; **Contact:** Okanogan National Forest, Methow Valley Ranger District, (509) 996-4003, www.fs.fed.us/r6/oka; **Notes:** NW Forest Pass required. Dogs prohibited at park boundary; **GPS:** N 48 30.292, W 120 43.126

When it comes to jaw-slacking, mouthwatering, eye-widening, horizon-spanning North Cascades views, Stiletto Peak makes the cut. And with all this amazing scenery in close proximity to the North Cascades Highway you'd think many a hiker would make a stab for Stiletto, right? Wrong. Most hikers just aren't cut out for this hike. The distance is too long, the climb too demanding. But for well-honed hikers, Stiletto promises more than just bountiful backcountry backdrops. You'll have the entire summit for yourself, sharpening your appreciation of real wilderness.

GETTING THERE

From Marblemount follow the North Cascades Highway (State Route 20) east for 51 miles to

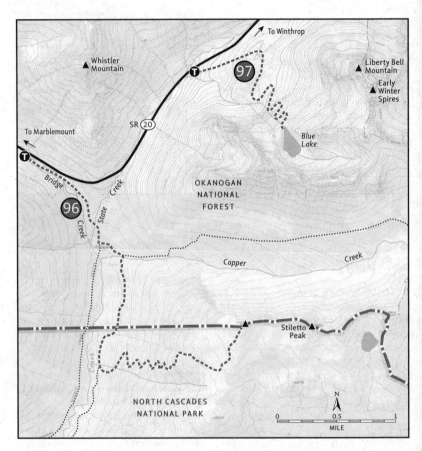

Rainy Pass. Continue east for 1.2 more miles to the Bridge Creek (Pacific Crest Trail) trailhead, on your left (elev. 4500 ft). Privy available.

ON THE TRAIL

Starting from the 4500-foot "low" point between Rainy and Washington passes, carefully cross SR 20 to pick up the Pacific Crest Trail. Trade highway noise for the soothing sounds of tumbling Bridge Creek as you follow the PCT. Gently descending, reach a junction after 1 mile (elev. 4250 ft).

The PCT continues right, following Bridge Creek to the Stehekin Valley. Head left on the Stiletto Spur Trail and after 0.3 mile come to another junction. Continue right; the trail leaving left ascends brushy slopes to Copper Pass (Hike 109), another option for quiet roaming. Cross Copper Creek and continue losing elevation, coming to an obscure junction in 0.25 mile. Avoid the trail that heads straight, unless you want to explore the scant remains of an abandoned mining camp.

Staying on the main trail, regain some lost

elevation and then lose it again. After crossing a braided brook, enter the North Cascades National Park. Four-legged hikers are not permitted past this point. A short distance beyond, about 2.5 miles from your start, reach a junction with the Stiletto Peak Trail (elev. 4000 ft).

From this point on, it's all business, no more gentle descents. The lightly maintained, in-danger-of-being-lost-forever trail marches up a steep shoulder of Stiletto through a series of unrelenting switchbacks. After 3 miles of merciless climbing, stop and acknowledge that you've just tackled 2100 vertical feet. Look around, too, and notice that trees have finally yielded to meadows and views at last.

The way, however, gets tricky now. The trail soon peters out at a saddle (elev. 6300 ft).

Approaching old lookout site on Stiletto Peak

Those inexperienced at routefinding may want to call it a day. Those confident enough to continue need to follow the ridge north, avoiding cliffs and rock on the slope's east side. You'll eventually find tread again, as well as rock steps that will deliver you to the 7223-foot precipitous shoulder, once home to a fire lookout.

From 1931 to 1952 some fortunate wardens reported for duty here. Their post is now marked by debris, but the far-sweeping views remain unblemished. Witness a landscape as wild as ever and now protected in national park and wilderness. Look north to Whistler, Cutthroat, and Liberty Bell, east to Black, Frisco, and Goode, south to Hock and McGregor, and west to the massive block of rock making up Stiletto's 7684-foot summit. Don't forget to look straight down into the Copper Creek valley, too. Holy vertigo Batman!

EXTENDING YOUR TRIP

A trail once ran from the saddle just below the lookout site all the way to Twisp Pass. Traces of tread still exist, and experienced routefinders shouldn't have a problem even in the overgrown meadows. It's about a 2-mile journey through parkland meadows and larch groves.

97 Blue Lake

RATING/ DIFFICULTY	ROUND-TRIP	ELEV GAIN/ HIGH POINT	SEASON
★★★/3	4.4 miles	1050 feet/ 6250 feet	July–Oct

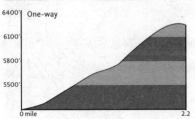

Map: Green Trails Washington Pass No. 50; Contact: Okanogan National Forest, Methow Valley Ranger District, (509) 996-4003, www.fs.fed.us/r6/oka; Notes: NW Forest Pass required; GPS: N 48 31.147, W 120 40.453

An uninspiring name for a pretty tarn tucked beneath the impressive Early Winters Spires. Short and sweet, this trail will leave you sitting by Blue's shimmering waters in no time. From a shoreline resting post marvel at the surrounding soaring walls of granite. Listen for clambering climbers scaling them. Despite the occasional clanking of carabiners, Blue Lake is a peaceful place above the busy state highway.

GETTING THERE

From Marblemount follow the North Cascades Highway (State Route 20) east for 51 miles to Rainy Pass. Continue east for 3 more miles to the trailhead located on your right, between mileposts 161 and 162. Privy available.

ON THE TRAIL

Start in dense timber, taking off east parallel to SR 20 before making a big switchback and leaving highway noise behind. Gradually ascending on well-beaten tread, take a break after 1 mile in a small clearing compliments of past avalanches. The views are good, but they get better—so carry on.

Return to forest and in 0.5 mile or so enter another clearing. In early summer a mosaic of blossoming flowers spreads out before you. Cast your eyes upward to Liberty Bell Mountain, proudly ringing above. Note a rough trail leading left—the climbers path for those towing the line to toll the bell.

The climb now eases, and after another 0.5 mile reaches Blue's outlet creek requiring a hop, skip, or jump. Enjoy nice views north to the

Opposite: Blue Lake

cloud-piercing peaks Whistler and Cutthroat, familiar landmarks along the North Cascades Highway. Now enter the basin bounding Blue Lake. Snoop around a dilapidating old cabin. Then settle on a sunny shoreline spot and soak up the scenery of the spectacular Spires.

EXTENDING YOUR TRIP

Just to the east of Washington Pass is the Lone Fir Campground, an ideal spot for setting up base camp to explore area trails. The 2-mile Lone Fir Loop Trail that takes off from the campground makes for a wonderful après dinner woodland stroll.

98 Driveway Butte

RATING/ DIFFICULTY	ROUND-TRIP	ELEV GAIN/ HIGH POINT	SEASON
★★★★/4	8 miles	3030 feet/ 5982 feet	Late May– Oct

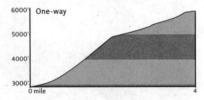

Map: Green Trails Washington Pass No. 50; **Contact:** Okanogan National Forest, Methow Valley Ranger District, (509) 996-4003, www .fs.fed.us/r6/oka; **Notes:** NW Forest Pass required; **GPS:** N 48 35.900, W 120 30.820

Here's a stiff climb to an old lookout site providing splendid viewing up deep, glacially cut valleys ringed by glacially carved summits. Enjoy an eagle's perspective of the West Fork Methow River, Early Winters Creek, Rattlesnake Creek, Robinson Creek, and Lost River valleys, pretty portals to rugged peaks and the Pasayten Wilderness. Melting out early, Driveway Butte
makes a good spring high-country probe— great, too, for enjoying blooms. In May and June half the way bursts with showy yellow arrowleaf balsamroot.

GETTING THERE

From Marblemount follow the North Cascades Highway (State Route 20) east for 70 miles to the turnoff for the Klipchuck Campground (Forest Road 300). From Winthrop follow SR 20 west for 17 miles to the turnoff. Drive FR 300 for 1 mile to the trailhead, located just before the campground entrance (elev. 2950 ft). Privy available.

ON THE TRAIL

Except during the autumn hunting season, expect to see few other two-legged trail users on this hike. Four-legged users, however, abound, especially deer. After late June when the balsamroot blossoms turn to seed, the butte is hot and dry. Carry plenty of water and sunscreen. Early season is best for a visit, but expect to encounter some snow midway; routefinding is easy if the skies are clear.

Begin with a very short stretch of level walking before heading up an old skid road. Through an open forest of ponderosa pine and Douglas-fir, waste no time gaining elevation. At 0.5 mile the trail swings east to slab up a sunny southern slope. Thousands of sunflowers, as balsamroot is colloquially called in these parts, help brighten the way. The trail was once used to drive cattle to the butte's high meadows for range, hence this peak's name. There are no cattle left to rustle, but plenty of lizards rustle in the low brush.

Humming "Wichita Lineman," undulate between patches of forest and wide-open former rangeland, climbing steeply and gaining 1800 feet in 2 miles on one heck of a driveway. The way levels as it enters what was once dense forest, now burnt snags and feisty new undergrowth thanks to a large wildfire that swept through shortly after the millennium. Near a creek crossing (dry by midsummer) a faint path leads right 0.5 mile to a 5500-foot view-granting knoll, an option for a shorter saunter.

The main trail continues left through a matchstick forest, crossing—depending on the season—either a series of snowmelt streams or dry draws. At 3.25 miles (elev. 5500 ft) the trail turns right (northeast), emerging in meadows and parkland below the butte. The tread disappears, but the way is quite clear—head straight

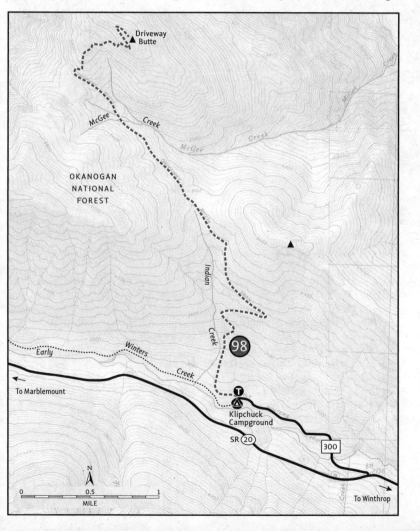

Goat Peak rises above the Methow Valley.

up the open south slopes of the butte, an oc-casional cairn providing a beacon.

At 4 miles crest the 5982-foot butte and reap your scenic rewards. To the north, 8726-foot Robinson Mountain dominates the ho-rizon, and Lost River is fully revealed. Look east down the Methow Valley with Goat Peak hovering above. Giants Gardner and Silver Star draw your attention southward, while the Harts Pass high country piques your interest to the west. Grouse, chickadees, nutcrackers, and bluebirds provide the score for this stun-ning preview.

EXTENDING YOUR TRIP

The Klipchuck Campground, adjacent to the trailhead, is a pleasant place to plop down for the night. On the next day take an easy 4-mile (500 ft gain) hike up the Early Winters Trail following the creek of the same name on a route used by Native Americans, explorers, and prospectors long before SR 20 laid claim to the way.

99 Cedar Falls

RATING/ DIFFICULTY	ROUND-TRIP	ELEV GAIN/ HIGH POINT	SEASON
★★★/2	3.5 miles	500 feet/ 3500 feet	May– early Nov

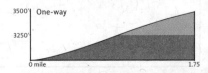

Map: Green Trails Washington Pass No. 50; **Contact:** Okanogan National Forest, Methow Valley Ranger District, (509) 996-4003, www .fs.fed.us/r6/oka; **Notes:** NW Forest Pass required; **GPS:** N 48 34.750, W 120 28.721

 Marvel at Cedar Creek careening down a series of rapids and crashing over a twin-tiered cataract into a deep narrow chasm. On a lightly traveled trail off of the busy North Cascades Highway, Cedar Falls makes an easy early or late-season jaunt. Cruise this way just after snowmelt and witness a deafening display of hydrologic force. Pretty wildflowers lining the trail help soften the trauma.

Cedar Falls

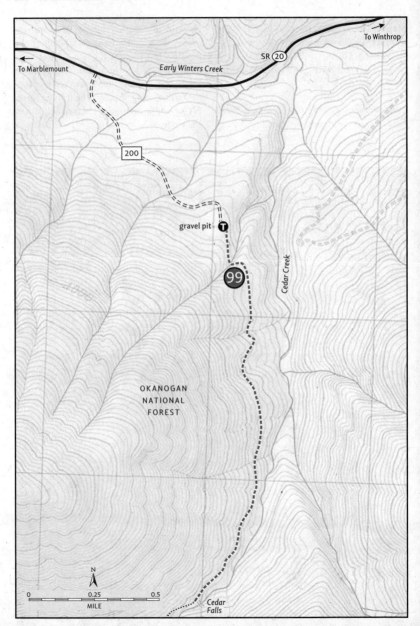

GETTING THERE

From Marblemount follow the North Cascades Highway (State Route 20) east for 70 miles to Klipchuck Campground. From Winthrop follow SR 20 west for 17 miles to the turnoff. Continue 0.25 mile from the turnoff, turning right onto Forest Road 200 (signed for Cedar Creek). Drive FR 200 for 1 mile to its terminus at a gravel pit and the trailhead (elev. 3000 ft). Privy available.

ON THE TRAIL

From the rather unattractive trailhead, head off into the woods on a wide and well-groomed path high above roaring Cedar Creek. Immediately come upon an unmarked junction with a primitive trail that goes right for 3.5 miles to Mudhole Lake, high on a shoulder of Silver Star Mountain. Climbing 3000 feet in 2 miles, it's a steep route. Continue straight on Trail No. 476, the more trodden and gentle path.

Soon pass through a gap in the forest that gives a glimpse north to Goat Peak and the cliffs below known as the Goat Wall. At 0.6 mile sneak a peek through the forest to across the creek valley and an impressive cascade tumbling down from Sandy Butte. At 1 mile the source of the continuous accompanying roar, Cedar Creek, can finally be seen as the trail gets closer to the crashing waterway.

Continue upvalley through groves of pine and fir. In spring, bouquets of yellow arnica and red paintbrush brighten the forest floor. As you head farther upvalley the forest canopy thins to reveal the steep slopes surrounding you.

At 1.75 miles, the sound of crashing water now intensely audible, you come to Cedar Falls. Thundering over granite ledges, the two-tiered cataract is an impressive sight. Above the falls a series of rapids prime the river for the plunge, while below a steep and narrow chasm swallows it after its turbulent display. Walk around to a couple of overhanging ledges for the best viewing, but be extremely careful on these exposed belvederes—this is no place for loose dogs or children.

EXTENDING YOUR TRIP

Hike not long enough? Continue up the Cedar Creek Trail, which offers good valley walking for miles. If you're really energetic make the 7-mile trek all the way to 6400-foot Abernathy Pass, a tight little notch on Abernathy Ridge.

POEM ON THE RANGE

Hikers who like to wax poetic while tramping the trails of the North Cascades may want to stuff in their rucksacks (if they haven't already) a book or two by Gary Snyder, Jack Kerouac, or Philip Whelan. Back in the 1950s this poetic trio had plenty of natural inspiration before them while sitting guard as fire lookouts in the North Cascades wilderness.

Crater Mountain, Sauk Mountain, Sourdough Mountain, and Desolation Peak are posts where the poets penned some of their works when not tending to mundane lookout tasks, or called out to suppress a fire. Two of the four peaks, Sourdough and Desolation, still retain their historical lookouts. All four of the peaks receive their share of poet pilgrims each hiking season.

Sauk is a fairly easy hike (Hike 49). Sourdough is challenging (Hike 83). Crater is for climbers, but its ridge is hikeable (Hike 90). And Desolation is backpackers' country, unless you spring for a Ross Lake water taxi to deliver you to the trailhead—a fair pittance for an aspiring writer or poet. Lookout poets admirer and writer (and one-time North Cascades volunteer fire lookout), John Suiter, penned a highly informative and engaging book, *Poets on the Peaks* in 2002. It's also a good book to tote around in your pack while hiking the inspiring North Cascades backcountry.

Harts Pass

An old road built for narrow-gauged vehicles to access mineral riches now provides hikers with easy alpine access. The highest road in Washington State, the gravel and narrow route to Harts Pass winds from the Methow Valley to the lookout tower at 7400-foot Slate Peak. You can only drive to the 7200-foot line, and from there it's an easy but visually overloading hoof to the summit. Some of the finest and easiest cloud-probing meadow rambling in the North Cascades waits for you at the handful of lofty trailheads at Harts Pass.

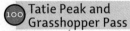

100 Tatie Peak and Grasshopper Pass

Tatie Peak

RATING/ DIFFICULTY	ROUND-TRIP	ELEV GAIN/ HIGH POINT	SEASON
★★★★★/3	5 miles	985 feet/ 7386 feet	July–Oct

Grasshopper Pass

RATING/ DIFFICULTY	ROUND-TRIP	ELEV GAIN/ HIGH POINT	SEASON
★★★★★/3	11 miles	1750 feet/ 7125 feet	July–Oct

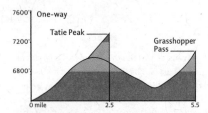

Map: Green Trails Washington Pass No. 50; **Contact:** Okanogan National Forest, Methow Valley Ranger District, (509) 996-4003, www.fs.fed.us/r6/oka; **Notes:** NW Forest Pass required; **GPS:** N 48 42.142, W 120 40.357

Ranking among the supreme ridge-running, cloud-probing, peak-peering jaunts in all of the North Cascades, the trek to Grasshopper Pass will have you hopping with joy with its nonstop horizon-spanning views of jagged ridges and colossal summits. Best of all, this alpine rapture is achieved with minimal effort. The trail starts high and stays high. And with the trail's gentle ups and down, most hikers young and old, two and four legged will have no problem making the journey.

GETTING THERE

From Winthrop drive the North Cascades Highway (State Route 20) west for 13 miles to the Mazama turnoff just past milepost 180. From Marblemount follow SR 20 east for 73 miles. Proceed north for 0.5 mile to Mazama. Turn left (west) at the intersection, following the paved road to Harts Pass (Lost River Road). The pavement ends in 6.7 miles, and the road becomes Forest Road 54. Follow this harrowing, at times narrow road for 12 miles to Harts Pass. Turn left onto FR 54-500 (signed for Meadows Campground) and in 2 miles come to road end and trailhead (elev. 6400 ft).

ON THE TRAIL

Start on a Cat track on the edge of a burn that scorched thousands of acres of high-country forest surrounding Harts Pass. In two minutes reach Trail No. 2000, the Pacific Crest Trail. The trail right heads to Canada. The trail left heads to Mexico via Grasshopper Pass—take it.

In no time break out of the forest into an open basin punctuated with tall larches. You may notice flagging and other disturbances below. They're remnants of the Brown Bear Mine. The region is littered with old mines, some still active, but none yielding much these days.

Gently climb, rounding the open basin, views expanding with each step, and reach a ridge crest at 0.75 mile. The way is all alpine now as the trail skirts steep slopes. Gaze south into the glacially carved South Fork Trout

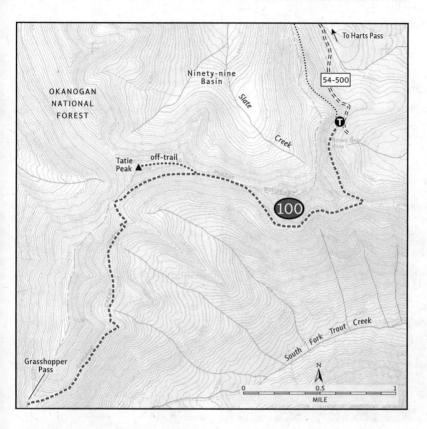

Creek valley. Its U-shaped symmetry indicates past glaciations (V-shaped valleys signify the past work of creeks and rivers).

At 2 miles (elev. 7000 ft) attain a small gap high on Tatie Peak's eastern shoulder. Marvel at the array of geological diversity at your feet. Shale, slate, sandstone, and granite—it rocks! Speaking of slate, the peak bearing that name can be seen off to the north. It's the one with the attractive fire tower gracing its summit.

Hikers comfortable with off-trail travel may want to continue along the ridge crest for 0.5 mile, climbing 400 feet to Tatie Peak's 7386-foot summit. It's not overly difficult; just

be aware of the drop-off along the northern slopes. Peak baggers can help themselves to a heaping of visual delights. The prominent summits of Jack, Crater, Azurite, Tower, Robinson, and Ballard can all be sampled from Tatie's wide-open perch.

The trail, however, forgoes those views, traversing Tatie's southern slopes to gently descend to another gap (elev. 6800 ft). Squeaky ground squirrels and whistling marmots will accompany you. Sneak a peek at the gap to impressive Mount Ballard and below to Slate Creek, where the mining community of Chancellor once bustled.

Pacific Crest Trail along ridge below Tatie Peak

Locate well-defined tread heading south, and follow it for about 0.5 mile to a 7125-foot knoll. Now revel in the shadows of all 8000-plus feet of impressive Mount Ballard and Azurite Peak. Admire, too, the prominent cloud-piercing Golden Horn and Tower Peak. And don't forget to set your sights downward to the confluence of crashing creeks that create the majestic Methow River.

EXTENDING YOUR TRIP

Spend the night at nearby Meadows Campground and enjoy supreme star gazing. Hike north along the Pacific Crest Trail to Harts Pass for quiet ramblings. Experienced hikers may want to locate the old Ninety-nine Trail that takes off from the PCT for the lonely ridge north of Tatie Peak. Solitude, spectacular scenery, and perhaps a spirit or two await you.

101 Windy Pass

RATING/ DIFFICULTY	ROUND-TRIP	ELEV GAIN/ HIGH POINT	SEASON
★★★★★/2	7 miles	1300 feet/ 6900 feet	July– mid-Oct

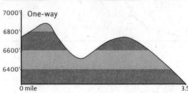

Maps: Green Trails Washington Pass No. 50, Pasayten Peak No. 18; **Contact:** Okanogan National Forest, Methow Valley Ranger District, (509) 996-4003, *www.fs.fed.us/r6/oka*; **Notes:** NW Forest Pass required; **GPS:** N 48 43.929, W 120 40.507

From this point, the trail continues to descend, now through alpine rock gardens and a majestic stand of larches. Pass this way in October and be wooed by a golden hue. Snow patches often blotch the heather meadows, providing the only water along the way. Bottoming out at 6500 feet in a boulder field, the way once again climbs and at 5 miles reaches 7125-foot Grasshopper Pass.

Don't call it quits here, however. Continue a little farther on the broad gap, leaving the trail just before it drops steeply to Glacier Pass.

Saunter to Windy Pass on a clear summer day and ask yourself a simple question. Does it get any better than this? Watch shadows cast by

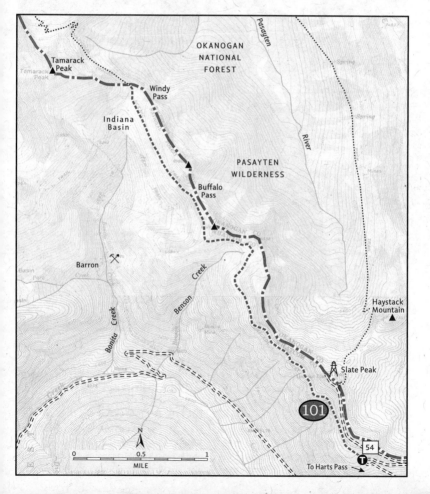

cotton-candy clouds dance across an awe-inspiring landscape of deep dark valleys and emerald ridges. Admire endless columns of icy and rocky spiraling peaks piercing the cobalt sky. Walk mesmerized through rapturous alpine gardens; waves of dazzling wildflowers gently swaying in warm breezes. Look out across some of the wildest wilderness remaining on the North American continent and let your senses whirl. Yet, you've hardly broken a sweat getting here. No, it doesn't get any better than this.

GETTING THERE

From Winthrop drive the North Cascades Highway (State Route 20) west for 13 miles to the Mazama turnoff just past milepost 180. From Marblemount follow SR 20 east for 73

Slate Peak in the distance

miles. Proceed north for 0.5 mile to Mazama. Turn left (west) at the intersection, following the paved road to Harts Pass (Lost River Road). The pavement ends in 6.7 miles, and the road becomes Forest Road 54. Follow this harrowing, at times narrow road for 12 miles to Harts Pass. Pass the campground and guard station, bearing right toward Slate Peak. Drive 1.4 miles to the trailhead at the first switch-back (elev. 6750 ft). Parking is limited.

ON THE TRAIL

From Mexico to Canada, Pacific Crest Trail No. 2000 snakes over 2600 miles along some of the most spectacular alpine country in the west. In Washington State, the PCT runs for

500 miles along the spine of the Cascades. And here, from Harts Pass, the trail makes its last hurrah on its way to its terminus in British Columbia's Manning Provincial Park. Through-hikers glow along this stretch of trail, completion of their arduous trek within reach.

For day hikers, this final section of the PCT is one of the best ways to get acquainted with this national scenic treasure. From Harts Pass to Windy Pass the trail winds along open slopes providing nonstop showings of spectacular alpine scenery. Best of all, it starts high and stays high, and when it does dip and climb, the rolling is gentle. If ever there was a stretch of trail for turning neophytes on to the wonderful world of hiking, it's right here.

From the lofty trailhead access the PCT in a clump of hardy larches. The trail skirts beneath the 7400-foot summit of Slate Peak. Below, Slate Creek drains a basin bearing scars from fortune seekers past and present. In the valley's mining heyday two boomtowns, Barron and Chancellor, hosted hardscrabble prospectors and profiteers. The towns have all but disappeared, but the surrounding hillsides still sport deep scars, ecologically devastating lesions. The mining claims are still active and less-than-enlightened extracting continues.

Lift your eyes from the basin, however, and gaze out at a landscape unblemished—awe-inspiring too, and punctuated with prominent peaks. Jack and Crater dominate the northwest. Baker also makes its presence known. Ballard and Azurite occupy the southwest. And straight ahead are a plethora of peaks in the Pasayten country.

Round Slate Peak into a small basin where melting snowfields provide the first waters for Benson Creek. Round a small knoll and marvel at the continuous floral shows displayed prominently along the trail. Arnica, anemone, aster, paintbrush, gentian, harebell, cinquefoil, phlox, and groundsel—they're all here and more.

The trail gently inches toward Buffalo Pass, but opts not to cross it, continuing instead along the western slopes of yet another knoll. Now losing a couple of hundred feet, the trail skirts Indiana Basin before making a short and easy ascent to Windy Pass (elev. 6257 ft). From here feast on views northeast into the heart of the half-million-acre Pasayten Wilderness, one of the largest roadless areas in Washington. Hiking just doesn't get any better.

EXTENDING YOUR TRIP

Want more and better views? Continue farther along the PCT to a higher unnamed pass, or if experienced in off-trail travel ascend 7290-foot Tamarack Peak. Before heading home make the 0.25-mile hike to the top of Slate Peak, one of the few remaining North Cascades summits with an active fire tower. Views are widespread, from the arid eastern fringes of the Cascades to the glacier-clad giants of the North Cascades National Park. Consider camping at Harts Pass or at nearby Meadows Campground and make the jaunt to Slate Peak on a moonlit, star-studded evening.

102 Silver Lake

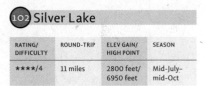

RATING/ DIFFICULTY	ROUND-TRIP	ELEV GAIN/ HIGH POINT	SEASON
★★★★/4	11 miles	2800 feet/ 6950 feet	Mid-July– mid-Oct

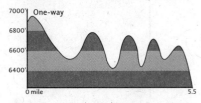

Maps: Green Trails Washington Pass No. 50, Pasayten Peak No. 18; **Contact:** Okanogan National Forest, Methow Valley Ranger District, (509) 996-4003, *www.fs.fed.us/r6/oka*; **GPS:** N 48 43.935, W 120 40.094

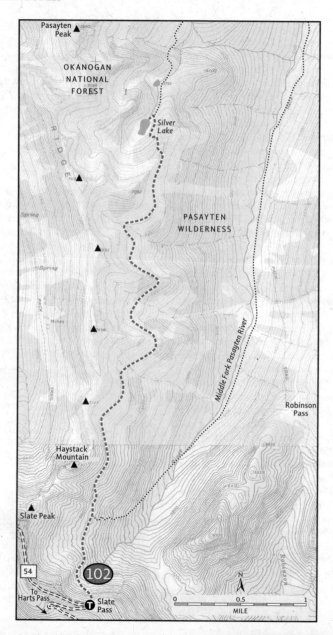

Pasayten
Peak

OKANOGAN
NATIONAL
FOREST

Silver
Lake

R I D G E

PASAYTEN
WILDERNESS

Spring

Spring

Mines

Middle Fork Pasayten River

Robinson
Pass

Haystack
Mountain

Slate Peak

54

To
Harts Pass

102

Slate
Pass

Robinson

N

0   0.5   1
MILE

Admire nearby lofty peaks while roaming miles of parkland meadows on a high ridge that parts two forks of the wild Pasayten River. Walk this way in midsummer and be dazzled by a wide array of blossoming beauties. Lupine, paintbrush, cinquefoil, aster, monkey flower, and an array of louseworts all add their strokes to this alpine easel. And Silver Lake? It's a wonderful backcountry body of water tucked in a basin beneath 7850-foot Pasayten Peak.

GETTING THERE

From Winthrop drive the North Cascades Highway (State Route 20) west for 13 miles to the Mazama turnoff just past milepost 180. From Marblemount follow SR 20 east for 73 miles. Proceed north for 0.5 mile to Mazama. Turn left (west) at the intersection, following the paved road to Harts Pass (Lost River Road). The pavement ends in 6.7 miles, and the road becomes Forest Road 54. Follow this harrowing, at times narrow road for 12 miles to Harts Pass. Pass the campground and guard station, bearing right toward Slate Peak. Drive 1.7 miles to the trailhead at the second switchback (elev. 6850 ft).

ON THE TRAIL

The trail to Silver Lake starts high and stays high, but much elevation is gained and lost along the way. Trail No. 498 starts with a short, steep climb of 100 feet to Slate Pass and amazing views—all before you've really gone anywhere. Slate Peak stands out immediately to your left. To the south and west are a cavalcade of North Cascades crests and summits as far as you can see. And to the north the U-shaped Middle Fork Pasayten River valley unfurls an emerald swath beneath craggy peaks.

Begin a steep descent into a heather and talus sloped basin where an obscure trail leads right toward Robinson Pass. Continue

straight through larches and meadows, admiring Slate Peak to your left hovering above you and Robinson Mountain on your right hovering above everything. Marmots and ground squirrels scurry about.

After 1 mile of fairly easy meandering and 1.5 miles from the trailhead, come to a junction with Middle Fork Pasayten Trail No. 575 (elev. 6500 ft). Stay left. The trail continues high on Gold Ridge, mainly in meadows, occasionally in subalpine forest groves. What it doesn't do, however, is hold a contour. Three times the way drops 200 to 300 feet, and three times

Silver Lake

it regains it. Several small creeks are crossed, but they may be dry come late summer. Pack sufficient water.

At 4.5 miles the trail climbs once more, this time more steeply, and once again it drops, again more steeply, losing over 400 feet this time. Now in a forested grove, locate an obvious but unmarked trail leading left. Take it. In no time you'll be admiring the glistening waters of Silver Lake.

Inviting shoreline meadows tempt you to nap. The shallow lake's warm waters welcome a foot soak. When the lake's level is low feel free to walk along a gravel shoreline to explore its marshy far end. Here among willows and cotton grasses, a stampede of elephant's head (a flowering figwort) flourishes. Of course, there's nothing wrong with just sitting by the lake and listening to the spotted sandpipers and watching trout snap flies as you rest up for the rolling return.

MEXICO TO CANADA

Putting in a long and hard day on the trail can certainly be challenging, but most likely rewarding as well. Can you imagine hiking for three, four, or five months? A small but growing group of hikers from coast to coast do just that each year on one of America's eight long-distance National Scenic Trails. The granddaddy of them all, the 2175-mile Appalachian Trail (AT) is the most popular. Completed in 1937, it winds its way from Georgia to Maine.

Here in the North Cascades, the Pacific Crest Trail finishes up its 2650 miles that started at the Mexican border. Officially completed in 1993, the Pacific Crest Trail, or PCT as it is lovingly called, became one of two of America's first national trails in 1968, along with the AT. Administered by the National Park Service, the National Trails System consists of congressionally designated trails. Inclusion in the system is based on a trail's cultural, historical, and scenic attributes as well as its draw for outdoor recreation.

The PCT, like most of the national trails, actually consists of many trails woven together to form one continuous corridor. While much of the PCT traverses deep wilderness far from population centers and roads, many good day-hiking opportunities exist where the trail crosses or comes close to roads.

The trail is well maintained and is cared for by several citizens groups, such as the Pacific Crest Trail Association. In the North Cascades take a day hike on this grand trail at Cutthroat Pass (Hike 95), Stiletto Peak (Hike 96), and from Harts Pass to Windy Pass (Hike 101), where it traverses some of the most spectacular scenery found anywhere within the National Trails System.

Opposite: Tarn on North Lake Trail

east slope

Methow River Valley

The sun-kissed Methow Valley has long had a reputation as one of the best places in the Northwest to glide across snowy trails in winter or cruise along single tracks in summer. But hikers need not shun the classic U-shaped valley for the hinterlands. In spring and fall the valley's trails are especially delightful to explore, especially the spring, when entire hillsides are streaked in a riot of blossoming wildflowers. Residents and visitors of the valley are an active lot. And thanks to a strong local trail association, they've got plenty of miles of interconnecting paths to be active on.

103 Lost River

RATING/ DIFFICULTY	ROUND-TRIP	ELEV GAIN/ HIGH POINT	SEASON
★★★/2	8 miles	300 feet/ 2700 feet	May–Nov

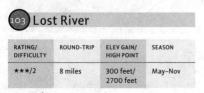

Maps: Green Trails Washington Pass No. 50, Mazama No. 51; **Contact:** Okanogan National Forest, Methow Valley Ranger District, (509) 996-4003, www.fs.fed.us/r6/oka; **Notes:** Rattlesnake habitat, be aware and keep dogs nearby; **GPS:** N 48 39.375, W 120 30.764

Amble 4 fairly easy miles alongside the delightful and wild Lost River. Follow the waterway into the Pasayten Wilderness, stopping at the base of a forbidding gorge. Here, where the river emerges from the darkness of the near-impenetrable chasm, imagine what lands lie farther upstream. But be sure to take time to appreciate the fully revealed wild country—big trees, mesmerizing rapids, and steep valley walls will not be lost on you.

GETTING THERE

From Winthrop drive the North Cascades Highway (State Route 20) west for 13 miles to the Mazama turnoff just past milepost 180. From Marblemount follow SR 20 east for 73 miles. Proceed north for 0.5 mile to Mazama. Turn left (west) at the intersection, following the Lost River Road for 7 miles to the trailhead, on your right and signed "Monument Trail" (elev. 2500 ft). The trailhead is 0.25 mile beyond end of pavement.

ON THE TRAIL

Monument Creek Trail No. 484 starts by a sign that says "Eureka Creek 4 miles." Why "Monument Creek"? Because that's where this trail eventually leads. Why "Eureka Creek"? Because its confluence with Lost Creek is where most hikers stop. Taking off into a stand of conifers, the trail finds Lost River soon enough. After slightly climbing above the swift-moving waterway, the trail moves in closer to hug its banks on several occasions.

Pass by stately ponderosa pines and across gentle flats while working your way up the river valley. After 2 miles or so the course gets a little rougher, intermittently crossing rocky slopes that challenge your footing and, in summer, your tolerance for heat. Expect to see snakes on these sunny basking spots, but not necessarily the ones that rattle. Once I spotted a rubber boa along the trail, a rather odd but interesting reptile. Owing its name to its loose skin and plump appearance, these serpents are docile. But if disturbed, they'll curl up and hold up their blunt strong tail, perhaps "striking" with it.

At just over 3 miles enter the Pasayten Wilderness, one of the wildest places remaining in Washington. One mile farther arrive at the confluence of Lost and Eureka creeks (elev. 2650 ft). On the bridge spanning Eureka, take a break to admire the creek's pretty waterfall and to gaze into the gorges that swallow both

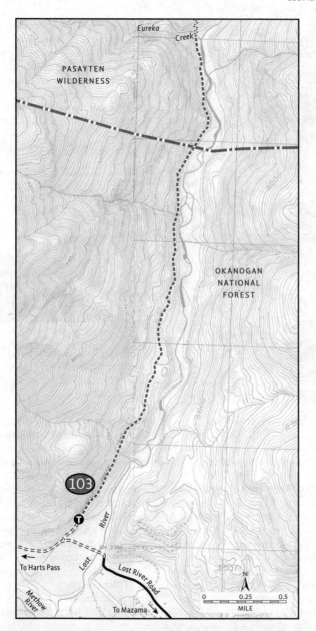

PASAYTEN
WILDERNESS

Eureka   Creek

OKANOGAN
NATIONAL
FOREST

103

Lost River

To Harts Pass

Lost River Road

Methow
River

To Mazama

N

0   0.25   0.5
MILE

A hiker stares into the Lost River gorge.

waterways from view. From this point upstream Lost River, earns its name.

EXTENDING YOUR TRIP

You can continue hiking beyond this point, but the journey is brutal. The trail ascends an insanely steep rib, climbing 4600 feet in 6 bone-dry miles to 7300-foot Pistol Pass before plunging 2700 feet in 3 knee-jarring miles to Monument Creek. Feel free, however, to push up the ridge 0.5 mile or so for some good views looking back down the Lost River valley. If you're interested in exploring a couple of other

nearby wild river valleys, consider Robinson Creek (trailhead 1.5 miles toward Harts Pass) and the West Fork Methow River (trailhead 2.5 miles toward Harts Pass). Both of these trails make good spring or fall hikes. Equestrians and hunters frequent them, but hikers are scarce. You'll find plenty of wildlife and, like along the Lost River, keep an eye out for rattlers.

104 Goat Peak

RATING/ DIFFICULTY	ROUND-TRIP	ELEV GAIN/ HIGH POINT	SEASON
★★★★/3	5 miles	1400 feet/ 7001 feet	June– late Oct

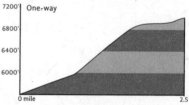

Map: Green Trails Mazama No. 51; **Contact:** Okanogan National Forest, Methow Valley Ranger District, (509) 996-4003, *www.fs.fed .us/r6/oka*; **GPS:** N 48 39.100, W 120 24.040

 Short and sweet and just a tad bit steep, this trail gets you to Goat Peak, sentinel over the Methow Valley with commanding views of its snaking river and the legions of nearby cloud-piercing peaks. Home to one of two active fire lookouts in the Methow (the other being Lookout Mountain, Hike 106), Goat was chosen for its stand-alone position over the rolling, prone-to-lightning-strikes terrain. But the views are striking too, so storm on over.

GETTING THERE

From Winthrop drive the North Cascades Highway (State Route 20) west for 8 miles, turning right onto Goat Creek Road at milepost 185 (the turnoff is just before the bridge over the Methow River). Continue on Goat Creek Road for 3.3 miles, turning right onto Forest Road 52. (If coming from the west, follow SR 20 east to the Mazama turnoff. Drive 0.5 mile to Mazama, then turn right onto Goat Creek Road and drive 1.9 miles, turning left onto FR 52.) Proceed on FR 52 for 2.8 miles, turning left onto FR 5225. In 6.5 miles turn right onto

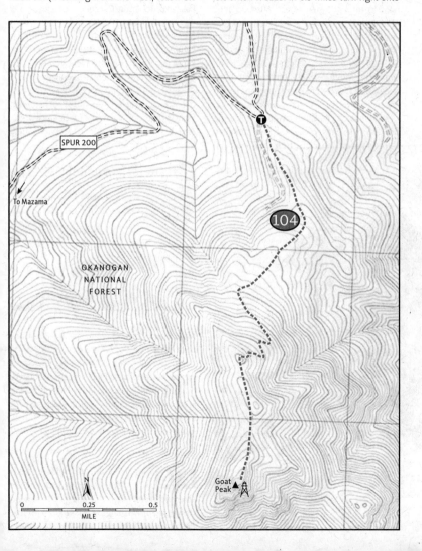

FR Spur 200 and drive 3 miles to the trailhead (elev. 5600 ft). Privy available.

ON THE TRAIL

From Goat Peak's mile-high trailhead, begin hoofing through open forest. After 0.5 mile of fairly easy ambling, the trail kicks into gear and rapidly gains elevation. Forest openings offer periodic peeks at surrounding peaks. After subduing a series of tight switchbacks on somewhat rough terrain, crest a small knoll (elev. 6850 ft), one of several that'll have you on a roll as you zero in on the lookout.

With most of the climb now past, enjoy the final 0.5 mile. Traversing meadows sprinkled with clumps of tenacious trees, you'll take in ever grander views. At 2.5 miles reach Goat's 7000-plus-one-foot summit. Tilt your water bottle back—you brought plenty, right? there's none along the way—and scan the horizons. Look north to the pinnacles of the Pasayten, Robinson, Osceola, and Pistol among them. The Tiffany Highlands hog the eastern horizon, while Azurite, Tower, and Cutthroat command the west. But it's the summits due south that'll siphon most of your attention, with Silver Star shining supreme among them.

Good spot for a fire lookout, huh? The first one was constructed here in 1923. The one in front of you has been in service since 1950. And the attendant? How long in service? You'll have to ask yourself.

105 Patterson Mountain

RATING/ DIFFICULTY	ROUND-TRIP	ELEV GAIN/ HIGH POINT	SEASON
★★★/3	3.7 miles	1100 feet/ 3500 feet	Apr– early Nov

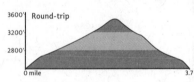

Map: Green Trails Sun Mountain No. 83S; **Contact:** Department of Natural Resources, Northeast Region (Colville), (509) 684-7474, *www.dnr.wa.gov;* **Notes:** DNR vehicle use permit required, available from agency or where hunting/fishing licenses are sold. If you don't have permit, park in small lot on south side of Patterson Lake Road, just beyond boat launch; **GPS:** N 48 27.718, W 120 14.630

Save this one for April or May when this normally drab peak is streaked in enough purple and gold to make a University of Washington Husky jump for joy. Patterned in lupine and larkspur, buckwheat

Author inspects summit privy.

Bitterroot in bloom

and balsamroot, Patterson is packed with showy blossoms in the spring. But there's more to meet your eyes than the fabulous floral show. Views far and near await you as well, from the sparkling waters of Patterson Lake to the glistening glaciers of the Sawtooth Ridge.

GETTING THERE

From Winthrop head east on State Route 20 for 0.6 mile, immediately turning right onto Twin Lakes Road (signed for the Winthrop National Fish Hatchery; the turnoff is just after crossing the Methow River). Follow Twin Lakes Road for 3 miles, turning right onto Patterson Lake Road (signed "Sun Mountain Lodge 6.4 miles"). Continue for 4 miles to the Patterson Lake boat ramp. Park on the south side of the road in a small pullout. The trail begins on the opposite side of the road (elev. 2400 ft). Additional parking is available 0.6 mile farther north at an alternative trailhead.

ON THE TRAIL

Directly across from Patterson Lake's boat launch, the trail begins climbing Patterson Mountain's sun-baked slopes. Most of the way is open to the elements. In winter, winds whip. In summer, temperatures scorch. But in spring and fall, this hike is a delight. Part of an extensive trail system developed and maintained by the Methow Valley Sports Trail Association, the Patterson trails primarily traverse Washington State Department of Natural Resources lands. But some private tracts are also crossed; respect postings.

In 0.3 mile after passing through a gate, reach a four-way junction (elev. 2650 ft). The trail left leads 0.7 mile across balsamroot, bitterroot, and basalt to the alternative trailhead near Patterson Lake's dam. The trail straight ahead is where you'll be returning from. Take the path right and begin your loop.

Angling across grassy slopes and the occasional aspen grove (lovely in autumn), steadily

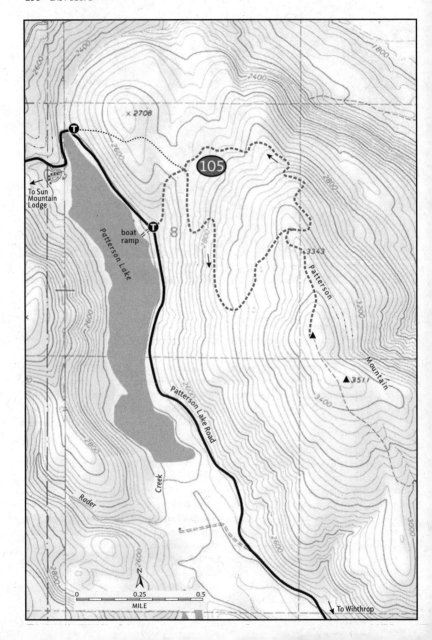

ascend. Views are nonstop. Patterson Lake shimmers below. About a mile from the junction a lone ponderosa pine shades you from the sun. A little farther, reach a junction (elev. 3200 ft). The spur right leads 0.5 mile along a ridge to attain Patterson's 3500-foot summit.

From the broad summit, feast on views: South to Hoodoo and the serrated Sawtooths. North to Winthrop and golden foothills, and Tiffany and North Twentymile peek from behind. East to Lookout Mountain and west to Goat and Gardner. Once satiated, retrace your steps to the junction.

Now complete the loop by heading right. Descending on northern slopes, behold—trees! In 1 mile return to the four-way junction. Your vehicle awaits you 0.3 mile ahead.

EXTENDING YOUR TRIP

There are plenty of nearby trails tying Patterson to the Sun Mountain Lodge's sprawling property, the Methow Valley, and the Okanogan

National Forest. Many of the trails are popular with mountain bikers, but in spring and fall the fat-tire aficionados are frequently absent. Trails in the Patterson Lake and Beaver Pond areas are particularly attractive for pedestrian travel.

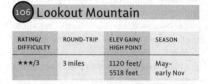

106 Lookout Mountain

RATING/ DIFFICULTY	ROUND-TRIP	ELEV GAIN/ HIGH POINT	SEASON
★★★/3	3 miles	1120 feet/ 5518 feet	May– early Nov

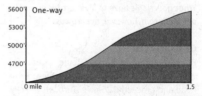

Map: Green Trails Twisp No. 84; **Contact:** Okanogan National Forest, Methow Valley Ranger District, (509) 996-4003, *www.fs.fed*

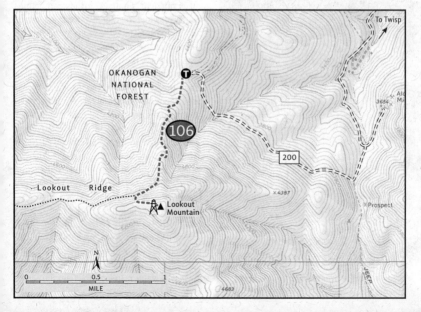

.us/r6/oka; **Notes:** Final 1.5 miles of access road can be rough. Park at gate and walk road if necessary; **GPS:** N 48 19.454, W 120 11.076

👪 ⚙ *From this landmark peak rising above the community of Twisp, you can look out over the placid Methow Valley and to lofty peaks north and south. Look out to the Sawtooth Ridge and also to the golden Columbia River plateau too. And look out from a fire tower lookout, one of a few still remaining in the region and still heeding Smoky's call. What you won't have to look out for on Lookout Mountain, however, are crowds.*

GETTING THERE

From Winthrop drive State Route 20 east for 11 miles to Twisp. Turn right onto Twisp River Road and proceed 0.25 mile. Turn left directly across from the Okanogan Rescue and Fire Department building, bearing right onto Lookout Mountain Road. In 0.2 mile bear left onto a gravel road that eventually becomes Forest Road 200. Drive 6.5 miles to the road end and trailhead (elev. 4400 ft).

ON THE TRAIL

Unmarked but obvious Lookout Mountain Trail No. 412 starts off on an old Cat track before settling into full-fledged trail. Open to multiple uses, including motorcycles, the trail is nevertheless lightly traveled and the tread is good and not chewed up, so hikers shouldn't shy away. The mountain is bone dry after snowmelt; don't forget your water bottle. The trail heads up a steep rib for 1 mile or so before easing up, traveling mainly under a forested canopy of pine and fir. In early summer the way is lined with shooting stars, spring beauties, and penstemon.

The trail then turns south, skirting the summit. At 1.2 miles (elev. 5350 ft), the lightly traveled and hard-to-follow Lookout Ridge Trail takes off right. Continue left instead, immediately leaving forest for meadows and ledges and a breathtaking view south to the soaring summits of the Sawtooth Ridge, Hoodoo and Oval peaks the most prominent.

But don't stop here. Continue for 0.25 mile to reach the 5518-foot summit and its handsome fire lookout. Now stroll around the open summit, absorbing the panorama. Get out the map and start identifying landmarks. Gardner, Patterson, Goat, and Robinson lie west. Tiffany, Bald, North Twentymile, and Granite are due north. The Columbia Plateau is to the east, and you already know what lies south—the Sawtooths. Directly below is the Methow Valley—what a sight!

EXTENDING YOUR TRIP

If you don't mind a little scouting, you can extend your hike by heading off on the Lookout Ridge Trail. Expect a handful of ups and downs, no water, no people, but plentiful views on this 4.6-mile trail.

Arrowleaf balsamroot beneath Lookout Mountain's lookout

THE UNTRAMMELED NORTH CASCADES

While most of the North Cascades is within national forest, that doesn't necessarily mean all the area is protected. National forests are managed for "multiple use." While some uses—like hiking—are fairly compatible with land preservation, other uses—like mining, logging, and off-road-vehicle use—are not.

Recognizing that parts of our natural heritage should be altered as little as possible, Congress passed the Wilderness Act in 1964 with bipartisan support (the House approved passage 373-1). One of the strongest and most important pieces of environmental legislation in our nation's history, the Wilderness Act afforded some of our most precious wild landscapes a reprieve from exploitation, development, and harmful activities such as motorized recreation. Even bicycles are banned from federal wilderness areas. Wilderness is "an area where the earth and community of life are untrammeled by man," says the legislation, "where man himself is a visitor who does not remain."

While the North Cascades had no shortage of qualifying lands back in 1964, only one area, Glacier Peak, was designated as wilderness. By 1968, however, the Pasayten was added, along with the new North Cascades National Park. The federal wilderness system would eventually include wilderness areas in national parks, as well as wildlife refuges and other federal lands. In 1984, a sweeping wilderness bill created five more wilderness areas in the region, and there are now more than 2 million acres of official wilderness:

San Juan Islands—353 acres

Mount Baker—117,528 acres

Stephen Mather (in North Cascades
    National Park)—634,614 acres

Pasayten—529,477 acres

Noisy-Diobsud—14,133 acres

Lake Chelan–Sawtooth—151,435 acres

Boulder River—48,674 acres

Glacier Peak—570,573 acres

Henry M. Jackson—100,356 acres

This seems impressive—Washington does rank fourth among the states in total wilderness acreage—but many conservationists (and this author) feel that it's not enough. The vast majority of our national forest lands are still under threat from development and motorized recreation. And while some of our public land base should be turned over for these uses, our last remaining unprotected roadless tracts of pristine wild country should not be.

In 2009 Congress added the Wild Sky Wilderness in the central Cascades to our state's wilderness areas. In the North Cascades, these large roadless areas deserve wilderness designation:

Mount Higgins and Pressentin Creek (Finney Block, Hikes 41 and 51)—28,000 acres

Helena Ridge (Mountain Loop Highway, Hikes 24, 26, and 27)—32,000 acres

Liberty Bell (North Cascades Highway, Hikes 91, 92, 95, 98, and 100)—112,000 acres

South Sawtooth (Sawtooth Ridge, Hikes 113, 114, and 115)—96,000 acres

Tiffany (Tiffany Highlands, Hikes 120 and 121)—24,000 acres

Long Swamp (Twentymile-Thirtymile region, Hike 119)—70,000 acres

Granite Mountain (Tiffany Highlands, Hikes 122 and 123)—28,000 acres

Whether these lands remain untrammeled and wild for future generations is a matter of public opinion and political will.

Twisp River Valley

A major tributary of the Methow, the Twisp River cuts a wide and deep valley in the Cascades' Sawtooth Range. Long a favorite stomping ground for equestrians and backpackers heading to the Lake Chelan National Recreation Area, the Twisp River valley has much to offer day hikers too. Scads of sparkling alpine lakes sit high in the surrounding rugged ridges. All of these gems require a little effort to reach, but their gorgeous environs make them well worth the sweat expended. And because the hikes aren't cakewalks and the trailheads are far from population centers, don't expect too much company on the trail.

107 Scatter Lake

RATING/ DIFFICULTY	ROUND-TRIP	ELEV GAIN/ HIGH POINT	SEASON
★★★/5	8.5 miles	3850 feet/ 7047 feet	July–Oct

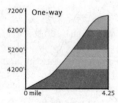

One-way

7200'
6200'
5200'
4200'

0 mile — 4.25

Map: Green Trails Stehekin No. 82; **Contact:** Okanogan National Forest, Methow Valley Ranger District, (509) 996-4003, www .fs.fed.us/r6/oka; **Notes:** NW Forest Pass required; **GPS:** N 48 26.089, W 120 31.205

⚙ *In an area of supreme larch hikes, Scatter Lake ranks among the best. Clamber up a steep and arduous trail to this secluded tarn tucked in a high cirque beneath the 8321-foot summit of Abernathy Peak. Once there, find a shoreline spot for sunning or set out to* explore the surrounding blueberry-carpeted, larch-lined, barren-sloped basin.

GETTING THERE

From Twisp follow the Twisp River Road west for 21.8 miles to the trailhead (elev. 3200 ft). The road is signed "Twisp River Recreation Area" and becomes Forest Road 44 at 10.8 miles, and becomes FR 4440 at the pavement's end at 18 miles. Privy available.

ON THE TRAIL

Start by warming up on Twisp River Trail No. 440. Immediately encounter a junction and head left. Shortly afterward reach another junction, and this time turn right onto Trail No. 427. The first mile or so is easy enough, the trail gradually climbing out of the Twisp River valley through an open forest of fir and pine. Enjoy window views out toward Twisp Pass.

The gentle grade becomes a thing of the past once Scatter Creek is encountered. On a bank high above the chattering creek, the trail changes direction and course to head straight up the narrow creek canyon. Soon enter the Lake Chelan–Sawtooth Wilderness Area, a 145,000-acre protected band of high peaks, alpine lakes, unbroken forest, and some prime Lake Chelan shoreline as well.

The hike now becomes a grind as switchbacks grow tighter and the trail gets steeper. The forest begins to open up and meadows appear, anticipation increases. You'll soon cross Scatter Creek—dip your bandana in cool, clear water and apply to your forehead. Carry on as switchbacks fade from existence and the trail gets even steeper. At about 3.5 miles reach a delightful meadow in a small basin (elev. 6500 ft). You're almost there. On steep slopes matted with blueberry bushes and punctuated with tenacious whitebark pines, subalpine fir, and larches, the trail makes its last climb to the lake.

Opposite: Scatter Lake in cirque beneath Abernathy Peak

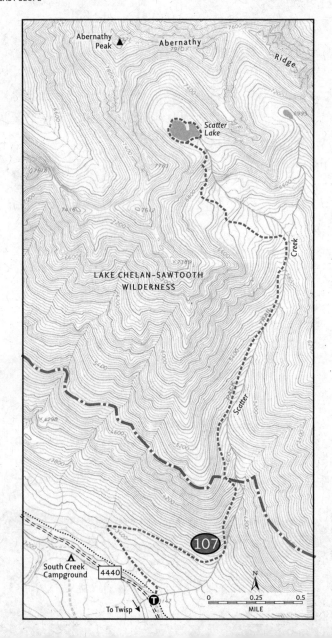

Rising above a small cascade, the trail enters the lake-housing cirque. A beautiful, shallow, larch-ringed tarn is immediately encountered. Scatter Lake, the real gem, is just a short distance farther. Soak your feet, soothe your soul, or just stare up at the barren slopes sliding into the lake. A 0.5-mile path circles the lake. Take your time.

EXTENDING YOUR TRIP
If reaching Scatter Lake wasn't too daunting, nearby Slate Lake (trailhead is downriver) offers a similar experience. Stats: 10-mile roundtrip, 3700 feet of vertical gain. Mystery, South Creek, and Poplar Flat campgrounds on the Twisp River make for good car-camping bases.

108 North Lake

RATING/ DIFFICULTY	ROUND-TRIP	ELEV GAIN/ HIGH POINT	SEASON
★★★★/3	9.8 miles	2200 feet/ 5800 feet	July–Oct

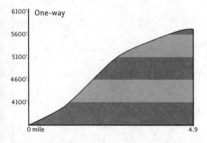

Map: Green Trails Stehekin No. 82; **Contact:** Okanogan National Forest, Methow Valley Ranger District, (509) 996-4003, www.fs.fed.us/r6/oka; **Notes:** NW Forest Pass required; **GPS:** N 48 27.514, W 120 34.053

Equestrians take to it. So did early prospectors and a few latter-day ones as well. But for some reason very few hikers find themselves on the trail to North Lake. Perhaps the nearby view-granting Twisp

Snowmelt creek flowing into North Lake

and Copper Pass trails siphon them away. But North Lake has views too—up-close and personal ones of lofty neighbors, 8321-foot Abernathy Peak and 8023-foot Gilbert Mountain. And the lake isn't too shabby either, cupped in a snowy and rocky cirque and waterfall fed. But I guess you'll have to take my word for it.

GETTING THERE
From Twisp follow the Twisp River Road west for 24.6 miles. The road is signed "Twisp River

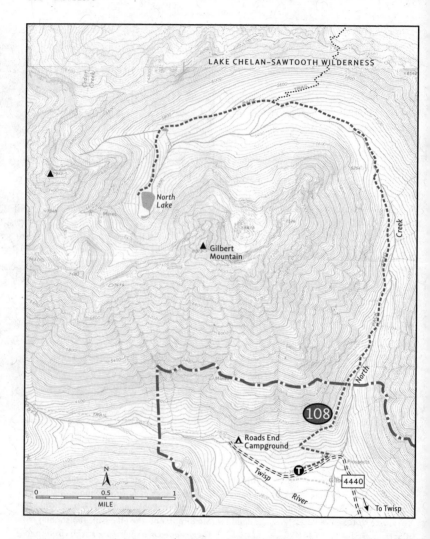

Recreation Area" and becomes Forest Road 44 at 10.8 miles, and becomes FR 4440 at the pavement's end at 18 miles. Turn right at the "Twisp Pass Trail" sign and in 0.1 mile come to a large parking lot and horse unloading area (elev. 3600 ft). Privy available.

ON THE TRAIL

From the trail register, head right on the North Creek Trail. The trail begins in an area that once housed the gold-mining boomtown of Gilbert. Nothing remains of it, but active claims still dot the area. Through open forest, the way is gentle at first, but the warm-up soon ends and you start climbing. After a series of long switchbacks the trail enters the North Creek valley (elev. 3900 ft). Now on a slope above the crashing creek, cross a couple of scree slopes before reentering forest. At 1.25 miles cross the wilderness boundary, and the way steepens.

Soon afterward encounter a creek and slide-prone area, but it shouldn't prove too tricky to negotiate. Now on improved tread the trail marches up the valley, undulating between cool evergreen groves and sun-kissed avalanche slopes. Stare back at the Sawtooth Range that hovers over the Twisp River valley and east up steep slopes to red-capped Abernathy Peak brushing the sky.

At 2.75 miles (elev. 5100 ft) you must cross bridgeless North Creek, a difficult maneuver in high water. Once over, the trail bends westward and pleasantly proceeds through groves of pine and spruce. At 3.4 miles reach a junction with the Cedar Creek Trail (elev. 5350 ft). Notice the old sign being swallowed up by an Engelmann spruce. It reads "Chelan National Forest," making it over fifty years old because the Chelan became the Okanogan National Forest in 1955.

Continue straight on good tread and an easy grade through delightful forest. At 4.2 miles enter a marshy meadow rife with orchids, asters, lupines, and mosquitoes. Pass a pretty tarn and hop over a babbling brook. Now hike the final stretch, an easy 0.7 mile through mature timber. At 4.9 miles reach pretty North Lake (elev. 5800 ft) sitting in a deep cirque on the north side of Gilbert Mountain.

Stretch out in the shoreline meadows or explore the basin. Kiss a waterfall. Discover a hidden "upper lake." Find remnants of old mining activity, but avoid being shafted (seriously, be aware of open pits). Wonder why this beautiful place remains off the radar for so many hikers.

EXTENDING YOUR TRIP
Follow the primitive Cedar Creek Trail 1.2 miles and 1000 vertical feet up to 6400-foot Abernathy Pass. Then scramble west along the ridge for views of Gilbert and Silver Star and down the Cedar and North Creek valleys.

109 Copper Pass

RATING/ DIFFICULTY	ROUND-TRIP	ELEV GAIN/ HIGH POINT	SEASON
★★★★/4	10 miles	3160 feet/ 6760 feet	July– mid-Oct

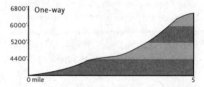

Map: Green Trails Stehekin No. 82; **Contact:** Okanogan National Forest, Methow Valley Ranger District, (509) 996-4003, *www.fs.fed.us/r6/oka*; **Notes:** NW Forest Pass required; **GPS:** N 48 27.514, W 120 34.053

Hike to a heathered high divide at the headwaters of the Twisp River. Following an old prospector's path first through lush forest then across sun-kissed slopes flush in floral splendor, the way isn't easy but it has its rewards. From the lofty pass enjoy up-close and personal views of some of the North Cascades more distinguished peaks. To the north Liberty Bell Mountain rings out, while Stiletto Peak sticks out like a knife in the south. Visit in fall and watch Copper turn to gold thanks to the larches.

GETTING THERE
From Twisp follow the Twisp River Road west for 24.6 miles. The road is signed "Twisp River Recreation Area" and becomes Forest Road

44 at 10.8 miles, and becomes FR 4440 at the pavement's end at 18 miles. Turn right at the "Twisp Pass Trail" sign and in 0.1 mile come to a large parking lot and horse unloading area (elev. 3600 ft). Privy available.

ON THE TRAIL

Three worthy trails disperse from this trailhead. Take the one heading west, Twisp Pass Trail No. 432. The way starts off easy enough as it parallels FR 4440 for 0.4 mile to its terminus at the appropriately named Roads End Campground. Now with road gone, enter the Lake Chelan–Sawtooth Wilderness. Following alongside the Twisp River, the trail alternates between lush groves of forest and warm, brushy avalanche slopes. The grade is gentle. In late spring songbirds are abundant in the shrubs and thickets lining the valley floor. Look for the elegant western tanager among the avian choir.

Eventually the grade steepens. At 2 miles, at the confluence of the North and South Forks of the Twisp River, come to a junction (elev. 4400 ft). The trail left heads to Twisp Pass (Hike 110). Instead, bear right onto Trail No. 426, the path less chosen. Following the North Fork in cool groves of old conifers, the trail marches up the broad valley. Cross the North Fork at 3.5 miles (elev. 5200 ft) and prepare to work. The way now climbs steadily and steeply. Hastily built by prospectors intent on reaching their claims, the trail heads for the pass in a most direct fashion.

Forest yields to meadows matted in heather and wildflowers. At 5 miles crest the 6760-foot pass. Wipe your brow and take in the views. Early Winters Spires, Stiletto Peak, and Frisco Mountain, all familiar sights along the North Cascades Highway, reveal different facades from your new outpost. The big snowy peak to the west is Goode Mountain. In fact, it's all good up here.

Early summer ascent of Copper Pass

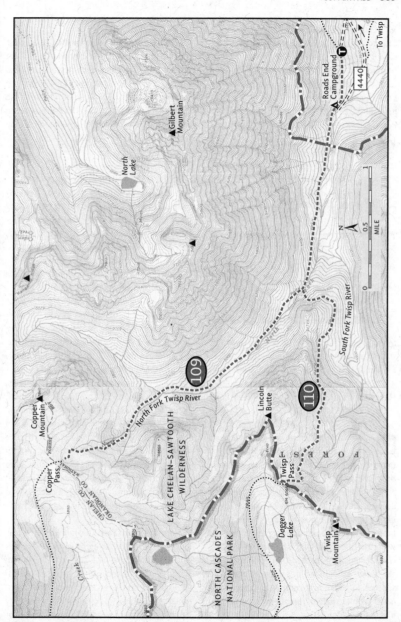

To Twisp

Roads End Campground

4440

North Lake

Gilbert Mountain

Cedar Creek

N

0   0.5   1
MILE

109

North Fork Twisp River

South Fork Twisp River

North

Copper Mountain

Copper Pass

LAKE CHELAN–SAWTOOTH WILDERNESS

CHELAN CO.
OKANOGAN CO.

NATIONAL

Lincoln Butte

110

Twisp Pass

F O R E S T

NORTH CASCADES NATIONAL PARK

Dagger Lake

Twisp Mountain

EXTENDING YOUR TRIP

The trail continues west for 4 more miles (though is more primitive), dropping into the herbaceous Copper Creek valley to connect with the Pacific Crest Trail 1 mile south of SR 20. For a loop, hike south on the PCT for 2 miles and then head 8 miles east on the Twisp Pass Trail to return to your vehicle.

110 Twisp Pass

RATING/ DIFFICULTY	ROUND-TRIP	ELEV GAIN/ HIGH POINT	SEASON
★★★★/3	9 miles	2460 feet/ 6064 feet	Late June– Oct

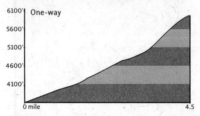

Map: Green Trails Stehekin No. 82; **Contact:** Okanogan National Forest, Methow Valley Ranger District, (509) 996-4003, www.fs.fed .us/r6/oka; **Notes:** NW Forest Pass required; **Notes:** Dogs prohibited beyond Twisp Pass; **GPS:** N 48 27.514, W 120 34.053

Glorious in autumn when golden larches set the hills aglow and crimson blueberry bushes light the meadows on fire, this dramatic portal into the North Cascades National Park makes a fine summer destination as well. During those warmer months enjoy alpine floral displays with glacier lilies, phlox, lupine, and paintbrush stealing the show. And while Twisp Pass in itself is a worthy objective, consider pushing farther. Drop down to Dagger Lake or wander a couple of miles of spectacular, open high country to explore polished granite shelves, remote grassy benches, and quiet hidden tarns.

GETTING THERE

From Twisp follow the Twisp River Road west for 24.6 miles. The road is signed "Twisp River Recreation Area" and becomes Forest Road 44 at 10.8 miles, and becomes FR 4440 at the pavement's end at 18 miles. Turn right at the "Twisp Pass Trail" sign and in 0.1 mile come to a large parking lot and horse unloading area (elev. 3600 ft). Privy available.

ON THE TRAIL

Take the trail heading west, Twisp Pass Trail No. 432. A fairly popular path among equestrians, the way is wide and well groomed and occasionally adorned with road apples. For its first 0.4 mile the trail parallels FR 4440 on its way to the Roads End Campground (a good place to stay over for an early start).

Leaving the road behind, enter the Lake Chelan–Sawtooth Wilderness and enjoy easy walking in a wild valley. Following alongside the Twisp River, the trail undulates between lush forest and warm, brushy avalanche slopes. Pass giant cottonwoods, deciduous behemoths among the colossal conifers. Pyramidal Lincoln Butte hovers above.

The grade eventually steepens. At 2 miles, at the confluence of the North and South Forks of the Twisp River, come to a junction (elev. 4400 ft). The trail right leads to Copper Pass (Hike 109). Stay left instead and cross the North Fork on a narrow bridge. Now steadily gaining elevation, the trail skirts Lincoln Butte and slabs up a series of benches. Thinning pines and a handful of ledges provide for good glimpses down the glacially carved Twisp River valley.

With the South Fork now far below, the trail works its way higher along Lincoln's southern slopes. Admire nice rock cribbing along the trail. Admire, too, growing views of South Creek Butte and Crescent, Hock, and Twisp mountains. Pass rock gardens, blueberry patches, heather meadows, and clumps of

Twisp Pass high country

subalpine fir. At 5.5 miles, in splendid park-lands, arrive at Twisp Pass (elev. 6064 ft). A well-weathered sign indicates you're only a few steps away from entering the sprawling North Cascades National Park.

EXTENDING YOUR TRIP

Dagger Lake lies within the park, beyond the pass another mile and 600 feet down. Four-legged hikers are not permitted, and they may very well be grateful for this. Swarming clouds of mosquitoes are not unheard of at the lake. A short way path leads left from the pass to a small tarn in the shadow of craggy Twisp Mountain. And supreme wanderings lie in the other direction along an abandoned but very obvious trail that heads north from the pass toward Stiletto Peak. Tread eventually peters out at a high basin below the old Stiletto lookout about 2 miles from the pass. Experienced cross-country travelers can connect with the Stiletto Peak Trail to bag the old lookout site (Hike 96) or can make a loop by dropping down to the Stiletto Spur Trail and returning on the Twisp Pass Trail. Or combine the main hike with the Copper Pass Trail (Hike 109) for another long loop choice.

111 Louis Lake

RATING/ DIFFICULTY	ROUND-TRIP	ELEV GAIN/ HIGH POINT	SEASON
★★★/3	10.5 miles	2300 feet/ 5351 feet	Mid-June– Oct

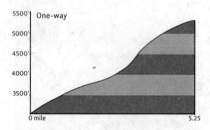

Map: Green Trails Stehekin No. 82; **Contact:** Okanogan National Forest, Methow Valley Ranger District, (509) 996-4003, www.fs.fed.us/r6/oka; **Notes:** NW Forest Pass required; **GPS:** N 48 26.368, W 120 31.872

Hike to a high hidden valley housing one of the largest alpine lakes in the Sawtooth Range. Under the watchful eyes of 7742-foot Rennie Peak, an 8000-plus-foot nameless neighbor and a junta of jagged pinnacles, Louis Lake's lofty surroundings are quite stunning. But despite such a rugged setting, the trek to Louis is most agreeable. Hoof this way in early summer before the horses arrive and enjoy a dazzling floral show as an added bonus.

GETTING THERE

From Twisp follow the Twisp River Road west for 22.4 miles to the trailhead at South Creek Campground (elev. 3050 ft). The road is signed "Twisp River Recreation Area" and becomes Forest Road 44 at 10.8 miles, and becomes FR 4440 at the pavement's end at 18 miles. Privy available.

ON THE TRAIL

Begin your hike from the South Creek Campground, not a bad place to hunker down the night before. Head up Trail No. 401 and cross the Twisp River on a bridge. At 0.3 mile the equestrian onramp merges from the left. Now on a well-groomed backcountry byway, South Creek babbling by your side, begin an easy ascent up a broad valley. Hovering summits surround you. The openness to the area has a Rocky Mountains ambience.

After 2 delightful miles on the South Creek Trail, come to a junction. Turn left onto Trail No. 428, descending a bit to a bridge crossing South Creek. Now in an impressive forest of old Douglas-fir, Engelmann spruce, and western white pine, begin climbing up the Louis Creek valley with the help of switchbacks. High above the creek, the trail works its way up the imposing valley. Avalanche chutes offer an occasional look out to the rocky ridges and serrated summits surrounding you. As you look back, Crescent Mountain and South Creek Butte command your attention.

At 4.25 miles the trail makes a bend westward. Louis Creek soon presents itself trailside. Come to Louis Lake 1 mile farther, in an open bowl of talus slopes and stark striated walls. Marvel at the large "driftwood" logs floating on the lake's surface and piled near its outlet, gifts from the avalanche gods. It's quite an impressive scene. Now sit your weary self down on one of those shoreline logs and savor the alpine serenity.

EXTENDING YOUR TRIP

You can follow the South Creek Trail for another 5 miles to South Pass, a 6300-foot notch in the Sawtooth crest. Or perhaps another Sawtooth lake is in order. The nearby Williams Creek Trail, off of FR 4430 (downriver), makes a 7.5-mile journey to remote Williams Lake. Gaining 3700 feet along the way, it's a grunt, but expect plenty of solitude as your reward. You won't be alone at Oval Lakes, however, one of the more popular hikes with equestrians in the Twisp River valley. Leaving from FR 44-080, it's 7.5

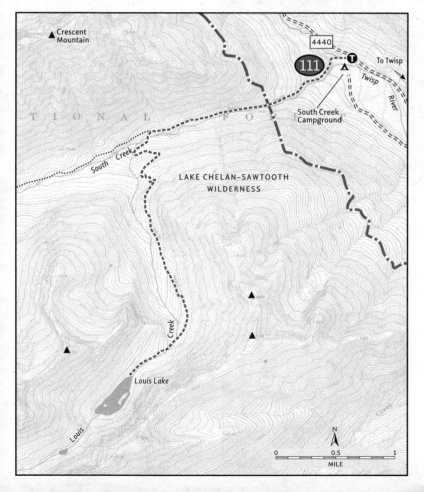

Louis Lake beneath Rennie Peak

dusty miles and 4000 feet of vertical just to the first lake. The area is spectacular and is worth the effort, but is better visited on an overnight in early summer or fall.

112 Libby Lake

RATING/ DIFFICULTY	ROUND-TRIP	ELEV GAIN/ HIGH POINT	SEASON
★★★/4	11 miles	3320 feet/ 7618 feet	July– mid-Oct

Maps: Green Trails Buttermilk Butte No. 83, Prince Creek No. 115; **Contact:** Okanogan National Forest, Methow Valley Ranger District, (509) 996-4003, www.fs.fed.us/r6/oka; **Notes:** NW Forest Pass required; **GPS:** N 48 16.556, W 120 17.402

Hidden in a high cirque in the hinterlands of Hoodoo Peak, Libby Lake is one of the loneliest and loftiest in the Sawtooth Range. And floating at an elevation of 7618 feet, it's also one of the highest alpine lakes in the entire Cascades. Surrounded by towering walls and tailings of talus, Libby's setting is stark. But its outlet is graced with rows of stately larches. In summer their delicate needles add soft green streaks to the barren basin, while in autumn their golden transformation adds light. It's a stiff climb, best attempted early to beat the Okanogan sun.

GETTING THERE

From Twisp drive State Route 20 east for 2 miles. Continue south on SR 153 for 9.4 miles, turning right onto Libby Creek Road, also known as County Road 1049 and signed "Blackpine Lake 12 miles." The turnoff is 1.3 miles south of Carlton. (From Pateros follow SR 153 north for 21 miles to the junction.) In 2.4 miles the pavement ends at a junction. Turn left onto FR 43, signed "Blackpine Lake 9 miles." In 5.2 miles turn left onto FR 24, signed "N FK Gold CR." In 1.2 miles turn right onto FR Spur 700, signed "Libby Lake Trailhead." And in 1.5 miles bear left onto FR Spur 750. Follow it for 1 mile to the road end and trailhead (elev. 4300 ft).

ON THE TRAIL

Trail No. 415 starts in an old cut. A few remnant ponderosas still stand, and swaying grasses and quaking aspens adorn the stumps. The trail wastes little time in attacking the ridge in front of it, steadily gaining elevation. In early summer, boughs of balsamroot turn the open

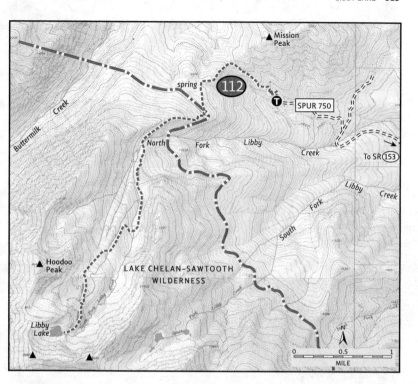

southern slope a sunny yellow. In the distance, Hoodoo Peak's hood peeks above the Libby Creek valley.

After about 1 mile of stiff climbing, crest the ridge and enjoy a bit of level hiking. In 0.5 mile you'll enter the Lake Chelan–Sawtooth Wilderness in a forest of lodgepole pine punctuated with granite glacial erratics. This is classic Okanogan Highlands topography. More stiff climbing ensues, than a slight descent as the trail crosses Libby Creek at about 2.5 miles (elev. 5800 ft).

Now in cool forest and across bogs and granite slabs, the trail works its way into a broad basin. Peer up at the imposing craggy walls encasing you and continue with more stiff climbing. At 5 miles stop to take a break and inspect an old cabin (elev. 7250). The final

grunt awaits. After pushing up a steep slope studded with larches, the trail finally relents, reaching the 1.5-mile-high lake. Its clear waters are rippled by cool breezes and probed by snowy fingers—Libby is made for looking not for soaking.

Admire the forbidding walls casting their long shadows across the lake. Ponder at what appears to be the ruins of an old rock dam at the lake's outlet. Built in 1911 by farmers far below, it was used for irrigation control. The gatekeeper must have been in one heck of a good shape.

EXTENDING YOUR TRIP

The nearby Blackpine Lake Campground is one of my favorite car-camping spots in the

Larches and talus above Libby Lake

Cascades. Spend the night there and walk its 0.4-mile wheelchair-accessible nature trail along the lake on a moonlit evening.

Gold Creek

The extreme southeastern corner of the North Cascades, the Gold Creek region, is often over-looked by hikers because the area is open to motorcycles. But don't believe that because a handful of dirt bikes ply these trails they're not worth your bootprints. This large roadless area is worthy of federal wilderness inclusion. Hikers must not shun these trails, or we may lose them to users less appreciative of nature's purity. Fortunately, motorcycle use here is moderate, and if you visit during the week you may not see anyone at all. The high-country lakes tucked in the nooks and crannies of the jagged Sawtooths are real gems, some of the prettiest alpine lakes in the Cascades, especially in autumn when their basins are aglow with cliff-clinging larches.

113 Crater Lakes

RATING/ DIFFICULTY	ROUND-TRIP	ELEV GAIN/ HIGH POINT	SEASON
★★★★/3	8.6 miles	2350 feet/ 6969 feet	Late June– mid-Oct

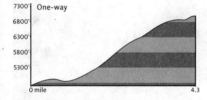

Map: Green Trails Prince Creek No. 115; **Contact:** Okanogan National Forest, Methow Valley Ranger District, (509) 996-4003, www.fs.fed.us/r6/oka; **Notes:** First 0.7 mile open to motorcycles; **GPS:** N 48 13.223, W 120 16.071

Tucked in a high cirque surrounded by sky-piercing peaks, the Crater Lakes epitomize rugged beauty. Among the most accessible of the alpine gems lacing jagged Sawtooth Ridge, reaching the Craters still exacts a fair amount of sweat and grit. But, while many of the nearby lakes often swirl in activity, Craters' environs generally remain calm. Hikers are few, horses rare, motorcycles barred. Come here in October when golden larches light up the steep valley walls and you'll swear you found the pearly gates.

GETTING THERE

From Twisp drive State Route 20 east for 2 miles. Continue south on SR 153 for 12 miles. At milepost 19 turn right onto Gold Creek Loop Road and drive 1.5 miles to a T intersection. Turn left onto County Road 1034, signed for Foggy Dew Campground. (From Pateros follow SR 153 north for 17 miles. Turn left onto Gold Creek Loop Road and drive 1 mile, turning left onto County Road 1034.) In 1 mile come to a junction and continue straight onto Forest Road 4340. The pavement ends at

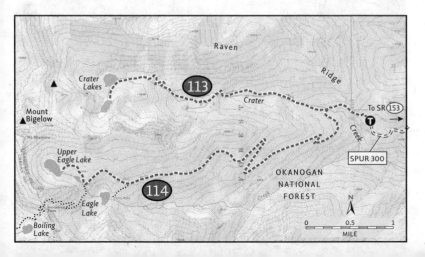

4 miles (bear right), and at 5.4 miles reach an intersection. Turn left onto FR Spur 300 and follow this rough-at-times road 4.6 miles to a large trailhead parking area (elev. 4700 ft).

ON THE TRAIL

Why the Crater Lakes and a dozen other nearby alpine lakes were ever left out of the Lake Chelan–Sawtooth Wilderness is beyond me. This is some of the finest backcountry east of the Cascade crest. Ecologically rich and graced with interconnecting trails, the Golden Lakes (a name given to this region by guidebook pioneers Harvey Manning and Ira Spring) should be a hiker's heaven. Instead, the Forest Service allowed (actually encour-

Upper Crater Lake

aged) motorized recreation in this region. A shame and a travesty. Now, I believe motorcyclists do indeed have a right to recreate on our public lands, but not on these lands. The Golden Lakes are far too fragile and far too valuable for wildlife and passive recreation to be a backcountry speedway.

Fortunately, motorcycles are prohibited on the Crater Lakes Trail. But you'll have to first endure 0.7 mile of dust and throttle on Eagle Lakes Trail No. 431. Beginning in open forest, the wide throughway gently climbs. In 0.25 mile stop and admire views over the Crater Creek drainage. Those two gorgeous lakes I've been extolling are up there in the shadows of Mount Bigelow, the prominent peak in front of you.

After a slight descent, cross Crater Creek (elev. 4825 ft) on a good bridge, enter a cool spruce grove and find the Crater Lake Trail taking off right. Immediately getting down to business, the trail climbs steeply up the narrow Crater Creek valley. At 1.25 miles from your start, cross the creek again and take a break before resuming your climb. Reach an outcropping and take another break, enjoying a good view east out to the Methow Valley sizzling in the sun. Start climbing again up more steep terrain.

At 4 miles rejoice as you enter a basin walled in by 8000-foot peaks. Lower Crater Lake (elev. 6814 ft) unfolds before you. Relax. As pretty as this lake is, Upper Crater is far more attractive. Recharge. Then work your way left (south) along the lakeshore to reach an inlet creek. Now on a somewhat defined path, follow the gurgling creek to reach the upper lake (elev. 6969 ft) in about 0.3 mile. Worth it, huh?

114 Eagle Lakes

RATING/ DIFFICULTY	ROUND-TRIP	ELEV GAIN/ HIGH POINT	SEASON
★★★/4	12 miles	2480 feet/ 7110 feet	Late June– mid-Oct

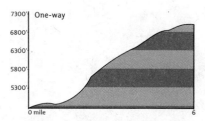

Map: Green Trails Prince Creek No. 115; **Contact:** Okanogan National Forest, Methow Valley Ranger District, (509) 996-4003, www.fs.fed.us/r6/oka; **Notes:** Open to motorcycles; **GPS:** N 48 13.223, W 120 16.071

> Hike to a pair of splendid lakes nestled high on the Sawtooth Ridge. Lower Eagle is perched in a peaceful grove of pines, while Upper Eagle sits in a lofty cirque flanked by spiraling crags and ribbons of larch. The trail is fairly easy, the grade never steep. It travels through big ponderosa and sweet-scented sage to glistening granite ledges, granting extensive views of nearby rock and distant hazy hills. Hot in the height of summer, this hike is a delight in early season when patches of snow prohibit wheels, or in early autumn when cool air blows down from the passes and the majestic larches turn the Eagles golden.

GETTING THERE

From Twisp drive State Route 20 east for 2 miles. Continue south on SR 153 for 12 miles. At milepost 19 turn right onto Gold Creek Loop Road and drive 1.5 miles to a T intersection. Turn left onto County Road 1034, signed for Foggy Dew Campground. (From Pateros follow SR 153 north for 17 miles. Turn left onto Gold Creek Loop Road and drive 1 mile, turning left onto County Road 1034.) In 1 mile come to a junction and continue straight onto Forest Road 4340. The pavement ends at 4 miles (bear right), and at 5.4 miles reach an intersection. Turn left onto FR Spur 300 and

Mount Bigelow reflected in tarn

follow this rough-at-times road 4.6 miles to a large trailhead parking area (elev. 4700 ft).

ON THE TRAIL

Eagle Lakes Trail No. 431 begins in forest thinned by past logging, but a few large ponderosa pines still grace the way. The trail is hot and dusty. Motorcycles have rutted and gutted the tread. Lament the degradation. Question how the Forest Service can allow such environmentally incompatible uses. Upon returning home, demand that your representatives in Congress correct this abuse of your public land.

After a short climb, the trail comes to a ledge granting good views of the Crater and Martin creek drainages. It's then a slow descent back into forest and shade, much appreciated on a hot summer's day. In 0.7 mile come to a junction just after crossing Crater Creek. The trail right climbs steeply to the Crater Lakes (Hike 113). Go left instead.

A short distance farther, ignore a side trail branching left. Through open lodgepole pine forest begin a steady climb. At 2.3 miles come to a junction with the Martin Creek Trail (elev. 5700 ft). Worthy destinations lie along this trail: Martin Lakes in 4.5 miles, Cooney Lake in 6.5 miles. Save them for another hike, preferably an autumn backpacking trip.

Continue right. As you ascend the forest thins, offering views out over Gold Creek basin and up toward the Sawtooth crest. Traverse grassy meadows, granite outcroppings, and sunny slopes flush in fragrant sage. At 4.5 miles (elev. 6700 ft) an obvious but unmaintained trail leaves left, dropping 200 feet to the forest-ringed Lower Eagle Lake.

Stay on the main trail for the upper lake. The climb eases. Now skirting a series of ledges, be sure to occasionally pause for the fine views of the lower lake twinkling below. At 5.5 miles (elev. 7050 ft) turn right onto a quiet side path. Motorcycles are barred on this short spur. Notice the soft delicate tread padded in larch needles, a far cry from the torn turf of the thoroughfare you left behind.

Pass a shallow tarn enveloped in showy larches. A half mile farther, arrive at Upper Eagle Lake (elev. 7110 ft). Cupped in a craggy, talus-laden cirque beneath 8135-foot Mount Bigelow, the lake sits in quite a dramatic setting. Find a spot along the shore to rest while the resident chickadees, chickarees, nuthatches, and nutcrackers serenade you.

EXTENDING YOUR TRIP

Beyond the Upper Eagle Lake junction, Trail No. 431 continues, passing another side trail to the lower lake before climbing to 7600-foot Horsehead Pass high on the Sawtooth Ridge. It's then a 1-mile and 500-foot drop to pretty Boiling Lake, set in a lofty and secluded basin.

115 Sunrise Lake

RATING/ DIFFICULTY	ROUND-TRIP	ELEV GAIN/ HIGH POINT	SEASON
★★★/4	13 miles	3730 feet/ 7228 feet	July– mid-Oct

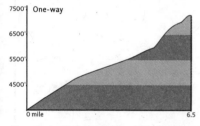

Map: Green Trails Prince Creek No. 115; **Contact:** Okanogan National Forest, Methow Valley Ranger District, (509) 996-4003, *www.fs.fed .us/r6/oka*; **Notes:** First 4.5 miles open to motorcycles; **GPS:** N 48 10.759, W 120 15.178

❎ ⚙ *Surrounded by golden lawns and groves of larch trees—their delicate needles littering the shoreline—Sunrise Lake will soothe your weary body and warm your wayfaring soul. Southernmost in a chain of dazzling alpine lakes perched high in the nooks and crannies of lofty and jagged Sawtooth Ridge, Sunrise Lake is a grand place to be any time of day.*

GETTING THERE
From Twisp drive State Route 20 east for 2 miles. Continue south on SR 153 for 12 miles. At milepost 19 turn right onto Gold Creek Loop Road and drive 1.5 miles to a T intersection. Turn left onto County Road 1034, signed for Foggy Dew Campground. (From Pateros follow SR 153 north for 17 miles. Turn left onto Gold Creek Loop Road and drive 1 mile, turning left onto County Road 1034.) In 1 mile come to a junction and continue straight onto Forest Road 4340. Follow this narrow but paved road for 4 miles to a junction near the Foggy Dew Campground. Turn left onto graveled FR Spur 200, bear right at an unmarked junction at 2.3 miles, and at 3.7 miles reach the road end and trailhead (elev. 3500 ft). Privy available.

ON THE TRAIL
Sunrise and a dozen other nearby alpine lakes were left out of the 150,000-plus-acre

Lone larch at Sunrise Lake

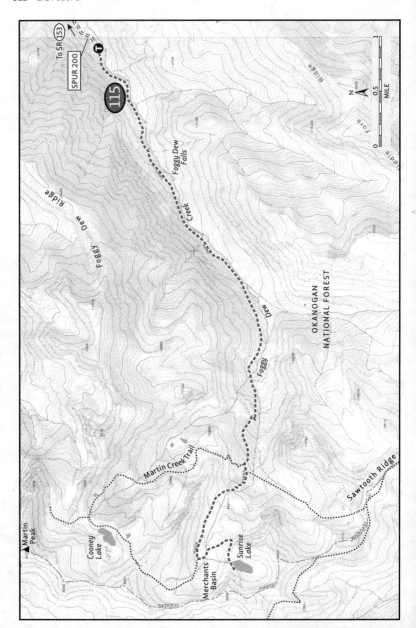

Lake Chelan–Sawtooth Wilderness. While the 100,000 acres of wildlands housing these crown jewels are currently managed as a roadless area, they are open to motorized travel. Does anyone else see the irony here? Roadless should be motorless! This area is far too precious for belched fumes and leaking oil; far too pristine to be a speed track; far too peaceful to be interrupted by throttles.

But don't let the presence of a few motorbikes discourage you from exploring this supreme corner of the North Cascades. The trails are open to you too, and hikers need to make their presence known so the Forest Service and perhaps Congress will right this terrible mismanagement of our public resources. Come early in summer or during the week for peace of mind.

Start by hiking up Foggy Dew Trail No. 417, which hugs the delightfully named Foggy Dew Creek for most of its way. The creek's melodious chattering may inspire you to recite poetry or hum Irish folk songs. The path is wide and well groomed and not too dusty. The grade is gentle, a true pleasure to walk.

Pass gurgling chutes and placid pools. Cross numerous tumbling side creeks, and at 2.5 miles take a break to admire Foggy Dew Falls (elev. 4900 ft) plummeting into a narrow cleft. Through a tunnel of lodgepole pine the trail marches deeper up the valley. Breaks in the canopy provide window views of the craggy surrounding ridges.

At 4 miles the trail parts ways with Foggy Dew Creek, following a tributary a short distance before crossing it on an old log bridge. The grade then steepens. At 5 miles reach a junction with the Martin Creek Trail.

Proceed left, continuing on a Foggy Dew Trail now closed to motorcycles. Rejoice! In 0.1 mile, in a cool grove of old-growth conifers, come to another junction. The trail left leads to the Sawtooth-straddling Summer Blossom Trail. Veer right to begin a steep

little climb over and around ledges and rock gardens with far-flung views out to the Columbia Basin.

At 6 miles enter Merchants Basin (6800 ft), a wide expanse of alpine meadows beckoning to be explored. Just beyond a cluster of campsites, a side trail takes off left and crosses a small creek. Follow it. Winding through big larches and Engelmann spruce, make one last climb. Finally, at 6.5 miles, enter the wide cirque that embraces sparkling Sunrise Lake. Larches grace the lake's outlet. Craggy 8000-foot spires reflect in its calm coves. If this doesn't qualify for wilderness protection, the sun doesn't rise in the east.

EXTENDING YOUR TRIP
From Merchants Basin you can continue 1 mile to a high ridge where a path drops 800 feet in 0.75 mile to gorgeous Cooney Lake. Then follow the Martin Creek Trail 2.75 miles back to the Foggy Dew Trail.

Chewuch River

North of the Methow Valley hub of Winthrop flows the Chewuch River, offering probing portals on the periphery of the sprawling Pasayten Wilderness. Much of the rugged roadless terrain that lies north of the Methow is the domain for equestrians and backpackers on multiday forays. But a handful of good day hikes give a satisfying taste of the wild region. With long ridges, long valleys, long stretches of forest both green and scorched, the Chewuch River region is also a long ways from the crowded cities of the Puget Sound.

116 Copper Glance Lake

RATING/ DIFFICULTY	ROUND-TRIP	ELEV GAIN/ HIGH POINT	SEASON
★★★/4	6 miles	2800 feet/ 6350 feet	Mid-June– Oct

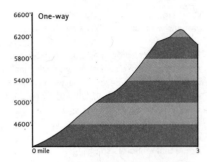

Maps: Green Trails Billy Goat Mountain No. 19, Mazama No. 51; **Contact:** Okanogan National Forest, Methow Valley Ranger District, (509) 996-4003, *www.fs.fed.us/r6/oka*; **GPS:** N 48 44.465, W 120 17.537

A Copper Glance? Perhaps. More likely golden views of towering cliffs reflecting in deep sparkling waters are *what you'll find. Little Copper Glance Lake sits in a rugged bowl of jumbled talus heaps sprinkled with delicate-needled larches under the reign of majestic 8000-plus-foot Isabella Ridge. An awesome sight indeed. But like the prospectors who built this trail, you must possess a tenacious spirit in order to reap this reward. The way is steep, rough, and a little bit tricky—but worth it.*

GETTING THERE

Follow the North Cascades Highway (State Route 20) east to Winthrop. Just before entering the town center, turn left onto West Chewuch River Road. In 6.75 miles reach the junction with the East Chewuch River Road (which comes from Winthrop) and continue north, now on Forest Road 51. Follow this paved road for 2.6 miles, turning left at Eightmile Ranch onto FR 5130 (signed "Billy Goat 17"). Continue for 12.4 miles (the pavement

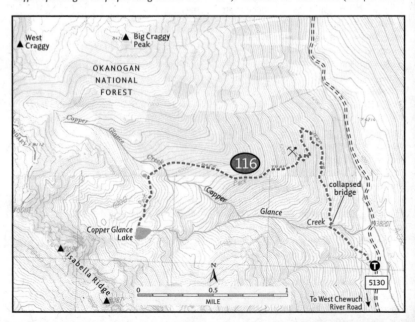

Copper Glance Lake in early summer

ends in 5 miles) to the trailhead at a gated old jeep road (elev. 3800 ft).

ON THE TRAIL

Start on an old jeep road, rapidly gaining elevation. In 0.4 mile Copper Glance Creek must be crossed. A sturdy bridge once provided safe passage, but time has taken its toll. The bridge has collapsed, making crossing in early season and during high runoff potentially dangerous. If the way looks unsafe, turn around and head for nearby Burch Mountain (Hike 117).

Once across, continue climbing. At 1.5 miles

the old road ends at a mine shaft (elev. 5200 ft). Narrow-gauge tracks lead into the damp darkness, which is hazardous to explore. Imagine instead what lingers in the blackness. Real trail now begins, but the way gets steeper. Valley views emerge, but the real treat is just ahead. A green carpet exploding with wildflowers rolls out beneath you while stark Isabella Ridge towers above.

At 2 miles resplendent meadows yield to old-growth forest. Continue ascending. Cross Copper Glance Creek once more (look for a log), then take a short break from upward mobility. Leveling off, the way skirts a marshy-shored little pond (elev. 6150 ft) before making one final steep and rocky climb of 200 feet to crest a ridge. Wow! In-your-face views of massive Isabella Ridge greet you.

It's now a 0.25-mile, 250-foot drop to the boulder-strewn, larch-laced basin embracing Copper Glance Lake. Find a good ledge to share with a sunning marmot and enjoy the spectacular scenery. Bookends West Craggy (elev. 8366 ft) and Sherman Peak (elev. 8204 ft) frame the clear lake. Jumping trout add a nice touch by rippling the cool deep waters.

117 Burch Mountain

RATING/ DIFFICULTY	ROUND-TRIP	ELEV GAIN/ HIGH POINT	SEASON
★★★★/4	10 miles	3200 feet/ 7782 feet	Late June–Oct

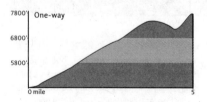

Map: Green Trails Billy Goat Mountain No. 19; **Contact:** Okanogan National Forest, Methow Valley Ranger District, (509) 996-4003, www

.fs.fed.us/r6/oka; **Notes:** NW Forest Pass required; **GPS:** N 48 47.066, W 120 19.060

Burch Mountain sits in the center of a rugged region riddled with old mines. Fortune seekers and strike-it-rich schemers once scampered and clambered all over this harsh landscape. Few found any lucre, and all that remains of their past presence are tailings and depressions, a few rusty relics, and wispy voices in the wind. From the lofty 7782-foot summit of this former lookout site, however, you can still strike it rich in visual rewards. Gaze out over impressive crags and spires, stark vertical walls, and deep, dark notches. Peer deep into the Pasayten Wilderness and out to the prominent peaks along its periphery.

GETTING THERE
Follow the North Cascades Highway (State Route 20) east to Winthrop. Just before entering the town center, turn left onto West Chewuch River Road. In 6.75 miles reach the junction with the East Chewuch River Road (which comes from Winthrop) and continue north, now on Forest Road 51. Follow this paved road for 2.6 miles, turning left at Eightmile Ranch onto FR 5130 (signed "Billy Goat 17"). Drive 16.5 miles to the road end and trailhead (elev. 4800 ft). The pavement ends at 5 miles, and the last mile is rough and may not be passable; you can park instead at the horse trailhead and access the trail from there. Privy available.

ON THE TRAIL
Trail No. 502A uses an old road for its first several hundred feet and then veers right on narrower tread. In 0.25 mile come to a junction (elev. 4800 ft). The trail left heads for Eightmile Pass, but you're off to Billy Goat Pass so stay right. Just beyond the junction, look off to your right for old mine pits.

The dusty trail now twists and turns under

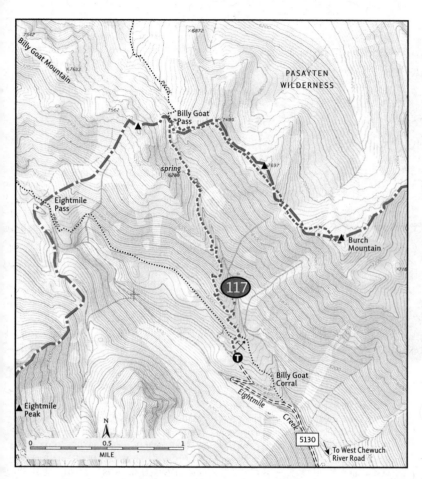

a thin canopy of Douglas-fir, steeply climbing to the pass. From forest openings along the way, an impressive fortress of surrounding peaks reveals itself. To the west, Isabella Ridge's Eightmile Peak, West Craggy, and Big Craggy Peak warrant a sigh. They're an awesome sight.

At about 1.75 miles enter a dense forest of subalpine fir and Engelmann spruce. With the valley walls narrowing, skirt a small creek, and then work your way through a grassy draw. At 2.75 miles crest Billy Goat Pass (elev. 6600 ft), a deep cleft shadowed by the stark ledges and vertical slopes of Billy Goat Mountain.

Continue for 0.1 mile, entering the Pasayten Wilderness in a thick grove of evergreens and dropping slightly to a junction at the edge of a meadow. The light tread leading right is the way to Burch Mountain—follow it. The way immediately gains ground, climbing 400

Glacier-carved Drake Creek valley

feet in 0.4 mile to reach a small knoll. Views north into the Pasayten are grand, but it gets better so keep going. Following a fairly open ridgeline graced with clumps of pine, the trail travels under cliffs and over knolls on its way to the summit.

In 1 mile from the pass, Burch's summit comes into full view, but you'll need to work a little harder to get there. The trail drops 200 feet to a larch-filled saddle before ascending the rocky summit cone. Through fields of granite and over alpine tundra, the final grunt to the 7782-foot former lookout site is extremely steep. But this lonely outpost is all yours now! Spin your head around. That's the Methow Valley and Abernathy Ridge to the south. The Tiffany Highlands, Mount Bonaparte, and the Kettle River Range fill the eastern horizon. To the north lie a plethora of Pasayten peaks. And to the west, staring you right in the face, is Isabella's intimidating lineup. Savor the scenic splendor and rest up for the return.

EXTENDING YOUR TRIP
Turn your hike into a long loop by heading north from Billy Goat Pass 2.2 miles to Drake Creek. Turn left (west), following Trail No. 502 for 3 miles to Jinks Creek. Then turn left again for a 4-mile return to the trailhead via Eightmile Pass. This option adds 6 miles and another 1000 feet of elevation gain to your journey.

118 Black Lake

RATING/ DIFFICULTY	ROUND-TRIP	ELEV GAIN/ HIGH POINT	SEASON
**/2	8 miles	780 feet/ 3982 feet	May–Oct

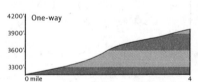

Map: Green Trails Coleman Peak No. 20; **Contact:** Okanogan National Forest, Methow Valley Ranger District, (509) 996-4003, www.fs.fed.us/r6/oka; **Notes:** NW Forest Pass required; **GPS:** N 48 46.985, W 120 09.680

Enjoy a gentle hike along a babbling creek to a pretty lake within the sprawling Pasayten Wilderness. Though Black Lake is named for its deep, dark waters, "black" also describes much of the surrounding forest. In 2003 a wildfire seared it, leaving charred stumps and blackened timber in its wake. This hike should be avoided on the hottest of days due to its lack of shade, but it's quite delightful in late spring when pioneering flowers paint the understory an array of vivid colors. Watch, too, nature regenerate herself as thousands of tenacious saplings restore the forest.

GETTING THERE

Follow the North Cascades Highway (State Route 20) east to Winthrop. Just before en-tering the town center, turn left onto West Chewuch River Road. In 6.75 miles reach the junction with the East Chewuch River Road (which comes from Winthrop) and continue north, now on Forest Road 51. Follow this paved road for 14.5 miles and turn left onto FR Spur 100 (signed "Lake Creek Trail 2"). Drive 2.5 miles to the road end at a corral and the trailhead (elev. 3200 ft). Privy available.

Talus along Black Lake

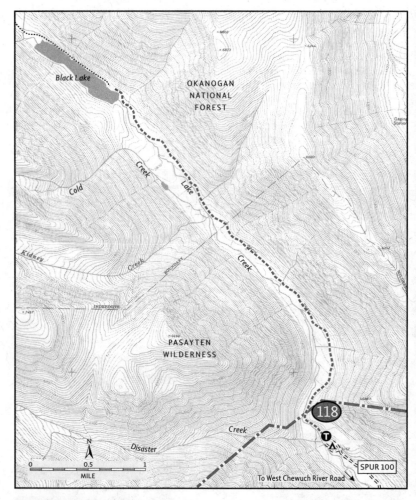

ON THE TRAIL

Trail No. 500 starts in a patch of pines and firs that escaped the great wildfire of 2003, but greenery soon succumbs to ghostly pallor. In 0.4 mile enter the Pasayten Wilderness and begin traversing a scorched landscape.

Aside from consuming the forest, the fire indirectly caused a series of landslides, be-

cause trees that had stabilized surrounding slopes went up in smoke. The devastation can be disheartening; it certainly was to me as I recalled the grand forest once standing here. But this is nature's way, and she knows what she is doing. A vibrant new forest is returning.

Fireweed is prolific along the trail; its

purple reigns, ruling the understory. Quaking aspens stake new ground, while blueberry bushes abound on the acidic soils. And as the forest is under reconstruction, Lake Creek continues its flow, filling the valley with sweet serenades. Birds also add sweet sounds. Woodpeckers play percussion on silvery snags, while kingfishers hold notes high in overhanging branches. Thrushes, flycatchers, and nutcrackers hum along.

At 2.2 miles cross a lazy side creek. A half mile farther, skirt a large talus slope. A short climb follows, and the trail continues meandering through burnt groves of pine and fir laced with trickling side creeks. At 4 miles arrive at Black Lake.

A nice sandy beach greets you with fine views of the surrounding high ridges, patches of fire-spared forest adding emerald streaks. Large landslides have disturbed this peaceful body of water by adding extra sediment, further stressing local populations of endangered bull trout. Hopefully, as the forest recovers the trout will once again flourish.

EXTENDING YOUR TRIP

The trail continues along the lake traversing sun-kissed talus slopes to arrive at the grassy west end in 0.7 mile. Crave solitude? Keep heading up the valley for as far as you like.

119 North Twentymile Peak

RATING/ DIFFICULTY	ROUND-TRIP	ELEV GAIN/ HIGH POINT	SEASON
★★★★/5	13 miles	4387 feet/ 7437 feet	June–Oct

7500'
6600' One-way
5700'
4800'
3900'

0 mile   6.5

Maps: Green Trails Coleman Peak No. 20, Doe Mountain No. 52; **Contact:** Okanogan National Forest, Methow Valley Ranger District, (509) 996-4003, *www.fs.fed.us/r6/oka*; **GPS:** N 48 42.172, W 120 06.299

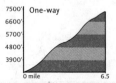 This is a long plod through forest singed, scorched (and a little bit spared) by the massive Tripod Fire of 2006 to a lonely outpost in the heart of one of the Okanogan's largest roadless areas. From lofty North Twentymile Peak, with its dollop

Hikers inspect historic lookout cabin.

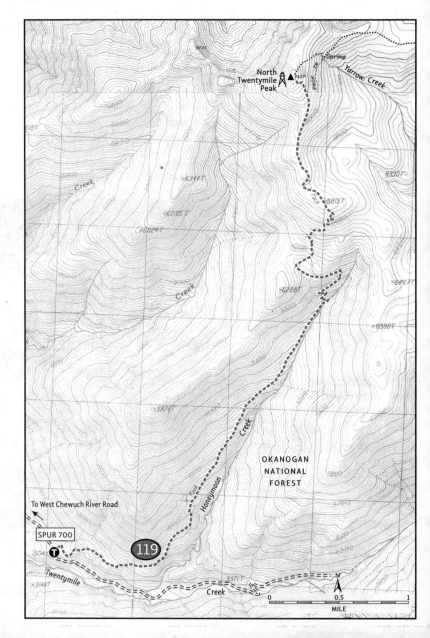

North Twentymile Peak

Spring

Yarrow Creek

×6344T

×6235T

×6024T

×6288T

×6467T

×6390T

Creek

Creek

Creek

×3828T

Honeymoon Creek

OKANOGAN NATIONAL FOREST

To West Chewuch River Road

SPUR 700

119

Twentymile

×3148T

Creek

N

0   0.5   1
MILE

*of meadows, feast on far-reaching views
from the Kettle River Range all the way to
the cloud-piercing guardians of the North
Cascades Highway. Scan deep valleys too,
including the Chewuch 1 mile directly below.
Then put down the binoculars and check out
the historical lookout that has sat guard on
this peak since 1923.*

GETTING THERE

Follow the North Cascades Highway (State
Route 20) east to Winthrop. Just before entering
the town center, turn left onto West Chewuch
River Road. In 6.75 miles reach the junction
with the East Chewuch River Road (which
comes from Winthrop) and continue north, now
on Forest Road 51. Follow this paved road for
11.2 miles, turning right onto FR 5010 just beyond the Camp Four Campground. Cross the
Chewuch River and bear right, heading south
on FR 5010. After 0.5 mile bear left onto FR Spur
700, and follow this somewhat rough road 1.6
miles to a gate and the trailhead (elev. 3050 ft).

ON THE TRAIL

Begin on old road through ponderosa pines
singed by the Tripod Fire that set over
175,000 acres of the Okanogan ablaze in the
summer of 2006. In 0.6 mile leave the old
road, veering left onto real trail (elev. 3350 ft).
Now start climbing up open southern slopes
that crackle in the heat of summer. Be sure to
pack plenty of water on this hike; by July water
is at a premium.

Steadily gaining elevation, steeply at times,
the way undulates between scorched landscapes of varying degrees and pockets of
greenery spared from the ravages of the great
conflagration. While the surroundings may not
always be aesthetically appealing, the forest
is recovering. Ponderosa and lodgepole pine
forests need fire for rejuvenation. The magni-
tude of the Tripod Fire is evident, its intensity
as well: pass by several granite boulders that

shattered from the heat of the fire, leaving behind a wake of flaky shards.

At about 3 miles (elev. 5000 ft) the trail
comes up along Honeymoon Creek and then
follows this delightful waterway for about
0.5 mile. The trail then commences a series
of short, steep switchbacks before making a
long traverse away from the creek valley and
then once again setting about some serious
climbing. As you ascend slopes of blackened
forest punctuated by verdant meadows, views
south begin to open up.

At 5.5 miles crest a 6800-foot knoll miraculously spared from the scorching. North
Twentymile's lookout-graced summit cone
comes into view. Next enjoy 1 glorious mile of
ridge running and tiptoeing through meadows
full of shiny granite slabs and the occasional
fluttering bluebird.

At 6.5 miles fling your pack off your sweaty
back and enjoy the 7437-foot summit. Two fire
lookouts command your attention: a "modern"
one built in 1947, and a historical one, a cu-
pola ground house constructed in 1923. One of
the last of its kind still standing, the structure
badly needs some reconstructive work if it is
to grace this peak well into the future.

Don't forget to take in the views too, from
Chopaka and the Loomis country to the north,
the Tiffany Highlands to the east, the Sawtooths to the south, and the wild Pasayten
country to the west. And immediately surrounding you are more than 70,000 acres of
unprotected roadless wilderness. It'll rebound
from wildfire, but not from motors and med-
dling. Federal wilderness protection would
suit this area just fine.

EXTENDING YOUR TRIP

From the summit a trail of sorts heads east
for over 10 miles of lonely ridges, meadows,
and forest. Pack map, water, and a sense of
adventure if inclined to explore this rarely
walked terrain.

BURNING CONTROVERSY

Fire is to the eastern slopes of the Cascades what rain is to the western slopes. And while both these natural occurrences shape the land and influence its flora and fauna, creating two very distinct facades of the Cascades, one is better accepted than the other. It seems like everyone complains about the rain, but no one is doing anything about it. Not so when it comes to fires.

Both the Forest Service and the Park Service long subscribed to a strict policy of fire suppression. After decades of this kind of forest-fire management, not surprisingly (or perhaps to some) eastern-slope ecosystems dramatically changed. Where fires once swept through, cleaning the forest floor of accumulated duff to create an open understory and allowing certain species to grow without competition, there are instead dense forest stands crowded with understory brush and years of accumulated matter.

In essence, tinderboxes were created, so when a fire now occurs it often burns with a vengeance. The Tripod Fire of 2006 scorched more than 175,000 acres, an area three-quarters the size of Mount Rainier National Park. Conservationists tend to favor a let-it-burn approach, allowing a natural balance to return to the forest. Timber owners and an ever-increasing rural population tend to want the fires fought head-on to protect their homes and resources. The Forest Service and Park Service are often swayed by stakeholders instead of being guided by forest ecology.

No matter how we choose to manage forests, one thing remains constant for all concerned: wildfires will continue to strike the region like they have for thousands of years. And depending on your point of view or personal stake, the consequences of our actions will be either positive or negative. But while we struggle to come up with acceptable fire-management polices, we can all agree that we want wildfire's future human toll to be zero.

On July 10, 2001, in the Thirtymile Creek drainage north of Winthrop, the state's second-deadliest forest fire took four young firefighters: Tom Craven, Karen Fitzpatrick, Devin Weaver, and Jessica Johnson. The Forest Service has placed a memorial at the spot where these brave men and women lost their lives. It can be visited by following the West Chewuch River Road (Forest Road 51) approximately 4 miles north of the Andrews Creek trailhead.

Tiffany Highlands

Welcome to Washington's big-sky country. With its gentle but lofty peaks, sprawling meadowed ridges and open slopes, and its abundance of sunshine, the Tiffany Highlands feel more like the Rockies than the North Cascades. The Tiffany Highlands exhibit characteristics of interior mountain ranges because the region teeters on the extreme eastern edge of the Cascades. The area is a transition zone between wet coastal and dry interior ecosystems and provides an important land bridge for certain migrating species. Much of the region remains roadless and wild, and its high undisturbed forests and meadows support lynx, wolverine, and the occasional grizzly. The Tiffany Highlands are a truly unique corner of the North Cascades.

120 Tiffany Mountain

RATING/ DIFFICULTY	ROUND-TRIP	ELEV GAIN/ HIGH POINT	SEASON
★★★★/3	6 miles	1740 feet/ 8242 feet	Late June–mid-Oct

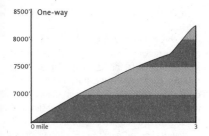

Map: Green Trails Tiffany Mountain No. 53; **Contact:** Okanogan National Forest, Tonasket Ranger District, (509) 486-2186, *www.fs.fed .us/r6/oka*; **GPS:** N 48 39.780, W 119 57.890

Rising to an elevation of 8242 feet, Tiffany Mountain is a lofty summit and one of the highest peaks in the Cascades that can be easily hiked. With a trailhead at 6500 feet, not much sweat needs to be expended to reach Tiffany's rocky and grassy wide-open summit. Centerpiece to the highlands sharing its name, Tiffany hovers over a windswept world of flower-bursting meadows and deli- cate alpine tundra at the extreme eastern reaches of the Cascades. Once the domain of solitary sheepherders, Tiffany now hosts intrepid hikers and solitude seekers.

GETTING THERE

From Winthrop head north on East Chewuch River Road (County Road 9137) toward Pearrygin Lake State Park. In 6.5 miles (just before the road crosses the Chewuch River), turn right onto paved Forest Road 37. The pavement ends at 7.5 miles, and at 13 miles come to a junction. Turn left onto FR 39, following this sometimes rough road for 3.2 miles to Freezeout Pass (at a cattle guard). The trailhead and limited parking are on the right side of the road (elev. 6500 ft).

ON THE TRAIL

Beginning at Freezeout Pass, Trail No. 345 takes off up Freezeout Ridge through a forest singed by wildfires in the summer of 2006. By late July the trail is lined with lupine, providing a purple pathway to the prominent peak. Arnica, daisies, and groundsell add golden touches.

Sprawling meadows in the Tiffany Highlands

After about 1.5 miles of gentle climbing, forest yields to flower-filled meadows punctuated with patches of krummholz (densely matted trees stunted by wind and snow). Swaying grasses and sedges engulf the dwarfed and contorted clumps of fir and pine. Lift your eyes from the bonsai forests and golden lawns and note Tiffany's summit cone coming into view. The trail skirts beneath it, traversing the mountain's wide-open southern slopes and arriving at a junction at 2.5 miles (elev. 7700 ft).

Turn left, following light tread 0.5 mile to reach the heavens.

At this lofty altitude, the elements can be extreme, making it quite difficult for plants to survive. But the alpine flora has adapted well, taking refuge behind weather-beaten boulders and in small protective depressions. Particularly striking are clusters of juniper clinging to lichen-encrusted rocks and outcrops.

Now, lift your nose up from the ground once more. It's time to take in the horizon-spanning

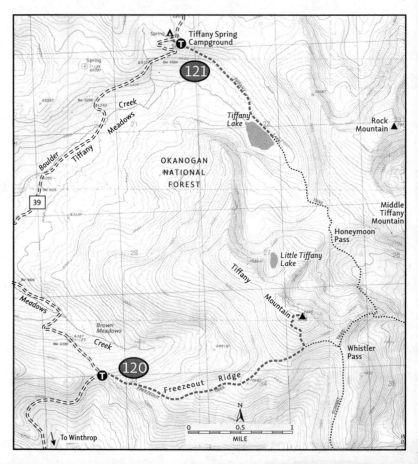

views from Tiffany's airy summit. In every direction an inspiring landscape unfolds. To the north are a panorama of Pasayten peaks, the Loomis country, and British Columbia's Snowy Mountain, and 1000 feet directly below is a little tarn in a stark cirque. Look south over high rolling ridges out toward Loup Loup Pass and the Beaver Meadow country. To the east the Okanogan Highlands bake in the sun. And west, the North Cascades crowd the skyline. It's a pretty big payoff for such a moderate effort.

EXTENDING YOUR TRIP

From the trail junction just before the summit you can continue hiking on Trail No. 345 to Whistler Pass. Then drop down on Trail No. 373 to Tiffany Lake (Hike 121), or head south for 2 glorious miles on the North Summit Trail to the Bernhardt Trail. Scramble up Clark Peak or hike 3 miles down the Bernhardt Trail, coming to FR 39 near Rogers Lake. Hoof up the road for just shy of 2 miles back to Freezeout Pass to complete a great loop.

121 Tiffany Lake

RATING/ DIFFICULTY	ROUND-TRIP	ELEV GAIN/ HIGH POINT	SEASON
★★★/1	3 miles	200 feet/ 6750 feet	Mid-June– mid-Oct

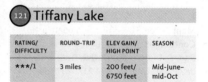

Map: Green Trails Tiffany Mountain No. 53; **Contact:** Okanogan National Forest, Tonasket Ranger District, (509) 486-2186, www.fs.fed .us/r6/oka; **GPS:** N 48 42.000, W 119 57.190

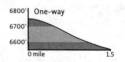

Enjoy an easy stroll to the largest alpine lake in the Tiffany Highlands. Ideal for introducing children to the backcountry, Tiffany Lake delights all

regardless of age. The marshy meadows and open pine groves teeming with wildlife may entice you to explore farther. But if a lazy afternoon is your plan, plop down beside this sparkling gem and let its gentle breezes and refreshing mountain air soothe your soul.

GETTING THERE

From Winthrop head north on East Chewuch River Road (County Road 9137) toward Pearrygin Lake State Park. In 6.5 miles (just before the road crosses the Chewuch River), turn right onto paved Forest Road 37. The pavement ends at 7.5 miles, and at 13 miles come to a junction. Turn left onto FR 39, following this sometimes rough road for 7.5 miles to Tiffany Spring Campground. Tiffany Lake Trail No. 373 begins across the road (on its east side) from the campground (elev. 6750 ft).

ON THE TRAIL

Perched in a high valley surrounded by lofty peaks, pristine Tiffany Lake poses as the precious centerpiece to the 24,000-acre Tiffany Roadless Area. This far-northeast corner of the Cascades contains unbroken alpine (albeit burnt) forests, botanically important subalpine parklands of sage, and critical habitat for grizzly bears.

Start out in an open forest of lodgepole pine, Douglas-fir, and Engelmann spruce. A pleasurable walk, it loses about 200 feet in elevation along the way to the lake. Despite being in a region that receives only 25 inches of annual precipitation, the valley you are slowly descending into is dotted with marshes, springs, and seeps. It's quite lush.

In just over 1 mile reach the sparkling and quiet lake. Tiffany Mountain, with its stark northern cirques, hovers above. Though Trail No. 373 is one of the more popular trails in the region, the concept of crowding is still unknown here. Saunter along the shoreline to stake out your own special spot for viewing

Tiffany Lake

and soaking. Napping and daydreaming are encouraged.

EXTENDING YOUR TRIP

There's plenty of wild terrain to explore beyond the lake. Continue on the trail for another mile, climbing 600 feet to Honeymoon Pass. Experienced off-trail travelers have two excellent options here: head north up steep and open slopes to reach rarely visited 7972-foot Middle Tiffany Mountain; or up steep slopes south to beautiful Little Tiffany Lake, tucked in a cirque 1000 feet below Tiffany Mountain's windblown summit. If a car shuttle can be arranged, consider hiking past Honeymoon Pass for 6 miles to the trail's eastern terminus on FR 38 at Salmon Creek; pack water. The Tiffany Spring Campground, with its six sites, makes a lovely base camp for further exploring the region.

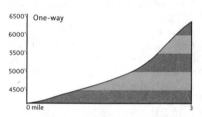

Map: Green Trails Tiffany Mountain No. 53; **Contact:** Okanogan National Forest, Tonasket Ranger District, (509) 486-2186, *www.fs.fed .us/r6/oka*; **GPS:** N 48 34.217, W 119 54.557

 *Hike an old sheep drive high into the roadless Granite Mountain hinterlands. Along the way traverse lonely meadows bursting with wildflowers. Take in views of the Okanogan Highlands and some of the least-known and hiked peaks in the state. The Conconully Reservoir sparkles below, set against rolling golden hills on the eastern edge of the North Cascades.*

GETTING THERE

From the junction of State Routes 20 and 215 in Okanogan, continue north on SR 215 for

122 Golden Stairway

RATING/ DIFFICULTY	ROUND-TRIP	ELEV GAIN/ HIGH POINT	SEASON
★★★/3	6 miles	2300 feet/ 6400 feet	June–Oct

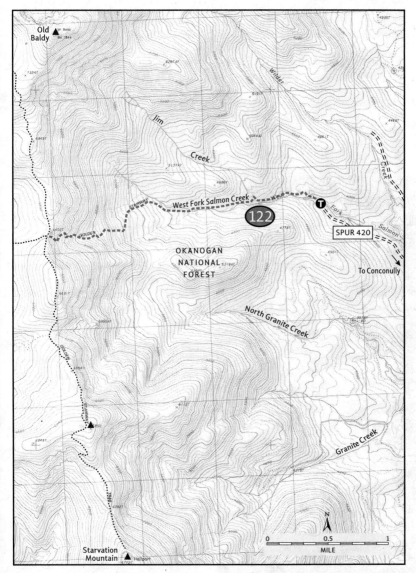

1 mile and turn left onto Pine Street just before the county courthouse (signed "Conconully 18 miles"). Stay on this arterial, which changes names several times (from Pine Street to Sixth Avenue to Orchard Grade to, finally, Conconully Road), for 19 miles to the old mining town of

Conconully. (From Omak reach Conconully Road by following Kermel Road off of SR 215.) Turn left at Conconully State Park onto Broadway Street (which becomes County Road 2017), following this paved road for 3 miles to a major intersection with Forest Roads 42 and 37. Bear right onto FR 37 and drive 5 miles. Turn left onto FR Spur 400, and in 0.8 mile bear left onto FR Spur 420 (signed "Golden Stairway Trail No. 345"). Avoiding spurs, continue 2 miles to the road end and trailhead

Muckamuck Mountain from Golden Stairway

(elev. 4100 ft). The last mile is rough and may require a high-clearance vehicle.

ON THE TRAIL

After making an initial hop over West Fork Salmon Creek, the trail comes to a logging spur and then heads left to parallel the lovely waterway. The next 1.5 miles are pure hiking delight as the trail winds through quiet forest (a little burnt from the Tripod Fire of 2006) and gains little elevation.

At 0.6 mile cross Jim Creek (elev. 4350 ft). At 1.2 miles cross the West Fork once more (elev. 4600 ft). The grade now steadily increases, culminating in a series of steep switchbacks. By this time, forest has yielded to flowery meadows and increasing views should help keep your mind off the toil. Stare straight out to the Conconully Reservoir and beyond to Bonaparte and the lonely peaks of the Colville Indian Reservation. The big meadowy mountain directly northeast is Muckamuck. One of my favorite Chinook words, it means "food" or "eat."

At 3 miles reach a forested notch (elev. 6400 ft) on a lofty ridge in the heart of the Granite Mountain Roadless Area. A refuge for lynx, this area is often encroached upon by illegal motorcycle riding. Lack of Forest Service presence allows the criminals to trespass with impunity.

EXTENDING YOUR TRIP

From the notch, you can venture north on Trail No. 369 to higher ground and better views. Old Baldy (elev. 7844 ft) makes a worthy scrambling destination. Or continue south on the Golden Stairway toward Starvation Mountain for 2 miles of ridge walking and great viewing. You can continue west as well, traveling 1.25 miles on Trail No. 526 to wildlife- (and mosquito-) rich Beaver Meadows. Conconully State Park makes an excellent base for exploring the region. Trails traverse Muckamuck Mountain, but you'll need a good map to find and follow them.

123 Beaver Lake

RATING/ DIFFICULTY	ROUND-TRIP	ELEV GAIN/ HIGH POINT	SEASON
★★/1	2 miles	400 feet/ 5500 feet	May–Oct

Map: Green Trails Loup Loup No. 85; **Contact:** Okanogan National Forest, Methow Valley Ranger District, (509) 996-4003, www.fs.fed.us/r6/oka; **GPS:** N 48 28.023, W 119 52.928

Enjoy an easy hike to a pretty little lake in the little-known Loup Loup region of the Okanogan. The only sizeable body of water in the 28,000-acre Granite Mountain Roadless Area, Beaver sits in a small forested bowl a mile above sea level. Here on the eastern extremes of the North Cascades, the sun shines long and hard. Beaver Lake invites foot and full-body soaking, a nice reprieve from the summer heat.

GETTING THERE

From Twisp follow State Route 20 east for 13 miles to Loup Loup Summit (pass). (From Okanogan follow SR 20 west for 19 miles.) Turn north onto Forest Road 42 (signed for a campground and ski bowl). In 0.5 mile bear right (signed for a campground and Conconully), and continue on FR 42 for another 2.4 miles to the pavement's end at a fork. Bear right, continuing on FR 42 for 0.8 mile to a junction. Turn left onto FR 4235 and follow it for 1.6 miles to another junction. Continue straight on FR Spur 100 (signed for Beaver Lake), coming to the unmarked trailhead in just shy of 2 miles at a gate and just after crossing Beaver Creek. Park

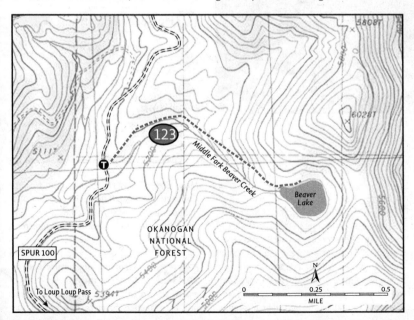

Beaver Lake

on the left; the trail begins on the right side of the road (elev. 5100 ft).

ON THE TRAIL

The trail begins in an open forest of uniform lodgepole pine. On smooth tread lined with juniper and blueberry bushes, easily gain elevation. In 0.25 mile, in a grove of old Engelmann spruce, ignore a side trail on the right (an old road) by continuing straight. At 0.6 mile commence a very short series of switchbacks, swinging around shards and slabs of granite.

And speaking of that solid igneous rock, the nearby mountain named after it rises to the north and can be glimpsed through the trees. Peeps of the snowy Sawtooth Ridge far to the west can also be caught along the way.

At 1 mile reach Beaver Lake near its marshy outlet. Continue on trail along the northern shore, passing well-used campsites to reach shoreline ledges—perfect places for snacking and contemplating. A few nice swimming spots are in the vicinity as well.

Enjoy this peaceful spot and reflect. In the late 1800s these hills were flourishing with human activity. Loup Loup once housed a bustling mining community of four hundred. *Loup* is French for "wolf," so perhaps two were spotted when the town was platted. And perhaps *le loup* will firmly reestablish his home in this corner of the North Cascades. Treating this lake kindly and keeping this area roadless are essential for making that happen.

124 Horseshoe Basin

RATING/ DIFFICULTY	ROUND-TRIP	ELEV GAIN/ HIGH POINT	SEASON
★★★★★/3	12 miles	1550 feet/ 7200 feet	June–Oct

Map: Green Trails Horseshoe Basin No. 21; **Contact:** Okanogan National Forest, Tonasket Ranger District, (509) 486-2186, *www.fs.fed .us/r6/oka*; **Notes:** NW Forest Pass required; **GPS:** N 48 54.515, W 119 54.244

A land of immense natural beauty teetering on the extreme eastern end of the North Cascades, Horseshoe Basin has long been a favorite destination for backpackers. With sprawling alpine tundra, shimmering tarns, a half-dozen wide-open, easy-to-scramble summits, and spectacular wildlife observing, it's no wonder visitors prefer to spend days here. But Horseshoe Basin's fairly easy approach and gentle terrain make it a dead ringer for day hikers too. You won't be able to experience it all. But you'll get a nice taste—and by traveling lightly in this precious area you'll leave less of an impact than all of those backpackers.

GETTING THERE
From downtown Tonasket turn left onto the Loomis Highway (signed "Many Lakes Recreation Area") and drive 16 miles northwest to the small village of Loomis. Bear right (north) onto County Road 9425 (Loomis-Oroville Road), and after 2 miles turn left onto Forest Road 39 (Toats Coulee Road). Follow this paved road 13.6 miles, turning right onto FR Spur 500 (signed "Irongate Trailhead"). Continue for 5.8 very rough and slow miles (high clearance necessary) to the trailhead at the road end (elev. 6150 ft). Privy and primitive camping available.

ON THE TRAIL
Setting out on the Boundary Trail (a 73-mile odyssey across the Pasayten), immediately enter wilderness and begin a slow descent on what was once a service road to a mine. In 0.25 mile cross a meadow with a nice view west to Windy Peak. Then enter lodgepole pine forest burnt to a crisp in the Tripod Fire of 2006, a conflagration that scorched over 175,000 Okanogan acres. Most of the way to Sunny Pass traverses the burn. A healthy forest will return, but in the meanwhile this hike can be

Alpine tundra on Horseshoe Mountain

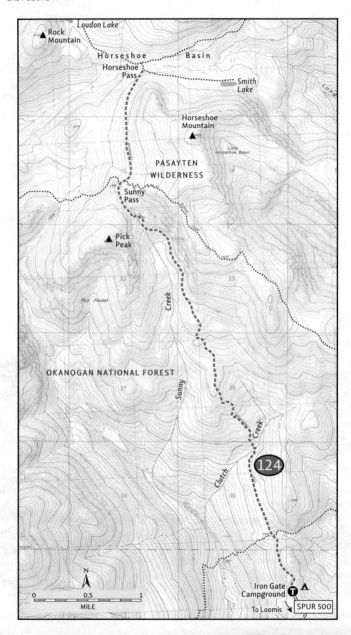

Loudon Lake

Rock
Mountain

Horseshoe   Basin

Horseshoe
Pass

Smith
Lake

Horseshoe
Mountain

PASAYTEN
WILDERNESS

Sunny
Pass

Pick
Peak

Pick Pocket

Creek

OKANOGAN NATIONAL FOREST

Sunny

124

Clutch

Creek

Iron Gate
Campground

To Loomis   SPUR 500

N

0   0.5   1
MILE

hot in summer (no forest cover) and potentially hazardous in strong winds (falling snags).

At 0.7 mile come to a junction with the Deer Park Trail and, shortly afterward, with the Clutch Creek Trail. At 1.5 miles cross a branch of Clutch Creek (elev. 6000 ft) and begin winding upward at a nice grade. Work crews with the Pacific Northwest Trail Association have nicely restored tread and repaired water bars damaged from the 2006 fire.

At 3.3 miles break out from the blackened snags (woodpecker heaven) into a lush verdant meadow garnished with a multitude of wildflowers (bluebird mecca). Sunny Pass shines ahead.

Continue upward through increasingly greener pastures, crossing gurgling creeklets and skipping through showy flower gardens to reach 7200-foot Sunny Pass at 4.8 miles. Horseshoe Basin, with its stable of stunning peaks carpeted in alpine tundra, spreads out before you. Take the trail to the right for closer inspection. In 0.1 mile ignore the Albert Camp Trail by continuing left. And after losing 200 feet in just over 1 mile, arrive dead-on in wide-open Horseshoe Basin. Sit and gape or consider your roaming options.

EXTENDING YOUR TRIP

By trail, you can head left 1 mile to Loudon Lake or right 0.8 mile to Smith Lake. Scrambling, you can head up 8106-foot Armstrong Mountain, 8076-foot Arnold Peak, 7617-foot Rock Mountain, or can head back to Sunny Pass and pick off 7620-foot Pick Peak. For the supreme scramble follow the Albert Camp Trail 1 mile to a 7700-foot shoulder of Horseshoe Mountain and then set out for the 7956-summit and its unparalleled view. For an interesting loop that adds 3.25 miles and 1000 more feet of elevation gain, return to your vehicle by first following the Albert Camp Trail 5.5 miles. Then take the Deer Park Trail 2 miles back to the Boundary Trail and then walk 0.6 mile to the trailhead.

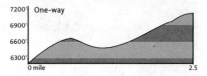

125 Disappointment Peak

RATING/ DIFFICULTY	ROUND-TRIP	ELEV GAIN/ HIGH POINT	SEASON
★★★★/3	5 miles	1200 feet/ 7160 feet	Mid-May– Oct

Map: Green Trails Horseshoe Basin No. 21; **Contact:** Department of Natural Resources, Northeast Region (Colville), (509) 684-7474, www.dnr.wa.gov; **GPS:** N 48 56.420, W 119 47.540

This fairly easy hike is a wonderful introduction to the wild and lonely Loomis State Forest, some of Washington's least-known public lands. Back in the 1990s, most of this wild country nearly succumbed to the chain saw. But thanks to a well-funded and well-publicized campaign spearheaded by Conservation Northwest, 25,000 acres of the Loomis was reclassified as a Natural Resource Conservation Area (NRCA). Home to lynx, wolverine, the occasional grizzly, and a plethora of wildflower species, there's nothing disappointing at all about Disappointment Peak.

GETTING THERE

From downtown Tonasket turn left onto the Loomis Highway (signed "Many Lakes Recreation Area") and drive 16 miles northwest to the small village of Loomis. Bear right (north) onto County Road 9425 (Loomis-Oroville Road), and after 2 miles turn left onto Forest Road 39 (Toats Coulee Road). Come to a V intersection in 7.75 miles, just beyond a cattle guard. Bear right (signed for Cold Springs Campground), following a rough gravel road 6.5 miles to Cold Springs Campground. Note

Loomis State Forest high country

these turns at confusing intersections: bear right at the first intersection, left at the second, and left at the third. Just beyond the campground and before the picnic area entrance, find trailhead parking on the right (elev. 6200 ft).

ON THE TRAIL

Bordering the Pasayten Wilderness to the west and British Columbia's Snowy Mountain Provincial Park to the north, the Loomis NRCA is in good company. This is an area of incredible biological diversity, a transition zone between the Cascades and the Okanogan Highlands. Rare fauna, much flora, and a handful of endangered flowering plants thrive here. The high-elevation forests of the Loomis provide some of the finest lynx habitat left in the entire Lower 48.

The trail to Disappointment Peak is via an old mining road. Gated and closed to all vehicles, the road is open only to foot traffic now. Follow it north through mature stands of lodgepole pine. The area is prone to wildfire, as evidenced by the surrounding ridges scarred and blackened from past conflagrations.

After a short climb the road-trail makes a gentle descent of about 200 feet into a lush boggy area. Signposts indicate that this microenvironment is within the Chopaka Mountain Natural Area Preserve. It's imperative that you stay on the trail so as not to disturb the myriad of rare plants growing here.

At 1 mile cross Disappointment Creek (elev. 6500 ft) in a cool forest of Engelmann spruce and whitebark pine before emerging into open meadows lined with sagebrush. The trail now climbs a south-facing slope, where in July and August the heat can be brutal. At 2 miles come to a junction near a fence line and spring (elev. 6850 ft). Trampled by grazing cattle, this spring is not the best water source. Turn left here to follow the more obvious track.

Soon emerge on a high saddle (elev. 6950 ft). Don't follow the road-trail down the north side of the ridge. Instead, leave it and follow tread west along an open ridge. After a 10-minute stroll arrive at the 7160-foot summit of Disappointment Peak, the western shoulder of Chopaka Mountain. Views are outstanding from this Loomis-country lookout. Peer west to the Horseshoe Basin high country and east to the lofty Loomis summits of Chopaka proper.

Not a disappointing hike at all and not a disappointing conservation achievement. Conservation Northwest, the organization responsible for protecting this region, is working hard to preserve roadless lands in the Kettle River and Selkirk ranges farther east.

EXTENDING YOUR TRIP
The track heading to the right from the spring leads 1 mile and 800 vertical feet up to the grassy and rocky summit of Joe Mills Mountain. Views are stupendous, reaching into British Columbia and the Pasayten country. An option for experienced hikers is to set out on the good but poorly marked trail from the Chopaka Picnic Area, near the trailhead, to Snowshoe Meadows. It's a 7-mile journey one-way, and the chances of running into a fellow hiker are slim to none.

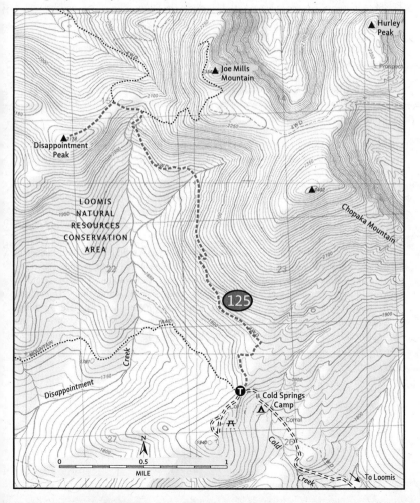

BEARLY MAKING IT

While the greater North Cascades ecosystem consists of some of the largest tracts of undisturbed wildlife habitat in the Lower 48, a few of its inhabitants are struggling to survive. This region is one of only five areas in the continental United States that still supports grizzly bears, but the North Cascades population consists of fewer than twenty-five individuals.

The grizzly is protected under the Endangered Species Act, and the federal government developed a recovery plan in 1997 to help the brown bear recover in the North Cascades. Predictably, not everyone in the region was thrilled about the prospect of one day possibly seeing the Monarch of the Mountains on their favorite hiking trail. Along with the expected opposition from ranchers, timber owners, and motor-vehicle recreationists (although not all of these folks oppose), a fair number of hikers, mountain bikers, and climbers also voiced disapproval.

The fact is, grizzly bears have been greatly maligned and misunderstood over the ages. Human encounters with grizzlies are rare. Human-caused deaths from grizzly bears are extremely rare. Each year more people are mauled by black bears than by grizzlies. Grizzlies generally shy away from human activity. They are an important component to a healthy North Cascades ecosystem.

Washington-based Conservation Northwest has initiated a campaign to help restore the grizzly to much of its historical North Cascades range. Through education and advocacy the organization hopes to enlighten Washingtonians into accepting and supporting grizzly recovery in the Evergreen State.

Conservation Northwest is advocating for gray wolf recovery in the region as well. Like the grizzly, wolves have also been persecuted and misunderstood. And like the grizzly, wolves are an integral part of a healthy North Cascades. But unlike grizzlies, wolf reintroduction and recovery tends to be less controversial. And wolves seem to be doing a better job of reintroducing themselves to their former range.

In October 2006, wildlife biologist Craig Flatten sent me a recording of a lone wolf howling, its call both eerie and magical, piercing the stillness of the autumn night. But this recording wasn't made in Alaska, where Craig worked for twelve years with the state department of fish and game. It was made one night in the Twisp River valley, where he was camping. The following morning Craig located fresh tracks on the river's sandy banks. Two years later Washington's first native-born wolf pups since the 1930s were documented. After a long absence, the call of the wild is returning to the North Cascades. Hopefully the grizzly too will find its way back home.

Appendix I: Recommended Reading

Maclean, John N. *The Thirtymile Fire: A Chronicle of Bravery and Betrayal.* New York: Henry Holt and Co., 2007.

Manning, Harvey, and Bob and Ira Spring. *Mountain Flowers of the Cascades and Olympics.* 2nd ed. Seattle: The Mountaineers Books, 2002.

Mueller, Marge, and Ted Mueller. *Afoot and Afloat: The San Juan Islands.* 4th ed. Seattle: The Mountaineers Books, 2003.

———. *Exploring Washington's Wild Areas.* 2nd ed. Seattle: The Mountaineers Books, 2002.

———. *Washington State Parks: A Complete Recreation Guide.* 3rd ed. Seattle: The Mountaineers Books, 2004.

Roe, JoAnn. *North Cascades Highway: Washington's Popular and Scenic Pass.* Seattle: The Mountaineers Books, 1997.

Suiter, John. *Poets on the Peaks.* Berkeley: Counterpoint Press, 2002.

Tabor, Rowland, and Ralph Haugerud. *Geology of the North Cascades.* Seattle: The Mountaineers Books, 1999.

Weisberg, Saul. *North Cascades National Park: The Story Behind the Scenery.* Las Vegas: KC Publications, 1988.

Whitney, Stephen R., and Rob Sanderlin. *Field Guide to the Cascades and Olympics.* 2nd ed. Seattle: The Mountaineers Books, 2003.

Appendix II: Conservation and Trail Organizations

Cascade Land Conservancy
615 Second Avenue, Suite 625
Seattle, WA 98104
(206) 292-5907
www.cascadeland.org

Conservation Northwest
1208 Bay Street #201
Bellingham, WA 98225
(360) 671-9950
www.conservationnw.org

Methow Conservancy
315 Riverside Avenue
PO Box 71
Winthrop, WA 98862
(509) 996-2870
www.methowconservancy.org

Methow Valley Sports Trails Association
PO Box 147
Winthrop, WA 98862
(509) 996-3287
www.mvsta.com

Monte Cristo Preservation Association
PO Box 471
Everett, WA 98206
www.whidbey.net/mcpa

Mount Baker Club
PO Box 73
Bellingham, WA 98227
www.mountbakerclub.org

The Mountaineers
300 Third Avenue W
Seattle, WA 98119
(206) 284-6310
www.mountaineers.org

Pacific Crest Trail Association
5325 Elkhorn Boulevard, PMB #256
Sacramento, CA 95842
(916) 349-2109
www.pcta.org

Pacific Northwest Trail Association
24854 Charles Jones Memorial Circle, Unit #4
North Cascades Gateway Center
Sedro-Woolley, WA 98284
(877) 854-7665
www.pnt.org

San Juan Island Trails Committee
http://sanjuanislandtrails.org

The San Juan Preservation Trust
PO Box 327
Lopez Island, WA 98261
(360) 468-3202
www.sjpt.org

Skagit Alpine Club
www.skagitalpineclub.com

Skagit Land Trust
325 Pine Street, Suite B
PO Box 1017
Mount Vernon, WA 98273
(360) 428-7878
www.skagitlandtrust.org

Student Conservation Association
689 River Road
PO Box 550
Charlestown, NH 03603
www.thesca.org

Washington's National Park Fund
PO Box 4646
Seattle, WA 98194
www.wnpf.org

Washington Trails Association
1305 Fourth Avenue, Suite 512
Seattle, WA 98101
(206) 625-1367
www.wta.org

Wilderness Society
1615 M Street NW
Washington, DC 20036
(800) 843-9453
www.wilderness.org

Index

About the Author

Craig grew up in rural New Hampshire where he fell in love with the natural world. A former Boy Scout, backcountry ranger in the White Mountains National Forest, and ski bum in Vermont, the outdoors is his calling! He has traveled extensively, from Alaska to Argentina, Sicily to South Korea, seeking wild and spectacular landscapes. He ranks Washington State, his home since 1989, among the most beautiful places on the planet and he has thoroughly hiked more than 13,000 miles of it from Cape Flattery to Puffer Butte, Cape Disappointment to the Salmo–Priest Wilderness.

An avid hiker, runner, kayaker, and cyclist, Craig has written about these passions for more than a dozen publications, including *Backpacker*, *Paddler*, *Northwest Magazine*, *Northwest Runner*, *AMC Outdoors*, *CityDog*, and *Northwest Outdoors*, and is the co-creator of Hikeoftheweek.com. Author of six books, among them *Day Hiking: Olympic Peninsula* and *Day Hiking: Central Cascades*, and co-author of two others, Craig is currently working on several other guidebooks for The Mountaineers Books.

He holds an AA in forestry from White Mountains Community College, and a BA in history and an MA in education from the University of Washington. He lives with his wife Heather and cats Giuseppe and Scruffy Gray in Skagit County, close to the North Cascades and the San Juan Islands.

Taking notes on Mount Pugh's summit

1% for Trails and Washington Trails Association

Your favorite Washington hikes, such as those in this book, are made possible by the efforts of thousands of volunteers keeping our trails in great shape, and by hikers like you advocating for the protection of trails and wild lands. As budget cuts reduce funding for trail maintenance, Washington Trails Association's volunteer trail maintenance program fills this void and is ever more important for the future of Washington's hiking. Our mountains and forests can provide us with a lifetime of adventure and exploration—but we need trails to get us there. One percent of the sales of this guidebook goes to support WTA's efforts.

Spend a day on the trail with Washington Trails Association, and give back to the trails you love. WTA hosts over 750 work parties throughout Washington's Cascades and Olympics each year. Volunteers remove downed logs after spring snowmelt, cut away brush, retread worn stretches of trail, and build bridges and turnpikes. Find the volunteer schedule, check current conditions of the trails in this guidebook, and become a member of WTA at *www.wta.org* or (206) 625-1367.

THE MOUNTAINEERS, founded in 1906, is a nonprofit outdoor activity and conservation club, whose mission is "to explore, study, preserve, and enjoy the natural beauty of the outdoors. . . ." Based in Seattle, Washington, the club is now one of the largest such organizations in the United States, with seven branches throughout Washington State.

The Mountaineers sponsors both classes and year-round outdoor activities in the Pacific Northwest, which include hiking, mountain climbing, ski-touring, snowshoeing, bicycling, camping, kayaking, nature study, sailing, and adventure travel. The club's conservation division supports environmental causes through educational activities, sponsoring legislation, and presenting informational programs.

All club activities are led by skilled, experienced instructors, who are dedicated to promoting safe and responsible enjoyment and preservation of the outdoors.

If you would like to participate in these organized outdoor activities or the club's programs, consider a membership in The Mountaineers. For information and an application, write or call The Mountaineers, Club Headquarters, 7700 Sand Point Way NE, Seattle, WA 98115; 206-521-6001. You can also visit the club's website at www.mountaineers.org or contact The Mountaineers via email at clubmail@mountaineers.org.

The Mountaineers Books, an active, nonprofit publishing program of the club, produces guidebooks, instructional texts, historical works, natural history guides, and works on environmental conservation. All books produced by The Mountaineers Books fulfill the club's mission.

Send or call for our catalog of more than 500 outdoor titles:

The Mountaineers Books
1001 SW Klickitat Way, Suite 201
Seattle, WA 98134
800-553-4453
mbooks@mountaineersbooks.org
www.mountaineersbooks.org

The Mountaineers Books is proud to be a corporate sponsor of the Leave No Trace Center for Outdoor Ethics, whose mission is to promote and inspire responsible outdoor recreation through education, research, and partnerships. The Leave No Trace program is focused specifically on human-powered (nonmotorized) recreation.

Leave No Trace strives to educate visitors about the nature of their recreational impacts, as well as offer techniques to prevent and minimize such impacts. Leave No Trace is best understood as an educational and ethical program, not as a set of rules and regulations.

For more information, visit *www.LNT.org*, or call 800-332-4100.

OTHER TITLES YOU MIGHT ENJOY FROM THE MOUNTAINEERS BOOKS

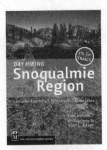

Day Hiking: Snoqualmie Region
Nelson & Bauer
Great hikes—done in a day!

Day Hiking: Olympic Peninsula
Romano
"Romano is one of the better guidebook writers around . . ."
—*Seattle P-I*

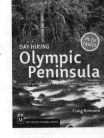

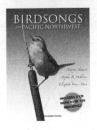

Birdsongs of the Pacific Northwest
Stewart, recordist; Whitney & Briars
Become an expert in identifying Northwest birds with this field guide and audio CD.

Nature in the City: Seattle
True & Dolan
The best places to experience wildlife and wild surroundings in the city.

Mountain Flowers of the Cascades and Olympics, 2nd Edition
Manning & Spring
Legendary Washington authors present 92 wildflowers in this handy pocket guide.

Digital Photography Outdoors, 2nd Edition
Martin
"A great all-in-one reference"
—*Digital Photography* magazine

The Mountaineers Books has more than 500 outdoor recreation titles in print.
Receive a free catalog at
www.mountaineersbooks.org.